SELECTED C[

NORTH[

CAROLINA

SELECTED CLIMBS IN
NORTH
CAROLINA

YON LAMBERT
HARRISON SHULL

THE MOUNTAINEERS BOOKS

Published by
The Mountaineers Books
1001 SW Klickitat Way, Suite 201
Seattle, WA 98134

First edition, 2002

Published simultaneously in Great Britain by Cordee, 3a DeMontfort Street, Leicester, England, LE1 7HD

Manufactured in the United States of America

Project Editor and Editor: Julie Van Pelt
Cover and Book Design: The Mountaineers Books
Layout: Mayumi Thompson
Mapmaker: Jim Miller/Fennana Design
Photographer: Harrison Shull *(www.shullphoto.com)*

Cover photograph: Arno Ilgner on the exposed Dollywood pitch (aka *Big Jugs and Wild Rides*) of his Whiteside Mountain headwall route, *Little Miss Dangerous* (IV, 5.10, A0)

Frontispiece: John Young riding the rivets and dowels on pitch 2 of *Remember Appomattox* (IV, 5.10, A2+), route 24 on the North Side of Looking Glass Rock

Library of Congress Cataloging-in-Publication Data

Lambert, Yon, 1971-
  Selected climbs in North Carolina / by Yon Lambert and Harrison
Shull.— 1st ed.
    p. cm.
  ISBN 0-89886-855-6 (pbk.)
  1. Mountaineering—North Carolina—Guidebooks. 2. Rock
climbing—North Carolina—Guidebooks. 3. North Carolina—Guidebooks.
I. Shull, Harrison, 1970- II. Title.
  GV199.42.N66 L36 2002
  796.52'2'09756—dc21
                                    2002008166

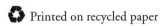

TABLE OF CONTENTS

Preface   9
Acknowledgements   11
Introduction   12

PIEDMONT

1. MOORE'S WALL   20
2. STONE MOUNTAIN   50

3. CROWDERS MOUNTAIN   69

NORTHERN BLUE RIDGE (THE HIGH COUNTRY)

4. SHIP ROCK   90

5. LINVILLE GORGE   103
   Hawksbill Mountain   107
   Table Rock   122
   North Carolina Wall   138
   Shortoff Mountain   163

SOUTHERN BLUE RIDGE

6. RUMBLING BALD
   MOUNTAIN   182
7. LOOKING GLASS ROCK   215
8. CEDAR ROCK   262

9. BIG GREEN MOUNTAIN   275
10. WHITESIDE MOUNTAIN   287

Appendix A: Ratings   316
Appendix B: Contact Information and Resources   317
Appendix C: Emergency Services   319
Route Index   320

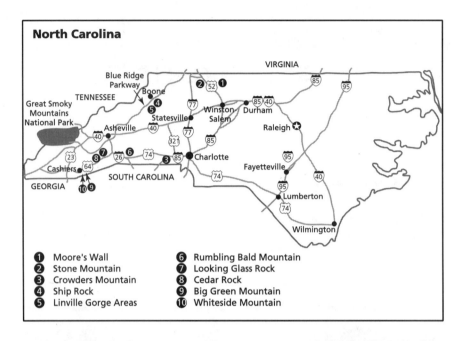

North Carolina

VIRGINIA

Blue Ridge
Parkway
Boone

TENNESSEE

Great Smoky
Mountains
National Park

Asheville

Statesville

Winston-
Salem

Durham

Raleigh ✪

Cashiers

GEORGIA

SOUTH CAROLINA

Charlotte

Fayetteville

Lumberton

Wilmington

① Moore's Wall
② Stone Mountain
③ Crowders Mountain
④ Ship Rock
⑤ Linville Gorge Areas

⑥ Rumbling Bald Mountain
⑦ Looking Glass Rock
⑧ Cedar Rock
⑨ Big Green Mountain
⑩ Whiteside Mountain

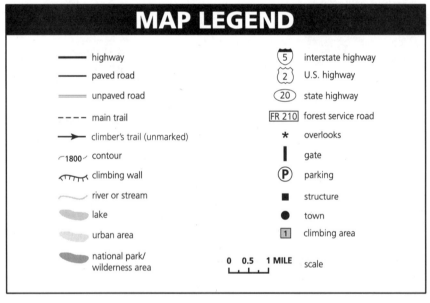

MAP LEGEND

——— highway	⑤ interstate highway
——— paved road	② U.S. highway
═══ unpaved road	⑳ state highway
- - - - main trail	FR 210 forest service road
➤ climber's trail (unmarked)	✻ overlooks
⌒1800⌒ contour	▌ gate
⟨⟨⟨⟨⟨ climbing wall	Ⓟ parking
～～ river or stream	■ structure
lake	● town
urban area	▣ climbing area
national park/ wilderness area	0 0.5 1 MILE scale

TOPO LEGEND

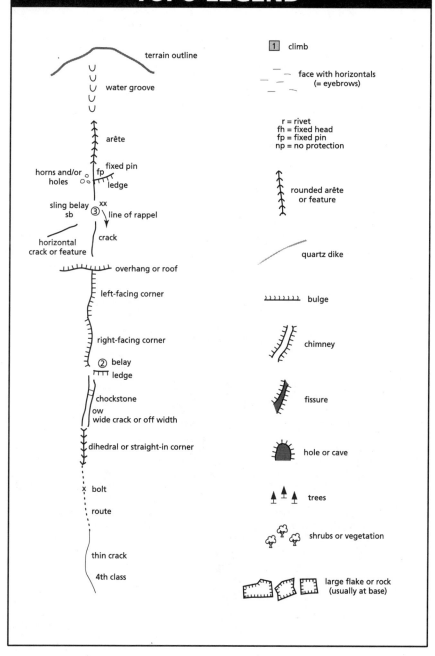

terrain outline

water groove

arête

fixed pin

horns and/or holes   fp

ledge

sling belay   xx
sb   line of rappel

crack

horizontal crack or feature

overhang or roof

left-facing corner

right-facing corner

② belay

ledge

chockstone

ow
wide crack or off width

dihedral or straight-in corner

x bolt

route

thin crack

4th class

1 climb

face with horizontals
(= eyebrows)

r = rivet
fh = fixed head
fp = fixed pin
np = no protection

rounded arête
or feature

quartz dike

bulge

chimney

fissure

hole or cave

trees

shrubs or vegetation

large flake or rock
(usually at base)

In memory of Doc Bayne
1952–2001

People have said that it can be disappointing to spend too much time with your
heroes. In the case of Doc Bayne, nothing could be further from the truth. A lifelong
Greenville, South Carolina, resident, Doc embodied Carolina climbing. He was bold
but soft-spoken, stubborn but easygoing—a former guidebook cover boy who
chummed with almost anyone willing to hang their way up one of his routes, which
were perhaps not always the hardest but certainly the most memorable.

Doc was killed in a hang-gliding accident on December 30, 2001, just a few weeks
before his fiftieth birthday. He left a ten-year-old son, Spencer, his parents, Betty and
Paul, as well as countless friends, acquaintances, and admirers. Doc was a rare man, a
mentor who lived up to a daunting reputation and kept building on it. This
guidebook was partly his vision and—as one of the last true standard bearers for
local ethics—it is now his legacy. He will be greatly missed, but never forgotten.

Doc Bayne at the High Anxiety Headwall crux of his Whiteside Mountain route,
Whippin' Boy

PREFACE

Welcome to North Carolina, the best backwater climbing area in America.

Here in the southern Appalachians, intimidating granite domes tower above lush mountain coves soaked in autumn colors. In the Piedmont, steep quartzite walls yield powerful sport climbs. Boulderers have their choice of numerous, world-class destinations scattered across the state. And connoisseurs of remote backcountry routes—free or aid—can find something to suit them in every season and in every grade. For everything but mountaineering, we can go head-to-head with any state in the union.

But now let's be honest: In contrast to the publicity heaped upon so many other East Coast cliffs, you probably haven't read much about North Carolina. Local climbers and our routes rarely make it into magazines. If Linville Gorge were in Kazakhstan it would probably draw more "elite" visitors.

Still, many locals couldn't be happier or prouder about our "backwater" status. That's partially why we decided to do this book. Don't misunderstand us. We're not out to expose North Carolina's great climbing for the sake of sheer publicity. Rather, we thought a new guide with more history and route descriptions might actually help to preserve our local character.

Ironically, it hasn't been an easy sell around here. Since the beginning, North Carolina has been a bastion of fiercely territorial and opinionated climbers. Although some of our best areas are well known, locals have long resisted publicity. When visiting writers arrived to explore, concerned climbers sometimes sent hate mail and threatened to boycott magazines. Those days are waning, but a few significant activists still turned their backs on this project.

There is no question that in North Carolina, a finite amount of rock calls for special vigilance. Access remains a particularly sensitive issue. However, our belief is that unless we're open about climbing—with everything from our history to first-ascent style—new climbers won't have any appreciation for what's happened here before. And that's not a good state of affairs.

So for the first new guide since Thomas Kelley's excellent *The Climber's Guide*

Mountain Laurel in bloom along the hike into Linville Gorge's North Carolina Wall

Access in North Carolina is not a right, it is a privilege. Please act responsibly.

to *North Carolina* (Earthbound Press, 1995, Third Edition), we chose to sacrifice volume in the name of perspective. Technically, this book is a "select" edition since it does not include all the routes in North Carolina. Instead, we focused on the history of major destinations and selected routes. We have also added as many new routes as possible.

Readers will hopefully note one additional difference between this book and Kelley's: the inclusion of first-ascent style where available. We did not do this to espouse one particular tactic over another. Frankly, we believe the manner in which a route went up is far less important than the first ascent party's candor about how they climbed it. Here in North Carolina, climbers have been pushing their limits—mostly in ground-up fashion—for many years. We have tried to capture some of the colorful modes of ascent by boiling first-ascent information down into a few short words—a nearly impossible task. Don't read too much into the phrasing or attempt to decode a clear definition of each style. Ground-up with aid isn't shorthand for anything. Instead, use the information to marvel at how some climbers tried ingenious, daring, or even seemingly suicidal solutions to limit their impact, increase commitment levels, *and* increase sheer difficulty. In this guide, a route's history and individuality is just as important as its number grade.

We don't say this to argue that all new first ascents should unfold in the manners detailed in this guide. However, if you have your eye on a new line, it might be wise to learn something about other routes in the area and the climbers who were there before you. Then determine how your contribution will serve as a logical extension of the area's ethic. In truth, North Carolina's "traditional" reputation is due as much to a protective streak for the region's limited rock supply as it is to a cadre of climbers clinging to old-fashioned ideas.

Hearing that, half of you will 86 this book in protest and return to your daily complaining on website message boards. We can't say we totally blame you. But even though we want to believe that climbers will someday agree on issues like the merits of guidebooks, chipping, chiseled aid placements, or squeeze jobs, we also recognize that some will continue to justify their actions in the name of pushing standards or public good. You could argue we've done that here.

Thankfully, the climbing community has proven itself fairly democratic, far-sighted, and generally capable of dealing with conflict. With this book, we merely want to help climbers better appreciate the value of what we have here in North Carolina.

If it can do that *and* get you to the base of a route, we've done our job.

Yon Lambert and Harrison Shull
Fall 2002

ACKNOWLEDGEMENTS

The authors wish to thank all those who contributed to this book with route information, photographs, interviews, suggestions, edits, and patience. We especially wish to thank Mike Fischesser for allowing us to use the transcripts of interviews he conducted in the early 1980s with some of the state's climbing pioneers.

Many additional climbers and friends assisted in the process. If we overlooked you, rest assured that it was stupidity and not an intentional omission. Special thanks goes to Alan Howell, Andy Kluge, Aram Attarian, Arno Ilgner, Bart Bledsoe, Biff Farrell, Bob Rotert, Bruce Burgess, Bryan Haslam, Burton Moomaw, Chris Caldwell, Chris Dorrity, Chris Rowins, Clarence Hickman, Doc Bayne, Doug Reed, Dudley Hammon, Eddie Begoon, Forrest Gardner, Gerald Laws, Henry Barber, Jack Strifling, Jeep Gaskin, Jim Beyer, Jim Corbett, Joe Lackey, John Provotero, Kenny Hibbits, Kris Kline, Kris Veersteegen, Lee Carter, Lynn Willis, Mark Lassiter, Monty Reagan, Nathan Brown, Pascal Robert, Porter Jarrard, Robert Hutchins, Robert McBride, Ron Dawson, Sandy Fleming, Sean Cobourn, Shannon Stegg, Stephen Scoff, Steve Longenecker, Thomas Kelley, Tim Fisher, Todd Wells, Tom Howard, Tom McMillan, Tyler Stracker, Wes Love, and Will Fulton.

Tommy Wagoner, Marshall Ellis, Matt Derstine, Andy Whittaker, Miera Crawford, Wade Carpenter, Art Rowe, Erin Bronk, Larry Trivette, Bambi Teague, and Alan Moore are among the public and private land managers responsible for these climbing areas. They have thoughtfully reviewed each section and helped ensure that the regulations presented are accurate and up-to-date.

Yon Lambert would also like to thank his family and his wife, Diane, for her patience and support. Harrison Shull hopes that all those who use this book will develop a newfound passion and respect for our climbing resources here in North Carolina.

INTRODUCTION

The challenge . . . exists in non-numerical space. You pass the bolt at the 5.12 "crux," and then the real ordeal begins. You climb there half knowing that your mind might visit places you would not willingly go. It's dangerous, and myths and superstition do a better job defending it than common sense. The essence—the justification, if there is any—lies in obscure, ineffable moments.
Jeff Achey, about Whiteside Mountain (*Climbing*, August 1, 1997)

Despite the name, *Selected Climbs in North Carolina* is actually a hybrid guidebook, providing a selection of some elements and more comprehensive treatment of others. It does not include every route—or even every "open" area—in the state. Climbers familiar with North Carolina will note significant omissions such as Pilot Mountain, a few cliffs at Crowders Mountain, Victory Wall, Devil's Cellar, and Sitting Bear. We made some hard choices, opting to exclude some areas in favor of longer route descriptions, including detailed route history where possible, and more local history for each cliff. As a result, the cliffs included in this guide are only a fraction of the climbing available in North Carolina. Many more routes may eventually show up in a comprehensive edition.

Some climbers feel that guidebooks diminish adventure, increase environmental impact, create access problems, or otherwise cause problems for the climbing community. We concede that this *can* be the case. However, we feel that a guidebook— done properly—can in fact work *for* us by preserving important factual information, local ethics and color, and by explaining to climbers where they should go and how we can visit these areas responsibly.

How to Use This Book
Routes in this guide are grouped into three geographic regions: Piedmont, Northern Blue Ridge (The High Country), and Southern Blue Ridge. Each region consists of the following climbing areas:
- Piedmont: Moore's Wall, Stone Mountain, and Crowders Mountain
- Northern Blue Ridge (The High Country): Ship Rock and Linville Gorge
- Southern Blue Ridge: Rumbling Bald Mountain, Looking Glass Rock, Cedar Rock, Big Green Mountain, and Whiteside Mountain

Each chapter of the guide begins with summary information about the overall climbing area described, including the type of climbing, rock type and height, number of routes, climbing season, and camping information.

We then include a climbing history for the area, followed by additional information on weather, restrictions and access issues, nearby emergency services, and specific gear recommendations. Driving directions from nearby towns and cites are

12

given under the heading Getting There. (Since this is a *climbing* guide and not a traveling guide, we highly recommend purchasing a detailed roadmap, atlas, or gazetteer to supplement these instructions.) Detailed approach directions then follow. These approach directions can be complex, depending on the number of walls described in a particular climbing area.

Next come detailed route descriptions for each wall or feature in the climbing area. The routes are numbered and described from relative access points. For instance, at Moore's Wall (chapter 1) the routes are listed right to left since the approach trail arrives at the cliff near the far-right (south) end. Conversely, at Looking Glass Rock (chapter 7), routes are listed counterclockwise around the dome, in order from left to right for ease of orientation. References to "left" and "right" assume you are facing the cliff (unless otherwise noted) and remember that all distances are estimates.

Topos are also included for each area and show as many routes as possible— including numerous climbs that are not mentioned in the text. Routes that are described in the text are numbered on the topos. Routes that are not described in the text are lettered on the topos. For instance, at Whiteside Mountain (chapter 10), the text includes a detailed description of *The Original Route* and *Traditions*. But the accompanying topos also include less-popular climbs such as *New Perversions*. This allows us to feature some of the best and most significant climbs in the state without having this guide balloon into a 900-page volume. The many additional routes on topos also keep the integrity of an area's routes intact and allow the additional routes to serve as landmarks. Note that while we have attempted to draw the topos as accurately as possible, they are not always perfectly proportional due to cliff orientation or the wandering nature of the routes.

A word about climb ratings: Part of the North Carolina tradition means that climbs often have been deliberately rated 5.11+ instead of 5.11d. The 5.11+ might mean anything from 5.11b to 5.12b. It says everything at once and yet tells you not much at all. To preserve this, we have given climbs letter grades in the text according to our interpretation or general consensus, but we have often labeled pitches on the topos with the purposely general +/- grades.

Ethics

North Carolina has a long and tortured history of ethical battles between old school and new, sport climbers and trad. However, rather than include our own diatribe about the idiosyncrasies of this region, we'll use this opportunity to outline some widely accepted local practices.

- Chipping or using artificial holds to make a route "go" are destructive and universally rejected by North Carolina climbers. Don't do it.
- Retro-bolting or adding new protection to established routes without consent of the first-ascent party is unthinkable and not worthy of additional comment.
- Squeeze jobs and excessive bolting are strongly discouraged. Consider the type of development that has gone up before your proposed line and make sure that your route will improve the area, not cause problems.
- Fixed anchors and protection should be camouflaged to blend with the rock. The use of chains and excessively large rappel systems is frowned upon.

- Bolts should be of the highest quality possible. Modern standards (plus the area's high amount of rainfall) dictate the use of stainless steel.

State Park Climbing Regulations

In addition to some private land and several national forests, climbing is allowed in four North Carolina State Parks: Hanging Rock (Moore's Wall, chapter 1), Stone Mountain (chapter 2), Pilot Mountain (not included in this guide), and Crowders Mountain (chapter 3).

Please follow these rules and regulations specific to the parks:
- Climbing is permitted only in designated areas. Check with the park office if you are unclear about open areas.
- Climbers must register before hiking in to the climbing areas. Each climbing area chapter tells where to register. Registration is free, and tracking climber numbers is the only way park officials can justify expanded facilities for climbers, so you have no excuse for not registering. Have your car license number handy.
- Use only established trails.
- Solo climbing is not recommended. Standard safety equipment and techniques must be used at all times.
- Do not sling trees or vegetation. If there are no anchors available on your route, then sling chock stones or place removable protection for anchors.
- Camping and fires are permitted in designated areas only. Alcohol is prohibited. Please do not litter.
- Pets are welcome but must be on a leash no longer than 6 feet.
- Please exit the climbing area well before closing time.

State parks also have specific rules regarding fixed anchors:
- No new fixed anchors are allowed. If you have concerns about an anchor, notify park management, who will in turn notify the Carolina Climbers Coalition for repair/replacement.
- All fixed anchors are installed and maintained through a cooperative agreement between the Division of Parks and Recreation and the Carolina Climbers Coalition. Unless you are involved in an approved repair or replacement project, leave your drill at home.
- The Division of Parks and Recreation does not install, maintain, inspect, or guarantee the worthiness or dependability of any fixed anchor. The decision to use any anchor rests with the climber.

Climber Activism: A History of the Carolina Climbers Coalition
By Aram Attarian, Ph.D., North Carolina State University

The Carolina Climbers Coalition, an advocacy group for climbers throughout North and South Carolina, has an interesting history. The origins of the organization can be traced back to the early 1970s. As the story goes, a nonclimber attempted to descend the Big Pinnacle at Pilot Mountain State

Park with a piece of rope. His descent terminated when the ledge he had lowered himself onto gave way, killing him. North Carolina State Parks responded by closing all state parks to rock climbing. Climbers responded to this closure by organizing themselves and initiating a letter writing campaign.

Part of this process also included setting up a series of meetings with state park personnel in the fall of 1973. Following these meetings, North Carolina State Parks reopened to climbing and the parks' first climbing policy was established. Areas such as the Big Pinnacle (Pilot Mountain State Park), the Hanging Rock (Hanging Rock State Park), and King's Pinnacle (Crowders Mountain State Park) remained closed to climbing due to concerns over natural resource protection and visitor safety.

In 1976 Mike Fischesser spearheaded a re-bolting project at Stone Mountain, which may have been one of the earliest such projects in the nation. The purpose of this project was to replace bolts that were placed in the late 1960s and early 1970s with Rawl ⅜-inch self-drive bolts and SMC hangers. The standard Stone Mountain routes received most of the attention.

Climbing in North Carolina progressed without too much concern or controversy through the 1980s and into the 1990s, when Burton Moomaw and Woody Keen, owners of Misty Mountain Threadworks, initiated the High Country Climbers Coalition (HCCC), centered in Boone. According to the founders, the HCCC formed as a way to get local climbers together. A couple of slide shows, a video premiere, and talks focused around the care of Ship Rock were the primary focus of this group. The annual Table Rock Road cleanup and one of the earliest "Climb Smart!" programs were also initiated by the group. The HCCC also conducted a survey to identify whether there was climber support to publicize North Carolina climbing areas in the mainstream climbing magazines. The majority of members didn't support this idea and subsequently a letter was sent to *Climbing* magazine requesting that North Carolina climbing not be publicized. The HCCC had met four or five times with thirty to forty people attending each meeting when the Howard's Knob issue surfaced.

According to bouldering guru John Sherman, Howard's Knob located in Boone, North Carolina, "is one of the finest bouldering areas in the country." In 1993, a 65-acre parcel of land containing the Howard's Knob boulders was purchased by a real estate developer who proposed to build on this land and closed it to climbing. Local residents, students, environmentalists, and climbers joined forces to oppose this development. With assistance from the Access Fund, this coalition formed the Watauga High Country Land Trust, whose mission is to preserve natural areas around Boone. Joey Henson, an active Boone climber, played a leading role in the formation of the land trust. The Watauga Land Trust approached the owner of Howard's Knob

Continued

about selling the property without success. The developer rejected several purchase offers and prepared to build a home on the property. This caused local activists to grow desperate. To show their concern local climbers climbed trees to prevent the bulldozers from moving in. In addition, Friends of Howard's Knob staged a rally to support preservation of "The Knob," and 500 people marched in the streets of Boone to no avail—bouldering at Howard's Knob is still not permitted.

The current Carolina Climbers Coalition (CCC) was created as a result of a rumor that spread throughout North Carolina in 1994. Climbers mistakenly thought that North Carolina State Parks would be closed to climbing as a result of a fatality at Crowders Mountain State Park. State park officials and climbers met in Charlotte and learned that a park closure was not planned but that a coalition would best serve the interests of both climbers and park officials. In January 1995 almost 100 area climbers met in Winston-Salem and voted unanimously to create the CCC to help preserve climbing access in the Carolinas.

Today, the CCC continues to involve itself with a variety of projects by working collaboratively with federal and state land managers and private landowners. Since its inception, the CCC has contributed a significant amount of time, effort, and financial support to preserve the diverse climbing resources and opportunities in the Carolinas.

Weather

Although many temperature snobs will argue otherwise, North Carolina is an excellent year-round climbing destination. A diverse selection of elevation and cliff orientation means that you can find places to climb where conditions are acceptable in both August and February.

Check out the table below for a convenient reference.

Cliff	Region	Orientation	Highest Elevation	Climbing Season
Moore's Wall	Piedmont	NW to NE	2,579 feet	Spring–Fall
Stone Mountain	Piedmont	S	2,300 feet	Fall–Spring
Crowders Mountain	Piedmont	SE	1,625 feet	Fall–Spring
Ship Rock	Northern Blue Ridge	SW	4,400 feet	Summer
Hawksbill Mountain	Northern Blue Ridge	NW	4,020 feet	Spring–Fall
Table Rock	Northern Blue Ridge	E	3,909 feet	Spring–Fall
North Carolina Wall	Northern Blue Ridge	W	3,200 feet	Spring–Fall
The Amphitheater	Northern Blue Ridge	S to N	3,200 feet	Spring–Fall
Shortoff Mountain	Northern Blue Ridge	W-NW	3,100 feet	Year-round
Rumbling Bald Mountain	Southern Blue Ridge	SW	3,200 feet	Winter
Looking Glass Rock	Southern Blue Ridge	ALL	4,000 feet	Year-round
Cedar Rock	Southern Blue Ridge	SW	4,056 feet	Fall–Spring
Big Green Mountain	Southern Blue Ridge	W	4,200 feet	Fall–Spring
Whiteside Mountain	Southern Blue Ridge	N Face, SE Face	4,930 feet	Year-round

Recommended Gear

North Carolina has everything from runout water grooves to steep endurance routes to bouldery crack climbs. Runouts are common, but less so nowadays with modern microgear.

Each chapter makes a special note if certain climbing gear or protection is particularly useful and we have made an effort to make suggestions on some particular routes. In the text, we have tried to note if a route is considered a sport climb (i.e., quickdraws only), although it is always wise to carry additional gear. Few routes will require more gear than listed below, and the vast majority will not need as much. So take this list for what it is: a recommendation.

Standard North Carolina Free-Climbing Rack

Slider nuts
One set of brass, copper-steel, or micro-sized wired nuts
One set of wired nuts
Two sets of three-cam units to 0.5 inch
Two sets of four-cam units 0.5 to 3 inches
Full-length runners or slings
10–12 quickdraws
Extra carabiners
Nut tool
Double ropes are not necessary but are helpful

Standard North Carolina Aid-Climbing Rack

Standard North Carolina free rack
3–8 knifeblades (KBs), 5 LAs, 2–5 angles (small sawed-offs), RURPs/beaks, hooks
5–20 circleheads, straight heads, and duckbills (depends upon route)

A Note About Safety

Safety is an important concern in all outdoor activities. No guidebook can alert you to every hazard or anticipate the limitations of every reader. Therefore, the descriptions of roads, trails, routes, and natural features in this book are not representations that a particular place or excursion will be safe for your party. When you follow any of the routes described in this book, you assume responsibility for your own safety. Under normal conditions, such excursions require the usual attention to traffic, road and trail conditions, weather, terrain, the capabilities of your party, and other factors. Keeping informed on current conditions and exercising common sense are the keys to a safe, enjoyable outing.

The Mountaineers Books

PIEDMONT —————————————————————

Opposite: *Art Brown latches onto the thank-god holds on* Bimbo's Bulge *(route 16) on the Circus Wall at Moore's Wall.*

1. MOORE'S WALL ─────────────────────

Climbing type: Traditional
Rock type: Quartzite
Height: 70 to 300 feet
Number of routes: 100+ (52 this guide)
Season: Spring through fall
Camping: Pay campsites available at Hanging Rock State Park (see appendix B)

Moore's Wall rises abruptly from the rolling hills and tobacco fields of the North Carolina Piedmont. And although it is far from the climbing hot spots of Asheville or Boone, this excellent quartzite wall ranks among the single best crags in the state— if not the entire Southeast. Located within the boundaries of Hanging Rock State Park, Moore's Wall is something of a blue collar climbing area. Though sprinkled with a few excellent, high-end sport routes, the essence of climbing here lies in dangling one-handed from a titanic jug while searching for that perfectly sized brass wire. That said, Moore's is an excellent learning area for aspiring leaders, too. Moore's also has a long history of bouldering and the locals continue to unearth new areas throughout the park. If bouldering is your bag, you'll want to check out the park's legal areas. This guide describes routes in the Hanging Garden area; on the Sentinel Buttress walls (Fire Wall, Sentinel Buttress proper, and Circus Wall); on Moore's Central Wall; and in the Amphitheater and North End.

History

> Some say that one's first impression of a mountain sticks in your mind the most. If this is true, then the awesome view of those cliffs at Hanging Rock have been indelibly etched in my memory. Although not the most fabulous mountains in the East, I have come to love and respect them as much as any I have seen or climbed elsewhere.
>
> **Chapel Hill climber George DeWolfe in an unpublished, underground guidebook (probably the state's first) on May 17, 1967**

While it is true that some rock climbing had already occurred in Linville Gorge, no other place in North Carolina saw as much activity as Hanging Rock State Park did in the early 1960s. In fact, one could easily argue that DeWolfe and companions such as Fess Green, Robert Mosely, and Charles Adams were the first genuine Tarheel craggers. Moore's Wall and its companion cliffs, Hanging Rock and Cook's Wall, must have posed an obvious allure for local climbers such as DeWolfe. Even though DeWolfe and friends certainly knew of the region's other cliffs such as Pilot Mountain and Sauratown, they focused their initial energies on Hanging Rock.

It is possible, of course, that another route saw an earlier ascent, but the first recorded rock climb at Moore's Wall occurred in August 1959 when DeWolfe and Tom Fawcett climbed the *Headwall Direct*. The climbers used 100 feet of ⅜-inch manila rope, two pitons (the first DeWolfe ever drove), and what the guide called "a

The cliffs at Moore's Wall as seen from Mickey Road

rather shaky belay." Although nowhere near the cutting edge of climbing (Royal Robbins and crew had climbed Half Dome in 1957), DeWolfe's ascent spurred a flurry of local action. For the next few years, climbers concentrated on appealing routes such as *Scrambled Eggs* (5.6), *The Sentinel* (5.5), and a variety of moderate routes at Hanging Rock itself (which is in the park's interior and now closed to climbing). The Duke University Outings Club was a driving force here, too. By the end of the 1960s when DeWolfe typed his guide, the park had approximately thirty routes.

Although climbers continued to visit, first-ascent action slackened considerably until around 1974, which we could call the beginning of a six-year golden era at Moore's. Armed with better gear and more willing to attempt the steep faces, Tom Howard led the way with ascents of *Raise Hell* and, later, *Air Show, Too Much Fun,* and *Zoo View* in 1976. We can only imagine Howard's delight as his hands latched onto the gigantic jugs that led the way out *Zoo View*'s second roof. In 1978, Bob Rotert managed a huge leap in difficulty when he free-climbed the amazing horizontal roof, *Aid Raid*—certainly one of the hardest routes in the state at that time. One other ascent that really shook the climbing community was *Wild Kingdom* over 1978 and 1979. By first following a left-arching corner and eventually a stunning crack through the impressive Fire Wall, *Wild Kingdom* followed the strongest single line at the cliff. In an ironic twist on the prevailing ethic, the second pitch of *Wild Kingdom* was actually previewed and equipped on rappel. Tom McMillan and Bob Rotert reasoned that the climbing was hard enough to warrant the tactic.

In the 1980s, with a host of classics now established, all the cliff really needed was a driving force to fill in the gaps. Tim Fisher stepped in to fill that role. A resident of Charlotte since 1985, he came to own land at the base of Moore's Wall that borders on Hanging Rock State Park land (if you follow the rutted dirt road to the circular pullout, you're on Fisher's property). This is probably the only reason climbers still have access to Moore's from this side of the park. While Fisher eventually made first ascents all over the state, Moore's Wall became his favorite crag and he maintains an amazing passion for the ethic here. Fisher knows that many climbers—even longtime partners—find his self-imposed style limitations imperious and archaic. Yet he has managed to squeeze some colorful and intricate routes out of this wall while adhering to a demanding code of ground-up climbing with little fixed protection. Although he likes to come off as crude or unapproachable, in person Fisher is ever positive and a bottomless source of beta.

Also in the 1980s, climbers such as David Petree and the legendary Eric Zschiesche made their mark on Moore's Wall. Petree grew up on a farm in nearby Rural Hall and grew tobacco for spending money as a teenager. Commonly seen hik-

Dan Krotz on the classic Zoo View *(route 17) on the Circus Wall*

ing trails in bare feet or climbing with a lit cigarette, Petree was something of a local Huck Finn. Nevertheless he teamed with John Provetero and John Regglebrugge to produce *Pooh Corner* and *Reckless Abandon*. As a joke, many locals even carried "cards" identifying themselves as certified "Men of Moore's"!

Zschiesche, meanwhile, began his career at Moore's as a teenage soloist in the early 1970s. Although he eventually moved away, he would return every so often in the 1980s to make some significant "first," usually inspiring the locals to climb harder in the process. Some say his most significant route is *Mighty Mouse*, but Zschiesche also climbed *The Middle Road* and *Nicotine*—opening locals' eyes about the use of in-situ protection on climbs at the highest grades. And Zschiesche is best known for his (occasionally nude) bouldering feats. Below the main walls at Moore's he spent countless days working on highball problems in the eponymously named Zschiesche Corridor. *Zen Spasm, Duck Soup,* and *The Ramp* are just a few of the "EZ" problems here, so spread out and enjoy.

Other North Carolina climbers have done some amazing things at Moore's Wall. In a busy period from 1985–88 Doug Reed pulled routes like *Plastic Cat* and unearthed a handful of other test pieces with Fisher and Porter Jarrard. Although Jarrard is probably best known for developing the Red River Gorge, he began under the tutelage of Fisher and spent many years honing his fitness and traditional climbing techniques at Moore's. Some think his route *Filet-O-Fish* is the best single-pitch line here. Jarrard was the climber who bolted *Zeus*—a former EZ top-rope project—and *Hercules* on the wild Hanging Garden.

Weather and Climbing Season

Moore's Wall, elevation 2,579 feet at its peak, faces northwest to northeast, which makes it an excellent March through November climbing area. Afternoon thunderstorms and hail are very common in the spring and summer. Moore's many roofs allow shelter, but lightning is common and people have been killed waiting out storms this way.

Restrictions and Access Issues

Moore's Wall is part of Hanging Rock State Park, which is managed by the North Carolina Division of Parks and Recreation. The park gates are locked except for the following hours:

- November through February: 8:00 A.M. to 6:00 P.M.
- March, October: 8:00 A.M. to 7:00 P.M.
- April, May, September: 8:00 A.M. to 8:00 P.M.
- June through August: 8:00 A.M. to 9:00 P.M.

In addition to the rules and regulations listed in this guide's introduction, please follow regulations specific to this park:

- **Closures.** The park closes a portion of Moore's Wall every year from January 15 until August 15 to allow peregrine falcon nesting. The closure includes all of the North End and extends nearly to the Amphitheater. In the past, the park has lifted this closure early.
- **Registration.** Climbers must register at either the park headquarters or the Tory's Den Trailhead, which is located off Charlie Young Road and below the parking area.

Emergency Services

Call Stokes County Emergency Medical Services Dispatch. The Stokes County Sheriff's Office is in Danbury, as is the nearest hospital, Stokes-Reynolds County Memorial Hospital. (See appendix C).

Gear

Bring a standard North Carolina free climbing rack. Microsized wired nuts, shallow Tri-Cams, removable bolts, and microcams are sometimes necessary.

Getting There

Moore's Wall is located north of Winston-Salem in Stokes County. From Winston-Salem, follow US 52 north toward Mount Airy for approximately 13 miles to exit 122 (Moore-RJR Drive). Turn left off the exit and drive east for approximately 4 miles. Moore Road turns into Mountain View Road and continues through two stoplights and one blinking red light until an intersection with NC 66 marked by several convenience stores. Turn left (north) onto NC 66 and drive 6.7 miles to Moore's Spring Road. (A sign on the left will point to Hanging Rock State Park, where there is camping.) Turn right onto Moore's Spring Road (SR 1001) and continue for 0.5 mile. Turn right onto Mickey Road (SR 2011) at a sign for Stoney Ridge Baptist Church. Continue for 0.8 mile. Turn right onto Charlie Young Road (SR 2028) and continue for 0.3 mile. To the right is Tory's Den Road. On the left, there is a parking area and park trail kiosk for the Tory's Den Trailhead. *Important*: You must stop and register here!

Once you have registered, drive up the dirt Tory's Den Road for 0.7 mile until you reach a Y intersection. This is private property. From here you have two options.

To the main parking area: Veer right here onto Tomahawk Road (which is often in poor condition) and follow it 0.5 mile until the road ends at an obvious, two-level marked parking area. Cars with high clearance may continue to a farther parking lot about 150 yards down this road, but this lot is sometimes overcrowded. The road ends in a cul-de-sac, which is sometimes hard to negotiate if packed with cars.

To the alternate parking area: If you have a high clearance vehicle, you may veer left at the Y intersection and continue up a hill to a narrow parking area just in front of a park boundary gate.

Approach

From the main parking area: Near the cul-de-sac at the end of the mountain road, a smaller jeep road heads right and up toward the cliff. Follow this road until it pinches down into a narrow trail through a scree field. You will pass the marked park boundary here. Continue on this trail following occasional blue blazes about 0.5 mile, past the Zschiesche Corridor, until it arrives at the Central Wall just underneath the route *Washboard*. Turn right for the Circus Wall, Fire Wall, and Hanging Garden, which are all within a few hundred feet. Turn left and hike about 0.5 mile to reach the Amphitheater. The North End is another 0.25 mile past the Amphitheater along the obvious trail.

From the alternate parking area: Hike around the park gate and follow the jeep road about 0.4 mile until you see a narrow opening in the woods on your right.

Follow this narrow trail through the woods until you reach a junction. Turn left for the Amphitheater and the North End, or continue straight, passing a large boulder on the way, to join the trail for the Circus Wall, Fire Wall, and Hanging Garden.

From Hanging Rock State Park: Hike the Moore's Wall Trail from the park. Trail maps are available from the park office.

Routes on Moore's Wall are numbered 1 through 52 and are presented right to left, beginning with the Hanging Garden area.

Hanging Garden Area

The Hanging Garden has the highest concentration of hard climbing at Moore's Wall. In recent years, several new lines have gone up and there are now several different anchors along the summit rim. The wall gets afternoon sun.

From the base of the Fire Wall, you'll see the Hanging Garden area up and to your right. Continue hiking to the right (west) for about 150 yards to reach a major gully leading up and left. Here, you can scramble up the gully (it's fourth class and not a good place for dogs) to reach the Hanging Garden. The first route you'll hit is *Pooh Corner*. Walk right for *First in Flight*.

Descent: For routes that top out on the rim, walk left and locate a weird-looking (but bomber) bolt and fixed pulley just beneath the rim above *Sentinel Buttress*. A double-rope rappel (110 feet) gains the Crow's Nest. From here, a single-rope rappel (80 feet) reaches the ground.

1. First in Flight   5.12a

This is the obvious 40-foot and 120-degree roof at the far right side of the Hanging Garden. There are some tough sequences, but placing the gear on this route may be the crux.

First ascent: Russell Erickson and Todd Skinner (1985).

Start: Off a block on the far right end of the Hanging Garden.

Pitch 1: Clip a rusty bolt hanger low on the wall, then climb up and right past a bolt and a fixed pin to the summit. No anchor. (40 feet). *Note:* It is possible to avoid the rusty bolt and boulder up to the first bolt of *Supercrimp*.

2. Supercrimp   5.13c/d

A direct and rarely repeated sport route up the insanely steep roof.

First ascent: Howie Feinsilber (1995).

Start: 10 feet left of *First in Flight* in a short, left-facing dihedral.

Pitch 1: Crank past six bolts to the summit. No anchor. (40 feet).

3. Pooh Corner   5.11a

An excellent "crack" climb up the overhanging white wall. If you're not used to steep climbing of this nature, *Pooh* may feel much harder than its rating!

First ascent: David Petree and Jon Regelbrugge (1986) to an obvious stance below final roof. Tim Fisher and Doug Reed pushed the route to the top.

Start: In a white corner on the far-right side of the Hanging Garden and just behind two hemlock trees.

Dudley Hammon in the steeps on First in Flight *(route 1)*

Pitch 1: Stem and jam up the corner to gain a right-facing flake at an overlap. Engineer moves past this to gain a good rest. Step left and continue to the summit past whopping jugs. Most parties set a natural belay here and then move left to rappel off *Stars and Bars.* (60 feet).

4. Porter's Pooh   5.11c

An excellent variation to its sister on the right. Steep and spicy, with one section where a successful on-sight may hinge on a pro-or-go decision!

First ascent: Porter Jarrard (1990, on-sight).

Start: See *Pooh Corner.*

Pitch 1: Stem and jam up the corner to gain a left-leaning ramp. Ape out this past gigantic holds until you can finagle a rest under the final headwall. Continue to the summit ledge. (60 feet).

5. Pygmalion   5.12d

Hard climbing abounds. Extremely fingery technical sequences and a lunge to a hidden clipping hold, which is the only jug on the route.

First ascent: Porter Jarrard (1990).

Start: This is the second bolt line 15 feet left of *Pooh Corner.* It starts in a short, left-facing dihedral, down and right of *Hercules.*

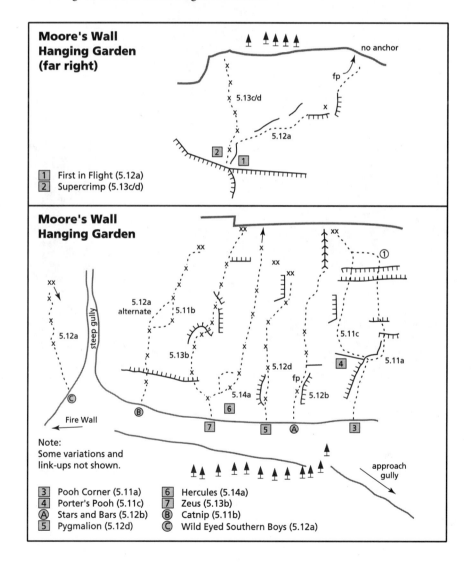

Moore's Wall Hanging Garden (far right)

no anchor

fp

5.13c/d

5.12a

1 First in Flight (5.12a)
2 Supercrimp (5.13c/d)

Moore's Wall Hanging Garden

steep gully

5.12a

5.12a alternate

5.11b

5.13b

5.14a

5.12d

5.12b

fp

5.11c

5.11a

Fire Wall

Note:
Some variations and link-ups not shown.

approach gully

3 Pooh Corner (5.11a)
4 Porter's Pooh (5.11c)
Ⓐ Stars and Bars (5.12b)
5 Pygmalion (5.12d)

6 Hercules (5.14a)
7 Zeus (5.13b)
Ⓑ Catnip (5.11b)
Ⓒ Wild Eyed Southern Boys (5.12a)

Tim Fisher in the steep finishing moves of Pooh Corner *(route 3)*

Pitch 1: Sport. Five bolts lead to a stance at the base of a right-facing corner with cold shuts. (50 feet).

6. Hercules   5.13c
A longtime project that was initially bolted in 1988, *Hercules* was finally climbed after a sustained effort.

Start: 10 feet left of *Pygmalion.*

Pitch 1: Sport. Precise footwork and a few long throws will get you through this 120-degree overhanging test piece. Seven bolts to cold shuts. (80 feet). *Note:* A variation between the second and third bolts reduces the difficulty somewhat.

7. Zeus   5.13b

This is the well-known and exceptionally steep sport climb that takes a strong line through the Hanging Garden. Excellent exposure and vicious moves.

First ascent: Harrison Dekker, Porter Jarrard, Eric Zschiesche (1989).

Start: 5 feet left of *Hercules*, down and right of a large hanging block.

Pitch 1: Sport. Climb out the wildly steep wall via crimpers and a few elusive moves. Six bolts and a pin. (80 feet).

Sentinel Buttress: Fire Wall

Sentinel Buttress is the most prominent area of rock on the right side of Moore's Wall. It includes there separate walls: Fire Wall, Sentinel Buttress, and Circus Wall.

Any line up the intimidating Fire Wall is an excellent tick. The upper part is nicknamed the "Billboard" for reasons that become obvious when you see the area. Although you'll note an unusual number of bolts, all of these routes are mixed with many spicy RP placements. The wall gets afternoon sun.

Descent: For routes that reach the rim, traverse left to the *Sentinel Buttress* rappel just beneath the rim. A double-rope rappel (110 feet) gains the Crow's Nest. From here, a single-rope rappel (80 feet) reaches the ground.

8. Riders on the Storm   5.11a

As the first line here, *Riders* helped break the aura of the Billboard. Though less popular than *Wild Kingdom*, it remains a committing and enjoyable lead.

First ascent: Tom Howard, Bob Rotert, Tom McMillan (1978, ground-up). Although initially a project of McMillan's, Rotert climbed above a scary pin (which today is the pin stack) and placed the bolt. Howard went up next and got the free ascent.

Start: Off an obvious 25-foot block with a spacious ledge under the Fire Wall.

Pitch 1: Step high to clip a stacked fixed pin. Move out left via slopey holds to get established under the huge left-facing dihedral/roof system. When you reach the first large roof, traverse right along the overhang to a bolt. Continue up and right to skirt the roof and then climb the face above leading to a large crack splitting the Billboard. Belay here. (5.11a; 130 feet).

Pitch 2: Climb the crack past the Billboard until it ends at a pin. Traverse right to gain the ledge below *Catnip*. (5.10b; 100 feet).

9. Wild Kingdom   5.11d

One of North Carolina's most classic hard routes, this line features two pitches of totally different styles. A mistake on the first pitch is a bad idea—excepting the initial pin stack, treat the other fixed gear as backup and not as primary protection!

First ascent: Tom McMillan and Bob Rotert climbed the route free with one point of aid in 1978. In 1979, Rob Robinson and McMillan returned for the all-free ascent.

Start: See *Riders on the Storm*.

Pitch 1: Climb *Riders* but continue into the dihedral past a pin and two bolts until

Moore's Wall
Sentinel Buttress:
Fire Wall

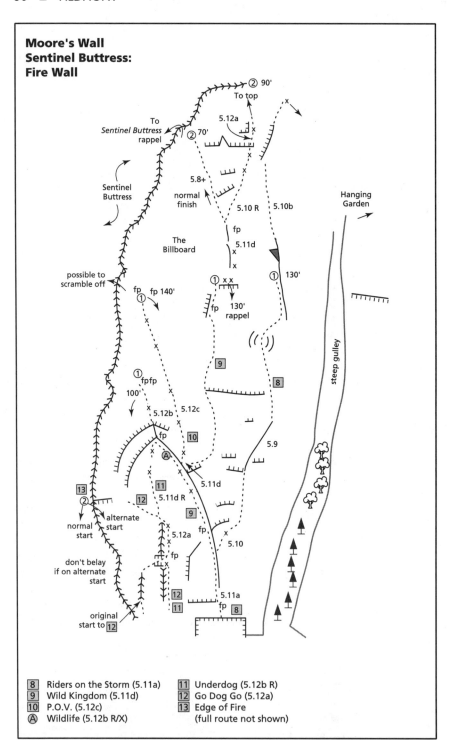

8 Riders on the Storm (5.11a)
9 Wild Kingdom (5.11d)
10 P.O.V. (5.12c)
Ⓐ Wildlife (5.12b R/X)

11 Underdog (5.12b R)
12 Go Dog Go (5.12a)
13 Edge of Fire
   (full route not shown)

you can move out right. (It is possible to clip a pin on *P.O.V.* to protect your second.) Move right and then straight up past two fixed pins to the anchor. (5.11d; 130 feet). *Note*: Watch for rope drag!

Pitch 2: Blast up the thin crack past two bolts and a pin via off-balance face holds and the occasional sloper until the difficulty eases. Continue up, aiming slightly left to a ledge and natural belay. (5.11d; 70 feet).

Note: Tim Fisher completed a direct alternate finish (sustained 5.12a), which tackles the summit roofs past some fixed gear, a pin, and one bolt.

10. P.O.V.   5.12c

The hardest line on the Fire Wall tackles the business on the first pitch of *Wild Kingdom* and accelerates into vicious crimpers.

First ascent: Porter Jarrard (1989, ground-up).

Start: Same as *Riders on the Storm*.

Pitch 1: From where *Wild Kingdom* fired out right on the first pitch (at the

Dudley Hammon bears down on the Billboard crux section of Wild Kingdom *(route 9).*

crux), continue straight up the steep wall past two bolts to a small arête. Claw your way past two final bolts and then aim for an easy crack on the left shoulder of the wall. Fixed anchors. (140 feet).

Note: A possibly unrepeated Doug Reed variation, *Wildlife* (5.12b R/X), continues up the dihedral where *P.O.V.* and *Kingdom* went right. Pull the roof past two pins and then finish on *Underdog* (see below). Be extremely careful of loose rock on this link-up.

11. Underdog   5.12b R
Here's a direct combo up the Fire Wall that features a full slate of cruxes.

First ascent: Porter Jarrard (1989, ground-up).

Start: 10 feet left of *Wild Kingdom* and off a block.

Pitch 1: Climb a crack leading to a tight dihedral capped by a small roof. Fire straight up through white rock (5.11d R), passing two bolts, a pin, and a final bolt to the anchor. (100 feet).

12. Go Dog Go   5.12a
This route climbs up to the Fire Wall arête and gains excellent position.

First ascent: Tim Fisher, Doug Reed (1987).

Start: On *Underdog.* The original start began 20 feet left, but *Underdog* created a better line.

Pitch 1: Climb *Underdog* to the roof, where you can move left past a bolt to a narrow ledge with a dowel. Follow a blunt arête past two more bolts, some RPs and a pin to the base of a steep white face. Traverse directly left 20 feet to the ledge where *Edge of Fire* finishes. (85 feet).

Note: It is also possible to continue up the face to the first bolt on *Underdog* and lower. If this calls to you, be sure to bring RPs for the 5.11d R face.

Sentinel Buttress: Sentinel Buttress and Circus Wall
Home to most of the early climbing at Moore's, today there are probably more forgotten routes on Sentinel Buttress proper and Circus Wall than established ones. Some of the undocumented lines include two direct start variations to *Sentinel Buttress, Staircase, Bugles, Crown of Thorns,* and *Warm-Up.* All of these routes were established in the late 1960s and range from 5.0 to 5.5. The Circus Wall gets sun by midafternoon.

Descent: Locate a weird-looking (but bomber) bolt and fixed pulley just beneath the rim above *Sentinel Buttress.* A double-rope rappel (110 feet) gains the Crow's Nest. From here, a single-rope rappel (80 feet) reaches the ground.

13. Edge of Fire   5.11b
Like *Welcome to Moore's* on the Central Wall, for years this line had an "R" rating associated with it for unknown reasons. Getting your sequence right is the key on the spectacular crux, but there is protection available.

First ascent: Lee and Pat Munson (1979).

Start: Either climb *Super Direct* to a stance under the right-leaning corner, or

Moore's Wall Sentinel Buttress

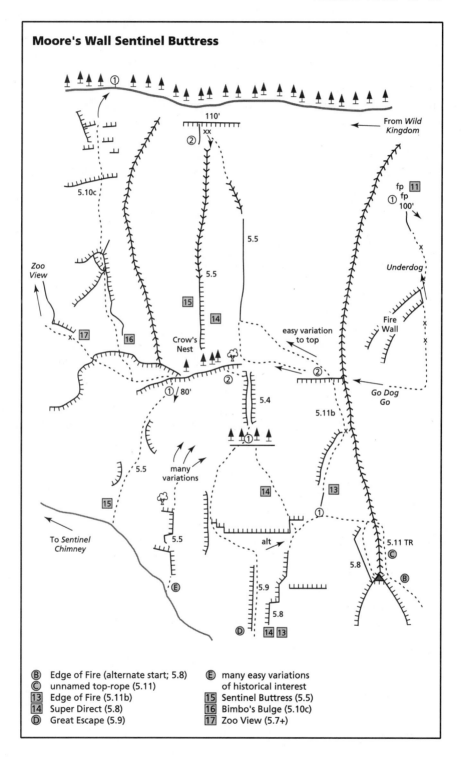

110'
5.10c
Zoo View
5.5
5.5
15
14
Crow's Nest
From *Wild Kingdom*
fp 11
fp 100'
Underdog
Fire Wall
easy variation to top
Go Dog Go
80'
5.4
5.11b
many variations
5.5
15
14
13
To *Sentinel Chimney*
5.5
alt
5.11 TR
C
5.8
B
5.9
5.8
D
14 13

- B Edge of Fire (alternate start; 5.8)
- C unnamed top-rope (5.11)
- 13 Edge of Fire (5.11b)
- 14 Super Direct (5.8)
- D Great Escape (5.9)
- E many easy variations of historical interest
- 15 Sentinel Buttress (5.5)
- 16 Bimbo's Bulge (5.10c)
- 17 Zoo View (5.7+)

traverse out left from the obvious ledge system under the main Fire Wall. If approached the second way this can be done in two pitches, but watch for rope drag.

Pitch 1: Follow either start to get established under the right-leaning corner.

Pitch 2: Stem and lieback up the wild, slabby corner until you're under an obvious cleft. Clip the bolt and make powerful moves through the cleft to gain low-angled ground. Belay on a pedestal. (5.11b; 100 feet if done as one pitch, 60 feet otherwise).

Pitch 3: Wander left and up the easy face to gain the Crow's Nest. (5.0; 40 feet).

14. Super Direct   5.8

The appealing crack on the front of Sentinel Buttress has a powerful start and then backs off to allow for some enjoyable face climbing.

First ascent: Unknown.

Start: On the obvious, right-facing crack and overhang at the low point of the buttress and just left of a large cave.

Pitch 1: Jam the flake past a roof and then move up and right via a crack system. Move right around another roof and traverse back left with your feet at the lip of the roof. Finish by wandering left to gain a stance beneath a large chimney. (5.8; 80 feet).

Pitch 2: Follow the chimney to gain the Crow's Nest. Many variations are possible here. (5.4; 40 feet).

Note: On the first pitch, it is possible to stop traversing earlier and climb through a nice 5.7 overhang. In this way a second pitch is possible that is well right of the Crow's Nest.

15. Sentinel Buttress   5.5

This is the classic moderate at Moore's Wall and the standard approach for *Bimbo's Bulge* and *Zoo View* farther to the left on the Circus Wall. Although the first pitch is extremely popular since it leads to the Crow's Nest, it is sometimes possible to find solitude on the second pitch. Watch for parties rappelling off both anchors since this route is the rap lane for the entire Sentinel Buttress.

First ascent: Robert Mosely, M. Davis (1963).

Start: Locate a small rise on a buttress where you can gain some polished, low-angled jugs.

Pitch 1: Climb the face to gain the Crow's Nest. (5.5; 80 feet).

Pitch 2: Move to the right side of the Crow's Nest and follow the obvious wide crack system to the summit rim. (5.5; 110 feet)

16. Bimbo's Bulge   5.10c

Thin face climbing leads to a wild, overhanging roof sequence.

First ascent: Rich Gottlieb, Jack Carter (1977).

Start: Same as *Sentinel Buttress.*

Pitch 1: Climb the face to gain the Crow's Nest, following *Sentinel Buttress.* (5.5; 80 feet).

Pitch 2: Move out left on the ledge and climb the steep, thin face to a triangular overhang. Blow over the first roof and get established under a second overhang. Get good small gear (0.4 inches) and blast for the summit. (5.10c; 100 feet).

17. Zoo View   5.7+

Possibly the best 5.7 in North Carolina. The "hero" holds on the second roof are unbelievable. Not recommend for leaders who are at their limit on sustained 5.7. Either many long slings or double ropes recommended.

First ascent: Tom Howard, Bruce Meneghin (1976, on-sight).

Start: Same as *Sentinel Buttress*.

Pitch 1: Climb the face to gain the Crow's Nest. (5.5; 80 feet).

Pitch 2: Edge carefully left out a precarious face to clip the lone bolt. Continue moving left around the corner to gain the base of a crack (stay low for good footholds). Follow the crack system into an alcove where you can prep for a grand finale roof finish. (5.7+; 140 feet).

Note: Watch for rope drag!

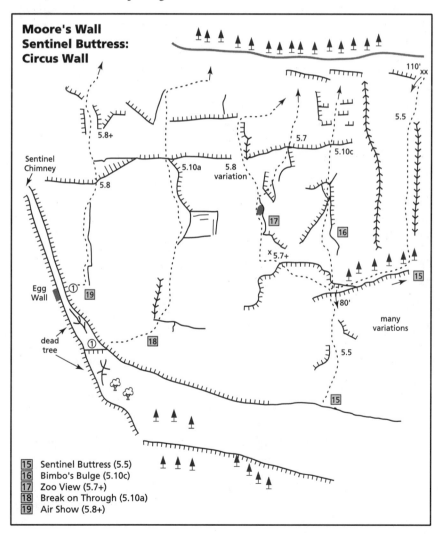

15 Sentinel Buttress (5.5)
16 Bimbo's Bulge (5.10c)
17 Zoo View (5.7+)
18 Break on Through (5.10a)
19 Air Show (5.8+)

18. Break on Through   5.10a

Locals swear this route's crux is a one-move wonder. Want to find out for yourself?

First ascent: Tom Howard, Tom McMillan (1978, on-sight).

Start: In Sentinel Chimney, the obvious cleft separating the Circus Wall from the Egg Wall to the left.

Pitch 1: Climb the Sentinel Chimney past the first dead tree to a ledge. Natural belay. (5.4; 50 feet).

Pitch 2: Move out right 10 feet to gain an awkward crack/corner. Follow it through an imposing overhang. Continue up and through a notch in a second overhang, then race for the rim on easier ground. (5.10a; 150 feet).

19. Air Show   5.8+

Steep and sustained with multiple cruxes, this may not be the best way to warm up. One false move high on the route and you may turn into a bottle rocket with report.

First ascent: Tom Howard, Bruce Meneghin (1976, on-sight).

Start: Same as *Break on Through*.

Pitch 1: Climb the Sentinel Chimney to the second of two dead trees. (5.4; 100 feet).

Pitch 2: From the belay, continue up the chimney a ways until you can move out right to a corner system. Follow it up and through a large overhang. Follow the face above using huge jugs, passing another corner and overhang. Moderate rock leads to the top. (5.8+; 100 feet).

The Central Wall

A collection of buttresses that ranges from slabby and casual to steep and horrifying, the Central Wall at Moore's stretches for several hundred yards in either direction and encompasses all types of routes.

Descent: There are several options: (1) It is possible to reach the summit rim and follow the cliff-top trail left to a junction near a large boulder. From here, follow the large gully to reach the base of the cliff between the main cliff and the Amphitheater. This is nontechnical and the best option if you have three or more people in your party. (2) There is a fixed anchor in a tree above the first pitch of *Welcome to Moore's*, which is between *Easy Hard* and *Shit Hook*. However, it is difficult to find since it is located partway down a vertical gully. (3) It is possible to make a fourth-class descent on rock to the right of *Washboard*. This descent is not advisable if you are unfamiliar with the route.

20. Hopscotch   5.3

A casual romp up a featured face with a fine view of the main Circus Wall. Many different variations exist and beginners will enjoy its exposure and great protection. However, *Hopscotch* has also been the scene of injuries due to the ledge-out potential and the severity of falling on featured, low-angled rock. Climb smart!

First ascent: Unknown.

Start: At the top of a large block just above the approach trail.

Pitch 1: Wander up the face just right of the overhang. Follow easy rock and a large crack system to the summit. (140 feet).

Art Brown pulls into the roof on Air Show *(route 19).*

21. Washboard   5.6

Amazing position, sinker protection, and memorable jugs. One of the best moderates around . . . even considering *Zoo View* is right around the corner!

First ascent: Unknown.

Start: At the base of a large dead tree that angles over the approach trail.

Pitch 1: Climb corner systems to an overlap. Step right and climb up fantastic face through a sea of incut jugs. Continue climbing just inside the corner until you can find a natural belay on a large ledge. (100 feet).

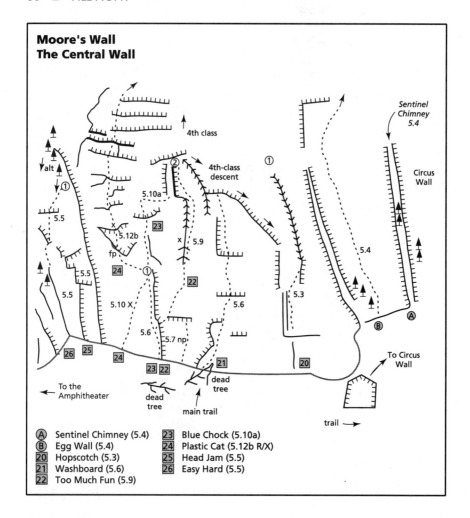

Moore's Wall
The Central Wall

Ⓐ Sentinel Chimney (5.4) |23| Blue Chock (5.10a)
Ⓑ Egg Wall (5.4) |24| Plastic Cat (5.12b R/X)
|20| Hopscotch (5.3) |25| Head Jam (5.5)
|21| Washboard (5.6) |26| Easy Hard (5.5)
|22| Too Much Fun (5.9)

22. Too Much Fun   5.9

Although a touch less difficult than *Blue Chock* (below), this route also offers nice position on the steep upper section.

First ascent: Bruce Meneghin, Tom Howard (1976, on-sight). Tim Fisher added the bolt on a later ascent.

Start: Look for a large flake above a landmark dead tree.

Pitch 1: Climb the first portion of *Blue Chock* until you can traverse right into a shallow corner. Continue up the corner past a bolt and to the base of a huge left-facing corner. With double ropes, this can be done as one pitch. (100 feet). Otherwise, set up a belay soon after the first bolt.

Note: Most parties unknowingly bail after the crux and finish on *Washboard*. The correct finish (5.8) goes up and left until you are level with the base of the dihedral on *Blue Chock*. Traverse right along the overhang. It is also possible to finish on *Blue Chock*.

23. Blue Chock   5.10a
Great crack and face climbing to a leering roof slot finish. Make "birthing" moves, then set up a belay nearby for a bird's-eye view!

First ascent: Paul Kinnaird, Robin Kinnaird (pre-1976).

Start: Same as *Too Much Fun.*

Pitch 1: Climb an obvious lieback flake above the dead tree to a stance just below a corner. (5.6; 50 feet).

Pitch 2: Pop over the corner and negotiate the crack through the steep wave of quartzite covered in electric green lichen. Traverse right into the corner (micronuts are handy) and grunt to the top (5.10a; 90 feet). *Note:* Many parties prefer to pull a 5.10a bulge midway out the second-pitch traverse.

Descent: Descend by walking off the fourth-class ledges right of *Washboard.*

24. Plastic Cat   5.12b R/X
This is one of the most serious routes at Moore's. The crux is well protected but it's the before and after that pose problems. . . . Double ropes recommended.

First ascent: Doug Reed, Tim Fisher (1987, ground-up with some aid).

Start: 10 feet left of *Blue Chock.*

Pitch 1: Climb the face left of *Blue Chock* (5.10 X) to a stance beneath a seam leading to a bulge with underclings. Crank past a fixed pin up to the bolt, nail the sequential crux, and hold on for 15 feet to a stance. Gear up and continue through overhangs with sporty pro. (140 feet).

25. Head Jam   5.5
Do not be deterred by the awkward slot about 40 feet above your head. Protection abounds and it leads to some excellent—and casual—corner climbing.

First ascent: Unknown.

Start: In cracks about 15 feet left of the huge left-facing corner.

Pitch 1: Climb cracks into the "head jam" slot. Either undercling or burrow your way left to a stepped crack system. Continue up the corner to fixed anchor. (110 feet).

26. Easy Hard   5.5
This route is often the scene of epic first leads. Nevertheless, it is also one of the best moderates around. Make sure to save some midsized pro for a crux near the end.

First ascent: Buddy Price, K. Savoy (1973).

Start: 50 feet left of *Head Jam* in a cleft splintered with cracks.

Pitch 1: Climb the obvious, lower-angled corner with excellent protection and many good stances. Eventually you will arrive at a small overlap; step right and pull through the face to a tree ledge. Belay here from fixed slings, or continue up the corner another 25 feet to the upper fixed anchor. (135 feet).

27. Welcome to Moore's   5.10d (no topo)
For years, this climb had a reputation as poorly protected and intimidating. Instead, it is one of the best lines here—a steep romp through buckets. Double ropes recommended.

First ascent: Tim Fisher, David Petree, Tim Schneider (1985). Fisher arrived at the cliff one day to find Petree and Schneider trying the upper roof. After Petree's first attempt failed, Fisher climbed up to meet them and proceeded to on-sight the crux pitch—bypassing Petree's in-situ protection in favor of his own.

Start: In a dirty corner about 75 feet left of *Easy Hard.*

Pitch 1: Climb the dirty, easy corner to the base of a short left facing corner. (5.5; 70 feet).

Pitch 2: Pull out right through the overhang and ape up to the diagonal crack 6 feet right of the main feature. Work some pro high into the flared corner, then step down and move left to gain gigantic jugs. Motor to a ledge with a natural belay. (5.10d; 50 feet).

Descent: Scramble off via descent gullies in either direction or locate a rappel tree 75 feet to the right and about 10 feet down a fourth-class chimney.

The Amphitheater

Between the Central Wall and the Amphitheater, there are several developed areas, a major (climbers-only) descent gully, and a park trail that leads up to the stone tower. This trail leads to an upper tier known as the Meat Puppet Crag.

Towering over a shady gully nearby on the left end of Moore's Wall (about 5 minutes from the Central Wall) is the Amphitheater. It is an imposing wall that offers everything from moderate face climbing to horizontal, 20-foot roofs. This is the place to be in warmer weather because it doesn't get sun until midafternoon.

Descent: For all routes right of *Almost Seven,* descend from fixed anchors at the top of *Stab in the Dark.* It is approximately 100 feet to the base. For *Almost Seven* and all routes to its left, descend from fixed stoppers at the top of this route. It is exactly 100 feet to the base from here.

28. Shit Hook   5.8+

New 5.8 leaders will not want to get lured onto this climb just because it looks slabby and the intimidation factor is low. It still packs a punch.

First ascent: Tom Howard, Rich Gottlieb, Bob Rotert (1978, on-sight).

Start: On the right-most side of the Amphitheater at a large, white, left-facing flake.

Pitch 1: Climb left-facing corner using edges and sloping liebacks to gain jugs out left. Continue up to an obvious ledge. (80 feet).

Note: Kenny Hibbits made the initial attempt and took a 20-foot ground-fall when he pulled off a block! Hibbits landed unhurt with the rock in between his legs.

29. Stab in the Dark   5.10d (5.8 R)

Get the tough stuff over with early, and then enjoy a nice (though somewhat run-out) arête.

First ascent: Tom McMillan, Rich Gottlieb, Bob Rotert, Tom Howard (1978).

Start: 35 feet left of *Shit Hook* and just right of the obvious low arête.

Pitch 1: Boulder your way into a pumpy stance where you can find some pro. Traverse left to gain the short hand and finger crack laced with thank-god jugs. Wander up the arête to a fixed anchor. (100 feet).

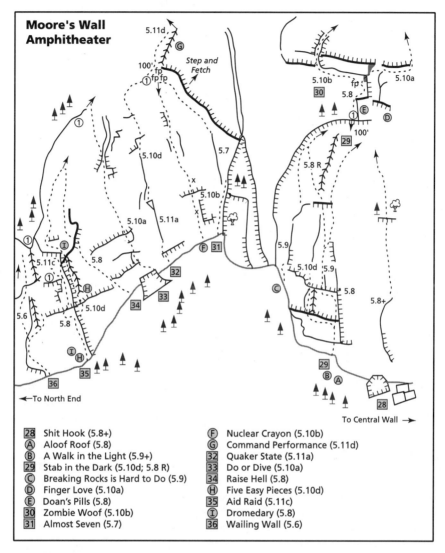

Moore's Wall
Amphitheater

5.11d
Ⓖ
100' fp
Step and
Fetch
①fp fp
5.10b
30
5.8
fp
5.10a
①
5.10d
5.7
Ⓔ
Ⓓ
100'
①
29
5.8 R
5.10d
X
5.10b
5.10a 5.11a
Ⓕ 31
5.9
5.11c
5.8
32
5.10d 5.9
Ⓒ
5.8
①
Ⓗ
33
5.8+
5.6
5.10d
34
5.8
Ⓘ Ⓗ
29
35
Ⓑ Ⓐ
36
28
←To North End
To Central Wall →

28	Shit Hook (5.8+)	Ⓕ	Nuclear Crayon (5.10b)
Ⓐ	Aloof Roof (5.8)	Ⓖ	Command Performance (5.11d)
Ⓑ	A Walk in the Light (5.9+)	32	Quaker State (5.11a)
29	Stab in the Dark (5.10d; 5.8 R)	33	Do or Dive (5.10a)
Ⓒ	Breaking Rocks is Hard to Do (5.9)	34	Raise Hell (5.8)
Ⓓ	Finger Love (5.10a)	Ⓗ	Five Easy Pieces (5.10d)
Ⓔ	Doan's Pills (5.8)	35	Aid Raid (5.11c)
30	Zombie Woof (5.10b)	Ⓘ	Dromedary (5.8)
31	Almost Seven (5.7)	36	Wailing Wall (5.6)

30. Zombie Woof   5.10b

A caver's delight! Depending on how you reach this wild slot way off the deck, it could be a full day of thrashing. Larger climbers may want to climb the crux as a lieback, which reportedly isn't much harder. Some large (3 to 4-inch) cams are helpful—even if you abandon all your gear for the final bit. Make sure you rack on the proper side of your body for the woof.

First ascent: Carlton Ramm, et al. (1978, ground-up).

Start: Climb either *Breaking Rocks is Hard to Do* (see topo) or *Stab in the Dark*.

Pitch 1: (aka *Breaking Rocks is Hard to Do*): Chickenwing through the alcove to gain a nice crack. Follow to a fixed belay. (5.9; 100 feet).

Pitch 2: Step left off the belay and gain a short 5.8 corner to a fixed belay. Bypass this and climb left into the roof. Lieback and jam out the steep roof until you can slither into the slot and "escape" by tunneling out to the summit. (5.10b; 60 feet).

31. Almost Seven (aka Golden Earring)   5.7

This route is extremely popular and rewarding. This long pitch requires crack climbing, a heady traverse (remember your second!), and super exposure despite the large roof looming above your head.

First ascent: Bruce Meneghin, Tom Howard (1976, on-sight).

Start: Either in the corner (more popular) or a crack 10 feet right (better).

Pitch 1: Climb the corner for a ways until you gain an excellent vertical crack system. Follow it until you can begin traversing left under the big roof. (100 feet).

Note: It is possible to climb a 5.8 finish (*Step and Fetch*) through the steep upper face.

32. Quaker State   5.11a

A superb, direct line up the center of the Amphitheater that should test your mettle. Once above the second crux, scour the wall for hidden pro on this aptly named classic.

Start: 20 feet left of *Almost Seven*.

First ascent: Rob Robinson, Tom McMillan (1978).

Pitch 1: Step onto the featured face and wander over a low overlap. Follow the arching crack to a triangular hole. Above, get a good rest and move into the thinning seam. Get pro high; move a little right and race for the top. (100 feet).

33. Do or Dive   5.10a

A classic sandbag that is a little runout to boot (hence the name). Make sure what pro you get is good.

First ascent: Tom McMillan, Jack Carter, Rob Robinson (1978).

Start: Begin on the right side of the large block.

Pitch 1: Traverse left out to the short vertical hand crack. Blast up the face through a series of small overlaps. At the overhang, look for good wires above to protect the crux. Pull the overhang and climb up to the crack. Load up on gear before heading to the big horizontal crack and cruise up the chimney to the top. Or, step left and climb straight up the face. (100 feet).

34. Raise Hell   5.8

A great route for intermediate leaders. Bring plenty of big gear.

First ascent: Tom Howard, Bill Newman (1974).

Start: At a large block at the base of the Amphitheater, just left of *Do or Dive*.

Pitch 1: Move left off the block and through steep, featured rock to a large chimney. Either follow this to the top or move out onto the face using large holds. (100 feet).

35. Aid Raid   5.11c

This is one of the most amazing (or galling) roofs around. Despite the steepness, for the most part *Aid Raid* is a romp through a juggy crack laced with buckets.

First ascent: Bob Rotert, Ted Anderson (1978, ground-up).

Fred Bahnson on the lower cracks of Do or Dive *(route 33)*

Start: Inside the corner, about 30 feet left of *Raise Hell.*

Pitch 1: Climb up the casual face to gain a large ledge. (5.8; 40 feet).

Pitch 2: Crank out the wild, horizontal roof until you can turn the lip by moving up and left. Belay in an alcove. (5.11c; 40 feet).

Pitch 3: Romp to the summit. (5.5; 60 feet).

36. Wailing Wall   5.6

History suggests this line was climbed in the early days, but was then overlooked for years until it was named in the mid-1990s. Nevertheless, it is a three-star moderate.

First ascent: Unknown.

Start: On the right side of the obvious arête at the bottom (left) side of the Amphitheater.

Pitch 1: Several variations exist. Either climb a chimney and face to a ledge or wander up the arête. Traverse under the roof, and step left past a crack system, then up a steep face with wonderful exposure, huge holds, and great gear. Belay from trees.

North End

This is a steep series of cliffs on the far left side of Moore's Wall that is actually the east end of the cliff. Although it is closed for a portion of each year for peregrine falcon nesting, it is well worth a visit during open season. The wall gets early morning sun.

Descent: Double ropes (or, in some cases, just a single 60-meter rope) will get you down many of the routes. In the case of the *Nutsweat* area, use the communal *Nutsweat* anchor. It is also possible to descend the Indian Head gully with a few short rappels.

37. Indian Head Direct   5.10+ (no topo)

The classic third pitch is amazing. Don't bail early, since you'll finish by standing on the 200-foot high Indian Head. This is the first large piece of rock you'll encounter after the Amphitheater. Double ropes recommended.

First ascent: Tim Fisher, Terry Jennings (1981).

Start: Directly under the obvious "Indian head" about 5 minutes beyond the Amphitheater. Look for a V slot with an overhang at the bottom.

Pitch 1: Climb through the overhang and slot to a nice belay ledge. (5.7; 40 feet).

Pitch 2: Climb the steep crack through the awkward bulge and continue on easier ground to a small ledge below the dark left-facing corner. (5.10c; 70 feet).

Pitch 3: Climb directly up the steep corner (look for no-hands rest) pulling over a block at the top. From here it is possible to bail in shame to the trees on the right. Instead, move directly left to gain a series of steep chimneys. Exit these into a wild open book, which you'll follow up and left to a ledge. From here, move left and up easy ground to the summit. (5.10d; 80 feet).

Descent: It is possible to scramble back down to the trees on the right. Two ropes will get you down in one rappel. Or scramble fourth class to the left (east) to the Indian Head gully for one 75-foot rappel.

38. Reckless Abandon   5.11a

A classic with great climbing and protection. It will feel harder than its grade if you miss the no-hands rest. Best done as one pitch.

First ascent: John Provetero, David Petree, Tim Fisher (1984, ground-up).

Start: Stroll up the long, sloping ledge that starts in the center of the cliff. This is the start of *Bat Attack, Death Wish,* and *Nutsweat.*

Pitch 1: Begin on *Nutsweat,* but move right through some chossy rock, passing a bolt, to gain a steep, featured crack. Climb past the obvious hole and through the vegetated corner. (5.11a; 90 feet).

Note: Doug Reed climbed a direct start (5.11c R/X) that is not for the faint hearted. Climb the tempting arête past a fixed pin to gain the crack system.

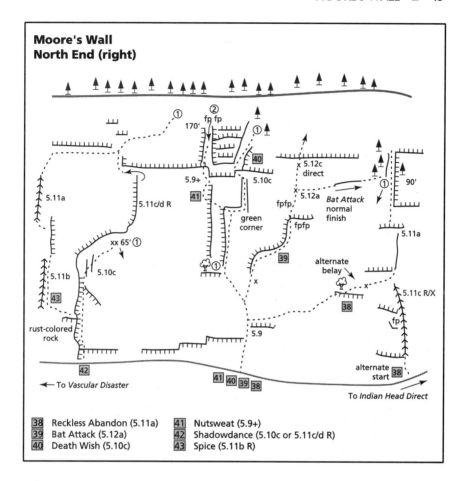

**Moore's Wall
North End (right)**

170'
fp fp
5.12c
direct
5.9+
5.10c
5.11a
5.11c/d R
40
5.12a
Bat Attack
normal
finish
green
corner
fpfp
fpfp
41
90'
5.11a
xx 65' ①
5.11b
5.10c
39
alternate
belay
5.11c R/X
43
x
38
fp
rust-colored
rock
5.9
42
5.9
38
← To *Vascular Disaster*
41 40 39 38
alternate
start 38
To *Indian Head Direct*

38	Reckless Abandon (5.11a)	41	Nutsweat (5.9+)
39	Bat Attack (5.12a)	42	Shadowdance (5.10c or 5.11c/d R)
40	Death Wish (5.10c)	43	Spice (5.11b R)

39. Bat Attack   5.12a

This route has been the scene of at least one genuine bat attack. All the same, if you're up to the burn, this killer lieback corner is quite a prize. Bring extra microcams and a ⅜-inch removable bolt.

First ascent: Monty Reagan aided this flake to the stance that now has fixed pins. The first ascent goes to Doug Reed and Tim Fisher (1986, A0 sieged). Fisher returned for the free ascent in 1988. Seth Tart added the direct finish described below.

Start: Same as *Reckless Abandon.*

Pitch 1: Climb the first pitch of *Nutsweat* to the base of the green corner, where you can get protection for the traversing moves into *Bat Attack.* (An RB hole also protects the first moves of the corner.) Thin liebacks take you up to the overhang where you can clip old angle pins. Move left to a second pair of pins and scour the wall for micropro. Crimp your way past the second bolt and trend right for the normal finish at a belay shared with *Reckless Abandon.* (95 feet).

Note: After the second bolt, move straight up past a third for the 5.12c direct finish (aka *New World Man*).

40. Death Wish   5.10c

Intimidating? Certainly. But this is hardly a grim reaper's special. Instead, you'll want to prepare for some thuggish (albeit well-protected) climbing through the upper roof system.

First ascent: Carlton Ramm (1979, ground-up).

Start: Same as *Reckless Abandon.*

Pitch 1: Climb the easy ledge up to short, vertical crack. Pop over an overhang to a good, exposed stance where the cracks split. Belay here. (5.9; 40 feet).

Pitch 2: Where *Nutsweat* goes left, go right. Follow steep cracks out to a ramp where you can power into a chimney. (5.10c; 50 feet).

Note: Can be done as one pitch.

41. Nutsweat   5.9+

To steal from Tennessee ace Rob Robinson: Just jumping out of the 5.8 nest? Not a good route for the fledgling 5.9 leader to grow on. Some 2.5- and 3-inch pieces may come in handy on the second-pitch traverse through the overhangs.

First ascent: Tim Fisher, Jim Overby (1981, on-sight).

Start: Same as *Reckless Abandon.*

Pitch 1: Climb the easy ledge up to a short, vertical crack. Pop over an overhang to a good, exposed stance where the cracks split. Belay here. (5.9; 40 feet).

Pitch 2: Climb the green corner to its top. Traverse left to a right-facing corner. Make a couple hard moves and traverse out on gigantic holds through the huge roof system. Belay in a cleft at a fixed anchor. (5.9+; 60 feet).

42. Shadowdance   5.10c or 5.11c/d R

Lightning struck this climb a few years back and locals think it literally blasted off some holds. Nevertheless, the 5.10c first section is an undisputed classic that often stays dry in rain. The ascent club is small for the second section (small brass and double ropes are mandatory) since the fall potential is long.

First ascent: Lee Munson, Steve Pachman (1984, ground-up, but cleaned and previewed on rappel).

Start: On the left side of a ledge in the open book.

Pitch 1: Stem through stunning rust-colored rock to reach a couple of thin seams above a slopey ledge. Work your way through these, back into the corner to a double-bolt anchor. (5.10c; 65 feet). For the full route, it's best not to belay. Instead, continue around the corner via insecure underclings, liebacks, and delicate smears. At the top of the corner, move left to a right-facing corner. Continue through a cleft to the ledge just above the *Nutsweat* anchor and belay. Downclimb to the anchor to rappel. (5.11c/d R; 115 feet).

43. Spice   5.11b R

This is another route that has only seen a handful of ascents because of the difficult and unprotected climbing.

First ascent: Tim Fisher, Bill Holtsford (1988, ground-up).

Start: Same as *Shadowdance.*

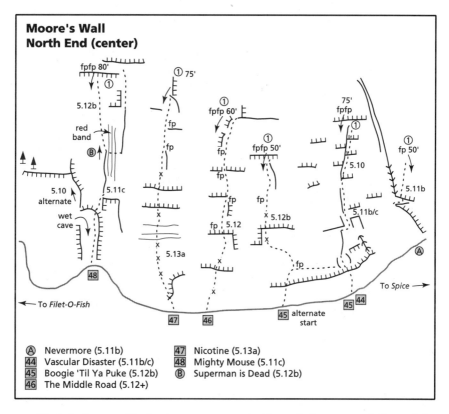

Moore's Wall
North End (center)

- Ⓐ Nevermore (5.11b)
- 44 Vascular Disaster (5.11b/c)
- 45 Boogie 'Til Ya Puke (5.12b)
- 46 The Middle Road (5.12+)
- 47 Nicotine (5.13a)
- 48 Mighty Mouse (5.11c)
- Ⓑ Superman is Dead (5.12b)

Pitch 1: Start as *Shadowdance,* except at the slopey ledge traverse left to a left-facing corner. Climb this, placing all the gear you can find. Step down and traverse left to climb the steep arête. Move right under the roof to gain the corner crack, eventually following this to steep jugs. Belay on the ledge just above the *Nutsweat* anchor. (115 feet).

44. Vascular Disaster   5.11b/c
At the health club, they call this a "fat-burning" workout! Power bouldering, wild liebacking, and steep jugs all wrapped together for an aerobic kick.

First ascent: Tim Fisher, Jim Overby (1985, ground-up).

Start: 200 feet down the trail from *Spice.* (On your way, you might want to take a side trail up to the excellent short crack, *Juggernaut* (5.10b). Several variations exist, but you're looking for a low roof where you can boulder up into a "scoop."

Pitch 1: Boulder over a low roof and fish in some low protection. Teeter your way up into a system of corners where the route rears and sprint through steep, well-protected bulges to a wad o' slings. (75 feet).

45. Boogie 'Til Ya Puke   5.12b
Most start this demanding route from *Vascular* and traverse left. But if you want to fully understand the route name, read on. . . . Double ropes recommended.

First ascent: Monty Reagan.

Start: Same as *Vascular Disaster.*

Pitch 1: From the stance above the *Vascular* boulder problem, trend up and left to a fixed stopper. Traverse straight left another 10 feet and move up to a bolt. Pull through the roof past an "eye" bolt and another fixed pin to a ledge with an anchor. (50 feet).

Note: It is possible to do a variety of unprotected and difficult direct starts. Some protect the harder starts by climbing yo-yo style off the first fixed pieces.

46. The Middle Road   5.12+

A classic mixed test piece that comes highly recommended despite a serious aura and few repeats. Technical, strenuous moves with no chance for a rest.

First ascent: Eric Zschiesche, Porter Jarrard.

Start: Begin off small sandy boulders and the left side of the *Vascular* roof.

Pitch 1: Climb past the low bolt to gain a slopey ledge. Move up aiming for a good horizontal, and then tweak past another bolt, a pin, and a fixed wire. Final hard moves lead to a short hand crack and eventually a nest of fixed stoppers and slings. (60 feet).

47. Nicotine   5.13a

An area test piece through steep waves of rock. Although it was the first 5.13 at Moore's, *Nicotine* is still rarely repeated.

First ascent: Eric Zschiesche, Porter Jarrard (1988).

Start: 20 feet left of *The Middle Road.*

Pitch 1: Follow the line of five bolts and two pins to a fixed anchor. (75 feet).

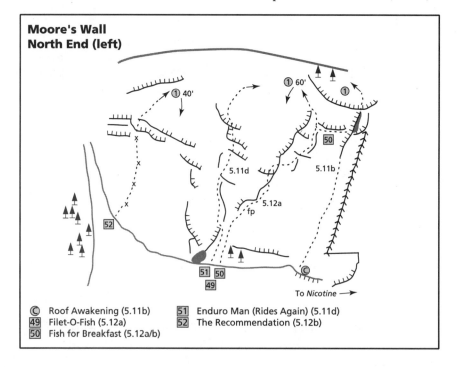

**Moore's Wall
North End (left)**

Ⓒ Roof Awakening (5.11b)
49 Filet-O-Fish (5.12a)
50 Fish for Breakfast (5.12a/b)
51 Enduro Man (Rides Again) (5.11d)
52 The Recommendation (5.12b)

48. Mighty Mouse   5.11c
Funky crack climbing and a few stopper moves demand all the attention you can muster.
    First ascent: Eric Zschiesche, Jim Williamson (1985).
    Start: On the far left side of the wall; begin by climbing a left-facing corner into the cave.
    Pitch 1: Follow the corner up to the big hole with the flat bottom. Ease out the right side of the hole until you can reach a jug. Insecure finger locks lead up through a thin seam where you can move right along a red band. Fire for the fixed anchors. (80 feet).

49. Filet-O-Fish   5.12a
Named in honor of Tim Fisher, this route is a burly affair with few moves harder than 5.11 and even fewer easier. Double ropes recommended.
    First ascent: Porter Jarrard, Doug Reed (1988, yo-yo).
    Start: At the base of a large slanted tree part way up the gully.
    Pitch 1: Climb the face behind the tree to the ledge. Step left to climb the bulbous steep face in the direction of a fixed pin. After the pin, move up and right to the final overhang. Hope you saved something for the finish! Pull the overhang and move left to the anchor. (60 feet).

50. Fish for Breakfast   5.12a/b
If you still have ammo in your guns at the top of *Filet*, try this short (20-foot) link that begins at the top of *Filet* and joins *Roof Awakening*.
    First Ascent: Tim Fisher, Robert Hutchins, Mike Turner (2000, ground-up).
    Start: Same as *Filet*.
    Pitch 1: Pull the final *Filet* overhang on the right and move right over steep ground. Don't pull up onto the ledge. Instead, climb up and spend some time on the thigh master before getting a stem below the roof. Pull the roof on the right and belay on the small ledge. Laps anyone? (80 feet).
    Pitch 2: Scramble to the top. Bear left and rappel off the pine down into a big cave.

51. Enduro Man (Rides Again)   5.11d
Do *you* have the staying power? *Enduro Man* will test your steep climbing ability.
    First ascent: Tim Fisher, Doug Reed, Jim Williamson (1986, yo-yo).
    Start: Same as *Filet*.
    Pitch 1: Climb up to the ledge as *Filet* above. Move farther left past a short chossy section and follow a weakness in the steep bulbous face. You might find a sloper or two. . . . (60 feet).

52. The Recommendation   5.12b
Crimpy and powerful climbing throughout, this was top-roped, cleaned, and bolted on the "recommendation" of Tim Fisher.
    First ascent: Doug Reed, Porter Jarrard (1988).
    Start: Follow the gully to the left side of the North End.
    Pitch 1: Follow four bolts through steep rock to anchors. (40 feet).

2. STONE MOUNTAIN

Climbing type: Multipitch, mostly bolted slab routes
Rock type: Granite
Height: Up to 500 feet
Number of routes: Approximately 70 (33 this guide)
Climbing season: October through April
Camping: Pay campsites are available at Stone Mountain State Park. For nearby private campsites, leave the park and go left onto Traphill Road from the Frank Parkway. Go right in 100 yards onto a gravel road; follow it a few hundred yards, past mobile homes, to campsites on left (there are more sites beyond powerlines). The owner will come by to collect fee (see appendix B).

Climbers usually fall into two camps when discussing Stone Mountain. Many disdain the area, considering it a futile anachronism (i.e., "friends don't let friends climb slab"). And then, of course, there are the few who find perverse joy in high stepping onto a friction dish 25 feet above their last protection. . . . Regardless of which side of the fence you stand, Stone Mountain is undeniably one of the most unique climbing venues in the East. Rising nearly 600 feet out of a meadow, the smooth swath of the South Face yields little in the way of obviously climbable features. Closer inspection, however, reveals some of the best friction climbing found in the country. An early pioneer, George DeWolfe, summed up the Stone Mountain mantra after summiting in October of 1966 and adding the following entry to the logbook: "The axe is ground, the soul is satisfied. The whole idea has got to be positive, never negative, or you'll never make it. For five trips I have had a negative attitude, but today it must have been, it had to be, positive."

History
The rich and storied history of climbing at Stone Mountain began in May of 1965 when George DeWolfe and John Thorne climbed *Entrance Crack* to reach Tree Ledge. DeWolfe remembers feeling completely inadequate gazing up at what is today called *The Great Arch* and trying to imagine liebacking the entire thing. Dismissing the route (known at the time as "The Dihedral Crack") as beyond their scope, they retreated. A determined DeWolfe, however, returned in August with Randy Constantine and started up the corner in oppressive heat and humidity. Dehydrated and out of water, they stalled about 150 feet from the top and retreated. They returned with the cooler temps of the fall to discover that Fess Green and Bill Chatfield had snagged the first ascent a few months earlier. Interestingly, DeWolfe and Constantine were two of twelve people who climbed *The Great Arch* that day.

DeWolfe returned the next weekend with Robin Wright and John Palmer and established "Punt Flake" which is now known as *No Alternative*. To their delight, as they topped out, Green and Chatfield were yelling at them from the field below for stealing "their" route. The irony of the situation was too much too ignore and it serves notice that even the very first climbers who developed lines on the immense South Face had a friendly rivalry that spurred route development. The remainder of

The South Face of Stone Mountain as seen from Wolf Rock

the 1960s quietly passed with climbers coming in and primarily repeating routes and occasionally establishing the odd new route here and there.

The 1970s got started with a bang thanks to the arrival of several strong climbers with a deep drive for first ascents. Bob Mitchell, already with gems at Looking Glass and Linville Gorge to his credit, rolled in with Will Fulton and established *Grand Funk Railroad* in 1971, which for some time was considered the hardest route at Stone Mountain. While climbers like Mitchell and Stan Wallace were merely visitors to the crag, the mid-1970s marked the rise to prominence of several climbers who were local to Stone. These local climbers honed their slabbing skills to such a degree that routes they established nearly thirty years ago are still very stiff today.

Kenny Hibbits, Gerald Laws, Robin Hinkle, Eric Zschiesche, Tom McMillan, and Bob Rotert were among this wave of bold first ascentionists. The friendly competition among these and other Stone Mountain climbers combined with the strong ground-up ethic of drilling bolts from stances on the lead created a legacy of routes that are more about mind control than brute strength. In January of 1974 McMillan teamed up with Jim McEver to establish the first 5.10 at Stone, *Rainy Day Women*. Reminiscing about the difficulty found on the first pitch, McEver recalls, "By the time I realized what I was in for, it was too late. I had to keep going or jump off." After getting the belay bolts in, he sank in complete exhaustion and started hallucinating. Later Rotert and Laws would join the pair to finish the route and establish a benchmark for others to chase.

It is worth noting that both McMillan and Rotert were high schoolers in 1974 when they arrived at Stone Mountain for a long Easter weekend. Over these short three days, they established three, classic full-length routes: *Mercury's Lead*, *Pandora's Way*, and *Electric Boobs*. Rotert recalls that *Rainy Day Women* had really opened their eyes to what was possible. "We were pretty amazed at the kind of holds that were on the face," he said recently. "We then figured that we could climb just about anywhere, so for *Mercury's Lead* we simply picked an arbitrary straight line halfway between *The Great Arch* and *Rainy Day Women.*"

Although locals such as Laws and Hibbits eventually took the lead in high-end route development, in 1978 two whirlwinds arrived from the Washington, D.C., area. Chris Rowins and Chris Kulczycki turned the Stone Mountain scene on its ears not only by climbing a longtime project (*The Great Brown Way*), but also by snatching three more classic 5.10s in short order: *Bombay Groove, Teflon Trip,* and *Banana Breath.* Rowins and Kulczycki also found the time to establish *Spiderman Swings South,* a fully free-climbable girdle traverse that crosses *The Great Arch.* While the audacity and skill displayed by these "outsiders" impressed the locals, Rowins and Kulczycki's opportunistic attitude grated on the locals' deeply spiritual feelings toward Stone Mountain.

Burton Moomaw rides the arête on Bombay Groove *(route 16).*

As a result, *Bombay Groove* was rechristened *Yankee Go Home!* by local climbers.

Such rivalries continued to push the grades even higher as talented younger climbers came onto the scene. The arrival of the Spanish Fire rock shoes in the mid-1980s had an impact too large to diminish. Laws remembers that not only were new and harder routes possible, but old test pieces were often brought down as much as a full number grade. Despite the arrival of this superior footwear, by the mid-1980s hopeful first ascentionists were running out of new routes to explore and Stone lapsed into somewhat of a decline with the development and popularity of newer climbing areas in the region. The arrival of sport climbing in the United States and a penchant for harder routes on steep stone left Stone Mountain in somewhat of a recession through the 1990s. You could climb there all weekend and maybe only see a few other parties.

In December 1997, the Carolina Climbers Coalition worked closely with the state park to initiate a massive rebolting project, replacing nearly 400 bolts on the South Face. The recent facelift has not made the runouts any less terrifying, but it has insured that the single bolt 25 feet below you will hold a fall if you slip. Word has spread about the great winter climbing on exciting moderate routes and traffic is starting to pick up again as a whole new generation of gym-bred climbers is getting a first taste of slab climbing North Carolina style.

Weather and Climbing Season

Stone Mountain's low elevation and southern exposure make cold clear days optimal. Climbing is best in cooler temperatures and insufferable in the heat and humidity in high summer.

Restrictions and Access Issues

Stone Mountain State Park is open year-round with the exception of Christmas Day. During periods of snowy and/or icy weather, the park may be closed due to hazardous driving conditions. Park hours are:

- November through February: 8:00 A.M. to 6:00 P.M.
- March, October: 8:00 A.M. to 7:00 P.M.
- April, May, September: 8:00 A.M. to 8:00 P.M.
- June through August: 8:00 A.M. to 9:00 P.M.

Emergency Services

Call 911 from a pay phone located just below the historic Hutchinson homestead at the base of the South Face. The closest hospital is the Hugh Chatham Memorial Hospital in Elkin (see appendix C).

Gear

Six to eight quickdraws and a light rack will work for most routes. Unusual protection needs are noted in the route descriptions. A 60-meter rope is highly recommended. Routes with 20 to 30 foot runouts between bolts are the norm at Stone Mountain and are considered well protected. Any route with an R or an X should be treated with the utmost respect.

Getting There

Stone Mountain is located 15 to 20 miles northwest of Elkin. From Charlotte, head north on Interstate 77 to exit 83 for US 21 north. After exiting, follow US 21 north for about 8 miles and then take a left onto Traphill Road (NC 1002). Signs for the park are at this intersection. After about 4 miles on Traphill Road, turn right onto the John P. Frank Parkway at Stone Mountain State Park signs. This continues about 2 miles directly into the park. Once inside the park, continue past the park office. The climbers' parking lot is about 2 miles farther down the main park road past the office. Park at the first bathrooms on the left.

Approach

From the parking area, hike the gravel road back to the restored Hutchinson homestead. From here, cross the creek on the right via the new bridge and head up the trail into the large field. Scope out the crag and then head to the registration kiosk at the tree line below Stone Mountain's South Face.

South Face

South Face routes are numbered from left to right. Routes 1 through 7 lie to the left and uphill from the area below the Tree Ledge in a steep, rocky drainage. Routes 8 through 12 start at ground level below the Tree Ledge. Routes 13 through 23 start off of the Tree Ledge itself. Routes 24 through 33 start at ground level right of the Tree Ledge.

Descent: There are two ways to descend the South Face of Stone Mountain: (1) Hike about 0.75 mile off the tourist trail, which is well blazed on the southwest shoulder of the mountain; or (2) rappel from the tree island above *The Great Arch*. This is not specifically a "rappel route," but the face has plenty of bolted stations to get down using some creative pendulums.

1. The Discipline   5.12a

This route vies with *Scimitar* (below) for the honors as Stone Mountain's hardest climb.

First ascent: Sandy Fleming, Steve Pachman (1983).

Start: 150 feet uphill of *Fantastic* at diagonal dikes with a bolt 15 feet up.

Pitch 1: Climb the dike to the first bolt below a bulge. Climb straight up past two bolts to the roof and clip a fixed pin and old bolt. Power over the roof on the exposed dike and up to a belay stance. (5.12; 100 feet).

Pitch 2: Climb the left-trending diagonal dikes to a natural belay at tied-off knobs. (5.6; 120 feet).

Pitch 3: Easy climbing leads to the top.

2. Fantastic   5.9+

This gem offers a Stone Mountain rarity—some great crack climbing.

First ascent: Gerald Laws, Buddy Price (1974).

Start: Just uphill of *Fleet Feet* below a diagonal crack.

Pitch 1: Surmount the large block and climb out the crack for about 30 feet. Then head up the sculpted face past two bolts to a flake. Follow this to a bolted anchor. (5.9+; 90 feet).

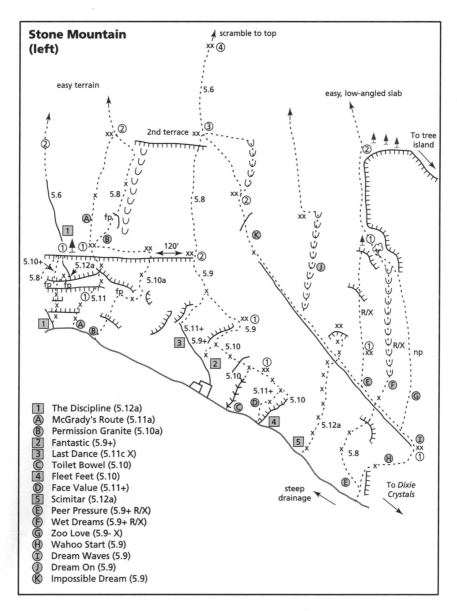

Stone Mountain (left)

Legend:
1 The Discipline (5.12a)
Ⓐ McGrady's Route (5.11a)
Ⓑ Permission Granite (5.10a)
2 Fantastic (5.9+)
3 Last Dance (5.11c X)
Ⓒ Toilet Bowel (5.10)
4 Fleet Feet (5.10)
Ⓓ Face Value (5.11+)
5 Scimitar (5.12a)
Ⓔ Peer Pressure (5.9+ R/X)
Ⓕ Wet Dreams (5.9+ R/X)
Ⓖ Zoo Love (5.9- X)
Ⓗ Wahoo Start (5.9)
Ⓘ Dream Waves (5.9)
Ⓙ Dream On (5.9)
Ⓚ Impossible Dream (5.9)

Pitch 2: Traverse left and up to a terrace passing one bolt. (5.9; 120 feet).
Pitch 3: Climb up to a second terrace. (5.8; 100 feet).
Pitch 4: Head up easier terrain to another bolted station. (5.6; 100 feet).
Pitch 5: Scramble off to the woods. (60 feet).

3. Last Dance   5.11c X

A stout test piece waiting for a worthy opponent. . . . Is that you?
First ascent: Jim Beyer, Bill Hoadley (late 1970s).

Start: Same as *Fantastic.*

Pitch 1: Continue out the *Fantastic* crack to its very end. Head straight up the flakes on your left. Climb the slab to the bolt on pitch two of *Fantastic* and then head up and left to the anchors. (5.11+; 150 feet).

Pitch 2: Finish on *Fantastic* or rap off.

4. Fleet Feet   5.10

Great flake climbing up to a slab crux. Few parties do more than the first pitch.

First ascent: Zeb Gray.

Start: At right-facing flake about 300 feet up the drainage from *Block Route.*

Pitch 1: Climb the flake on natural pro to its end. Move up and left passing two bolts to a belay. (5.10; 70 feet).

Pitch 2: Traverse left and up a bit to a bolt and the continue left passing another bolt before joining *Fantastic.* (5.10; 90 feet).

Bryan Haslam bears down on the ultracrimpy Scimitar *(route 5).*

5. Scimitar   5.12a
This is possibly the hardest route at Stone Mountain. The crux of this crimpfest is often simply finding a way to let go to clip the bolts.

First ascent: Mike Fischesser, Gerald Laws, Robin Hinkle (1994, rap-bolted).
Start: 30 feet right of *Fleet Feet.*
Pitch 1: Crimp, edge, and curse your way up amazing micro-edges past nine bolts. (120 feet).
Descent: Rappel down and left to the anchors on *Fleet Feet* and then to the ground.

6. Dixie Crystals   5.9
Pure friction fun on rock-shoe friendly rock. Bring a single 4-inch piece.

First ascent: Gerald Laws, Kenny Hibbits (1978).
Start: On a large block below a vertical dike just uphill from a black streak, 20 feet uphill of *White Way Direct.*
Pitch 1: Head up and right passing flakes and two bolts to a bolted station at a horizontal break. (5.8; 70 feet).
Pitch 2: Climb up past The Navel to a bolt and then straight up passing another to a bolted station. (5.9; 100 feet).
Pitch 3: Climb past one bolt angling up left to a bolted station. (5.9; 100 feet).
Pitch 4: Climb up and left to an alcove and follow the corner above to the top. (5.7; 100 feet).

7. White Way Direct   5.9
This crystal-pinching adventure is a great warm-up for the *Great White Way* proper.

First ascent: Gerald Laws, Buddy Price (1974).
Start: Just up the drainage from the *Block Route* at downward diagonaling dikes.
Pitch 1: Climb up to the flake and clip the bolt. Head out right to another bolt that leads to easier terrain and then to the belay at a small tree. (90 feet).

8. Block Route   5.8
Many climbers claim that the better protection makes this the preferred way to access Tree Ledge. Originally known as the "friction start" to "The Dihedral Crack" and rated at 5.6.

First ascent: Unknown.
Start: On the apron below the left end of Tree Ledge at a crack with vegetation in it.
Pitch 1: Climb to the crack and up past a small tree and bolts to a wildly scooped face. Climb up to a short left-facing corner. Wiggle, squirm, and flop like a beached whale right onto the face and head to the top. (120 feet).

9. U Slot   5.7
Another popular way to get to the Tree Ledge if *Entrance Crack* is a mob scene.

First ascent: Unknown.
Start: At a left-facing corner 20 feet up with trees at the base.
Pitch 1: Climb the hand crack just on the outside of the arête formed by the

Jack Igelman gets into the groove on Great White Way *(route 13).*

corner. At the top of the crack trend up and right to the overlap and then head straight for the trees. (120 feet).

10. Crystal Lizard   5.8
A headier way to get to the Tree Ledge than the previous two lines.
    First ascent: Unknown.
    Start: Right of *U Slot* at some pods 20 feet up with large trees growing out of them.
    Pitch 1: Head up past the multiple tiny quartz dikes passing two bolts. Climb up to the overlap and head to the tree ledge. (110 feet).

11. Entrance Crack   5.4 R
This is the most common access route to the Tree Ledge. The wide crack may accept large big-bros. Most go without.

First ascent: George DeWolfe, John Thorne (1965).

Start: Under the far-right end of the Tree Ledge, locate the large crack.

Pitch 1: Climb the hand crack to a pine tree. Step up and left and finish up the wide crack to Tree Ledge. (120 feet).

12. Dirty Crack   5.8
The increase in traffic has cleaned up this gem. Don't let the name fool you!

First ascent: Unknown.

Start: In the obvious right-facing corner 30 feet to the right of *Entrance Crack*.

Pitch 1: Climb the corner past a few small trees to the right end of Tree Ledge. (120 feet).

13. Great White Way   5.9
The quintessential water groove route at Stone Mountain. If you don't have fun on this one, you should check your pulse!

First ascent: Gerald Laws, Buddy Price (1974).

Start: 20 feet left of *The Great Arch* at a small tree.

Pitch 1: Step to the left side of the left water groove and climb past two bolts on the face to gain the groove. Stay in the groove past two more bolts to a belay stance. (5.9; 110 feet).

Pitch 2: Follow the deepening groove to a bolt, and then negotiate a long run up to a belay left of the groove. (5.8; 110 feet).

Pitch 3: Follow groove up to trees. (5.6; 50 feet).

14. Between the Ways   5.10c
A completely different flavor of climbing than the groove routes to the right and left.

First ascent: Mike Fischesser (1994, rap-bolted).

Start: Directly between the two "ways."

Pitch 1: Climb the steep wall between the grooves past three bolts to where the angle kicks back. Continue up past three more bolts to an anchor. (5.10c; 165 feet).

Pitch 2: Trend up and right to eventually join *Great Brown Way* at the first bolt on pitch 2. Continue in this groove to the top. (5.9; 130 feet).

15. Great Brown Way   5.10c
This astounding groove was reported in *Climbing* magazine in the mid-1970s as "potentially the hardest route at Stone Mountain . . . if it could even be climbed." After years of unsuccessful attempts by the locals, Chris Kulczycki quickly led the crux after two short falls.

First ascent: Chris Kulczycki, Chris Rowins (1978).

Start: At the dark water groove immediately left of *The Great Arch*.

Pitch 1: Climb past a flake to gain the water groove. Clip a bolt and make some tenuous moves up to another bolt. You're out of the woods now—scamper up to the bolted station right of the groove. (5.10c; 120 feet).

Pitch 2: Continue up the water groove past another bolt to the trees. (5.9; 150 feet).

16. Bombay Groove (aka Yankee Go Home) 5.10a

Awesome arête-pinching with intimidating exposure. Chris Rowins and Chris Kulczycki established this route and *Great Brown Way* on back-to-back days! The tour de force from these two "outsiders" upset the locals, hence the route's second name.

First ascent: Chris Rowins, Chris Kulczycki (1978).

Start: On *Great Brown Way.*

Pitch 1: Climb to the first bolt of *Great Brown Way* and traverse out right to the arête. Move up the arête passing one bolt to the shared bolted belay on *Great Brown Way.* (5.10a; 120 feet).

Pitch 2: Head back right to the arête and up to the bolt. Head up the groove to the right of the *Great Brown Way* to the trees. (5.9+; 150 feet).

Note: An unprotected 5.10 direct start was on-sight soloed by Doug Reed. It pulls the overhanging and awkward arête immediately above the start of *The Great Arch.*

17. The Great Arch 5.5

By far the best-known route at Stone Mountain, *The Great Arch* is an anomaly in that it follows a continuous splitter dihedral rather than blank slab. Regardless, it is a classic in every sense of the word, and it will be crowded on weekends.

First ascent: Bill Chatfield, Fess Green (1965).

Start: At the far-left end of the Tree Ledge.

Pitch 1: Follow the corner to a bolted station right of the corner. (5.5; 130 feet).

Pitch 2: Follow the corner to a bolted station on the left wall. (5.5; 100 feet).

Pitch 3: Follow the corner past a bolt at the wide section to the tree island. (5.4; 150 feet).

18. Mercury's Lead 5.9-

This route was originally rated 5.10, but the advent of sticky rubber has rendered this dog's bark worse than its bite.

First ascent: Bob Rotert, Tom McMillan (1974).

Start: The first route right of *The Great Arch.*

Pitch 1: Climb past two bolts to a ledge. Either traverse left to belay at *The Great Arch* anchors or move right and build a gear (2 inch max) belay in flakes. (5.9; 90 feet).

Pitch 2: Cross the slab up and right past the anchor for *Storm in a Teacup.* Then move up the J hook to a bolt. Head straight up to one more bolt and then right to anchors. (5.7; 150 feet).

Pitch 3: Easier climbing leads to the tree island. (5.4; 60 feet).

19. Storm in a Teacup 5.10a

This route climbs on the left edge of the white splotches that are easily seen from the field below the crag. Originally rated 5.9.

First ascent: Sandy Fleming, Lezley McIlveen (1986).

Start: The first bolted line to the right of *Mercury's Lead*.

Pitch 1: Climb a straight line past three bolts and the "splotches" to a belay at the base of the J hook. (5.9+; 150 feet).

Pitch 2: Step out right of the J hook and climb nearly straight up past no bolts to the anchors on top of pitch two of *Mercury's Lead*. (5.8; 90 feet).

Pitch 3: Climb to the tree island. (5.4; 60 feet).

20. Rainy Day Women   5.10a

The first-ascent party noted in the original logbook, "If I had to describe it in a word, it would be intense—definitely intense." This was Stone Mountain's first 5.10.

First ascent: Jim McEver, Tom McMillan, Bob Rotert, Gerald Laws (1974).

Start: Just left of center on the Tree Ledge. The first bolted line right of *Storm in a Teacup*.

Pitch 1: Climb up to a bolt and then angle up and right past another to anchors. (5.10; 80 feet).

Pitch 2: Climb off the belay heading for a lone bolt up and slightly left. Continue straight up to a bolted station. (5.9; 100 feet).

Pitch 3: Climb straight up to a bolt and then head sharply left and up to use the bolted station on *Mercury's* and *Storm in a Teacup*. (5.7; 110 feet).

Pitch 4: Climb to the tree island. (5.4; 60 feet).

21. Banana Breath   5.10a

A testy and sustained route.

First ascent: Chris Rowins, Chris Kulczycki (1978).

Start: 20 feet right of *Rainy Day Women*.

Pitch 1: Climb up the flakes at the base heading for a bolt on the slab 25 feet up. Continue straight up past two more bolts and at the third bolt, belay on a single bolt. (5.10; 100 feet).

Pitch 2: Climb directly up past two bolts to the pitch 2 belay of *Yardarm*. (5.9; 150 feet).

Pitch 3: Finish on *Yardarm*.

22. Yardarm   5.8-

A popular route that sees a lot of traffic. The runouts are on some of the more featured terrain found at Stone Mountain.

First ascent: Jim Dailey, Stan Wallace (1972).

Start: 20 feet right of *Banana Breath* at some flakes at ground level.

Pitch 1: Climb up and right to a bolt at 25 feet. Continue up and right a long ways to another bolt that leads to a bolted belay on top of a flake. (5.8; 150 feet).

Pitch 2: Climb up and left past some overlaps. Clip a bolt and head up decreasingly steep ground past another bolt to a belay. (5.8; 150 feet).

Pitch 3: Exit pitch—either scramble off left to the tree island or traverse right to a bolted rap station.

Randy Franklin awash in a sea of granite on Yardarm *(route 22)*

23. No Alternative   5.5

This route is a mirror image of *The Great Arch*. This was the second route climbed at Stone Mountain and was originally known as *Punt Flake*. Bring a light rack to 3 inches.

First ascent: George DeWolfe, Robin Wright, John Palmer (1965).

Start: In the large, left-facing corner on the right end of Tree Ledge.

Pitch 1: Climb the flakes and corner to its end. (5.4; 200 feet).

Pitch 2: Move straight up to a bolt at 75 feet and then continue up moderate terrain to another bolted station. (5.5; 150 feet).

Pitch 3: Easy terrain leads off to the trees at the top.

24. The Pulpit   5.8

Some say that this is the best-protected route at Stone Mountain.

First ascent: Unknown.

Start: At an arcing left-facing corner/flake just right of *Dirty Crack*.

Pitch 1: Climb up the flake and then right to a sloping ledge with a bolt 25 feet up. Move right to a bolt and up to a shallow steep groove to a bolt. At the top of the groove angle up and right past one bolt to a belay. (5.8; 160 feet).

Pitch 2: Climb up past two bolts. At the second, trend up and left to a bolted belay passing an old fixed pin. (5.8; 120 feet).

Pitch 3: Head up and right over easy ledges to a small left-facing corner and then traverse hard right over a water groove to a belay stance known as The Oasis. (5.8; 150 feet).

Pitch 4: Traverse up and right to the *Grand Funk* dikes. Pass the belay (clip it for pro) and head straight up the face to a large flake (The Pulpit) with a bolted belay above. (5.7; 165 feet).

Pitch 5: Easy terrain leads off the top. (165 feet).

25. Purple Daze   5.11a

More than one hardman has tasted humble pie on this sustained route.

First ascent: Jess Tucker, Vince Davis, Pat Land.

Start: Just right of the mossy seam where *The Sermon* starts.

Pitch 1: Climb thin face past four bolts to a natural belay (medium to large cams) at flakes. There is a single bolt on top of these flakes. (5.11a; 150 feet).

Pitch 2: Move left to join *The Pulpit,* or move up and right on unprotected ground to The Oasis. (5.9; 150 feet).

Pitches 3 and 4: Finish on *The Pulpit.*

26. Strawberry Preserves   5.10c

To protect the opening moves, the first-ascent party tossed their rope over a tree branch that no longer exists. During the rebolting effort in 1997, the first bolt was added to make the route "climbable." It's still no picnic.

First ascent: Eric Zschiesche, Robin Hinkle, Lindsay Broome (1979).

Start: 15 feet right of the mossy seam.

Pitch 1: Climb up and clip a bolt at 25 feet. Continue straight up past two bolts to a belay. (5.10c; 120 feet).

Pitch 2: Climb up to The Oasis ledge above. (5.8; 100 feet).

Pitches 3 and 4: Finish on *The Pulpit* or rappel.

Elizabeth Pendleton liebacks the flakes of No Alternative's *first pitch (route 23).*

Stone Mountain (center)

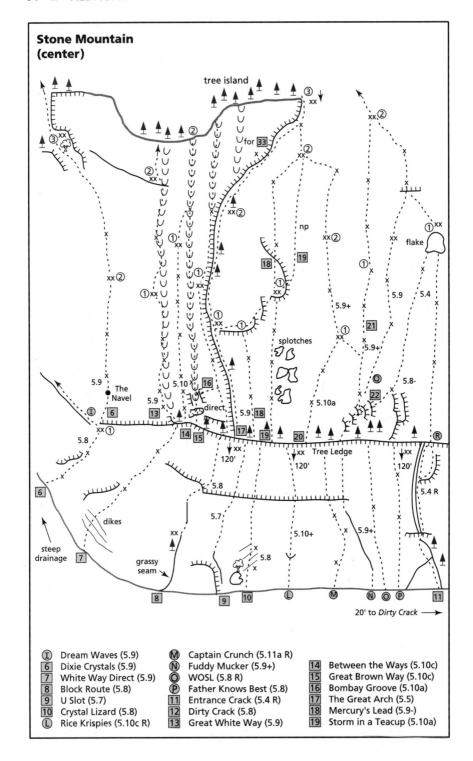

①	Dream Waves (5.9)	Ⓜ	Captain Crunch (5.11a R)
6	Dixie Crystals (5.9)	Ⓝ	Fuddy Mucker (5.9+)
7	White Way Direct (5.9)	Ⓞ	WOSL (5.8 R)
8	Block Route (5.8)	Ⓟ	Father Knows Best (5.8)
9	U Slot (5.7)	11	Entrance Crack (5.4 R)
10	Crystal Lizard (5.8)	12	Dirty Crack (5.8)
Ⓛ	Rice Krispies (5.10c R)	13	Great White Way (5.9)
		14	Between the Ways (5.10c)
		15	Great Brown Way (5.10c)
		16	Bombay Groove (5.10a)
		17	The Great Arch (5.5)
		18	Mercury's Lead (5.9-)
		19	Storm in a Teacup (5.10a)

Stone Mountain
(center continued)

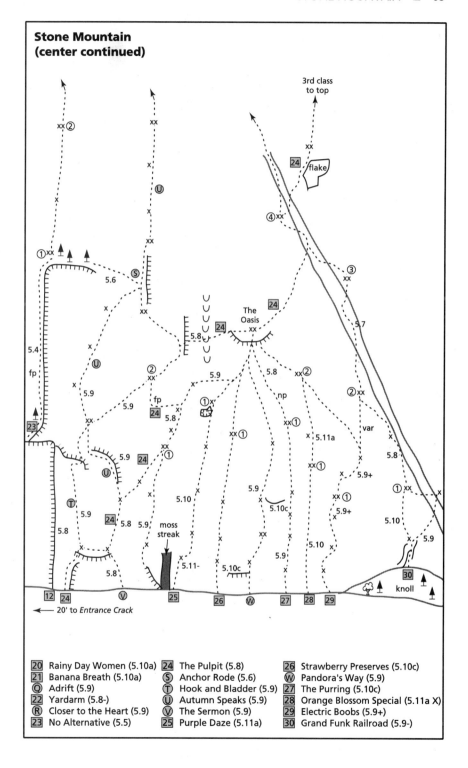

3rd class to top

The Oasis

moss streak

flake

knoll

var

← 20' to *Entrance Crack*

20 Rainy Day Women (5.10a)	24 The Pulpit (5.8)	26 Strawberry Preserves (5.10c)
21 Banana Breath (5.10a)	S Anchor Rode (5.6)	W Pandora's Way (5.9)
Q Adrift (5.9)	T Hook and Bladder (5.9)	27 The Purring (5.10c)
22 Yardarm (5.8-)	U Autumn Speaks (5.9)	28 Orange Blossom Special (5.11a X)
R Closer to the Heart (5.9)	V The Sermon (5.9)	29 Electric Boobs (5.9+)
23 No Alternative (5.5)	25 Purple Daze (5.11a)	30 Grand Funk Railroad (5.9-)

27. The Purring   5.10c
This is hard climbing, but it's better protected than your average Stone Mountain route.
First ascent: Sandy Fleming, David McClain (1990).
Start: 20 feet right of *Pandora's Way* and 20 feet left of the brown streak of *Orange Blossom*.
Pitch 1: Climb a straight line up ever steepening rock past four bolts to a bolted belay stance. (5.10c; 120 feet).
Pitch 2: Climb with no pro but on much easier terrain to The Oasis ledge. (5.8; 100 feet).
Pitches 3 and 4: Finish on *The Pulpit* or rappel.

28. Orange Blossom Special   5.11a X
A testy benchmark authored by two Stone Mountain masters at the height of their powers or at the depth of their insanity. You choose. A long-gone tree branch was used as pro on the first ascent.
First ascent: Kenny Hibbits, Gerald Laws (1979).
Start: At the brown water streak right of *The Purring*.
Pitch 1: Tie in to a rope and solo to the anchors. (5.10 X; 70 feet).
Pitch 2: Climb past one bolt to easier ground and anchors. (5.11; 100 feet).
Pitch 3: Climb to The Oasis ledge. (5.8; 80 feet).
Pitches 4 and 5: Finish on *The Pulpit* or rappel.

29. Electric Boobs   5.9+
A fascinating journey over some surrealistically sculpted and scooped stone. This route rarely climbs "above" the bolts—get creative and look for the path of least resistance.
First ascent: Bob Rotert, Tom McMillan (1974).
Start: 25 feet left of *Grand Funk Railroad* below wavy white rock.
Pitch 1: Climb past large scoops and waves past three bolts to an anchor. (5.9+; 90 feet).
Pitch 2: Zig up right a bit and zag back left to a bolt. Move out a tenuous traverse to the right and clip a bolt. Head up and left to join the shared belay on top of pitch 2 of *Orange Blossom Special*. (5.9+; 150 feet).
Pitch 3: Head to The Oasis exactly like pitch 3 of *Orange Blossom Special*. (5.8; 80 feet).
Pitches 4 and 5: Finish on *The Pulpit* or rappel.
Note: For a variation, don't stop at the pitch-1 anchors. Rather, keep climbing pitch 2 and then at the second bolt, head straight up to the bolted anchor on *Grand Funk Railroad*. Finish on this route.

30. Grand Funk Railroad   5.9-
Arguably the best full-length route at Stone Mountain. It is unique in that it generally follows the same feature for its entire length. Some brass can be useful.
First ascent: Bob Mitchell, Will Fulton (1971).

Start: At the top of the knoll that is 300 feet right of *Entrance Crack* and below a series of seams and small cracks.

Pitch 1: Climb the initial seams and pockets up to a depression and a bolt. Traverse right past a shallow groove and then up over the "tracks" to a bolt. Climb another 20 feet to an anchor. (5.9; 100 feet).

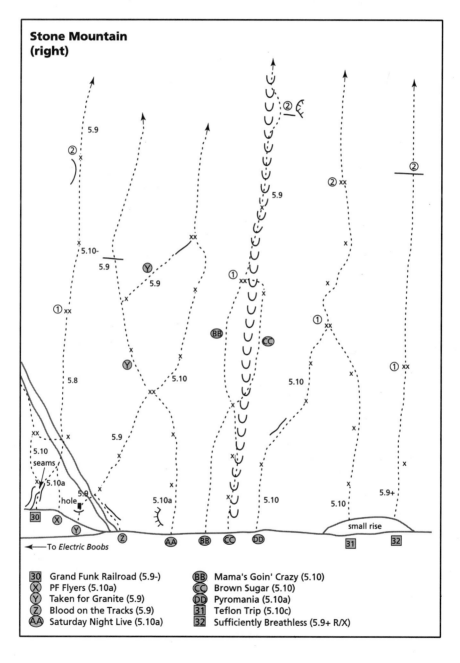

Stone Mountain (right)

30	Grand Funk Railroad (5.9-)	BB Mama's Goin' Crazy (5.10)
X	PF Flyers (5.10a)	CC Brown Sugar (5.10)
Y	Taken for Granite (5.9)	DD Pyromania (5.10a)
Z	Blood on the Tracks (5.9)	31 Teflon Trip (5.10c)
AA	Saturday Night Live (5.10a)	32 Sufficiently Breathless (5.9+ R/X)

Pitch 2: Climb up the dikes passing a bolt about 20 feet up. Continue another 20–30 feet before traversing out left over the groove and up to the bolted anchor. (5.8; 80 feet).

Pitch 3: Climb 20 feet to a pocket near the tracks and then head up the tracks to a bolted anchor. (5.7; 150 feet).

Pitch 4: Follow the dike up and left. (5.6; 150 feet).

Pitch 5: Easier terrain leads to the top.

31. Teflon Trip   5.10c

The more polished granite on this route requires you to be at the top of your friction skills.

First ascent: Chris Rowins, Chris Kulczycki (1978).

Start: 70 feet down and right of *Grand Funk Railroad,* at a small rise along the base.

Pitch 1: Pick your way through the lichens to clean rock and a bolt. Climb straight up passing two more bolts to a bolted station. (5.10; 120 feet).

Pitch 2: Climb up to a bolt at 25 feet and then angle up and right to another. Then cruise up to the anchors above. (5.10; 150 feet).

Pitch 3: Easy terrain leads to the top.

32. Sufficiently Breathless   5.9+ R/X

This route is another standard-setting line that sees little traffic. It did not get completely retro bolted in 1997 and still requires a light rack.

First ascent: Bob Rotert, Ewell Culbertson (1974).

Start: 20 feet right of *Teflon Trip.*

Pitch 1: Climb to the first bolt at 45 feet and then head to the anchors another 35 feet up. (5.9+; 80 feet).

Pitch 2: Climb straight up keeping a dike on your left. Belay at a horizontal crack. (5.9+; 120 feet).

Pitch 3: Climb straight up a full rope length to a huge block of quartzite and belay. (5.9; 150 feet). There are no anchors here, so assume a firm stance!

Pitch 4: Scramble off to the top.

33. Spiderman Swings South   5.10d (no topo)

This route is a girdle traverse of the full South Face. Little is known about this route, so take the general description below with a grain of salt. Bring a light rack.

First ascent: Chris Rowins, Chris Kulczycki (1978).

Start: Hike right of *Sufficiently Breathless* until you can walk up the very low-angled rock.

Pitches: The general beta for this one is to angle up and left until you are about 300 feet up and then start traversing left. Use all the bolts and belays that you can as you traverse. You want to intersect *The Great Arch* in the middle of pitch 3. Locate a bolt just over the lip, and make the crux move up onto the face. Traverse left until you get to easy terrain that allows you to downclimb.

3. CROWDERS MOUNTAIN

Climbing type: Top-roping, traditional, sport
Rock type: Quartzite
Height: 40 to 100 feet
Number of routes: Approximately 140 (41 this guide)
Climbing season: Fall through spring
Camping: Pay campsites available at Crowders Mountain State Park (see appendix B)

Often snubbed for being too crowded, too chossy, too retro-bolted, or too hot, no cliff in North Carolina seems to get the bum rap as often as Crowders Mountain. Nevertheless, though it may not be a world-class destination, this Piedmont cliff near Charlotte is rightfully popular because the best routes occur on beautiful quartzite. Beginning and intermediate climbers will be especially pleased with the variety and those of you seeking harder challenges should find something to keep you busy at Red Wall or Hidden Wall. The cliff line at Crowders Mountain is jumbled and it may take a visit or two to learn the lay of the land. But visit on a weekend and rest assured there will be somebody around to offer directions. The amount of polish on some of the more popular routes is testament to the climbing traffic this cliff receives. This guide includes routes on Hidden Wall, Practice Wall, David's Castle, Red Wall, and on walls in The Fortress area.

History

Crowders Mountain did not become a protected state park until 1974, but climbers have likely been visiting this area since well before then. The first known ascent occurred in 1974 when Kip Connor and Derek Brown climbed the obvious corner system of *Middle Finger* on the Middle Finger Wall. In December 1974, Gil Harder and Connor also climbed a route on David's Castle that they initially called *Peaches and Cream* (5.6, A1). That route is now known as the excellent, left-facing corner *Instant Karma,* and went free to Cal Swoager and Wes Love in 1982. Another obvious line, *The Caterpillar,* may have already been climbed by then, too.

After those early ascents it was somewhat quiet at Crowders Mountain for the next few years. But locals began to rediscover the quartzite walls in the early 1980s. A resurgence of activity began as the obvious features on larger walls fell in rapid succession. Routes such as *Gastonia Crack* and *The Bear* may have seen earlier ascents, but the real classics went to several Piedmont climbers who realized the potential here. Love and Doug Reed were two of the most active. This team joined up to complete some of Crowders's best single pitches and Love remembers that the team would often take turns leading. Having the ever-hungry Reed on his heels gave Love the motivation to climb with no falls lest he give up the sharp end (and usually the glory!). At the time, strong ethics led the duo to shun fixed protection and fixed ropes, resulting in some bold and brilliant ascents. Later, some dim-witted wannabe decided that routes such as *Energy Czar* and *Welcome to Crowders* needed bolts—and the formerly bold leads were sterilized into dime-a-dozen face climbs.

Layout of the cliffs along the south side of Crowders Mountain State Park

In 1998, the Carolina Climbers Coalition spearheaded a rebolting project that included approximately three dozen routes. This included replacing old pitons and bolts as well as installing a number of new belay and rappel stations along the rim. Unfortunately, the well-meaning bolting project also bled over to some of the other walls at Crowders Mountain. New routes began popping up extremely close to established lines, effectively rendering the bold, older lines meaningless. Placing new bolts or pitons at Crowders Mountain is illegal and will result in serious bans for the climbing community. Do not do it.

Weather and Climbing Season
The main walls at Crowders are relatively low elevation (1,625 feet), face southeast, and see abundant sun. As a result, popular areas such as Practice Wall, David's Castle, and Red Wall can be miserable in the heat of summer. But smaller cliffs such as Hidden Wall, The Fortress, or the backside of Middle Finger Wall offer shade and breezes.

Restrictions and Access Issues
Crowders Mountain State Park is operated by North Carolina Division of Parks and Recreation. There are no major raptor or other restrictions. The park gates close at night and the park is open during the following hours:
- November to February: 8:00 A.M. to 6:00 P.M.
- March, October: 8:00 A.M. to 7:00 P.M.
- April, May, September: 8:00 A.M. to 8:00 P.M.
- June to August: 8:00 A.M. to 9:00 P.M.

In addition to the rules and regulations listed in the introduction, please follow regulations specific to this park:

- **Registration.** Climbers must register before hiking in to the climbing areas. There is a registration kiosk at the trailhead for the Linwood Road access and the park office.
- **Minimum impact.** Use only established trails. All climbs must be accessed from the ridge top, Backside, or Tower Trails.

Emergency Services

Call 911 from a pay phone at the building at the Linwood Road access. Gaston Memorial Hospital is a short distance away in Gastonia (see appendix C).

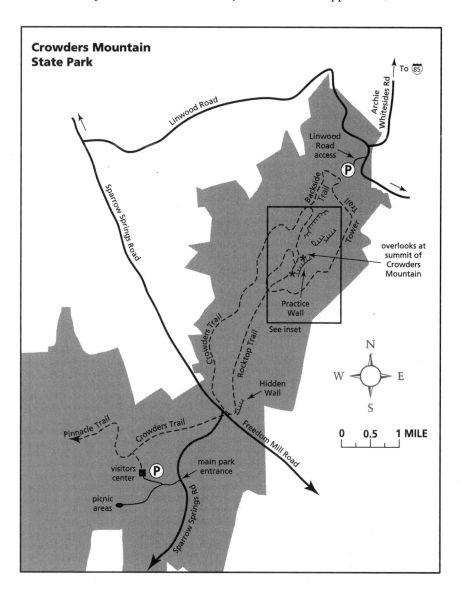

Gear

The standard climbing rack at Crowders Mountain is probably a top-roping kit. Bring several long (20- or 30-foot sections) pieces of webbing and a piece of carpet to help protect your ropes from abrasion on the sharp rock. For lead climbing, a standard North Carolina free climbing rack is sufficient.

Getting There

Crowders Mountain is located 29 miles west of Charlotte. From Interstate 85 outside of Charlotte, follow the interstate south to exit 13 (Bessmer City/Edgewood Road). Follow Edgewood Road south for 0.6 mile to a junction with West Franklin Road (US 29/74). Signs for Crowders Mountain State Park will direct you to the right. These are for the park office and Hidden Wall and will *not* direct you to the main climbing areas.

For the park office and Hidden Wall: Turn right at the junction of Edgewood Road and West Franklin Road (US 29/74), and follow it for 2 miles. Turn left onto Sparrow Springs Road (SR 1125) and follow it for 2.6 miles. Turn right (also onto Sparrow Springs Road) and go 0.6 mile to signs for Crowders Mountain State Park. Turn right onto State Park Road and follow it to the park office/visitors center and parking.

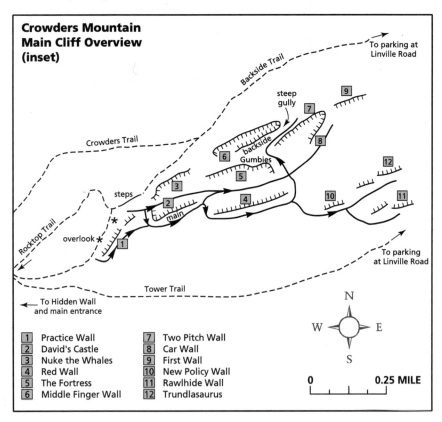

Crowders Mountain Main Cliff Overview (inset)

1 Practice Wall	7 Two Pitch Wall
2 David's Castle	8 Car Wall
3 Nuke the Whales	9 First Wall
4 Red Wall	10 New Policy Wall
5 The Fortress	11 Rawlhide Wall
6 Middle Finger Wall	12 Trundlasaurus

For the main climbing areas (Linwood Road access): Continue straight through the light where the road becomes Archie Whitesides Road (SR 1122). Follow this for 1.8 miles until the road dead-ends onto Linwood Road. Turn left and go 0.1 mile to a parking lot on the right. The Linwood Road access (which was overhauled in early 2001) includes bathrooms, kiosks, and registration forms. It is the only place to access the Backside Trail, which leads to the main climbing areas.

Approach

For Hidden Wall: Park at the park office/visitors center. Follow the Crowders Trail for 1 mile to the intersection of Sparrow Springs Road and Freedom Mill Road. Cross Sparrow Springs Road and continue on the Rocktop Trail (which is on the right) for a short distance until you can skirt around right (southeast) to the base of Hidden Wall.

For the main climbing areas (Practice Wall, David's Castle, Red Wall, and walls in The Fortress area): From the Linwood Road access, follow the Backside Trail 0.9 mile up a steep, gravel jeep road. Do *not* break off the trail and bushwhack (a fence has recently been erected as a further deterrent). The Backside Trail ascends a long flight of stairs to the top of Practice Wall. Climbers may negotiate a ridge-top trail along the summit ridge to access the other climbing areas. The approach takes about 25 minutes from the parking area to the top of Practice Wall.

Routes are numbered 1 through 41, beginning on Hidden Wall and continuing on the clustered main walls to end on Middle Finger Wall.

Hidden Wall

This is a small, out-of-the-way area that will appeal primarily to hard sport climbers. The routes here are generally short and powerful, often featuring wild crux sequences on vicious crimpers. Many an up-and-coming Charlotte-area hardman has trained on these routes in anticipation of bigger things to come. Hidden Wall gets morning sun.

Descent: Rappel the routes or walk off.

Note: There are numerous additional routes both left and right of the main faces that are neither in the text nor on the topos.

1. Anthrax   5.11d

This face-climbing variation to *Elastic Rebound Theory* is worth the effort.

First ascent: Diab Rabie, Scotty Greenway (1989).

Start: 50 feet right of cliff's left end, look for a bolt beside a right-facing corner.

Pitch 1: Sport. Start on *Elastic* and cut left after the fourth bolt for a short extension to cold-shut anchors. Eight bolts to shuts. (65 feet).

2. Elastic Rebound Theory   5.11c

Sloping jugs lead to a crimpy roof and a balancy 5.11 finale.

First ascent: Doug Reed (1986, ground-up). Continuation: Eddie Pain, Alvino Pon (1989).

Start: Same as *Anthrax*.

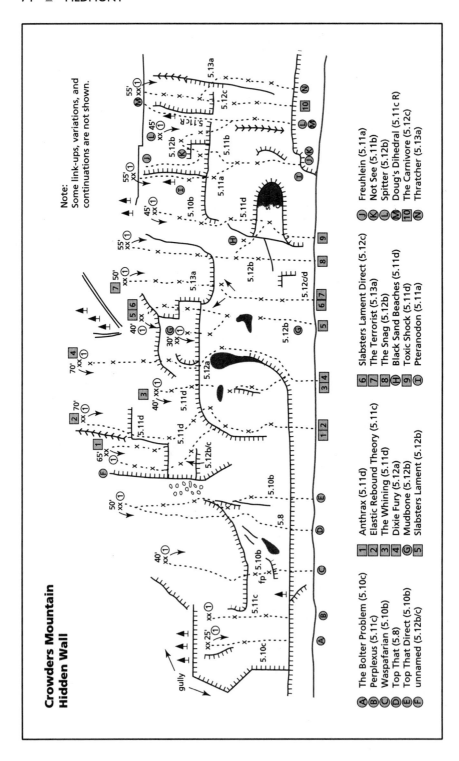

Pitch 1: Mixed. Climbs the roof to a corner right of the arête. Six bolts to shuts. (70 feet).

3. The Whining   5.11d
Some consider this the best route here: a classic combo of steep flakes, huecos, and pockets through roofs to a sloper crux.
First ascent: Scotty Greenway, Diab Rabie (1988).
Start: 15 feet right of *Elastic*, and just left of an ugly chimney.
Pitch 1: Sport. Climb the series of flakes out a roof system. Four bolts to shuts. (40 feet).

4. Dixie Fury   5.12a
This burly roof crack is one of the wall's earlier lines and still probably one of the best.
First ascent: Doug Reed (ground-up).
Start: At *The Whining*.
Pitch 1: Mixed. Scramble up to a bolt just before the cave. Fire the jam crack out the roof, gaining a flake. Gun to the top past four additional bolts. (70 feet).

5. Slabsters Lament   5.12b
Difficult pockets lead to the classic upper face.
First ascent: Diab Rabie (1989).
Start: 30 feet right of *Dixie Fury* at a face with a smattering of "holes."
Pitch 1: Sport. Pumpy and steep, this route follows a corner system up to a steep headwall with three bolts and cold-shut anchors. Look for the no-hands rest! Four bolts total. (40 feet).

6. Slabsters Lament Direct   5.12c
The lower face adds more difficult and technical climbing.
First ascent: Doug Reed (1989).
Start: 8 feet right of *Slabsters Lament*.
Pitch 1: Sport. Four bolts to shuts. (40 feet).

7. The Terrorist   5.13a
Climb the technical moves of *Slabsters Lament Direct* to a bouldery roof. Blast out the face above and negotiate a technical face.
First ascent: Scotty Greenway (1990).
Start: Same as *Slabsters Lament Direct*.
Pitch 1: Sport. Five bolts to shuts. (50 feet).

8. The Snag   5.12b
Thin, dynamic moves on some of the best rock at Hidden Wall.
First ascent: Scotty Greenway (1988).
Start: 10 feet right of *The Terrorist*, beneath small overlap and pin.
Pitch 1: Sport. A low, bouldery crux on the vertical face leads to a shallow crack system and jugs. Four bolts to shuts. (55 feet).

9. Toxic Shock   5.11d
You might want to have a Ph.D. in finger pockets for this one.
>**First ascent:** Doug Reed.
>**Start:** 20 feet right of *The Snag* under a small cave.
>**Pitch 1:** Sport. Gun out of the cave and past four bolts to shuts. (45 feet).

10. The Carnivore   5.12c
Thin flakes on the low face bar the way to some excellent 5.10 climbing.
>**First ascent:** Scotty Greenway (1991).
>**Start:** At the far-right end of main wall and right of a large hole.
>**Pitch 1:** Sport. Crimp up to some pumpy moves above the overlap. Five bolts
to shuts. (55 feet).

Practice Wall
The Backside Trail will deposit you at the top of this quartzite blade, which is home
to some of the most popular and best-known routes at Crowders Mountain. The

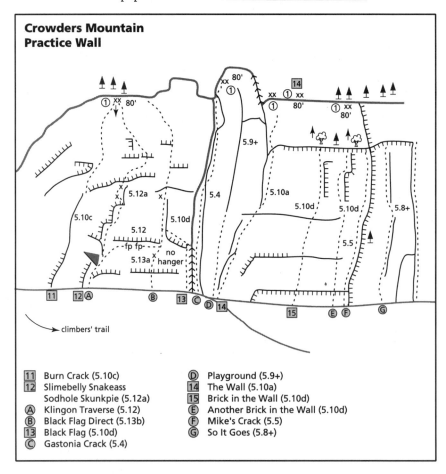

Crowders Mountain Practice Wall

11 Burn Crack (5.10c)	Ⓓ Playground (5.9+)
12 Slimebelly Snakeass	14 The Wall (5.10a)
Sodhole Skunkpie (5.12a)	15 Brick in the Wall (5.10d)
Ⓐ Klingon Traverse (5.12)	Ⓔ Another Brick in the Wall (5.10d)
Ⓑ Black Flag Direct (5.13b)	Ⓕ Mike's Crack (5.5)
13 Black Flag (5.10d)	Ⓖ So It Goes (5.8+)
Ⓒ Gastonia Crack (5.4)	

Adam Fox pulls through the upper section of Burn Crack *(route 11).*

top-rope setups are obvious (refer to topo); skirt around to the right (south) of the cliff to access from below. If you choose to lead one of these routes, it is a good idea to keep an eye on the cliff above. It is not unusual for people to drop top-ropes without checking.

The summit ridge above Practice Wall is a popular hangout area for park visitors because of its fine views of the Piedmont and neighboring Charlotte. Climbers should be aware that objects do occasionally fall from the top.

Descent: Rap the routes or walk off.

11. Burn Crack 5.10c

This is easily one of the best pitches at Crowders.

First ascent: Cal Swoager, Wes Love (1982).

Start: About 25 feet right of the crag's far left side, beneath an obvious hand crack.

Pitch 1: Boulder up steep ground to gain the hand crack. Flared jams and awkward moves allow access to good flakes. Double-bolt anchor. (80 feet).

12. Slimebelly Snakeass Sodhole Skunkpie 5.12a

A famous early hard route that took many attempts and is now (sadly) usually top-roped.

First ascent: Shane Cobourn (1985, ground-up).

Start: 5 feet right of *Burn Crack*.

Pitch 1: Finesse your way through steep flakes to a stance in the shallow corner. Palm up the rounded flake to long reaches past two bolts. Fire out to the right and get a short rest before chugging onward to a double-bolt anchor. (80 feet).

13. Black Flag 5.10d

First ascent: Doug Reed (1986).

Start: 20 feet right of *Skunkpie*.

Pitch 1: Crank up the arête and trend left to gain a good horizontal crack system. Step up the corner to clip single bolt, then gallop through good edges and flakes. (80 feet).

Note: The direct start is 5.13a, but there is no hanger at the first bolt.

14. The Wall 5.10a

This is a very popular route among top-ropers but it is seldom led.

First ascent: Thomas Kelley, Gary Mims.

Start: 50 feet right of *Black Flag*.

Pitch 1: Climb right-angling flake system to a system of steps where you can bump up aiming for an obvious thin crack. Follow it to the summit ledges. (80 feet).

15. Brick in the Wall 5.10d

This is also a popular top-rope route, but is somewhat harder than its brother next door.

First ascent: Doug Reed, Wes Love (1985).

Start: 20 feet right of *The Wall*.

Pitch 1: Thin face holds and long reaches guard some exquisite face climbing. (80 feet).

David's Castle

By hiking northwest along a polished and faintly blazed trail on the summit ridge, you will negotiate through some clefts and eventually gain a perch overlooking the backside of this impressive buttress. While the backside offers a few good moderate routes over a shady gully, the front side (the main wall) is a beautiful white, orange, and gray wall that gets morning sun. Climbers should be prepared to occasionally share this cliff with rappellers. Additionally, erosion is fast becoming a problem in the gullies around

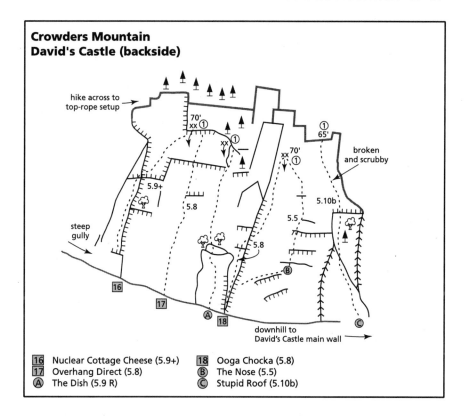

Crowders Mountain
David's Castle (backside)

hike across to top-rope setup

70' xx ①

xx ①

① 65'

xx 70' ①

broken and scrubby

5.9+

5.8

5.10b

5.5

steep gully

5.8

B

16

17

A 18

downhill to David's Castle main wall →

C

16	Nuclear Cottage Cheese (5.9+)	18	Ooga Chocka (5.8)
17	Overhang Direct (5.8)	B	The Nose (5.5)
A	The Dish (5.9 R)	C	Stupid Roof (5.10b)

David's Castle. The backside access gully can be slick and polished and it is not easy to negotiate with dogs.

Descent: Rappel routes or walk off where possible.

Backside
16. Nuclear Cottage Cheese   5.9+
Well-protected but pumpy for the new 5.9 leader!

First ascent: Wes Love, Rodney Lanier (1985).

Start: Look for left-facing flakes at the far left side of the buttress.

Pitch 1: Climb up the blocky face and past a small roof to gain an airy and exciting finish. Double-bolt anchor. (80 feet).

17. Overhang Direct   5.8
Varied climbing and perhaps a touch less difficult than the other routes on this section of wall.

First ascent: Wes Love, Clarence Hickman (1985).

Start: 10 feet right of *Nuclear Cottage Cheese*.

Pitch 1: Climb straight up a rutted face beneath a flake. Cut back left and follow the flakes right of *Cheese* to good horizontals and a massive ledge with a double-bolt anchor. (70 feet).

18. Ooga Chocka   5.8

A very popular top-rope route, *Ooga* should be on the list of anyone aspiring to climb some of North Carolina's classic cracks. An awesome blend of hand jamming, stemming, and the occasional thank-god face hold.

First ascent: Tom Howard, Bob Rotert.

Start: In brown rock beneath an obvious hand crack in the corner.

Pitch 1: Climb the corner to a small roof, then gun for a double-bolt anchor. (70 feet).

Main Wall

19. Psychotic Reaction   5.10b/c

Bouldering anyone? This line is short, au naturel, and fun.

First ascent: Wes Love, Doug Reed (1986).

Start: Under an obvious roof on the left.

Pitch 1: Follow a right-arching seam and corner to chain anchors. (25 feet).

20. Two Step   5.10

Similar to its midget neighbor but with bolts and, as a result, far more popular.

First ascent: Doug Reed, Wes Love (1987).

Start: 10 feet right of *Psychotic Reaction*.

Pitch 1: Follow the direct line up a seam to the anchor. Two bolts. (25 feet).

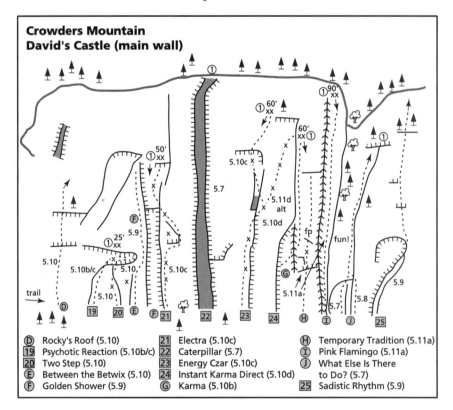

Crowders Mountain
David's Castle (main wall)

Ⓓ Rocky's Roof (5.10)	21 Electra (5.10c)	Ⓗ Temporary Tradition (5.11a)
19 Psychotic Reaction (5.10b/c)	22 Caterpillar (5.7)	Ⓘ Pink Flamingo (5.11a)
20 Two Step (5.10)	23 Energy Czar (5.10c)	Ⓙ What Else Is There
Ⓔ Between the Betwix (5.10)	24 Instant Karma Direct (5.10d)	to Do? (5.7)
Ⓕ Golden Shower (5.9)	Ⓖ Karma (5.10b)	25 Sadistic Rhythm (5.9)

21. Electra   5.10c

Beautiful rock and devious climbing make *Electra* an enduring classic.

First ascent: Doug Reed, Ben Fowler, Wes Love (1986).

Start: 25 feet right of *Two Step*.

Pitch 1: Sport. Climb the shallow corner and seam past a flake. Five bolts to shuts. (50 feet).

22. Caterpillar   5.7

A gaping chimney that cleaves the entire David's Castle.

First ascent: Unknown.

Start: In the obvious chimney, 8 feet right of *Electra*.

Pitch 1: Stem, chimney, and jam up the feature to the top of the cliff. (80 feet).

23. Energy Czar   5.10c

This excellent route was once a bold and memorable 5.11a. The sad retro-bolting job has left it neutered and far easier.

First ascent: Doug Reed, Wes Love (1987, on-sight with no fixed protection).

Start: 15 feet right of *Caterpillar* under a dramatic right-facing arête and corner.

Pitch 1: Sport. Stem and crimp your way up the corner until you can reach out left. Pull a small roof via gigantic holds and make a little run past friable rock to a ledge. Four bolts to double-bolt anchor. (60 feet).

Note: A difficult variation (5.11d) goes up and right past three additional bolts to a separate anchor.

24. Instant Karma Direct   5.10d

One of the best lines at Crowders, *Karma Direct* would be a three-star route most anywhere.

First ascent: Gil Harder, Kip Conner. Rodney Lanier, and Wes Love made the first free ascent. Cal Swoager and Wes Love did the *Direct* in 1987, on-sight.

Start: 20 feet right of *Energy Czar*, following a left-facing corner.

Pitch 1: Climb the stunning, thin corner to the upper crack. (60 feet).

25. Sadistic Rhythm   5.9

If you choose to top-rope this route, beware of the swing. The route is steep and strenuous.

First ascent: Doug Reed, Wes Love (1987).

Start: 50 feet right of *Instant Karma Direct* in a wide, right-slanting dihedral.

Pitch 1: Follow the right-arcing corner through a wide section and onto the face. (60 feet).

Red Wall

Red Wall is a short distance northeast of David's Castle. There is no official trail, but climbers' trails allow easy access. Red Wall is broken into two distinct areas: the small left side and the right side, which opens up after a vegetated area into an impressive, red-colored area that gives the wall its name. These cliffs get morning sun.

Unmarked climbers' trails contour northeast from the right side of Red Wall to

Crowders Mountain
Red Wall

Ⓐ unknown
26 Silence the Critics (5.12b)
27 Desperately Seeking Juggage (5.11b)
Ⓑ Target Practice (5.8)
Ⓒ Opinionated (5.9)
Ⓓ Spring Fling (5.8)
Ⓔ Spring Swing (5.8)
Ⓕ Beer Wolf (5.9+)
Ⓖ Spring Fever (5.7)
Ⓗ Spring Break (5.8)
Ⓘ Red Wall Chimney (5.3)

28 Welcome to Crowders (5.12a)
29 T.K.O. (5.12a)
Ⓙ Red Red Wine (5.11b)
30 Scramble My Feedback (5.10a)
31 911 (5.8)
32 Master Beta (5.10c)
33 Axis (Bold as Love) (5.11c)
34 Fashion (5.12b)
35 The Gimp (5.10d)
Ⓚ Tom Tom Club (5.9 R)

To Resurgence Walls

the long-overlooked Resurgence Walls (which are not in this guide). A trail that climbs up the hillside from this side of Red Wall leads to the cliff top near The Fortress.

Descent: Walk off where possible or rappel the route.

Left Side
26. Silence the Critics   5.12b
Initially attempted by Shane Cobourn on lead and then rap-bolted by another party, Cobourn flashed the first ascent of this route as his "comeback" from knee surgery.

First ascent: Shane Cobourn (1990).

Start: Climb off a ledge to a flake.

Pitch 1: Sport. Three bolts to cold shuts. (30 feet).

27. Desperately Seeking Juggage   5.11b
Work your way up the right side of the pillar.

First ascent: Scotty Greenway, Monica Browne.

Start: 4 feet right of *Silence the Critics*.

Pitch 1: Sport. Climb past three bolts to the *Silence* anchor. (30 feet).

Right Side
28. Welcome to Crowders   5.12a
Though short, this is an awesome stretch of difficult climbing that went ground-up with no fixed gear and only one fall because of bad rock—the broken hold also pushed the difficulty to 5.12. Sometime in the 1990s, this route regrettably received the "treatment."

First ascent: Cal Swoager, Wes Love (1982, on-sight).

Start: Step onto the wall on its left side and trend right following a seam.

Pitch 1: Sport. Power up the seam to a short flake, where you can trend right. Three bolts to double-bolt anchor. (50 feet).

29. T.K.O.   5.12a
Abysmally small holds and long reaches allow a more direct line up the gorgeous face.

First ascent: Doug Reed.

Start: 20 feet right of *Welcome to Crowders*.

Pitch 1: Sport. Crimp and high-step up the face to a bolt. Long moves lead past waves of orange rock. Three bolts to shuts. (40 feet).

30. Scramble My Feedback   5.10a
This striking burnt-orange dihedral is a landmark on the Red Wall.

First ascent: Wes Love, Doug Reed, Clarence Hickman (1987, ground-up).

Start: 10 feet right of *T.K.O.*

Pitch 1: Climb small ledges to the obvious dihedral. Lieback and stem past a bolt and then romp to the summit. (70 feet).

31. Master Beta   5.10c
Although it has some loose holds, *Beta* is a gentle warm-up for the harder routes on this wall.

First ascent: Steven Lilliard.
Start: 30 feet right of *Scramble My Feedback*, off a large flake.
Pitch 1: Sport. Climb up the face angling slightly right. Six bolts to shuts. (70 feet).

32. Axis (Bold as Love)   5.11c
A climb worthy of the Hendrix reference despite a tiny section of vegetation.
   First ascent: Doug Reed (1986). First free ascent by Bob Rotert and Wes Love (1986).
   Start: Same as *Master Beta*.
   Pitch 1: Trend up the face aiming for a right-angling crack system. Follow it through one difficult section past a bolt and fixed pin. No anchor. (90 feet).

33. Fashion   5.12b
No fads here! This kind of climbing will never go out of style.
   First ascent: Doug Reed.
   Start: 5 feet right of *Axis*.
   Pitch 1: Angle up and right aiming for the obvious right-leaning seam. Pass one old bolt via a fierce section of crimpers. Five bolts to anchor. (80 feet).
   Note: It is possible to do a direct start past one bolt at 5.11d.

34. The Gimp   5.10d
Here's a popular new addition that stole some thunder from the *Tom Tom Club*.
   First ascent: Diab Rabie (1996).
   Start: 5 feet right of *Fashion*.
   Pitch 1: Sport. Climb huge jugs up exposed rock to the *Fashion* anchor. (80 feet).

35. Tom Tom Club   5.9 R
An alluring arête with an exposed finish.
   First ascent: Wes Love, Clarence Hickman (1986, on-sight).
   Start: 5 feet right of *The Gimp*.
   Pitch 1: Trend up the enjoyable arête—ignoring *The Gimp* bolts if possible—and stay straight when the sport line goes left. (90 feet).

The Fortress Area
A trail climbs up the hillside from the Red Wall to reach several cliffs that are in a concentrated and popular area of the park. They include Nuke the Whales, The Fortress, Middle Finger Wall, Two Pitch Wall, and Car Wall (see Crowders Mountain main-cliff overview map). Take some time to explore.
   Descent: Rappel most routes or walk off where possible.

The Fortress
36. Fortress Fingers   5.10b
Looks hard . . . and feels it, too! This is a short but sweet feature.
   First ascent: Wes Love, Rodney Lanier (1983).

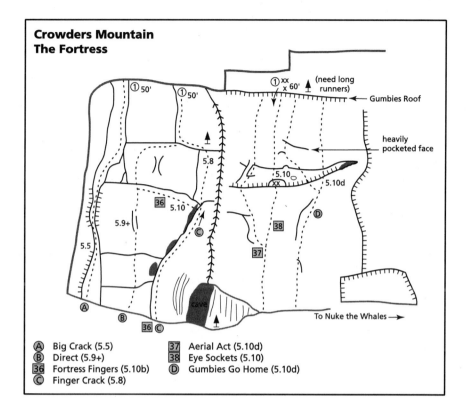

**Crowders Mountain
The Fortress**

Gumbies Roof

heavily pocketed face

5.10d

To Nuke the Whales →

(need long runners)

Ⓐ Big Crack (5.5)
Ⓑ Direct (5.9+)
36 Fortress Fingers (5.10b)
Ⓒ Finger Crack (5.8)
37 Aerial Act (5.10d)
38 Eye Sockets (5.10)
Ⓓ Gumbies Go Home (5.10d)

Start: 8 feet left of the outside arête at a right-slanting flake system.

Pitch 1: Climb the crack until you can step left along a short but difficult finger crack. Angle up and right to the anchor. (50 feet).

37. Aerial Act   5.10d

The exact date is unknown, but sometime in the mid-1980s Shane Cobourn free-soloed the first ascent of this route in a moment of extreme daring.

First ascent: Shane Cobourn.

Start: On a face right of the cave, aiming for the obvious weakness in Gumbies Roof.

Pitch 1: Saunter up the easy face. Power your way out the roof via a good crack and jugs. Gun for the big ledge with a three-bolt anchor. (60 feet).

Note: A top-rope setup requires long runners.

38. Eye Sockets   5.10

The name used to be self-explanatory, but now the route is mainly just a steep, pocketed wall.

First ascent: Shane Cobourn, Doug Reed, Sean Cobourn.

Start: Same as *Aerial Act.*

Pitch 1: Climb the face aiming for a bolt inside two large huecos in the roof. Crank over the lip and climb the face to the ledge. (60 feet).

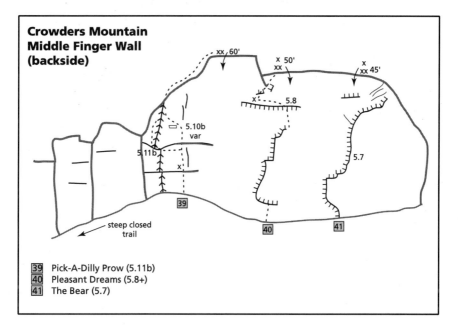

**Crowders Mountain
Middle Finger Wall
(backside)**

39 Pick-A-Dilly Prow (5.11b)
40 Pleasant Dreams (5.8+)
41 The Bear (5.7)

Middle Finger Wall (Backside)

39. Pick-a-Dilly Prow   5.11b

Short but awe-inspiring. This is another bold lead that took several strength-sapping attempts—the low crux was initially protected with a pin/skyhook combination!

First ascent: Wes Love, Ben Fowler (1987).

Start: On the left side of Middle Finger under the obvious arête.

Pitch 1: Fire past a low bolt to gain a precarious position under the arête. Move out left to gain the devious overhanging crack and flake system. Gun up the arête for shuts. (60 feet).

Note: It is possible to take a 5.10b variation. See topo.

40. Pleasant Dreams   5.8+

Hard moves off the deck keep the riff-raff away.

First ascent: Doug Reed, Sean Cobourn.

Start: 20 feet right of *Pick-a-Dilly Prow* at the obvious chalked low roof.

Pitch 1: Climb up to a right-facing flake system. Follow to a ledge and three-bolt anchor. (50 feet).

41. The Bear   5.7

An excellent albeit casual romp to the summit of the Middle Finger.

First ascent: Unknown.

Start: 10 feet right of *Pleasant Dreams.*

Pitch 1: Pick the easiest line up the steep face. Three bolt anchor. (45 feet).

Opposite: *Chris McGowan pocket hunting on* Eye Sockets *(route 38)*

NORTHERN BLUE RIDGE
(THE HIGH COUNTRY) —————————

Opposite: *Kathy Thore walks a fine line on* Boardwalk *(route 13) on the Main Tier of Ship Rock.*

4. SHIP ROCK

Climbing type: Multipitch and single-pitch traditional
Rock type: Metasandstone—primarily quartz, chlorite, and mica
Height: 200 feet max, most shorter
Number of routes: Approximately 70 (26 this guide)
Season: Summer is best; spring and fall are close seconds.
Camping: For free U.S. Forest Service camping, head south on the Blue Ridge Parkway to just past mile 311 and go left on Old Jonas Ridge Road; follow it 1 or 2 miles to find campsites near the road. Don't camp on private property. Pay campsites are available on the Blue Ridge Parkway: Linville Falls Campground is 13 miles to the south, and Julian Price Campground is about 5 miles to the north.

When the heat of the summer sets in, Ship Rock is the place to be. Its looming gray tiers are primarily the domain of the trad climber seeking steep and pumpy routes with generally abundant protection. However, big holds on steep stone make even the easier-rated routes pack a pump of several grades harder. But don't let this keep

Ship Rock as seen from the Linn Cove Viaduct on the Blue Ridge Parkway

you away from Ship Rock. The wide array of classics from 5.7 to 5.12 makes it worth a visit. Add the proximity to the wealth of climbing in Linville Gorge (chapter 5) and to the world-class bouldering around Boone, and Ship Rock becomes a must-visit crag on any North Carolina high-country tour. Routes described in this guide are on Ship Rock's Main and Upper Tiers; the Lower Tier has been omitted.

History

Ship Rock saw very limited activity prior to 1980. Before that, the Linn Cove Viaduct section of the Blue Ridge Parkway was not yet completed, thus making the approach much more difficult. The crag was probably first visited by climbers in the fall of 1979 when Tom Howard, Dan Perry, Tom McMillan, and Andy Hayes bushwhacked up to the cliffs from US 221. Intrigued by the obvious potential, the next summer they went in and did the first route, *Borrowed Time*. Howard remembers that they knew the rocks had potential, but the climbers were so busy developing more readily accessible crags like Table Rock, Hawksbill, and the North Carolina Wall that they felt no rush to get on Ship Rock. Soon that sentiment changed as the parkway neared completion and access became much easier.

The steep and intimidating roofs at Ship Rock offered a change of pace in many respects from the heavily featured climbing found on the North Carolina Wall and at Table Rock, the two closest climbing areas. Climbers had become accustomed to pushing their limits on the steep faces of these Linville Gorge walls. So, buoyed by these successes, Perry and Lee Carter came back to Ship Rock a few months after *Borrowed Time* to work on what would become the second route on the wall, *Linn Cove Lullaby*. Eschewing bolting, they fixed a no. 1 hex in the crack at the crux of pitch two and were having some difficulties when Tom Howard came walking up. They lowered a rope to him, brought him to the belay ledge, and promptly gave him a shot at the crux. Howard pulled the moves and finished what has become a certain classic. With the psychological barrier down, other routes began to appear and fixed gear soon became accepted as the only way to protect the blanks between gear placements.

Seeking to escape the steamy summer conditions, the next wave of Ship Rock developers came up from Charlotte in the mid-1980s. Doug Reed led the charge along with Vernon Scarborough, Chip Self, Wes Love, and Byron Bridges, among others. They took the acceptance of fixed gear one step further and created very technically difficult routes up blank expanses of rock. Routes like *Chromium Chain*, *Revival*, *First Flight*, and *Artistic Arête* are prime examples of this trend that was led by the driven Reed. He felt that Ship Rock marked a change in direction for himself as well as others seeking to push the limits: "It was the logical step towards the acceptance of sport climbing that would come in the late 1980s."

That being said, sport climbing has never been fully embraced in North Carolina, and Ship Rock stands as a prime example of the quality routes that can be created with the restrained use of fixed gear where needed. For the most part, Ship Rock was fully developed by the end of the 1980s, but sporadic development has occurred in later years when very difficult routes like *Castaway* filled in obvious blank lines. Lost a bit in the glare of nearby Boone's world-class bouldering, Ship Rock nevertheless stands as one of the best places in the Carolinas to find respite from high summer.

Restrictions and Access Issues

The National Park Service manages Ship Rock as part of the Blue Ridge Parkway corridor and currently there are no serious access restrictions. Practice minimum impact ideals by rappelling off the top of the Main and Upper Tiers rather than descending the fragile vegetated hillsides on either end of the crag. Currently there are bolted rap stations above *Boardwalk*, *Harpoon*, *Lost at Sea*, *Edge of a Dream*, and *Castaway*.

Emergency Services

Call the Blue Ridge Parkway's "Parkwatch" emergency number. The closest hospital is Watauga Medical Center in Boone. (See appendix C.)

Getting There

Ship Rock looms directly over the Blue Ridge Parkway (BRP) near mile marker 303. From Boone, take NC 105 south to the junction with US 221 in Linville. Turn left and follow US 221 to the junction with the parkway at the top of the mountain. Go north on the parkway for 2 miles and Ship Rock will be above you on the left. Continue almost 0.5 mile farther to park at the Rough Ridge Overlook (the first pullout north of Ship Rock). Please do not park on the grassy shoulders immediately below Ship Rock!

Approach

From Rough Ridge Overlook, hike back south along the grassy shoulder of the parkway for about 0.5 mile. Cross the bridge and pass a road-cut on the right. Look for a trail heading up into the woods to the base of the rock. The first routes that you pass are six lines on the Lower Tier, none of which are covered in this guide.

Main Tier routes are described first, followed by routes on the Upper Tier. Routes are numbered 1 through 26 and follow along the wall, right to left, in each area.

Main Tier

To reach the Main Tier, follow the trail a few hundred feet past the Lower Tier routes. Traverse to the right under a low roof for routes 1 and 2. Scramble up and left to access routes 3 through 22.

Descent: Use the bolted rap station above *Boardwalk* and *Harpoon*.

1. Chromium Chain   5.11c

Don't underestimate the looks of this one . . . it packs a hell of a pump!

First ascent: Doug Reed (1985).

Start: 75 feet right of *Revival* just below a clean-cut right-facing corner.

Pitch 1: Climb the corner past three fixed pins and some gear. Make an awkward exit from the roof and head to the rhododendrons. (60 feet).

2. Patio Roof   5.12b

The chalked holds and bail slings attest to both the appeal and difficulty of this roof. The bolt, while not placed on the first ascent, has been allowed to remain.

First ascent: Maurice and Doug Reed (1986).

Start: Locate the fixed gear in the large roof immediately left of *Chromium Chain*.

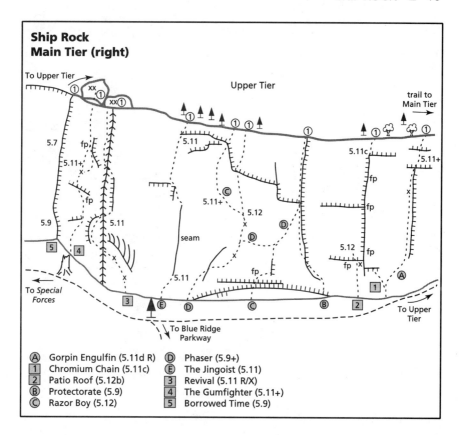

Ship Rock
Main Tier (right)

Ⓐ Gorpin Engulfin (5.11d R)	Ⓓ Phaser (5.9+)
1 Chromium Chain (5.11c)	Ⓔ The Jingoist (5.11)
2 Patio Roof (5.12b)	3 Revival (5.11 R/X)
Ⓑ Protectorate (5.9)	4 The Gumfighter (5.11+)
Ⓒ Razor Boy (5.12)	5 Borrowed Time (5.9)

Pitch 1: Climb up to the roof and then connive some way to get out the roof past a fixed pin and a bolt. Finish on *Chromium Chain*. (65 feet).

3. Revival   5.11 R/X

Though rarely led, wires on the old bolts and some brass make for a worthy endeavor.

First ascent: Doug Reed, Byron Bridges.

Start: At the arête a few feet right of *The Gumfighter* and just left of where the trail hits the rock.

Pitch 1: Climb up past two bolts without hangers. Continue left to the thin right-facing flake that arches right out a small roof to a big jug on the arête. Head straight up the overhanging arête to the anchor. (90 feet).

4. The Gumfighter   5.11+

A classic one-move wonder. Doug Reed later free-soloed that one move barefoot, though!

Start: Left of *Revival* and directly above a broken-off pine tree.

First ascent: Maurice Reed, Doug Reed, Vernon Scarborough.

Pitch 1: Climb up through some steep terrain past a fixed pin to a no-hands stance just above the lip at a bolt. Crimp up and right to dual fixed pins before heading up the crack to the bolted anchor on the upper large block. (70 feet).

Bill Saul in the business on The Gumfighter *(route 4)*

5. Borrowed Time   5.9

A short boulder problem off the ground leads to a very enjoyable and easier crack/
corner. This was the very first route established at Ship Rock.

    First ascent: Tom Howard, Dan Perry (1980).

    Start: The corner left of *The Gumfighter.*

    Pitch 1: Boulder up into the corner and follow it to the trees. (60 feet). You
arc now in the mini-amphitheater below the Upper Tier. Walk off or climb on the
Upper Tier.

6. Special Forces   5.11a R

The bolts got upgraded on this slabmaster's special, but falling on the way to the second bolt is still not an option.

First ascent: Doug Reed, Vernon Scarborough.

Start: 40 feet left of *Borrowed Time*, below an obvious bolt.

Pitch 1: Climb past the first bolt and make some tenuous, thin slab moves up to a stance at the second bolt. Desperately thin slab crimping leads up and right to a left-facing corner. Follow this past a fixed pin to a rhododendron-covered ledge with cold shuts. (75 feet).

7. Artistic Arête   5.13a

This route sees some aspiring redpointers but few successes.

First ascent: Doug Reed (1986).

Start: The bolted arête right of the start to *Hindu Kush*.

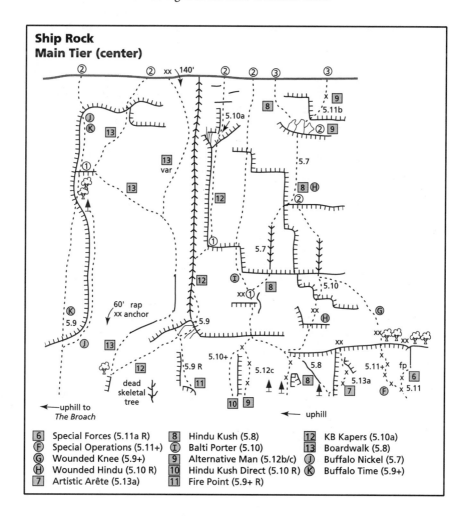

**Ship Rock
Main Tier (center)**

6 Special Forces (5.11a R)	8 Hindu Kush (5.8)	12 KB Kapers (5.10a)
F Special Operations (5.11+)	I Balti Porter (5.10)	13 Boardwalk (5.8)
G Wounded Knee (5.9+)	9 Alternative Man (5.12b/c)	J Buffalo Nickel (5.7)
H Wounded Hindu (5.10 R)	10 Hindu Kush Direct (5.10 R)	K Buffalo Time (5.9+)
7 Artistic Arête (5.13a)	11 Fire Point (5.9+ R)	

Pitch 1: Climb the arête and face to the right past two bolts to a ledge with cold shuts. (70 feet).

8. Hindu Kush   5.8

This is one of two must-do 5.8s at Ship Rock! Big jugs and a lot of exposure.

First ascent: Bob Mitchell, Dan Perry (1981).

Start: Just left of *Artistic Arête*. A small pine is about 10 feet up the route.

Pitch 1: Follow the crack past the small pine to flakes that traverse left. Head straight up and left through steep rock to a huge horizontal flake that sticks out. Pull up and mantel onto this flake and belay at bolts. (5.8; 75 feet). *Variation:* Start 20 feet left and climb straight up past two bolts to join the traverse. (5.9).

Pitch 2: Head up and right to a corner/roof that you pull out to the right. Move up to a short corner above a roof and then fire up and right across face to a good ledge. (5.7; 80 feet).

Pitch 3: Climb a short vertical crack and then head up big jugs moving slightly left to gain a ledge with some large boulders. Stay left of the roof and head to the top. (5.7; 70 feet).

9. Alternative Man   5.12b/c

The first-pitch crux is popular due to its bolts. The upper pitches are excellent too.

First ascent: Mark Terrant, Galen Howell (1991).

Start: At the bolted arête just right of the "trampled" area below *Fire Point*.

Pitch 1: Climb the devious arête past two bolts and then up to the bolt for *Hindu Kush Direct*. Finish at the *Hindu Kush* first-pitch anchors. (5.12b/c; 70 feet).

Pitch 2: Climb *Hindu Kush* to the ledge with large boulders. (5.7; 120 feet).

Pitch 3: Climb out the prowlike roof to the right. Clip a bolt and slab your way to the top. (5.11b; 40 feet).

10. Hindu Kush Direct   5.10d R

Like *Fire Point*, this a great lead up a clean corner but it has devious protection. Be sure you are solid at the grade for this one.

First ascent: Doug Reed, Mike Grimm (1986).

Start: In the left-facing corner just left of the bolted arête of *Alternative Man*.

Pitch 1: Climb the strikingly clean corner on small gear. Exit the corner at the top and head up to a bolt. Climb up and slightly right to the big roofs. Pull the roof and belay at the first-pitch anchors for *Hindu Kush*. (65 feet).

11. Fire Point   5.9+ R

That's *fee-ray*—like the shoes! There is some tricky pro on the first 30 feet, so folks not solid at the grade should err on the side of caution.

First ascent: Tom Howard, Dan Perry (1984).

Start: In the right-facing corner left of *Hindu Kush Direct*. This is where the main rappel touches down.

Pitch 1: Climb up the corner on thin pro to join either *Boardwalk* or *KB Capers*.

Pitch 2: Finish on your chosen route.

12. KB Capers   5.10a

Fun and exposed climbing leads to the "mystery move" on the second pitch.
   First ascent: Jim Okel, Dan Perry (1981).

Michael Williams exits the first-pitch roof of KB Capers *(route 12).*

Start: On *Boardwalk* or *Fire Point.*

Pitch 1: Climb up either start to where they meet and rail out right to horizontals angled up to the arête underneath a roof. Pull around the arête and then head up the arête and face to a right-facing corner on the right side of the arête. (5.9; 70 feet).

Pitch 2: Climb up the corner to a roof where you have to move a bit right to pull the devious sequence of moves through the upper roof. Climb easier ground to the top. (5.10a; 100 feet).

13. Boardwalk   5.8

This is the area's classic and most crowded route. It is also the location of the main rap station—so avoid belaying at the midway bolted station on busy weekends unless you like ropes tossed on your head; there's plenty of natural pro out right for natural anchors.

First ascent: Lisa Perry, Dan Perry (1982).

Start: 20 feet left of *Fire Point.* There is a large horizontal crack at chest level at the base of the route and a dead, but still standing, tree.

Pitch 1: Via any number of means (left is easier), access the easier stone up and right from the bushes. Climb up passing a roof on the left to a horizontal that traverses out right toward a good vertical crack left of the arête. Climb the cracks and horizontals left of the arête until you can angle left across the face to a belay stance in the bushy corner. (5.8; 70 feet).

Pitch 2: Traverse up and right off the ledge aiming for the weakness on the left side of the roof above. Pull the roof and head to the bolted anchor at the top. (5.8; 50 feet). *Variation:* Where route trends left on pitch 1 to gain the bushy belay in the corner, continue straight up big holds angling right to pass the bulge near the arête. Continue up and left to the anchors at the top. (5.8; 150 feet).

Descent: A rappel on a 60-meter rope will not reach the ground. Either rappel twice or be prepared to downclimb easy terrain.

14. The Broach   5.11d

You better have your dial set to aggro for this overhanging pumpfest.

First ascent: Doug Reed (1985).

Start: 75 feet uphill of *Boardwalk* at some dark water streaks just above two dead trees.

Pitch 1: Climb up and right across blocky terrain to the base of a corner that has a smooth and slabby right side. Move up this corner system until you can climb up and right over roofs to gain a horizontal crack below a huge overhang. Traverse out under the roof following this diagonal crack. Big guns will get you out to the lip where you head straight up to the top. (140 feet).

15. First Flight   5.11b

If you get pumped, you may take flight off this gem.

First ascent: Doug Reed, Maurice Reed, Vernon Scarborough.

Start: Same as *The Broach.*

Pitch 1: Climb *The Broach* to where it breaks right to the roofs. Here follow a good crack up and left past a fixed pin to face climbing that leads back right to a right-facing corner and a gear belay. (5.10b; 100 feet).

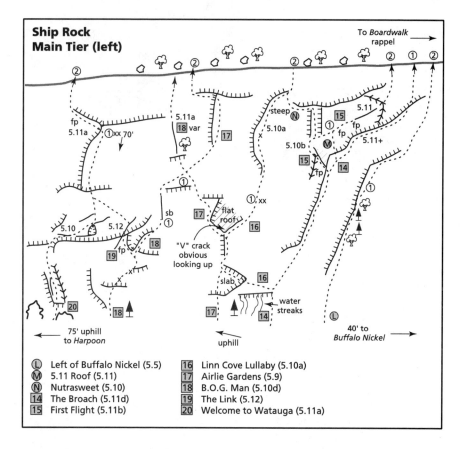

**Ship Rock
Main Tier (left)**

To *Boardwalk*
rappel

Left of Buffalo Nickel (5.5)
- Ⓛ Left of Buffalo Nickel (5.5)
- Ⓜ 5.11 Roof (5.11)
- Ⓝ Nutrasweet (5.10)
- 14 The Broach (5.11d)
- 15 First Flight (5.11b)
- 16 Linn Cove Lullaby (5.10a)
- 17 Airlie Gardens (5.9)
- 18 B.O.G. Man (5.10d)
- 19 The Link (5.12)
- 20 Welcome to Watauga (5.11a)

Pitch 2: Traverse out right past two fixed pegs in the horizontal crack. Turn the arête and climb easier ground to the top. (5.11b; 50 feet).

16. Linn Cove Lullaby   5.10a

Big jugs and dizzying exposure make this one full-value!

First ascent: Tom Howard, Dan Perry, Lee Carter (1980).

Start: Same as *The Broach.*

Pitch 1: Wander up past the water streaks to a small ledge. Traverse up and left across a slab that ends at a right-facing corner capped by a flat roof split by a V crack. Climb up and right under the roof and then up over a bulge to a bolted belay. (5.9; 70 feet).

Pitch 2: Climb up to a bolt and then continue up the corner until it arches right and ends. Head to the top on juggy horizontals. (5.10a; 70 feet).

17. Airlie Gardens   5.9

A definite classic with great position and exposure!

First ascent: Tom Howard, Dan Perry (1982).

Start: 20 feet uphill from *Linn Cove Lullaby.*

Pitch 1: Climb straight up to the roof split by the V crack on *Linn Cove Lullaby.*

Mike Grimm pulls the steep crux of Linn Cove Lullaby *(route 16), with Goose Kearse belaying.*

Head left out the thin crack and pull over the lip into a short corner. Move over another bulge and then left to a good stance. (5.9; 70 feet).

Pitch 2: Climb the right-facing corner up to the roof where you make a very exposed traverse out left from under the roof. Pull over the lip and climb to the top. (5.9; 60 feet).

18. B.O.G. Man   5.10d

Powerful moves on really steep terrain. The initials stand for "Bolts-on-Grand-father"—these are believed to be the first bolts ever placed on Grandfather Mountain.

First ascent: Tom Howard, Thomas Kelley (1982). Doug Reed did the second-pitch variation in 1986.

Start: 20 feet uphill from *Airlie Gardens* and immediately uphill of a large tree.

Pitch 1: Climb up to the base of a small roof that has two bolts above it. Boulder powerful moves up and right to the second bolt. Balance up and right to a small, but good, stance. Move up and left to gain a handrail that rides out the overhang to the right and then fight the pump to access the belay stance at slings. (5.10d; 80 feet).

Pitch 2: Head up and right to finish on pitch two of *Airlie Gardens* (5.9; 50 feet). *Variation:* Angle up and left from the pitch-one belay to the base of a splitter, overhanging crack with a bush at the base. Climb the steep crack to easier terrain above. (5.11a; 60 feet).

19. The Link   5.12

This route has a great variety of moves, decent pro, and should be on the tick list of the 5.12 Ship Rock climber.

First ascent: Doug Reed.

Start: Same as for *B.O.G. Man.*

Pitch 1: Instead of riding the rail out right on pitch one of *B.O.G. Man*, head up and left past a large flake to a fixed pin. Crimp up and right to a strong move at the lip. Pull onto the slabby face above and climb to the *Welcome to Watauga* first-pitch anchors. (5.12; 80 feet).

Pitch 2: Finish on *Welcome to Watauga.* (5.11a; 40 feet).

20. Welcome to Watauga   5.11a

Get ready for some outrageous heel hooking on an airy lip traverse.

First ascent: Wes Love, Rodney Lanier. Shannon Stegg and Jim Okel made the first free ascent.

Start: 20 feet uphill from *B.O.G. Man* locate a right-facing corner 20 feet up.

Pitch 1: Climb the corner to the top and get good pro up and right in the big water-streaked flake. Wild traverse moves out right access the face above. Then climb up the overhanging corner to a bolted anchor. (5.10b; 70 feet).

Pitch 2: Traverse left out the large roof on thin holds past a fixed pin and then pull the lip to a large crack that takes you to the trees. (5.11a; 40 feet).

21. Harpoon   5.10a (no topo)

Bomber locks and jams make this sweet, if not too short, crack a classic.

First ascent: Jim Okel, Tom Howard, Lee Carter (1981).

Start: 75 feet uphill from *Welcome to Watauga* on a wall that faces downhill. This wall holds the last routes uphill on the Main Tier.

Pitch 1: Climb the obvious hand and finger crack on the right side of the wall to the bolted station on a ledge. (50 feet).

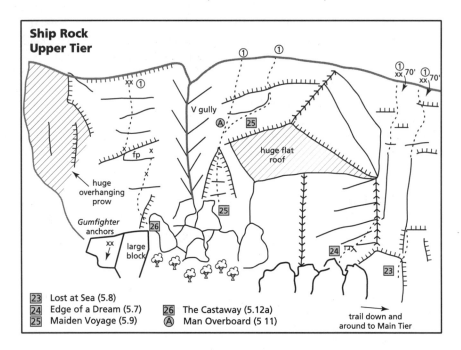

Ship Rock
Upper Tier

V gully

huge flat roof

huge overhanging prow

Gumfighter anchors

large block

trail down and around to Main Tier

23	Lost at Sea (5.8)
24	Edge of a Dream (5.7)
25	Maiden Voyage (5.9)
26	The Castaway (5.12a)
A	Man Overboard (5 11)

22. The Anguish of Captain Bligh 5.11b/c (no topo)

A masterpiece of sequential fingerlocks and arête climbing.

First ascent: Maurice Reed, Doug Reed, Vernon Scarborough.

Start: 15 feet left of *Harpoon.*

Pitch 1: Climb the seams and locks up to a wild sequence on the arête. Eventually, move right onto the face to join *Harpoon.* (50 feet).

Upper Tier

From the far-right side of the Main Tier, take a trail that starts right of *Chromium Chain* (see Main Tier right-side topo) and curls up and around through rhododendrons to the base of a short wall. Head left along this wall for 100 feet to access these next four routes, which are in a small amphitheater with jumbled blocks at the base.

Descent: Use the rap stations above *Lost at Sea, Edge of a Dream,* or *Castaway.*

23. Lost at Sea 5.8

A classic in the same style as *Edge of a Dream.*

First ascent: Joanne Keen, Woody Keen.

Start: 20 feet to the right of *Edge of a Dream* at a short left-facing corner.

Pitch 1: Climb the short corner and pull right around a sharp arête. Pull through large holds to a crack on the left side of a roof that leads to easier ground and bolted anchors. (70 feet).

24. Edge of a Dream 5.7

Big holds with equally big exposure more than make up for the brevity of this great line.

First ascent: Tom Howard, Dan Perry (1980).

Start: Left side of the arête on the far-right side of the small amphitheater.
Pitch 1: Climb up large horizontals and jugs on the face aiming up and right for the arête. Turn the arête and follow a nice crack to a bolted belay. (70 feet).

25. Maiden Voyage   5.9
Fun moves that keep you guessing from below.
First ascent: Trip Collins, Clyde Mann.
Start: On the left side of the amphitheater and just right of a V-notch gully.
Pitch 1: Climb over triangular blocks to a good stance. Move up and right to gain a thin crack under a roof. Pull through this feature out right and then head to the top past big holds. (65 feet).

26. The Castaway   5.12a
A relatively recent addition to Ship Rock that is getting rave reviews from those in the know. Bring a light rack to 1 inch.
First ascent: Lynn Willis (1997).
Start: Left of the V-notch gully, locate a small dihedral with fixed gear above.
Pitch 1: Once in the corner, head up past two bolts to large roof. Clip a fixed pin and then rail out the overhang past another bolt. Pull up onto the hanging slab and climb the face to the bolted anchors. (70 feet).

5. LINVILLE GORGE

Linville Gorge dominates the landscape in North Carolina's "high country," a mountainous region in the northwestern section of the state. A 14-mile canyon cleaved by the Linville River, the gorge is formed by Linville Mountain on the west and Jonas Ridge on the east. For many reasons other than its congressional wilderness designation, climbers consider this the last great "wilderness" climbing area in the southern Appalachians. The gorge is a jumble of fractured and hard-to-reach ridgelines; secret bouldering coves; and imposing, improbable, multipitch walls. The gorge areas covered in this guide are Hawksbill Mountain, Table Rock, North Carolina Wall and The Amphitheater, and Shortoff Mountain. There are several other worthwhile climbing areas in the gorge, so have fun exploring.

In November 2000, a series of wildfires exploded across the 10,900-acre Linville Gorge Wilderness. By the time firefighters got the fires under control, approximately 6,000 acres had burned—including huge swaths near Shortoff Mountain, Table Rock, The Chimneys, and North Carolina Wall. The fires, possibly started by cigarettes or campfires, have deeply scarred this fragile area, and visitors should be aware that many areas in the gorge have changed considerably. In some places, old trails have simply vanished, and climbers should be especially attentive about relying on burned vegetation for handholds or anchors.

Restrictions and Access Issues
All of the climbing areas in this section, except Table Rock, are in the Linville Gorge Wilderness and as such fall under the congressional wilderness designation. Among

other wilderness area restrictions, this means no power equipment is allowed.

In addition to the rules and regulations listed at the front of the guide, please follow regulations specific to this area:

- **Peregrine falcon closures.** The U.S. Forest Service closes portions of Linville Gorge each year between January 15 and August 15 for peregrine falcon nesting. While the Forest Service often lifts these bans well before August 1, it does not always remove the signs at trailheads in Linville Gorge. Unless you like uncertainty and disappointment, you would do well to confirm which cliffs are open before you make plans to climb in Linville Gorge. The U.S. Forest Service posts restrictions and annual peregrine falcon closures on its website, *www.cs.unca.edu/nfsnc,* but this site changes often. You can also find updated closure information at *www.carolinaclimbers.org.*
- **Road closures.** The access road to the Table Rock Picnic Area is generally gated from January 1 to April 1 because of weather conditions. While the cliffs may be open, this gate closure will add a steep, 1.4-mile, uphill hike to your trip. In spring, it is wise to check in advance with the Forest Service.

Camping

Permits are required for overnight camping in the wilderness area only on weekends and holidays during from May 1 through October 31. You can obtain these free permits by contacting the district ranger's office in Nebo, Monday through Friday, 8:00 A.M. to 4:30 P.M. (see appendix B). Walk-in permits, for the current week only, are available at the Linville Gorge Information Cabin, located on Kistler Memorial Highway on the western rim of the gorge. The cabin is open from April through October, seven days a week, 9:00 A.M. to 5:00 P.M.

Free camping is available along FR 210 en route to the Table Rock Picnic Area, but do not camp in the picnic area's parking lot. Once on the trail toward The Chimneys, you cross the wilderness boundary and there are many flat, shady spots available for tent camping (permit required).

Water

It is best to bring your own water any time you visit Linville Gorge, especially if you are camping at one of the legal spots above the Table Rock Picnic Area or off FR 210. However, there are some unreliable possibilities for additional water (don't forget your filter):

- If camping down in the gorge, consider the Linville River.
- A seasonal spring near Little Table Rock, approximately 500 feet from the junction of the Little Table Rock Trail and the white-blazed Mountains-to-Sea Trail (MST).
- A seasonal spring near the route *Tarantula* at the North Carolina Wall.
- A seasonal spring running down The Amphitheater gully.
- A seasonal spring near the approach gully for Shortoff Mountain.

Emergency Services

The closest hospital is Grace Hospital in Morganton. (See appendix C.)

Gear

A standard free-climbing rack works fine for most Linville Gorge routes. Be prepared for many placements in horizontal slots; extra TCUs always come in handy. Many routes tend to wander a bit, so double ropes or additional long slings would be advisable.

Getting There

There are northern and southern access points for Linville Gorge climbing areas. To access the climbing areas on the east side of the gorge (Hawksbill Mountain, Table Rock, and the North Carolina Wall), drive to the northern access at Table Rock Road. From Asheville and points west, follow Interstate 40 to exit 72 for US 70 and Old Fort. Follow US 70 east to Marion. Before Marion, turn left onto US 221 heading north for Linville Falls. Follow US 221 to Linville Falls and turn right onto NC 183 heading east. After about 0.2 mile, you will pass a right turn for Kistler Memorial Highway—not a highway at all—and the western rim of Linville Gorge. This road leads to the Linville Gorge Information Cabin, where you can get a camping permit (see Camping above).

Follow NC 183 for 4 miles to a junction with NC 181. Turn right (south) on NC 181 headed for Morganton and go approximately 2.5 miles. At the bottom of a hill, turn right (west) onto Gingercake Road (SR 1264) at a sign for the Linville Gorge Wilderness Area and the Table Rock Picnic Area. At 0.3 mile, veer left onto the first fork, Table Rock Road (SR 1261). This shortly becomes FR 210, which is gravel. See each climbing area for remaining driving directions and approaches.

The southern access to Linville Gorge takes you to a parking area for Shortoff Mountain. See the Shortoff Mountain section below for complete driving directions and approach.

Overview of Linville Gorge looking downstream from Wiseman's View

Table Rock

The Chimneys

North Carolina Wall

Shortoff Mountain

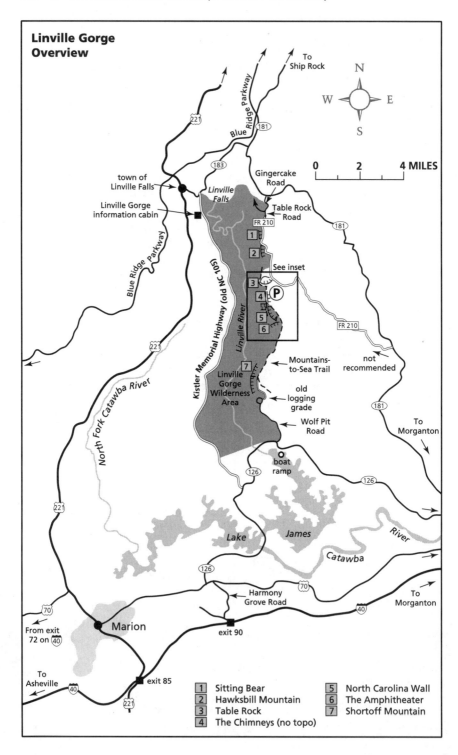

Linville Gorge Overview

N
W · E
S

To Ship Rock

Blue Ridge Parkway

221

181

183

town of Linville Falls

Linville Gorge information cabin

Linville Falls

Gingercake Road

Table Rock Road

FR 210

181

0   2   4 MILES

Blue Ridge Parkway

221

Kistler Memorial Highway (old NC 105)

Linville River

1

2

See inset

3

4

P

5

6

FR 210

Mountains-to-Sea Trail

not recommended

7

Linville Gorge Wilderness Area

old logging grade

Wolf Pit Road

181

To Morganton

North Fork Catawba River

boat ramp

126

126

Lake   James   River

Catawba

126

Harmony Grove Road

70

To Morganton

40

70

Marion

exit 90

From exit 72 on 40

To Asheville

40

exit 85

221

1	Sitting Bear	5	North Carolina Wall
2	Hawksbill Mountain	6	The Amphitheater
3	Table Rock	7	Shortoff Mountain
4	The Chimneys (no topo)		

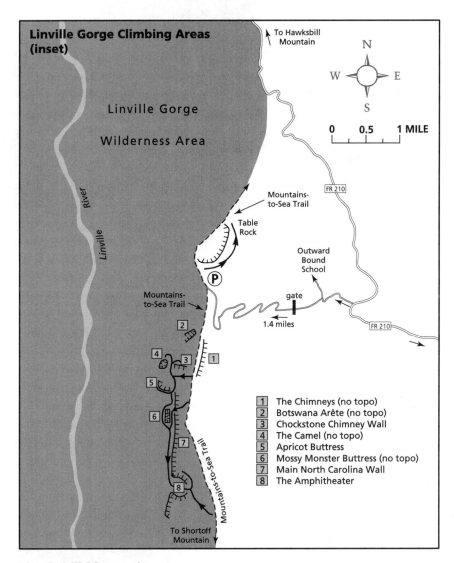

Linville Gorge Climbing Areas (inset)

To Hawksbill Mountain

Linville Gorge Wilderness Area

N
W E
S

0   0.5   1 MILE

Linville River

Mountains-to-Sea Trail

FR 210

Table Rock

Outward Bound School

P

Mountains-to-Sea Trail

gate

1.4 miles

FR 210

Mountains-to-Sea Trail

2

4 3 1

5

6

7

8

1   The Chimneys (no topo)
2   Botswana Arête (no topo)
3   Chockstone Chimney Wall
4   The Camel (no topo)
5   Apricot Buttress
6   Mossy Monster Buttress (no topo)
7   Main North Carolina Wall
8   The Amphitheater

To Shortoff Mountain

Hawksbill Mountain

Climbing type: Traditional
Rock type: Metasandstone
Height: 70 to 180 feet
Number of routes: Approximately 75 (24 this guide)
Climbing season: April through October
Camping: See Linville Gorge introduction

This area is a multitiered series of overhanging cliffs on the northwest-facing flanks of Hawksbill Mountain. Named because its profile from afar resembles a hawk's bill (duh), the cliff has a short approach and some of the best single-pitch lines in the

The three tiers of Hawksbill Mountain as seen from Wiseman's View

entire gorge. The cliff's orientation and dense vegetation often keeps Hawksbill pleasantly cool on hot summer days. Hawksbill is not well-known among many southeastern climbers, but more than one visitor has bemoaned not visiting sooner.

This guide includes routes on the Main Wall, Lower Hawksbill, and previously hidden Middle Hawksbill. Upper Hawksbill routes, high on the mountain, are not in this guide.

History

Despite its relatively small size, Hawksbill occupies a special place in local climbing lore. Home to previous guidebook cover shots such as *Lost in Space* and *The Fat Lady*, this cliff was also the scene of the infamous "Hawksbill Summit" in the mid-1990s, which cast a pall on new route development for several years. Today, the metamorphosed rock of Hawksbill still sees far fewer climbers than nearby Table Rock, but the routes here are some of the best in the state.

Tom Howard and Rich Gottlieb made the first visit to Hawksbill in the winter of 1977–78 on a cold, rainy day. Despite the weather, the climbers immediately recognized Hawksbill's potential and agreed to return as soon as possible. In the summer of 1978, Howard returned with Bill Newman and completed the *Hawksbill Traverse*. Unbeknownst to them, Gottlieb and Tom McMillan had already swiped that line! On the same day, Howard also tried the line that would eventually become *Lost in Space*. Using all passive protection (the only thing available at the time), Howard climbed out the intimidating roof—and promptly took a long fall, spraining his ankle. Undeterred, Howard returned the following spring for the free ascent. Although the route was not ahead of its time in terms of difficulty, Howard's willingness to go for it on steep ground with questionable gear still keeps these routes exciting and challenging for modern climbers.

Just when it seemed the Main Wall was climbed out, some intrepid climbers blundered through the steep rhododendron hillside below this wall and found Lower Hawksbill. This cliff proved a gold mine of hard, single-pitch climbs, and new developers such as Thomas Kelley, Doug Reed, Bruce Burgess, and others cashed in on the potential. Meanwhile, and true to his reputation as an explorer, Howard was one of the first climbers to bushwhack past the Main Wall and discover that the cliff band reappeared after many climbers assumed it dwindled out. This lower section of the Main Wall became known as Middle Hawksbill and saw some development around 1988, when Howard and Kelley returned to snag a few traversing crack lines. But Burgess and Jeff Burton really got to work in the early 1990s when they established four very difficult, hook-bolted lines on the cliff.

Mark Dew strikes a balance on King of Kings *(topo only) at Lower Hawksbill.*

Around 1993, a band of local climbers led by Mike Fischesser began visiting the cliff and developing rappel-bolted routes. About eighteen routes went in before the state's climbing cognoscenti got wind of the development style and rounded up the posse. In late winter of 1995, a large and diverse group of climbers came together to discuss the situation at Fischesser's cabin not 40 minutes from the cliff. The short version of the Hawksbill Summit went like this: After agreeing to first climb the routes and evaluate them individually, a few renegades went in and began "removing" the routes ahead of the others. Fischesser protested at first, then did a sudden 180-degree turn. He came in the next morning to remove the rest of the routes himself—mainly by simply unscrewing the bolt hangers. About two dozen of the climbers present went on to sign a letter to the regional climbing magazine *Boulderdash* with a proclamation called "The Traditional Proposal." It read, in part, "While we realize that we are only a minority of the over 2,000 climbers in North and South Carolina, the following signatures do represent a majority of the main first ascentionists and people who have maintained the traditional style of climbing in the Carolinas. . . . Similar to a museum or national park concept, we would like to propose to the climbers of North and South Carolina that Carolina climbing remain a region where all can go to learn, experience and enjoy the craft of adventure climbing from the ground up using traditional style."

Obviously, this did not sit well with some of the young locals. But "The Traditional Proposal" has nonetheless survived for seven years. It is up to the next generation of activists to decide whether they will continue to value this ethic or cast it aside as old-fashioned and misguided.

Weather and Climbing Season
Hawksbill Mountain (elevation 4,020 feet) faces northwest and is an excellent warm-weather destination (although insects can be brutal in spring and early summer). The cliff starts getting sun in midafternoon.

Getting There
Follow the driving directions to Table Rock Road and FR 210 given in the Linville Gorge introduction. Pass the Sitting Bear climbing area pullout on the right (area map only) after about 2.5 miles on FR 210. After approximately 3 miles on FR 210, there is a pullout on the left for the Jonas Ridge Trail. The approach trail for all the Hawksbill Mountain walls (Main, Middle, and Lower) begins on the right, across the road.

Approach
Across from the parking area, follow the steep trail up an old rutted road for 0.5 mile to a junction on the ridgeline.

For the Main Wall: Turn sharply left at the junction on the main trail and continue another 0.1 mile to another indistinct trail on the right, occasionally marked by a pile of downed limbs. (Continue 0.1 mile on the main trail to the summit if you want to explore the Upper Hawksbill routes not in this guide. Hike west from the summit until you can scramble and downclimb to a series of tree ledges underneath roofs.) The narrow, indistinct trail to the right will deposit you near *Star Trekin'* on the Main Wall.

For Middle Hawksbill: From *Star Trekin'* on the Main Wall, continue 400 feet down the hill.

For Lower Hawksbill: From the junction on the ridgeline, continue another 20 feet to an old, wooden signpost. Veer left through dense woods for about 5 minutes to emerge near *Hairy Canary.*

Routes are numbered 1 through 24 from left to right, starting on Hawksbill's Main Wall, continuing on Middle Hawksbill, and finishing on Lower Hawksbill.

Main Wall

1. Winged Mongrel   5.10a

An excellent mix of crack climbing and jugs, this route is steeper than it looks!

First ascent: Tom Howard, Jim Downs (1979, ground-up).

Start: At left-most side of cliff on a bushy pedestal.

Pitch 1: Move up the face and angle left to where a roof and angling crack system meet. Follow the corner up and right until you can monkey-bar onto the face

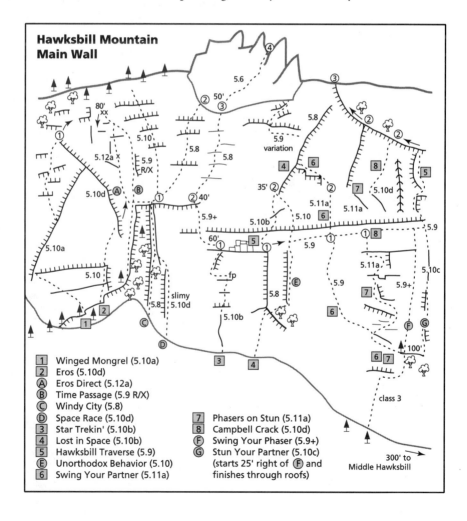

Hawksbill Mountain Main Wall

1. Winged Mongrel (5.10a)
2. Eros (5.10d)
Ⓐ Eros Direct (5.12a)
Ⓑ Time Passage (5.9 R/X)
Ⓒ Windy City (5.8)
Ⓓ Space Race (5.10d)
3. Star Trekin' (5.10b)
4. Lost in Space (5.10b)
5. Hawksbill Traverse (5.9)
Ⓔ Unorthodox Behavior (5.10)
6. Swing Your Partner (5.11a)

7. Phasers on Stun (5.11a)
8. Campbell Crack (5.10d)
Ⓕ Swing Your Phaser (5.9+)
Ⓖ Stun Your Partner (5.10c)
(starts 25' right of Ⓕ and finishes through roofs)

using huge jugs. Continue up the face to a natural belay near the top of the cliff.

Descent: Move right to rappel from two bolts atop *Eros Direct.* (80 feet).

2. Eros 5.10d

More sustained than its partner to the left, but with the same huge holds and great pro.

First ascent: Tom McMillan, Tom Howard (1979, ground-up).

Start: 20 feet right of *Winged Mongrel* beneath a shallow, right-facing corner.

Pitch 1: Move up the corner and cut left around a roof. Continue up the face to the base of a wildly steep crack and roof system. Ape out left on huge holds and exit onto the face (can be a little dirty). Continue up the face to a natural belay near the top of the cliff.

Descent: Move right to rappel from two bolts atop *Eros Direct.* (80 feet).

3. Star Trekin' 5.10b

Parties often climb the crux first pitch as a warm-up for other routes through the roof.

First ascent: Jim Downs, Tom Howard (1979, ground-up).

Start: 50 feet right of a dirty corner system beneath a shallow seam.

Pitch 1: Follow the seam directly up to a small overlap. Some long reaches past an old fixed piece will force you left. Bigger holds at a corner allow access to the natural belay. (5.10b; 60 feet).

Pitch 2: Step left off the ledge and aim for good holds on the clean white wall. Traverse to the right and continue up to another good ledge. (5.9+; 40 feet).

Pitch 3: Step off the ledge at some blocks and fire directly up a steep face past good horizontals that eat protection. Belay at a blocky, triangular roof. (5.8; 50 feet).

Pitch 4: Thread your way through roofs to exit at the summit. (5.6; 25 feet).

Descent: Hike through rhododendrons to gain a short cliff line barring the summit. Negotiate this and then follow a trail north (left) off the summit for about 0.2 mile until you can find a faint climbers' trail on the left. This trail will take you back to the Main Wall in about 10 minutes.

4. Lost in Space 5.10b

For many years this was the poster route of Linville Gorge. Midsized camming units (0.5 to 0.75 inch) protect the roof crux but the corner above is fantastically exposed, too!

First ascent: Tom Howard, Jim Downs (1978-79).

Start: Under a right-facing corner.

Pitch 1: Trend up the face a ways until you can gain the obvious corner. (5.8; 60 feet).

Pitch 2: Blast up over the roof with some long reaches and heel hooking. Traverse right along a horizontal and belay. (5.10b; 35 feet).

Pitch 3: Continue up a ramp and corner system that confronts you with a short crux up high. Great pro and excellent exposure make this a real treat. Belay at the summit. (5.8; 70 feet). *Note:* It is possible to traverse left under an overlap high on this pitch for a 5.9 finish with nice roof climbing.

Descent: Same as *Star Trekin'.*

Opposite: *Lee McGuffey savors the exposure on* Lost in Space *(route 4).*

5. Hawksbill Traverse   5.9

Included for posterity's sake, this weird route avoids the issue by slinking right under the huge roof. There is a short, steep section near the end. Bring an ample supply of larger cams (2 to 3 inches).

First ascent: Tom McMillan, Rich Gottlieb (1978).

Start: On *Star Trekin'*.

Pitch 1: Climb the first pitch of *Star Trekin'*. (5.8; 60 feet).

Pitch 2: From the first belay on *Star Trekin'* traverse right and keep going. The traverse is a little unsettling. Good hands but occasionally no feet! Make sure to protect your second and use those larger cams. Belay in an alcove atop routes 6 and 7. (5.9; 60 feet or 80 feet).

Pitch 3: Continue right past one funky section and look for an opportunity to move up onto the smaller headwall. Follow a corner system to the summit. (5.9; 50 feet).

Descent: Same as *Star Trekin'*.

6. Swing Your Partner   5.11a

Does this gigantic roof really go? See for yourself. The traditional start to this route is via *Lost in Space* to the *Hawksbill Traverse*. A direct start may have been climbed earlier but it was not documented until 2001.

First ascent: Bill Newman, Tom Howard (1980, ground-up). Howard and Jim Okel made the first free ascent in 1980. Andy Kluge and Bruce Burgess did the direct start in 2001.

Start: Follow the trail 100 feet downhill from *Star Trekin'* to a mossy slab. Work your way up tree ledges and right under a vegetated roof to a narrow ledge (the *Phasers on Stun* ledge). Note that the traditional start to *Swing Your Partner* has been *Lost in Space*.

Pitch 1: From the *Phasers* ledge, climb up the slab aiming for a ledge just left of the right-leaning corner/roof. Move up and right for a clean, steep face under the roof. Belay or continue for the endurance pump. (5.9; 70 feet).

Pitch 2: The first few moves are stomach churning, but the protection is excellent and the climbing eases on the headwall. Belay in a horizontal. (5.11a; 30 feet).

Pitch 3: Move left along the steep face to a series of "steps" that deposit you on the upper pitch of *Lost in Space*. (5.8; 80 feet).

Descent: Same as *Star Trekin'*.

7. Phasers on Stun   5.11a

Here's a recommended and long-overlooked two-pitch route that is excellent as an independent line or as a direct start to *Campbell Crack*.

First ascent: Bruce Burgess and Lea Crandall climbed the first pitch on-sight in 1991. Burgess and Andy Kluge returned in 2001 to add the second pitch.

Start: Follow the trail 100 feet downhill from *Star Trekin'* to a mossy slab. Work your way up tree ledges and right under a vegetated roof to a narrow ledge (the *Phasers* ledge).

Pitch 1: Climb a left-angling ramp aiming for a ledge. Trend up and right— and then back left—following a short, shallow corner until you can pull onto the steep face. Continuous climbing leads to a small roof. Move left and pimp up a final slab to the belay in the *Hawksbill Traverse* horizontal. (5.11a; 80 feet).

Pitch 2: Monkey your way out the roof on a left-rising rail (3.5- to 4-inch gear) until it is possible to fire straight up the steep face to another good horizontal. Traverse up and left to a hanging ledge. Roll up on to the ledge. Climb the steep face and thin seam just right of the arête for another 25 feet to a nice belay near the top. (5.11a; 75 feet).

Note: Can be climbed as one, long 165-foot pump festival.

Descent: Same as *Star Trekin'*.

8. Campbell Crack   5.10d

Although short, this is simply a must-do route that starts from the upper tier. Altitude and attitude: Gunks-style climbing that looks out over the entire upper Linville Gorge.

First ascent: Doug Reed, Tom Howard (1983).

Start: Get to *Hawksbill Traverse* or start on *Phasers on Stun*.

Pitch 1: Either traverse right along the *Hawksbill Traverse* for approximately 80 feet or climb *Phasers on Stun* for an excellent direct approach.

Pitch 2: One of the best. Blast off the belay and into a steep, left-angling crack on the headwall. Small and midsized units are helpful here. Continue straight up and through a weakness or move left on a rail with holds so big it is impossible to fall . . . or so it seems. (5.10d; 70 feet).

Descent: Same as *Star Trekin'*.

Middle Hawksbill

This cliff is on the same contour lines as the Main Wall, but since it is somewhat downhill it has long been regarded as a separate area. Middle Hawksbill saw some sporadic development in the late 1980s and early 90s, but faded into obscurity after the Hawksbill Summit. We have only described a select number of routes. Please note that many other lines exist here that are not on the topo.

Descent: Rappel the routes.

9. Line of Fire   5.12c

Crimp strength and a few big moves are needed to fire this one.

First ascent: Bruce Burgess, Lea Crandall (1994).

Start: 300 feet downhill from the last Main Wall routes.

Pitch 1: Begin at a left-facing corner on the left end of a clean, gently overhanging wall. Climb past five bolts to cold shuts. (50 feet).

10. Pascal's Route   5.12c/d

The edges on this route are razors and the holds—as well as the bolts—are pretty well spaced. Stick-clip anyone?

First ascent: Pascal Robert.

Start: 15 feet right of *Line of Fire*.

Pitch 1: Three bolts lead to a single bolt anchor. (50 feet).

11. Tips Ahoy   5.12c/d

A crimping test piece that didn't see a redpoint ascent until some time after it was bolted.

First ascent: Jeff Burton (1994). The first free ascent is unclear.

Start: 10 feet right of *Pascal's Route*.

Pitch 1: Follow a line of five bolts to a double-bolt anchor. (50 feet).

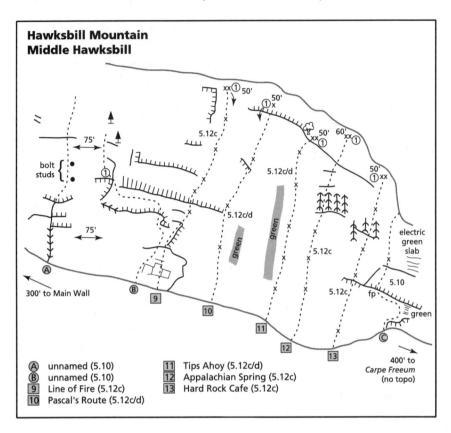

**Hawksbill Mountain
Middle Hawksbill**

Ⓐ unnamed (5.10)
Ⓑ unnamed (5.10)
9 Line of Fire (5.12c)
10 Pascal's Route (5.12c/d)

11 Tips Ahoy (5.12c/d)
12 Appalachian Spring (5.12c)
13 Hard Rock Cafe (5.12c)

12. Appalachian Spring   5.12c

This mixed pitch was the first established in this impressive sector of Middle Hawksbill. Bring quickdraws plus 0.4-inch, 1-inch, and 2.5-inch cams.

First ascent: Bruce Burgess, Lea Crandall (1993).
Start: 8 feet right of *Tips Ahoy.*
Pitch 1: Three bolts past some vicious crimpers lead to a series of rounded pinches and good horizontals. Double-bolt anchor. (60 feet).

13. Hard Rock Cafe   5.12c

Some incredibly sequential climbing bars the anchors.

First ascent: Bruce Burgess, Jeff Burton (1994).
Start: 25 feet right of *Appalachian Spring.*
Pitch 1: Follow a line of four bolts to the top. (50 feet).

14. Carpe Freeum   5.11c (no topo)

A brilliant line with steep climbing, bomber gear, and a stout crux. Bring extra 2- to 2.5-inch cams.

First ascent: Tom Howard, Lee Carter (1991).
Start: Hike another 400 feet down the wall past many routes with stripped bolt

hangers to find the impressive, steep wall with an overhanging crack and corner about 40 feet up. This starts just right of a large, low roof.

Pitch 1: Juggy climbing leads you up and then right to a 2-foot roof. Fire up into the hanging, left-facing corner and then jam and stem the dihedral to a cushy belay ledge. Scramble a little higher to rap from a tree. (85 feet).

Lower Hawksbill

15. Hairy Canary   5.11a

Huge roofs separated by a short face section. It is possible to do this route in a light rain because of the roofs, although pulling over the top can be a little awkward.

First ascent: Thomas Kelley, Lee Carter.

Start: 20 feet right of a large corner system with a lone bolt.

Pitch 1: Pull over a low roof and step move into position beneath a wrapper handrail jug. Clip the bolt and ape up on gigantic holds. Finish on a slabby, dirty face. (55 feet).

Descent: Rappel from bushes.

16. America under Attack   5.12d/13a

A steep, incipient seam that may wreak havoc on your tendons.

First ascent: Biff Farrell, Chris van Leuven, Chad Hilliard (2001).

Start: Around an arête, 50 feet right of *Hairy Canary*. Begin off a jumbled pile of large boulders.

Pitch 1: Mixed. Move past sweeping diagonals to a vertical seam. Follow this desperate feature to a ledge and then the summit. Four bolts, two fixed pieces. (75 feet).

Descent: Rappel the route.

17. The Diving Board   5.11d

Powerful climbing down low gives way to a sustained romp through buckets.

First ascent: Doug Reed, Thomas Kelley, Tom Howard, Lee Carter.

Start: 8 feet right of *America under Attack*.

Pitch 1: Power directly up beneath two bolts through a low roof and corner. Move right to another bolt and continue up the corner system aiming for the teeter-totter "diving board." (70 feet).

Descent: Rappel from slung rhododendrons; bring something to back it up.

18. The Fat Lady   5.11a

Is it crack climbing or jug hauling? More of the latter. With textbook TCU placements, this route is perhaps more manageable than it used to be.

First ascent: Lee Carter, Tom Howard, Thomas Kelley (ground-up).

Start: 30 feet right of a bulging face beneath a tree ledge, look for the obvious wide crack leading to ledge.

Pitch 1: Climb a blocky, wide corner to a spacious ledge. (5.8; 30 feet). *Note:* Although the route can be done as one pitch, this awesome belay ledge is hard to pass up.

Pitch 2: Blast up the fantastic splitter to a huge rail. Move right onto a thank-god

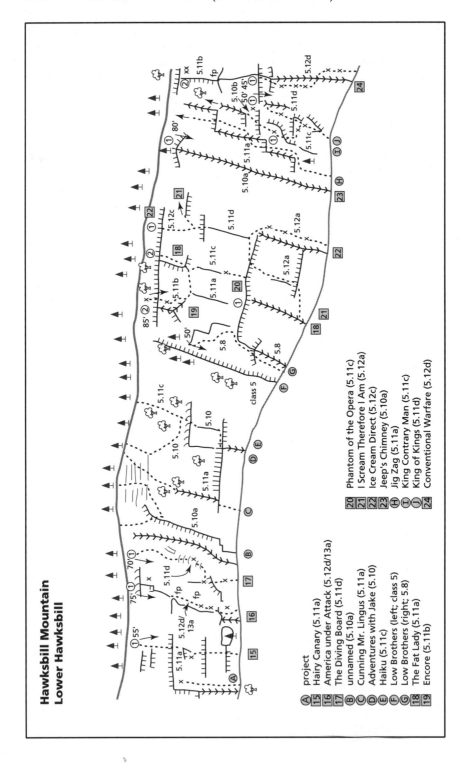

Hawksbill Mountain
Lower Hawksbill

Ⓐ project
15 Hairy Canary (5.11a)
16 America under Attack (5.12d/13a)
17 The Diving Board (5.11d)
Ⓑ unnamed (5.10a)
Ⓒ Cunning Mr. Lingus (5.11a)
Ⓓ Adventures with Jake (5.10)
Ⓔ Haiku (5.11c)
Ⓕ Low Brothers (left; class 5)
Ⓖ Low Brothers (right; 5.8)
18 The Fat Lady (5.11a)
19 Encore (5.11b)

20 Phantom of the Opera (5.11c)
21 I Scream Therefore I Am (5.12a)
22 Ice Cream Direct (5.12c)
23 Jeep's Chimney (5.10a)
Ⓗ Jig Zag (5.11a)
Ⓘ King Contrary Man (5.11c)
Ⓙ King of Kings (5.11d)
24 Conventional Warfare (5.12d)

ledge, then up through a right-facing corner system (occasionally wet) to the top. Remember: It ain't over 'til. . . . (5.10d; 55 feet).

Descent: Set up a natural belay. Then move left and above *Encore* for a single cold shut. A single 55-meter rope will reach the ground.

19. Encore   5.11b

Considered by many to be the only way to finish *The Fat Lady*, this combo makes for one of the best pitches in the state.

First ascent: Bruce Burgess, Galen Howell (summer 1990, ground-up).
Start: Same as *The Fat Lady.*

Kelly Brown steels himself for the Encore *finish (route 19) to* The Fat Lady *(route 18).*

Pitch 1: Climb the first pitch as *Lady.* (5.8; 30 feet).

Pitch 2: Climb the *Lady* crack to the roofs, continuing slightly left to a hanging corner where the wall steepens. Clip a bolt and yard for the top. (5.11b; 55 feet).

Descent: Rappel from a single cold shut. A single 55-meter rope will reach the ground.

20. Phantom of the Opera   5.11c

This splitter will clean your pipes if you're not careful! One pitch goes ground to summit on this nice variation linking the initial corner and final roof of *The Fat Lady.* Bring some brass wired nuts.

First ascent: Bruce Burgess, Galen Howell (1989, ground-up).

Start: In *The Fat Lady* corner.

Pitch 1: Climb the initial corner of *Fat Lady.* Work your way up to bolt, then crimp up to a good hold just before the seam. Finish on the standard *Lady* roof. (80 feet).

Descent: Same as *Lady.*

21. I Scream Therefore I Am   5.12a

Powerful crack climbing with technical (but good) gear. Bring some brass wired nuts.

First ascent: Kris Kline, Bruce Burgess (1988, ground-up). Kline also did the first free ascent in 1988.

Start: 20 feet right of *The Fat Lady.*

Pitch 1: Start up the *Lady* corner, but move quickly right along a rail at a roof to a strenuous, bottoming crack. Continue up to the ledge and climb the small corner to a thin seam. Once past the small overlap, exit on a ledge system to the right. (55 feet).

Descent: Rappel from trees.

22. Ice Cream Direct   5.12c

Sustained and technically demanding, this route is an enduring Linville Gorge test piece. Rarely on-sighted (or even climbed), suitors will need to prepare for thin nutting well into the meat of the route. Can you hang on? Bring some brass wired nuts.

First ascent: Doug Reed, Tim Fisher (1987, ground-up with some dogging).

Start: 15 feet right of *I Scream Therefore I Am.*

Pitch 1: Engineer moves up the overhanging corner past three bolts to a ledge. Join *I Scream* up the small corner and thin seam and don't move right to rest on *I Scream.* Continue up another seam and fire a long move to a third ledge below the headwall. One final pull gains the rim and a belay in bushes. (80 feet).

Descent: Rappel from trees.

23. Jeep's Chimney   5.10a

The suffer quotient on this corner is too low to earn bonus points since good stems and face holds allow for very little serious thrashing. As a result, it has seen at least one nude ascent. Bring extra 3- to 4-inch camming units.

Matt Massey sets up for the business on Ice Cream Direct *(route 22).*

First ascent: Jeep Barrett, Steve Owen (1987).
Start: 50 feet right of *I Scream Therefore I Am.*
Pitch 1: Chickenwing up the wide corner that allows the occasional chimney-stem rest. Follow past a recess at the top to trees for the belay. (80 feet).
Descent: Rappel from trees.

24. Conventional Warfare   5.12d

The longtime area test piece is perhaps even harder now that some holds have broken.

First ascent: Bruce Burgess, Sam Stevenson (1989, ground-up from hooks). Burgess did the first free ascent in 1991.

Start: 30 feet right of *Jeep's Chimney.*

Pitch 1: Negotiate demanding face climbing and stemming up a steep right-facing corner to a ledge. Natural belay with medium-sized gear. (5.12d; 45 feet).

Pitch 2: Climb the upper corner and crack system past a fixed pin to double-bolt anchor. (5.11b; 30 feet).

Descent: Rappel the route.

Table Rock

Climbing type: Multipitch traditional
Rock type: Chillhowie quartzite
Height: 70 to 300 feet
Number of routes: Approximately 60 (30 this guide)
Climbing season: April through November
Camping: See Linville Gorge introduction

Table Rock is one of the mainstays of North Carolina climbing. With an assortment of bolted multipitch routes in the 5.5 and 5.6 range and some excellent moderates like *White Lightning* (5.8), it is probably the premier beginning and intermediate cliff in the state. Used as a multipitch climbing experience location by North Carolina Outward Bound School since the late 1960s, Table Rock stays busy almost all week during peak season. The wall itself is not the most aesthetic of destinations since the gray quartzite is a little drab and broken by numerous tree ledges. Still, the best routes are fun, exposed, and challenging. Its elevation (3,909 feet at the summit) means this cliff is acceptably cool even during the worst of summer. Below and west of Table Rock proper, there are a couple of smaller cliffs including Little Table Rock and Devil's Cellar. These areas offer some solitude from the main walls and a few worthy routes. The Chimneys, which are a short hike opposite Table Rock, offer convenient top-roping and some good bouldering.

History

Very little history exists about climbing in North Carolina prior to 1960, but it is a good bet that at least some early routes went up in the vicinity of Table Rock—one of the state's most significant climbing landmarks. For instance, Morganton climber Jim Anthony made a few unrecorded ascents in the Linville Gorge area and probably climbed the 90-foot *Two Pitch* (5.4) at Table Rock. But prior to the opening of North Carolina Outward Bound School at Table Rock, there was precious little activity.

To open the school, the English climber John Lawrence moved to North Carolina in the summer of 1967. It was a fortuitous move for local climbers. In his youth, Lawrence's parents often vacationed in the English Lake District and Lawrence also spent several years in the Royal Marines special forces. Later,

Overview of Table Rock as seen from the Mountains-to-Sea Trail

Lawrence went on to serve as an Outward Bound instructor in Australia for several years before he came to North Carolina. He remembered that—not counting some tentative forays by locals—there wasn't much happening in terms of rock climbing when he arrived.

"The (only) people there before us were Green Berets," Lawrence said. "Everywhere we went, we found evidence of them. At the Chimneys, we'd get up cracks where you would never think and we'd find pins." That very year, Lawrence added his first route to the wall: *Cracker Jack*. Previously credited to other parties, Lawrence has said in interview transcripts that he feels confident his ascent of this imposing slot with Dave Mashburn in 1967 was the first. "One's never sure of these things," Lawrence said. "But the story I heard was Brad Shaver and Mickey Craig climbed it in March 1971 and they named it *Cracker Jack* because they found an old bunch of gear in it and they cleaned it out, so it was like a Cracker Jack box."

Many climbers point to the ascent of *Second Stanza* by Lawrence and Chuck Sproull in 1968 as the wall's other important early ascent. In following a series of corners, cracks, and chimneys, the climbers knocked off a striking natural line. The route did not go free until two years later when Bob Gillespie and partners knocked it off in November 1970 at 5.8. (Lawrence has said that he aided the roof crux because it was "dirty as hell.")

Another early activist at Table Rock was Karl Rohnke. A tall, athletic javelin thrower whose nickname was "Skip" (as in *Skip to My Lou*), Rohnke was reportedly quite strong and his exploits included the first free ascent of nearby Sitting Bear. Most climbers now believe that he bolted most of the early routes at Table Rock—not the U.S. Army. Longtime climber Steve Longenecker has spoken about old photos of Rohnke "bolting up *My Route* and some things on Table Rock."

Over the next three decades, climbing standards advanced slowly at Table Rock. A few notable ascents occurred around 1976 when Bob Rotert and Diff Ritchie sent

Fresh Garbage and Brad Shaver and Ritchie also nabbed the difficult *Mourning Maiden*. Both routes were among the area's first 5.10s. Table Rock has always had an undeserved reputation as a "teaching" cliff unworthy of serious efforts by the state's best climbers. But it's more likely that Table Rock lagged behind the standards of most other areas because hard natural lines are just not abundant. Although many of the early classics were bolted, climbers of the 1980s generally avoided those tactics in part because Table Rock is such a landmark for the climbing community as a whole. So, save one or two routes, we could almost write off the entire decade in terms of first-ascent activity. Most of the action in Linville Gorge took place elsewhere—notably on Hawksbill and Shortoff Mountains.

Instead, some of the most interesting climbing on Table Rock during this time actually took place at the private boulders of Outward Bound's base camp. Over the course of twenty years and into the early 1990s, around 100 problems went up. Luminaries such as John Sherman even visited to poke around on problems like *Short Jam*. The Outward Bound area is closed to the general public, but if you're in a class you might consider asking a guide for the tour.

In 1992, past Outward Bound program director and local climber Mike Fischesser established a couple of face climbs at Table Rock immediately left of *The Cave Route*. The *Ellie Raynolds Memorial Buttress* and *Just Say Moo* share anchors and have provided many climbers with enjoyable leads. Fischesser's work likely inspired a few other locals to reevaluate Table Rock and suddenly some new lines started going up. Among the most significant are Gary Butler and Brady Robinson's steep 1996 effort *Helios* and the two *Aphid* climbs near *Peek-A-Boo*. Fischesser also proved there are some fun moderates left to bag when he and Zachary Lesch-Huie unearthed the four-pitch *Hidden Crack* in 1999.

Weather and Climbing Season

Table Rock (elevation 3,900 feet) faces generally east except for the North End, which still sees sun part of the day. Afternoons at Table Rock are generally shady and cool. Beware spring and summer thunderstorms, especially lightening.

Getting There

Follow the driving directions to Table Rock Road and FR 210 given in the Linville Gorge introduction. Continue on FR 210 approximately 8.5 miles to the Table Rock Picnic Area.

Approach

The approach for all areas on Table Rock is very easy. Follow the white-blazed Mountains-to-Sea Trail north out of the picnic area parking lot toward Table Rock. At 0.25 mile, look for a knee-high, railroad-tie barrier on the right. Follow this trail along the base. In about 50 yards, you'll come to a small trail on the left that leads up to the South End of Table Rock. Continue right along the base for East Face and North End routes.

Routes are numbered 1 through 30 and are left to right around Table Rock, starting on the South End and ending on the North End.

South End

This is technically the left end of the east face, which is visible from the parking lot. The far-left (south) side of this area is vegetated.

Descent: Walk off.

1. Cracker Jack   5.8

Suitors can get a good look at this intimidating crack and chimney system from the Table Rock Picnic Area. Binoculars only make the anticipation worse.

First ascent: John Lawrence, Dave Mashburn (1967).

Start: Locate an obvious dihedral where the approach trail meets the base.

Pitch 1: Follow to a left-facing corner system capped by a vegetated roof. Climb right and around the roof until you can continue up a big boulder in the base of a wide crack. (5.7; 130 feet).

Pitch 2: Follow the obvious wide crack up to the chimney, and then grunt your way to the summit rim. (5.8; 75 feet).

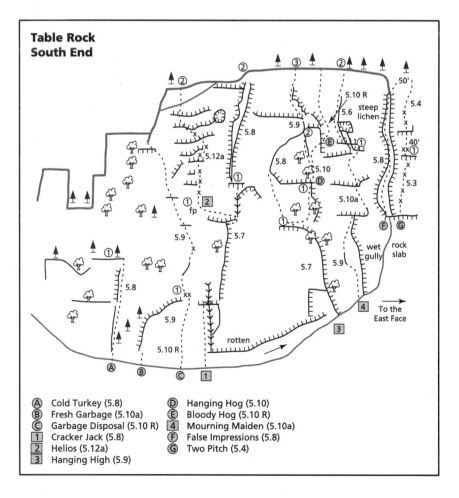

**Table Rock
South End**

Ⓐ Cold Turkey (5.8)
Ⓑ Fresh Garbage (5.10a)
Ⓒ Garbage Disposal (5.10 R)
[1] Cracker Jack (5.8)
[2] Helios (5.12a)
[3] Hanging High (5.9)
Ⓓ Hanging Hog (5.10)
Ⓔ Bloody Hog (5.10 R)
[4] Mourning Maiden (5.10a)
Ⓕ False Impressions (5.8)
Ⓖ Two Pitch (5.4)

2. Helios · 5.12a

This towering feature should have been climbed long ago! As it is, the line offers some well-protected steep climbing.

First ascent: Brady Robinson, Gary Butler (1996).

Start: In the *Cracker Jack* corner.

Pitch 1: Climb the first part of *Cracker Jack* past the licheny roof and then traverse back left to a hole with a fixed pin. Natural belay. (5.7; 120 feet).

Pitch 2: Climb up through a series of roofs on the increasingly difficult face past six bolts. Medium gear protects the upper section. (5.12a, 70 feet).

Note: You can do this as a one-pitch direct by climbing straight through the lichen roof of *Cracker Jack* (5.11), but beware of rope drag.

3. Hanging High 5.9

An excellent, steep line up the South End of Table Rock. On the original line, a long traverse avoids the gigantic roof. The *Hanging Hog* variation (see topo) is vegetated but tackles a decent crack.

First ascent: Guy Jacobson, Percy Wimberly. The first free ascent went to Brad Shaver and Mickey Craig in 1974. Jim Okel and Tom Howard did the steep *Hanging Hog* variation in 1982.

Start: Locate the right-angled corner about 100 feet right of *Cracker Jack* and past a huge, rotten roof.

Pitch 1: Climb the right most (easier) of two left-facing dihedrals. Exit this and traverse left for the belay. (5.7; 100 feet).

Pitch 2: Climb around the left end of the big roof, then up and right to a hanging belay at a laurel bush. (5.8; 60 feet).

Pitch 3: Jam, stem, and huff your way up the overhanging crack until you can exit right onto the easy face. Follow it to the summit. (5.9; 75 feet).

4. Mourning Maiden 5.10a

One of the early 5.10s at Table Rock, this route remains a demanding line that can burn unwary parties.

First ascent: Brad Shaver, Diff Ritchie (1976).

Start: 15 feet right of *Hanging High* at the left-facing dihedral.

Pitch 1: Climb a casual face to a left-facing dihedral. Continue to an overhang with a sharp lip. Pull it to gain the delicate face above and a second overhang. Once you pull this and are situated under a third overhang, trend right and into a chimney for the belay. (5.10a; 130 feet).

Pitch 2: Follow the chimney to a ledge with some loose blocks. Continue up the face to the summit. (5.6; 70 feet).

East Face

The main wall (East Face) at Table Rock is an obvious landmark for miles around. Many tree ledges, rhododendrons, and moss hummocks interrupt the wall, but in between there is plenty of excellent and exposed climbing. Sun in the morning; cool and shady in the afternoon.

Descent: Rappel the routes unless otherwise noted.

5. Talking about Mudflaps, My Baby's Got 'Em   5.11 (no topo)

An obscure but challenging route. With more traffic this could brighten up nicely.

First ascent: Jeff Burton, Lyle Dean (1990).

Start: Follow the trail past the South End to a steep, mossy wall. *Mudflaps* starts right of the wet corner system and off a high ledge.

Pitch 1: Stem and lieback up the sharp corner with a low pin. Trend left under the roof, passing another pin, to gain a vertical white face with good holds and a high bolt. Follow through a bulge to a natural belay. (5.11; 75 feet).

Pitch 2: Climb the right side of a flaky pillar until you can step right to a short corner. Crank up the steep face through a weakness to the summit. (5.10; 75 feet).

Descent: Rappel from trees.

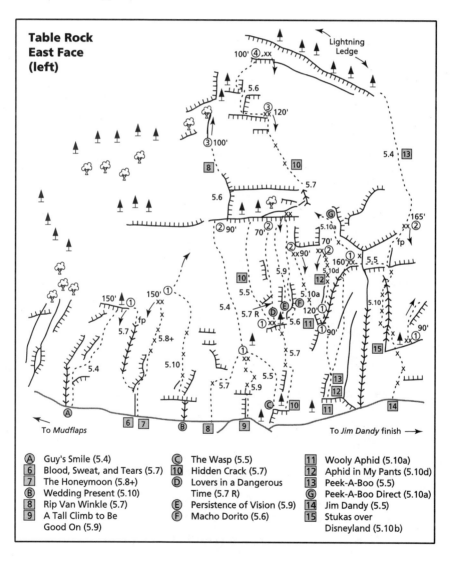

Table Rock East Face (left)

Ⓐ Guy's Smile (5.4)	Ⓒ The Wasp (5.5)	11 Wooly Aphid (5.10a)
6 Blood, Sweat, and Tears (5.7)	10 Hidden Crack (5.7)	12 Aphid in My Pants (5.10d)
7 The Honeymoon (5.8+)	Ⓓ Lovers in a Dangerous	13 Peek-A-Boo (5.5)
Ⓑ Wedding Present (5.10)	Time (5.7 R)	Ⓖ Peek-A-Boo Direct (5.10a)
8 Rip Van Winkle (5.7)	Ⓔ Persistence of Vision (5.9)	14 Jim Dandy (5.5)
9 A Tall Climb to Be Good On (5.9)	Ⓕ Macho Dorito (5.6)	15 Stukas over Disneyland (5.10b)

6. Blood, Sweat, and Tears 5.7

This is an old classic that never seems to lose its luster. Clean and very fun face climbing.

First ascent: Jim Dailey (1973).

Start: On the right side of a bulge about 100 feet right of a huge alcove and tree ledges. Begin about 10 feet above the trail and off a rhododendron ledge.

Pitch 1: Either face climb up the seam (hard and unprotected) or start in the obvious cracks on the right. Trend left to a clean face, eventually passing a fixed pin to gain a tree ledge. (150 feet).

Descent: Rap from slings on a pine.

7. The Honeymoon 5.8+

This is one of the newer routes at Table Rock with some good face climbing.

First ascent: Jim Toman, Zachary Lesch-Huie, Mike Fischesser (1999).

Start: Same as *Blood, Sweat, and Tears*.

Pitch 1: Climb the first part of *BST*, but continue straight up the right-facing flake aiming for bolts. Climb past four bolts and some gear to a bolted belay. (150 feet).

8. Rip Van Winkle 5.7

A "sleeper" hard section down low leads to some fun, easy climbing.

First ascent: Paul Cobb, Tom McMillan (1972).

Start: Below orange-looking overhangs and 75 feet right of *Honeymoon*. Start at the base of a shallow dihedral with a large block on the right.

Pitch 1: Climb the shallow corner to an old bolt where you can begin making a rising traverse to the right around a slight ridge. The wall steepens briefly before you can climb a crack to a large block. Belay at new bolts. (5.7; 100 feet).

Pitch 2: Climb the corner and gain a casual face split with crack systems that leads to a huge tree ledge for a belay. (5.4; 90 feet).

Pitch 3: Walk to the right side of a ledge and locate a large left-facing corner. Climb this past 2 vertical steps, then into a wide crack for the belay. (5.6; 100 feet).

Pitch 4: Trend up and right through lower-angled rock onto a bushy ledge that gains Lightning Ledge. (5.6; 80 feet).

Descent: Walk off from Lightning Ledge.

9. A Tall Climb to Be Good On 5.9

Somehow ignored in the past, this is a newer route offering a nice mix of crack and face climbing.

First ascent: Ron Dawson, Mark Bishop (1993).

Start: 20 feet right of *Rip Van Winkle* atop an apron.

Pitch 1: Climb a short dihedral to a small roof with a bolt. Continue up the face past two more bolts and a bulge. Double-bolt anchor. (70 feet).

10. Hidden Crack 5.7

Proof that not all the classic moderates have been climbed! A lot of bushy stuff and tree ledges up higher, but this is a great route nonetheless.

First ascent: Mike Fischesser, Zachary Lesch-Huie (1999).

Start: Right of *A Tall Climb to Be Good On*, third-class up a corner system to gain a tree ledge.

Pitch 1: Move up and right from the ledge through low-angled rock to a blocky corner. Follow it until you can gain the right side of a buttress and clip a bolt. Follow clean rock, trending slightly left past two bolts. The belay is just left of a small tree. (5.7; 100 feet).

Pitch 2: Stroll up the cleanest section of an easy slab to gain the gigantic tree ledge. Double-bolt belay. (5.5; 70 feet).

Pitch 3: Climb straight off the belay through small ledges, passing a small tree and aiming for a bolt on the left side of an arête. Traverse right, then move up on big holds, angling left past two bolts on a great face. It is a little tricky to gain the sloping belay ledge. (5.7; 120 feet).

Pitch 4: Traverse 25 feet left until you pass a left-facing flake and overhang. Climb this angling right to a small ledge. Here, reach around left for a good TCU placement, and then romp up to Lightning Ledge for a belay. (5.6; 100 feet).

Descent: Walk off.

11. Wooly Aphid   5.10a

A companion face climb to its harder neighbor to the right.

First ascent: Mike Fischesser, Zachary Lesch-Huie (1999).

Start: 150 feet right of *Hidden Crack* and in the *Peek-A-Boo* corner. You'll have to follow the main trail up to a good ledge under a huge, wide gully capped by a roof at 150 feet. Many people climb partway up the gully to clip an old bolt. For full value, start lower at the right-facing flake.

Pitch 1: Climb the right-facing flake past low-angled rock until you can step left to gain a ledge with a vertical crack. Belay here with medium cams. (5.4; 90 feet).

Pitch 2: Climb the crack to a bulgy face. Gain two bolts and stroll to a double bolt anchor. (5.10a; 90 feet).

12. Aphid in My Pants   5.10d

Technical face climbing that demands precise footwork and crimp strength.

First ascent: Mike Fischesser, Zachary Lesch-Huie (1999).

Start: Same as *Wooly Aphid.*

Pitch 1: Climb the right-facing flake past low angled rock to a tiny ledge within the corner, slightly above the *Wooly Aphid* ledge. (5.4; 120 feet).

Pitch 2: Continue up the thin crack (TCUs) to gain a face. High step and slap past five bolts to a double-bolt belay. (5.10d; 70 feet).

13. Peek-A-Boo   5.5

It is hard to seriously recommend one-move wonders, but here is one worth all 300 feet of climbing!

First ascent: Bob Mitchell, Bob Gillespie (1970).

Start: Same as *Wooly Aphid.*

Pitch 1: Follow the low-angled face and occasional vertical cracks on the left side of the apron until you can traverse right to a double-bolt belay. (5.4; 160 feet).

Pitch 2: Here's your move: Clip a bolt and then step across the void to gain the right wall. Continue right along the line of least resistance to a corner. Then move up to a belay ledge with double bolts. (5.5; 80 feet). You can rappel from a double-bolt anchor to the top of the first pitch of *Jim Dandy*. Then make a second rappel to the ground. Or . . .

Pitch 3: Low-angled rock leads to Lightning Ledge. (5.4; 80 feet).

Descent: Walk off from Lightning Ledge.

14. Jim Dandy   5.5

The earliest climbers at Table Rock were into naming routes after themselves. But at least this one is fitting!

First ascent: Karl Rohnke, Jim Merritt (1968).

Start: Begin about 20 feet right of the *Peek-A-Boo* gully.

Pitch 1: Climb the casual face up and over the bulge and past three bolts up to a tree ledge. Double-bolt anchor right of the pine tree. (5.4; 90 feet).

Pitch 2: At the right end of the ledge, climb a short vertical section to gain a ramp. Follow this up and right for about 50 feet until you hit a corner. Climb another 50 feet to a bolted belay. (5.4; 130 feet).

Pitch 3: Climb the slabs past bolts to gain Lunch Ledge. Belay in the trees. (5.3; 75 feet).

Descent: Either rappel from here or continue to the summit via *Cave Route*.

15. Stukas over Disneyland   5.10b

Many climbers had eyed this arête for years. The first-ascent team didn't add it easily, either. Gary Butler's hook popped and sent him for a 20-footer while drilling a bolt.

First ascent: Ron Dawson, Gary Butler (1996).

Start: On *Jim Dandy*.

Pitch 1: Climb *Jim Dandy* to the tree ledge belay. (5.5; 90 feet).

Pitch 2: Climb up the right side of the overhanging arête to gain a bolt, move out to the left side of the arête passing three more bolts. A final bolt allows you to gain *Peek-A-Boo* just after the step-across move. (5.10a; 165 feet).

Descent: Rap from the fixed belay to the first pitch of *Jim Dandy*.

16. Skip to My Lou   5.6

For the most part, this is casual face climbing with a couple of challenging cruxes. Bring a light rack.

First ascent: Karl Rohnke.

Start: About 25 feet right of *Jim Dandy*. Either scramble up to the first ledge of *Jim Dandy* or climb through a break in a low roof section.

Pitch 1: Follow bolts until you are even with a big tree on the left. Traverse right onto the vertical wall with a small, arching undercling crack. Climb this up and right to a bowl with double bolts. (5.6; 165 feet).

Pitch 2: Climb past a bolt and make a rising traverse up and right to Lunch Ledge. (5.6; 90 feet).

Pitch 3 and Descent: Either finish on *Cave Route, My Route,* or walk off to the right and downclimb a vegetated third-class gully.

17. Slippin' into Darkness (aka Helmet Variation)   5.9

Helmet Buttress (which is left of this route) was one of the early climbs at Table Rock. This line has been called *Helmet Variation* (see the topo for yet another *Helmet Variation*), but most Outward Bound folks call it *Slippin' into Darkness. Slippin'* offers some excellent crack climbing and great pro.

First ascent: Mickey Craig, Tom Howard, Jim Dailey (1973). Howard also free climbed both variations in the late 1970s.

Start: On the right side of the Helmet Buttress, under the obvious right-facing corner.

Pitch 1: Climb the right-facing corner to a small tree ledge. Continue up the clean hand and finger crack to a double-bolt anchor. (75 feet). *Note:* It is possible to do another 5.6 face pitch to a double-bolt anchor.

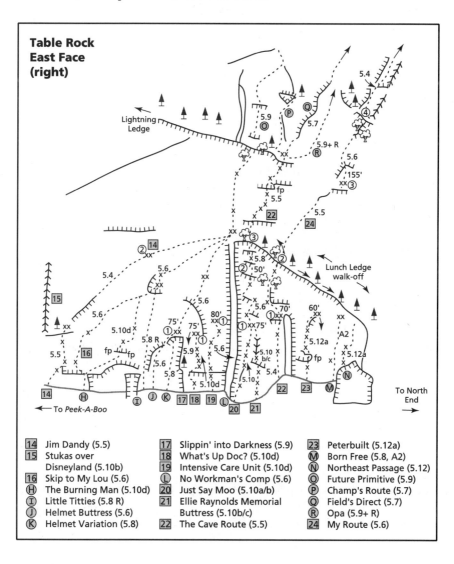

Table Rock East Face (right)

14 Jim Dandy (5.5)	17 Slippin' into Darkness (5.9)	23 Peterbuilt (5.12a)
15 Stukas over	18 What's Up Doc? (5.10d)	Ⓜ Born Free (5.8, A2)
Disneyland (5.10b)	19 Intensive Care Unit (5.10d)	Ⓝ Northeast Passage (5.12)
16 Skip to My Lou (5.6)	Ⓛ No Workman's Comp (5.6)	Ⓞ Future Primitive (5.9)
Ⓗ The Burning Man (5.10d)	20 Just Say Moo (5.10a/b)	Ⓟ Champ's Route (5.7)
Ⓘ Little Titties (5.8 R)	21 Ellie Raynolds Memorial	Ⓠ Field's Direct (5.7)
Ⓙ Helmet Buttress (5.6)	Buttress (5.10b/c)	Ⓡ Opa (5.9+ R)
Ⓚ Helmet Variation (5.8)	22 The Cave Route (5.5)	24 My Route (5.6)

18. What's Up Doc? 5.10d

This is not an extremely popular route, but it's definitely worth the effort if you're into technical faces.

First ascent: Doc Klein, Ron Dawson, Jeep Barrett.

Start: 20 feet right of *Helmet Buttress.*

Pitch 1: Climb up to the first bolt and make precarious moves on polished quartzite to gain a ledge. Step right a little and trend up and left past four more bolts to double-bolt anchor. (75 feet).

19. Intensive Care Unit 5.10d

Initially a variation of *What's Up Doc,* this route is now an independent line. We might call it "Psych Ward" instead, since it's not the most appealing line.

First ascent: Ron Dawson, Mark Bishop (1996). Kris Kline later added the direct start.

Start: 10 feet right of *What's Up Doc.*

Pitch 1: Climb up the awkward and devious face to the right side of the *Doc* ledge. Wander up and right past bolts and plenty of lichen to anchors. Five bolts total. (80 feet).

20. Just Say Moo 5.10a/b

Basically a wandering start to *Ellie Raynolds Memorial Buttress, Moo* offers nice variety and a good pump.

First ascent: Mike Fischesser, Pete Luellen (1992).

Start: 100 feet right of *Intensive Care Unit,* at a slab and left of the prow.

Pitch 1: Climb over a low, easy roof to gain a bolt and work up and right via the weird crack. Pull another, harder, roof past two bolts and clip a final bolt before gaining the anchors atop *Ellie.* (75 feet).

21. Ellie Raynolds Memorial Buttress 5.10b/c

This is actually a three-pitch climb, although some just do the first pitch, which is reachy and sequential. The climbing higher is exposed and certainly as good as *The Cave Route.*

First ascent: Mike Fischesser, Pete Luellen (1992).

Start: 10 feet right of *Just Say Moo.*

Pitch 1: Wander up the slab past three spinning bolts. Negotiate the small roof with a bolt and climb past a final bolt before the anchor. (5.10b/c; 75 feet). Rappel or . . .

Pitch 2: Thread your way past a roof and across some ledges past three bolts. (5.6; 50 feet).

Pitch 3: Surmount an overlap past one bolt to gain the top of the buttress. (5.8; 75 feet).

Descent: Walk off third class via Lunch Ledge.

22. The Cave Route 5.5

This route is well protected and exposed. Most parties climb to Lunch Ledge and third-class down from there. Alternately, continue to the summit via the normal finish or via any of several routes that lead from the ledge.

First ascent: Unclear, possibly early Outward Bound instructors or U.S. Army.

Start: 50 feet right of *Ellie Raynolds Memorial Buttress*, just left of the huge, left-angling cave.

Pitch 1: Wander up the bolted face to gain a double-bolt belay at a good stance. (5.4; 70 feet).

Pitch 2: Move out left around the corner, and then up a short ramp. Climb right up a crack until it ends and move right into the trees. Beware rope drag. (5.5; 50 feet).

Pitch 3: Climb off the tree ledge via a bolted face to a roof. Continue up to an anchor on Lightning Ledge. (5.5; 60 feet).

Descent: Walk off from Lightning Ledge.

23. Peterbuilt   5.12a

This is a funky, steep, one-pitch route included more for historical purposes than for quality.

First ascent: Peter Noebels, Jim Walker.

Start: 20 feet right of *The Cave Route* gully under a pin.

Pitch 1: Ape your way up to a pin. Then make hard, slopey moves past the bolts to gain a double-bolt belay. (60 feet).

24. My Route   5.6

From Lunch Ledge, this route climbs a dramatic and mostly clean face to the summit of Table Rock.

First ascent: Karl Rohnke and R.D. McLean (1968).

Start: In the middle of Lunch Ledge, usually gained by climbing *The Cave Route*.

Pitches 1 and 2: Same as *The Cave Route*.

Pitch 3: Climb the nicely featured and exposed face following bolts past scoops, dikes, and jugs to gain a bolted belay in a notch. (5.5; 155 feet).

Pitch 4: Exit the notch out left and move left a little before taking the line of least resistance up to another bushy ledge. Natural belay. (5.6; 50 feet).

Pitch 5: Climb the right-angling ramp system past bolts to the summit. Exposed and enjoyable! (5.4; 40 feet).

Descent: Walk off.

North End

Far less crowded than the zoo-like East Face, this area has some excellent routes. Higher wind usually means the wall stays cooler in summer despite morning sun.

Descent: Rappel the routes unless otherwise noted.

25. Second Stanza   5.8+

The best route on this part of the wall, *Second Stanza* has a ton of variety and challenging moves.

First ascent: John Lawrence, Chuck Sproull (1968). Bob Mitchell, Steve Longenecker, and Roy Davis returned to nab the first free ascent in 1970.

Start: 200 feet right of *The Cave Route*. Hike around a corner and up a gully to a ledge.

Jennifer Jenson exits the pitch-2 roof of Second Stanza *(route 25).*

Pitch 1: Climb a left-facing flake to gain a ledge beneath a broken crack. (5.6; 50 feet).

Pitch 2: Continue up the wide, serrated corner. Awkward and exposed; bring some larger pieces. Belay at a stance midway up the next corner. (5.7; 70 feet).

Pitch 3: Climb out left and pull the roof at a steep notch. Continue up and right via a left-leaning crack until you gain the upper tree ledge on *My Route*. (5.8+; 60 feet).

Pitch 4: Finish via the last pitch of *My Route*. (5.4; 40 feet).

26. On Misty Edge   5.11c

An ego-bruising affair. The two Peters were masters at discovering bold lines others had overlooked.

First ascent: Peter Young, Peter Noebels (1985).

Start: 15 feet right of *Second Stanza* under shallow vertical cracks.

Pitch 1: Follow the cracks straight up to the first ledge on *Second Stanza*. (5.9; 50 feet).

Pitch 2: Step out right and climb past a low overlap to gain a difficult seam. Gun for the top past one fixed pin and some steep jugs! (5.11c: 75 feet).

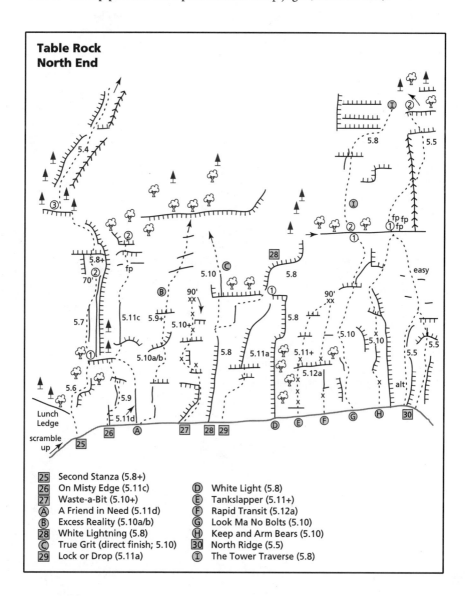

Table Rock North End

25	Second Stanza (5.8+)	
26	On Misty Edge (5.11c)	Ⓓ White Light (5.8)
27	Waste-a-Bit (5.10+)	Ⓔ Tankslapper (5.11+)
Ⓐ	A Friend in Need (5.11d)	Ⓕ Rapid Transit (5.12a)
Ⓑ	Excess Reality (5.10a/b)	Ⓖ Look Ma No Bolts (5.10)
28	White Lightning (5.8)	Ⓗ Keep and Arm Bears (5.10)
Ⓒ	True Grit (direct finish; 5.10)	30 North Ridge (5.5)
29	Lock or Drop (5.11a)	Ⓘ The Tower Traverse (5.8)

27. Waste-a-Bit   5.10+

... of time? Not on this new classic, which is already quite popular. Bring a light rack including a 4-inch piece.

First ascent: Ryan Beasley, Curt Koontz, John Meyers (2001).

Start: 25 feet right of *On Misty Edge.*

Pitch 1: Climb a right-facing flake with some wide gear to a stance. Teeter past four bolts with some hard clips and a few pieces of gear to a double-bolt anchor. (90 feet).

28. White Lightning   5.8

This is the first pitch of *True Grit Direct* followed by the second pitch of *White Light.* The combo is really the only way to approach these features since the original lines are now gardens. This may be the best 5.8 at Table Rock.

Start: 50 feet right of *On Misty Edge* in an obvious dihedral.

First ascent: Peter Young and John Lawrence climbed the obvious but vegetated *White Light* in 1971. A year later, Peter Prandoni and Young returned to do *True Grit* all the way through the roof cracks and up to the vegetated bush line and summit.

Pitch 1: Climb the clean, white corner to its top. Move a little right to gain the roof, where you will traverse about 20 feet right to an obvious ledge. (5.8; 90 feet).

Pitch 2: Climb up through the right-facing corner via excellent jams. Turn a lip to gain an open book corner, and then move up and eventually straight right across moss hummocks for a natural belay. (5.8; 70 feet).

Pitch 3 or Descent: A couple of lines continue to the top, or rappel from fixed pins on *North Ridge.*

29. Lock or Drop   5.11a

Classic go-for-broke crack climbing.

First ascent: Thomas Kelley, Kris Kline.

Start: Same as *White Lightning.*

Pitch 1: Climb the first few moves of *White Lightning* until it is possible to step right onto the face. Be careful with your pro at the small overlaps. Launch up into a pumpy crack system that finally backs off at the very end. Find a natural belay with medium and large pieces just beneath the *White Lightning* corner. (5.11a; 80 feet).

Pitch 2 and Descent: Finish on *White Lightning.*

30. North Ridge   5.5

This route—which is actually the northeast ridge—is *the* vantage point on Table Rock as well as being steep and strenuous for the grade.

First ascent: Bob Gillespie, Bob Mitchell (1970).

Start: Follow the cliffside trail up to an obvious flat spot beneath the ridge.

Pitch 1: Follow the corner until you can step out right through an overhang. Continue up great holds until the wall slabs off. Trend left to gain a three-pin belay. (5.5; 130 feet).

Opposite: *Burton Moomaw on the classic pitch-2 dihedral of* White Lightning *(route 28)*

Pitch 2: Step up and right via a deceptively difficult crack, eventually reaching a crack under a roof. Move right around the roof, then back up and left to gain the gravely ledge. Go up the small trail, climb onto a big rock ledge and belay. (5.5; 70 feet).

Pitch 3: Climb a long, easy pitch to the summit. (5.5; 70 feet).

Descent: Walk off.

North Carolina Wall

Climbing type: Multipitch traditional
Rock type: Metamorphic (metasandstone and quartzite)
Height: 70 to 500 feet
Number of routes: Approximately 90 (29 this guide)
Climbing season: April through November
Camping: See Linville Gorge introduction

Wilderness is relative here on the East Coast. But even though Linville Gorge is one of the state's most popular areas, climbing at the North Carolina Wall or The Amphitheater is about as close to true wilderness climbing as it gets east of the Rockies. North to south, you'll encounter The Chimneys (not in this guide), Chockstone Chimney Wall, Apricot Buttress, the main North Carolina Wall, and finally The Amphitheater.

The routes aren't especially long, but many factors combine to make this area of Linville Gorge an excellent entrée to the demands of multipitch adventure climbing. The main North Carolina Wall in particular has languished in obscurity for many years. At first blush, it is hard to understand why. After all, it is a stunning, 500-foot wall in a pristine setting. But considering the combination of seasonal closures, a

The main North Carolina Wall as seen from the Apricot Buttress

Shortoff Mountain 7 miles away

Main North Carolina Wall

Gold Coast Cliffs

Mossy Monster Buttress approach gully

Mashburn's Pinnacle (not in guide)

To Apricot Buttress

difficult approach, and vast sections of blank rock, perhaps it is not such a mystery after all. So: Is the juice worth the squeeze? You be the judge.

History

By 1970, climbing was already well established in the Piedmont and at Table Rock, where Green Berets and Outward Bound instructors had climbed some of the more obvious routes. But locals such as John Lawrence—an Outward Bound guide—knew there was much more opportunity below the gorge rim. In transcripts of interviews made by longtime local Mike Fischesser in the early 1980s, Lawrence recalled that he remembers the area being almost deserted.

"[We never climbed there because] we were always a little bit frightened that something would happen," said Lawrence, who spent a goodly portion of one summer hacking a trail down into The Amphitheater anyway.

Instead, it was up to 19-year-old Western Carolina student Bob Mitchell, Looking Glass Rock pioneer Steve Longenecker, and Bob Gillespie to make the first ascent of arguably the area's most famous route. Mitchell had been in during the winter and noticed a line at The Amphitheater capped by a headstone that reminded him of an Egyptian sarcophagus. So, on a hot day in early spring 1970, the trio returned gunning for it. Despite Lawrence's work, there was no sign of a trail.

"I don't know how [Mitchell] ever found it," Gillespie said in the same Fischesser interview transcripts. "You just walked to the rim and he said, 'Here's the place where you enter the bushes.' You kept going down and pretty soon you got to the rocks."

After a short entry pitch, Longenecker remembers that it was Gillespie who led a crux hand crack. Instead of aid climbing, however, the trio found surprisingly easy climbing and a few hours later Longenecker was the first to the summit.

"I'm belaying and here comes [Mitchell] who didn't have a shirt on," Longenecker said. "I didn't realize until he came to the top that he had nothing on except his shoes. First ascent and first nude ascent."

The Mummy—named for that "headstone" cap rock—remains one of the best beginner's leads in North Carolina. Mostly 5.3 with a touch of 5.5, the three-pitch route probably sees 75 percent of today's traffic in The Amphitheater. About a year later, Greenville, South Carolina, climber Art Williams trekked down into the area to swipe the other classic: *The Daddy* (5.6). Longer and a touch harder, a toss-up it's over who got the better line!

Despite its formidable reputation, the North Carolina Wall also first saw development in April 1970 when Mitchell and Gillespie teamed up for *Bumblebee Buttress*. When Mitchell and Gillespie saw this wall from across the gorge, the first line they picked out was the obvious corner to the right of *Bumblebee Buttress*. But they ended up choosing *Bumblebee* simply because it looked more interesting upon closer inspection. They were right. Their line ended up being the choice route on the wall, a long, steep corner system with a wild headwall near the summit. "We used to pick stuff that was, for us, pretty iffy," Gillespie said.

The duo climbed the route wearing old leather shoes and homemade knickers. One section—a wide, left-facing corner about 130 feet up the face—nearly repelled the team and forced Mitchell to turn over the lead for one of the few times in his life.

Ron Dawson leads off on the pitch-3 arête of The Mummy *(route 27).*

And although they brought chocks along with them, Mitchell used tiny pins nestled in the face for protection on the last headwall pitch. Near the summit, they spied some mountain laurel filled with bees, including a bumblebee, and hence the name.

Over the next ten years, climbers continued to wander into both areas and ended up bagging the occasional gem. In 1973, Bob Rotert and Tom McMillan hiked over to the outcropping left of the Mossy Monster Buttress and unearthed *Apricot Jam* on what is now known as Apricot Buttress. The same pair also collaborated again six years later on the intimidating *Captain Hook's Nameless Nightmare.* On the first ascent, McMillan prerigged his harness with a hook so he could let go to rest on the final steep pitch. He climbed until he pumped out and then hung on a hook until he excavated a bomber hex placement for solid protection. This was one of the first times this style was used on such an outrageous route in North Carolina.

Still, considering the main North Carolina Wall's size—almost 0.5 mile wide and 500 feet tall—and steepness, perhaps no other cliff in North Carolina has since yielded so little in the way of climbable rock. In the subsequent two decades, only a few new lines have gone up, and many parties have gone in with big plans only to be thwarted by steep, blank rock. For instance, on the first ascent of the *Pixie Wall* (5.11+), Doug Reed and Chip Self hiked in intending to do a line through the huge roof to the left. However, when that face proved more formidable than planned, they started up the face via an alternate line and finished in a few hours. "A real nonstory but a nice route," Reed said. Maybe so, but at the time of its ascent, this route was the hardest in Linville Gorge.

In 1987, Kris Kline, a land surveyor from Asheville, and North Carolina guidebook author Thomas Kelley also straightened out *Rinky Dink* and gave it a much better direct finish than the original, wandering, free line. The same pair also added some of the overlooked classics in The Amphitheater. In the years since, route development has occurred sporadically. Of particular note are the efforts of Winston-Salem climber Nathan Brown, who has unearthed some long-overlooked areas and climbed some fantastic features in impeccable style. Though small, the Chockstone Chimney Wall (developed by Brown and partners) is a gorgeous, steep, and north-facing wall. Similarly, Brown's routes on the main North Carolina Wall tackle spectacular sections of rock that must have initially called out to gorge pioneers who left them untouched for future generations.

Kelley still thinks the main North Carolina Wall holds immense promise for a committed, talented free climber. "There's no reason to think that climbing techniques and skill levels haven't risen enough to take on walls like [this] from the ground up," he said. And, in truth, all it takes is a visit or two to learn of the potential.

Weather and Climbing Season

Although the west-facing North Carolina Wall (elevation 3,200 feet) can serve as a solar collector in warm weather, it can also be cold and quite bitter in the winter. The approach gully is often more windy and cooler than the wall itself. Like the rest of the gorge, North Carolina Wall sees a fair amount of spring and summer thundershowers. The routes get afternoon sun.

While somewhat cooler, The Amphitheater is also best climbed from spring through fall purely because of the wilderness area closures (see the Linville Gorge introduction). Routes such as *The Open Book* and *Turkey Beard* get afternoon sun. All the routes near *Land of the Little People* stay pleasantly cool and shady.

Gear

Bring a standard North Carolina free climbing rack. *Important:* By mid-2001, some of the routes on the North Carolina Wall had dubious anchors and bad bolts. Be extremely careful of all fixed gear in this area of Linville Gorge since much of it is aging and suspect.

Getting There

Follow the driving directions to the Table Rock Road and FR 210 given in the Linville Gorge introduction. Continue on FR 210 approximately 8.5 miles to the Table Rock Picnic Area.

Hiking into this area is probably the trickiest approach in this guide because of the combination of dense vegetation and unmarked trails. A forest fire in 2000 obscured the already faint trails and made access even more difficult. None of the climbing areas in this section are suitable for small children or dogs. Please read the approaches carefully and give yourself ample time to explore on your first visit.

Approach

Hike south out of the Table Rock Picnic Area parking lot past the pit toilets and the picnic ground. The very large, well-maintained trail you are following is the Mountains-to-Sea Trail (MST). After a short hike (about 0.5 mile or 15 minutes), you will pass the popular top-roping area known as The Chimneys. Stay on the trail as it follows the ridge and continue through rhododendron tunnels until you reach the end of The Chimneys at 0.8 mile. From here, follow the approach directions below for your selected area.

For Chockstone Chimney Wall and Apricot Buttress: Continue beyond The Chimneys a short distance (about 100 feet) and take the first unmarked trail on the right. (During raptor season, the Forest Service often posts closure notices here.) You're on the correct trail if you pass a slab of exposed rock about 30 feet from the turnoff from the MST. Follow this trail for 0.1 mile to the gorge rim. (It is possible to scramble atop the Apricot Buttress here for a good overview of the North Carolina Wall.)

For the Chockstone Chimney Wall, take a steep, wet, north-facing gully from the gorge rim (the southwest-facing gully opposite leads to Apricot Buttress). At the bottom of the gully and when facing Table Rock, turn right for the Chockstone Chimney Wall. (Continue left for a formation called The Camel. This pillar has one obscure 5.9 route on its north face.)

For the Apricot Buttress, from the gorge rim carefully maneuver into a steep, southwest-facing gully between the buttress and the main North Carolina Wall. Prepare for a tricky class 3 or class 4 descent. At the bottom of the gully, *Apricot Jam* begins immediately to your right.

For the main North Carolina Wall: Continue beyond The Chimneys another 0.2 mile on the MST to the second unmarked trail on the right, at a tree with two trunks and a white blaze. (During raptor season, the Forest Service often posts closure notices here.) Turn right (west) and follow the trail on a gentle descent for about 3 minutes to a trail junction.

Make a quick dogleg by turning left and then almost immediately right into a tunnel through the rhododendron. Continue down the trail to a clearing. From here, follow the second-class gully until it ends just behind the Mossy Monster Buttress. The gully is steep and often wet, but there is no need for a fixed rope.

Once you reach the chasm separating the buttress and the main wall, cut left behind the buttress and into the narrow corridor. You will emerge between the main wall and the gully, but you must follow the trail to the right (under the Mossy Mon-

Overview of The Amphitheater as seen from the trail to the top of the Mummy Buttress

ster Buttress) and then negotiate one final steep gully to gain a climbers' trail beneath the cliff. If you turn left here, it is about 5 minutes along the cliff to reach *Pixie Wall* on the main wall. *Note:* It is also possible to turn right and follow a faint trail away from the North Carolina Wall to reach the Apricot Buttress.

For The Amphitheater: Continue beyond The Chimneys approximately 0.5 mile on the MST until you encounter the third unmarked spur trail heading downhill to the right (west). (During raptor season, the Forest Service often posts closure notices here.) A good landmark to look for in order to find the right trail for The Amphitheater is three large quartz chunks exposed in the trail. Immediately after these chunks will be a 10-inch pine growing halfway into the left side of the trail. The tree has a large white dot painted on it and has a large chunk of rock stuck into its first fork. The Amphitheater trail is immediately across from this tree. Take this trail downhill until you hit a large flat rock.

For both The Amphitheater's north side and south side (or headwall), continue downhill a few hundred feet to the obvious descent gully on your left. Descend the gully. Or, instead of descending the gully, you can reach routes on the north side by continuing out onto the point above *The Open Book* and rapping in with two ropes. This is a good place to view the entire Amphitheater and get your bearings.

For The Amphitheater's Mummy Buttress area, turn left at the large flat rock, and follow the trail as it contours along the rim of the gorge. Continue over the top of the Reggae Wall and scramble down a steep gully on the far side of the Reggae Wall. Traverse back right below the Reggae Wall, and then down to the top of the Mummy Buttress. Descend the gully between the Mummy Buttress and the main wall.

Routes are numbered 1 through 29, from Chockstone Chimney Wall through the Main North Carolina Wall and ending on The Amphitheater.

Chockstone Chimney Wall

Though small, this steep and beautiful wall is between The Chimneys and the Apricot Buttress. It faces due north and stays cool and shady during high summer. It is well worth a visit.

Descent: Rack up and stash your gear before descending gully to routes. Walk off.

1. Changing Corners   5.10b/c

The most diverse line on this wall goes from a chimney to an awesome arête and then steps left to finish on a steep splitter.

First ascent: Nathan Brown, Myles Small, Steve Beeson (1999, ground-up from hooks).

Start: At the right end of the wall in a wide crack.

Pitch 1: Begin in the chimney and climb past overlaps to a rhododendron ledge. (5.10a; 30 feet).

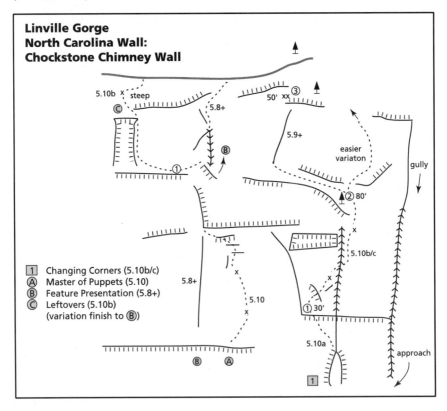

Linville Gorge
North Carolina Wall:
Chockstone Chimney Wall

1 Changing Corners (5.10b/c)
Ⓐ Master of Puppets (5.10)
Ⓑ Feature Presentation (5.8+)
Ⓒ Leftovers (5.10b)
   (variation finish to Ⓑ)

Pitch 2: Climb out onto the arête passing a bolt to gain thin holds and then jugs. Continue past another bolt and find a natural belay on a tree ledge. (5.10b/c; 80 feet).

Pitch 3: Move left from the ledge around a corner. Pull a small roof and continue up the overhanging crack. Double bolt belay. (5.9+; 50 feet).

Apricot Buttress Area

This interesting buttress is often the first stop for aspiring North Carolina Wall climbers because of its classic namesake. The routes are generally straightforward and follow obvious features.

Descent: Rack up and stash your gear before descending gully to begin routes. Scramble off the top of the buttress after climbing.

(There is another wall on the left—north—end of North Carolina Wall between the Apricot Buttress and Mossy Monster Buttress. This area is unique with many horizontals, pockets, and other bizarre features. There are three 100-foot routes that end at a rap station below an upper band of rotten rock. Unfortunately, this wall is often wet.)

2. Apricot Jam   5.9+

A classic Bob Rotert sandbag. You get the hardest moves over with quickly and then things open up nicely.

First ascent: Bob Rotert, Tom McMillan (1973).

Start: Immediately right of the approach gully at an obvious deep dihedral.

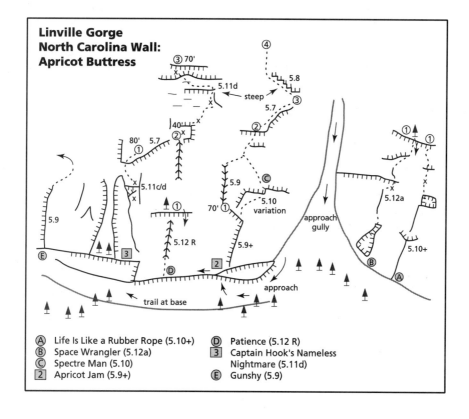

**Linville Gorge
North Carolina Wall:
Apricot Buttress**

Ⓐ Life Is Like a Rubber Rope (5.10+)   Ⓓ Patience (5.12 R)
Ⓑ Space Wrangler (5.12a)   ③ Captain Hook's Nameless
Ⓒ Spectre Man (5.10)   Nightmare (5.11d)
② Apricot Jam (5.9+)   Ⓔ Gunshy (5.9)

Pitch 1: Jam your way up the deceptively difficult crack to gain a notch under a large roof. (5.9+; 70 feet).

Pitch 2: Step left around the overhang and move into a straight-in corner. Follow this to a moderate face and a ledge for a belay. (5.9; 60 feet).

Pitch 3: Climb diagonally right to a bulge, then wander about 30 feet right until you can move up and underneath a stair-stepped, left-facing corner. Natural belay. (5.7; 70 feet).

Pitch 4: Follow the exposed hanging corner to the summit. (5.8; 100 feet).

3. Captain Hook's Nameless Nightmare   5.11d

Long regarded as an ultra-serious endeavor because of aging gear, this route got a facelift with new stainless bolts in 2000.

First ascent: Tom McMillan, Kenny Hibbits, Bob Rotert, Eric Zchiesche, Lindsay Broome (1979).

Start: Continue about 30 feet left of *Apricot Jam* and scramble to a higher tier.

Pitch 1: Climb the crack to a pair of bolts at a blocky area. Move into a cleft where you can find a belay. (5.11c/d; 80 feet).

Pitch 2: Follow the corner up and right to a good stance above an arête with a lone bolt. Belay here. (5.7; 40 feet).

Pitch 3: Step off a block and move out right to a bolt. Continue straight up to a horizontal where you can traverse right a few feet to gain a steep crack with another bolt. Climb up to a narrow ledge, move left, and then gun past a final bolt. (5.11d; 70 feet).

Main North Carolina Wall

Routes 4 through 8 start from the base of the main North Carolina Wall. Routes 9 through 12 start on the wall's Tarantula Ledge. Obviously this wall has much potential, though much of it is hard. Not all of the wall's routes are listed below or are on the accompanying topos. If you think you are doing a new route, it would be wise to make doubly sure. There has been a good bit of unreported climbing in this area.

Descent: Rack up and stash your gear on the rim before descending to routes. Scramble off from top. More detail given for some routes.

4. Pixie Wall   5.11c/d

Rarely repeated, this route is just plain eerie. Prepare for long pitches, scary bolts, and hard climbing on steep ground. Crisp edges and good pro on the technical crux make any attempt worthwhile, though.

First ascent: Doug Reed, Chip Self (1987, ground-up in a single push).

Start: Hike underneath the gigantic, blank roof that bars much of this cliff. Begin just right of this feature and on the left side of a large flake.

Pitch 1: Follow the flake to a left-arching corner system and past two horrible bolts. Clip a bolt and pin to negotiate the somewhat loose roof. Climb up into "don't fall" territory and then aim slightly left to a belay on a block at a bolt. (5.11a; 100 feet).

Pitch 2: Climb straight off the belay through a sketchy roof and onto the steep wall above. Protection is difficult. Gain a mossy ledge just before the crux, which has good gear and excellent climbing. (5.11c/d; 120 feet).

Pitch 3: Wander up the face above, taking the line of least resistance. (5.7; 100 feet).

Pitch 4: More of the same until the wall eventually kicks back. (5.8; 80 feet).

5. Never Never Land   5.12a R

Ever the enigmatic climber, leave it to "KK" to find this hidden and desperately hard line sandwiched between two classics. This route involves long runouts on 5.9 and some creepy protection placements.

First ascent: Kris Kline (1997, solo, ground-up, pro placed on aid).

Start: Off a block about 20 feet right of *Pixie Wall.*

Pitch 1: Climb the slab to gain three bolts. Sketch your way past these and around a left-facing corner and ledge system. Continue to a hanging block. (5.9 R). Maneuver past this and up to another bolt. Crank the small roof to gain a good horizontal that takes plenty of pro. (5.12a; 140 feet).

Pitch 2: Climb right to gain the *Rinky Dink* corner and finish via the direct version described below. (5.11d; 100 feet).

6. Rinky Dink Direct   5.11b

Although this route desperately needs some TLC, it is an awesome line. Steep and varied climbing keeps your interest throughout. Bring double ropes or many shoulder-length runners for the second pitch.

First ascent: Brad Shaver, Bob Mitchell, Art Williams (1972). Jim Okel, Tom Howard, and Shannon Stegg did the first free ascent of the original *Rinky Dink* in 1980. Kris Kline and Thomas Kelley made the first free ascent of *Rinky Direct* in 1987.

Start: In an obvious left-facing crack/flake 75 feet right of *Never Never Land.*

Pitch 1: Jam, stem, and lieback to gain a ledge. Clip an ancient pin and edge up the ramp until you can clip a second pin. Angle left and pull a roof to gain a good crack. Climb this up to an alcove with two old bolts. (5.10c; 100 feet).

Pitch 2: Move left off the belay and under a large roof. Climb right past two pins and onto the exposed face with another pin. Continue past two more fixed pins and a bolt, moving out right through steep rock and a wild pedestal. (5.11b; 120 feet).

Pitch 3: Continue up the face past excellent incuts and several steep (but easy) sections. Belay on a spacious ledge with a small tree. (5.8; 100 feet).

Pitch 4: Climb straight off the ledge to the summit. (5.7; 80 feet).

Note: There is a new direct start to the original *Rinky Dink*, which is shown on the topo only. *Rinky Direct* (5.12, A0) has been led free but has not yet been redpointed.

7. Bumbledink   5.9

When it was climbed in the days before TCUs, this route had a bad reputation for long runouts. It is more manageable with modern microgear. The first-ascent party calls the second pitch one of the most memorable on the wall. Strong words . . .

First ascent: Tom Howard, Jim Okel, Dan Perry (1981).

Start: On the blank looking slab about 75 feet right of *Rinky Dink Direct.*

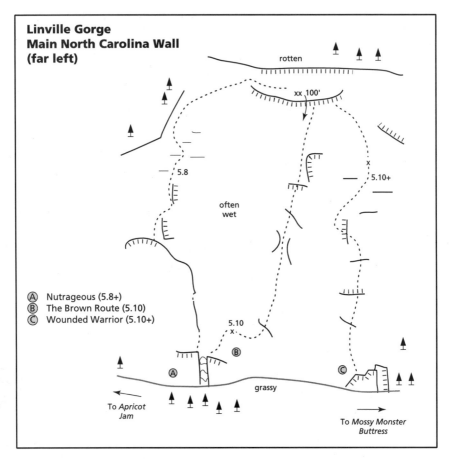

**Linville Gorge
Main North Carolina Wall
(far left)**

rotten

xx 100'

5.8

often
wet

5.10+

Ⓐ Nutrageous (5.8+)
Ⓑ The Brown Route (5.10)
Ⓒ Wounded Warrior (5.10+)

5.10
x

Ⓑ

Ⓐ

Ⓒ

grassy

To *Apricot
Jam*

To *Mossy Monster
Buttress*

Pitch 1: Climb the unprotected, slabby face with good edges to a ledge. (5.9;
100 feet).

Pitch 2: Follow the crack until you can gain an exposed, featured face with nice
horizontals. (5.9; 120 feet).

Pitch 3: Wander up the face to the summit rim; many variations are possible.
Either simul-climb or do a short fourth pitch. (200 feet).

8. Bumblebee Buttress   5.8

An enduring classic. The first-ascent party nearly called this route *Hang-Ups* because
they were not optimistic about two daunting corners, especially one bomb-bay roof
up high.

First ascent: Bob Mitchell, Bob Gillespie (1970).

Start: Midway down the North Carolina Wall, on a ledge about 10 feet above
the trail.

Pitch 1: Climb the deep, left-facing corner to gain an arête. Move up and left to
another ledge. Continue up the corner via excellent jams and stems to belay at a good
stance beneath the bomb-bay roof. (5.8; 100 feet).

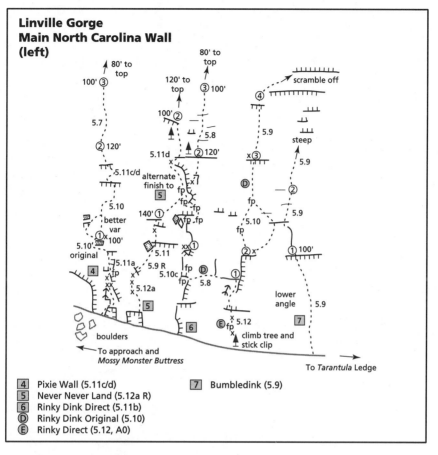

**Linville Gorge
Main North Carolina Wall
(left)**

	Pixie Wall (5.11c/d)
4	Pixie Wall (5.11c/d)
5	Never Never Land (5.12a R)
6	Rinky Dink Direct (5.11b)
Ⓓ	Rinky Dink Original (5.10)
Ⓔ	Rinky Direct (5.12, A0)

7	Bumbledink (5.9)

Pitch 2: Finagle your way past the bomb-bay slot and climb the crack to a great ledge at the top of the buttress. (5.8; 100 feet).

Pitch 3: From the ledge, move right and up the headwall aiming for a bulge. Bypass this a little bit right, and then continue up to another good ledge. (5.8; 70 feet).

Pitch 4: Wander up the lower-angled face to the summit. (5.5; (100 feet).

Descent: An obvious and well-maintained climbers' trail leads through the dense rhododendron to the cliff-top trail that runs parallel to the gorge rim.

9. Mitzeitzusparen   5.9+
This German name translates roughly to "with time to spare."

First ascent: Tom Howard, Dan Perry.

Start: After *Bumblebee Buttress* and aptly named *The Corner,* continuing along the cliff base for a long distance leads to *The Limey* (not in this guide). Instead, when you get the opportunity, third-class up some mossy slabs to gain an area known as the Tarantula Ledge. *Mitzeitzusparen* starts about 100 feet right of where you gain the Tarantula Ledge and about 30 feet right of a vegetated gully.

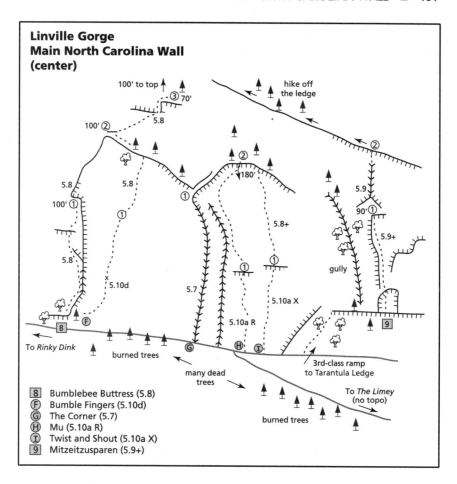

Linville Gorge
Main North Carolina Wall
(center)

8 Bumblebee Buttress (5.8)
Ⓕ Bumble Fingers (5.10d)
Ⓖ The Corner (5.7)
Ⓗ Mu (5.10a R)
Ⓘ Twist and Shout (5.10a X)
9 Mitzeitzusparen (5.9+)

Pitch 1: Climb the shallow, right-facing corner system to the top of a block. (5.9+; 90 feet).

Pitch 2: Climb through a bulge to a shallow weakness. Follow this to its end and climb off on the face to a huge ledge. (5.9; 90 feet).

Descent: Follow the ledge system left to the top of the main North Carolina Wall.

10. Freebird   5.11b/c

Named less for Lynyrd Skynyrd than for the flying you could do if you blow it at a bad time. Don't break a crucial, semi-detached flake low on this spectacular, long pitch. Bring at least one each of 3- and 4-inch cams.

First ascent: Chris Kinghorn, Nathan Brown (1999, ground-up).

Start: 25 feet right of *Mitzeitzusparen* above a grassy spot.

Pitch 1: Climb past a bolt to the flake. Two fixed pins protect a thin face and an overlap. Move left across the overlap, then angle up and right past horizontals and

Opposite: *Will Byrom, with Tony Jones belaying, tackles the upper roof on pitch 2 of* Bumblebee Buttress *(route 8).*

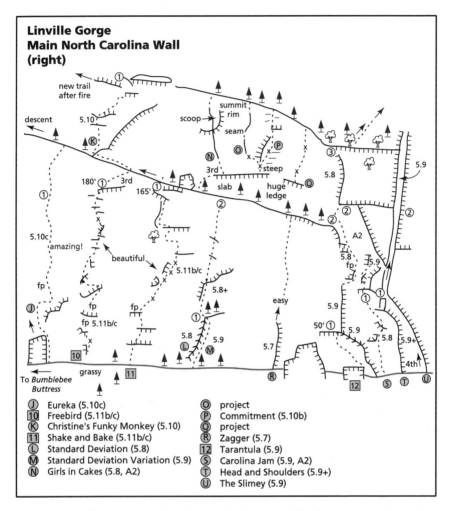

Linville Gorge
Main North Carolina Wall
(right)

Ⓙ Eureka (5.10c)
⑩ Freebird (5.11b/c)
Ⓚ Christine's Funky Monkey (5.10)
⑪ Shake and Bake (5.11b/c)
Ⓛ Standard Deviation (5.8)
Ⓜ Standard Deviation Variation (5.9)
Ⓝ Girls in Cakes (5.8, A2)

Ⓞ project
Ⓟ Commitment (5.10b)
Ⓠ project
Ⓡ Zagger (5.7)
⑫ Tarantula (5.9)
Ⓢ Carolina Jam (5.9, A2)
Ⓣ Head and Shoulders (5.9+)
Ⓤ The Slimey (5.9)

flakes, eventually passing another bolt. Wide horizontals lead to some pockets and a natural belay. (5.11b/c; 180 feet).

Descent: You can third-class off from here via the huge ledge system. Or, for one additional pitch try *Christine's Funky Monkey* (5.10). Climb off the "descent" ledge just left of a left-facing flake. Scramble through rhododendron to a trail constructed after the year 2000 fires.

11. Shake and Bake   5.11b/c

This new addition to the North Carolina Wall is one of the wildest lines off the Tarantula Ledge. The upper section climbs a gorgeous face near a green streak.

First ascent: Nathan Brown, Mark Winebrenner, Jason Gunn (1998, ground-up from hooks).

Start: 25 feet right of *Freebird*.

Pitch 1: Climb past a small overlap and then a ledge to a hidden pin. Four bolts lead past a sustained face to a horizontal where the difficulty eases. Climb to an optional belay on a ledge about 15 feet right of a moss pad. Step left for a nice 5.7 crack to another ledge for the belay. (5.11b/c; 165 feet).

Descent: You can third-class off from here. See *Freebird* for additional options.

12. Tarantula 5.9

A choice dihedral, some devious gear placements, and generally enjoyable climbing make this route an excellent adventure.

First ascent: Bob Mitchell, Ron Cousins (1972).

Start: 200 feet right of *Shake and Bake*. Follow the trail behind a large boulder and into a narrow corridor. *Tarantula* begins off a block 50 feet right of the corridor.

Pitch 1: Climb off the block and traverse left under the large roof. Belay at a ledge under the dihedral. (5.9; 50 feet). *Note:* It is possible to do a direct start.

Pitch 2: Climb the excellent dihedral until you can exit right onto a stance (good micro wired nuts here) and follow the crack above up to a fixed piece. Trend left to a belay. (5.9; 100 feet).

Pitch 3: Continue up shallow corners and past one tree ledge. (5.8; 120 feet).

The Amphitheater: North Side

Routes 13 through 16 are on the north side of The Amphitheater. They are best accessed via the main approach gully. At the base of the gully, keep the rock on your right and scramble down to your desired route.

Descent: Rack up and stash your gear before descending gully to routes.

13. The Prow 5.4

A classic moderate in an incredible wilderness setting. A great introduction to climbing in Linville Gorge.

First ascent: Jed Williamson, Mark Calkins, Andy Damp (1970).

Start: After descending the gully, scramble down and right until you get to the very end of a tree-covered ledge extending out onto the slab. This start avoids the pitches below that are not worthwhile.

Pitch 1: Climb straight up off the left end of the ledge to a roof, where you will trend left to the base of a left-leaning crack for a belay. (5.4; 90 feet).

Pitch 2: Climb up the crack to a belay at a ledge with blocks. (5.3; 120 feet).

Pitch 3: Climb the dihedral to its end and follow steep face to a ledge. (5.4; 100 feet).

Pitch 4: Wander up easy, lichen-covered rock to top. (Easy fifth class; 50 feet).

14. The Open Book 5.11b

A burly boulder problem at the start leads to some of the best jams and stems in the gorge. Don't miss it!

First ascent: Guy Jacobson, Gil Harder (1978). Bob Rotert, Randy Mann, and Ted Anderson did the first free ascent.

Start: From the gully, scramble right along the base of the rock to the first ramp. Scramble third-class ground, up and right to a pod 30 feet below the roof.

Pitch 1: Scamper up to the roof and boulder through the bulge, passing a bolt and

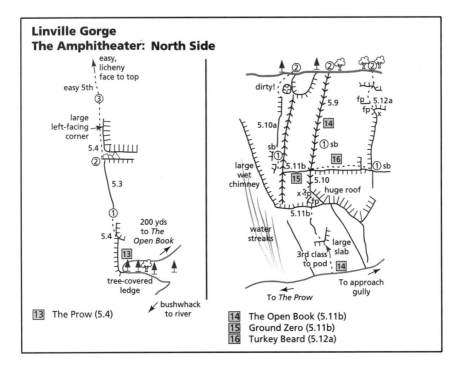

Linville Gorge
The Amphitheater: North Side

13 The Prow (5.4)

14 The Open Book (5.11b)
15 Ground Zero (5.11b)
16 Turkey Beard (5.12a)

two pins. Continue 50 feet up the fantastic corner to a hanging belay. (5.11b; 100 feet).
Pitch 2: Climb the corner to the tree-covered ledge at the top. (5.9; 70 feet).

15. Ground Zero   5.11b
A fine route that deserves more traffic.

First ascent: Thomas Kelley, Gary Mims (1987). Kris Kline and Thomas Kelley made the first free ascent later that same year.

Start: On *The Open Book*.

Pitch 1: After the roof and about 40 feet up *The Open Book* corner, traverse left out a thin horizontal crack to flakes on the arête. Step around the arête and head up to a semihanging belay. (5.11b; 100 feet).

Pitch 2: Ascend the overhanging hand crack to the steep face and on up to a belay ledge. (5.10a; 80 feet).

16. Turkey Beard   5.12a
A tour-de-force for the aspiring North Carolina 5.12 trad climber.

First ascent: Doug Reed, Chip Self (1986).

Start: On *The Open Book*.

Pitch 1: About 35 feet up *The Open Book* corner, traverse out right on a ledge. Step over to the base of a steep corner for a hanging belay. (5.11b; 100 feet).

Pitch 2: Climb the corner to a bolt. Step up and left to an old ring-angle pin (clip it long!) and then up and left again to another fixed pin. Fire over the bulge and straight through more roofs to the top. (5.12a; 100 feet).

Biff Farrell, with Chad Oliver belaying, climbs through the crux on Turkey Beard *(route 16).*

The Amphitheater: South Side (Headwall)

Routes 17 and 18 are on The Amphitheater's south side, or headwall. To access these routes, scramble down the main approach gully and then hug the rock to the left until you can third-class up onto a ledge at your first opportunity.

Descent: Rack up and stash your gear before descending gully to routes.

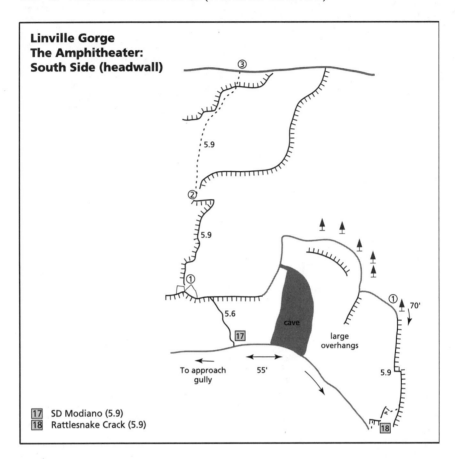

Linville Gorge
The Amphitheater:
South Side (headwall)

17 SD Modiano (5.9)
18 Rattlesnake Crack (5.9)

17. SD Modiano   5.9

Another nice moderate on a wall that sees little traffic.

First ascent: Mike Dunn, Sean Cobourn (1982).

Start: Below the right-facing corner system just left of the center of the wall.

Pitch 1: Climb up and left across easy ground to the base of the corner. (5.6; 60 feet).

Pitch 2: Climb the face to gain the blocky corner, which leads to a nice belay stance below a roof. (5.9; 70 feet).

Pitch 3: Pull left out the small roof/corner and follow good edges and horizontals straight to the top. (5.9; 60 feet).

18. Rattlesnake Crack   5.9

A gem in the bushes that's worth the time to find.

First ascent: Tom Howard, Bruce Meneghin (1977).

Start: At a corner 100 feet right of *SD Modiano* past a large overhang.

Pitch 1: Climb the clean dihedral through a slight roof to a belay at the trees. (70 feet).

The Amphitheater: Mummy Buttress Area

Routes 19 through 29 climb on or near The Amphitheater's Mummy Buttress. Therefore, the best approach option is to hike across the top of the gorge rim to the summit of the Mummy Buttress (see the Approach section above).

Descent: Rack up and stash your gear on the rim before descending to routes.

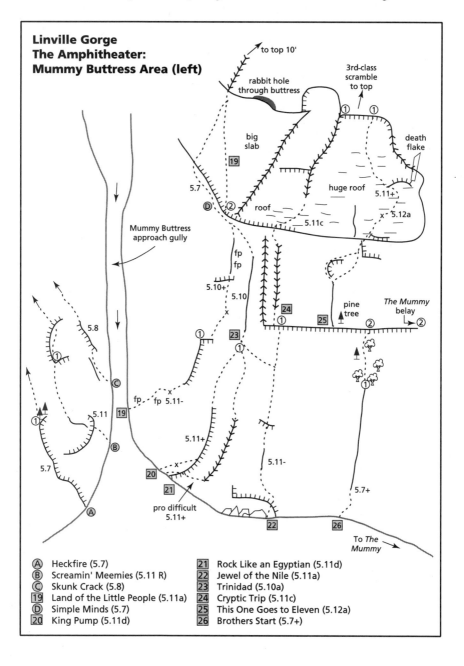

**Linville Gorge
The Amphitheater:
Mummy Buttress Area (left)**

Ⓐ Heckfire (5.7)	21 Rock Like an Egyptian (5.11d)
Ⓑ Screamin' Meemies (5.11 R)	22 Jewel of the Nile (5.11a)
Ⓒ Skunk Crack (5.8)	23 Trinidad (5.10a)
19 Land of the Little People (5.11a)	24 Cryptic Trip (5.11c)
Ⓓ Simple Minds (5.7)	25 This One Goes to Eleven (5.12a)
20 King Pump (5.11d)	26 Brothers Start (5.7+)

19. Land of the Little People   5.11a
A deceptively difficult route in the descent gully that stays cool in summer.

First ascent: Thomas Kelley, Ralph Fickel, Mark Stroud (1986).

Start: At the bottom of the approach gully, locate a seam on the left wall (to the left as you descend gully) with two fixed pins to a bolt.

Pitch 1: Climb the seam past two dubious knifeblades to a bolt. Step right to a broken crack and corner system that leads to a nice belay stance. (5.11a; 80 feet).

Pitch 2: Move up and right from the belay to a bolt that leads to steep liebacks over a small roof. Continue up the corner to another roof. Traverse left a bit and pull the roof to belay above the lip. (5.10+; 100 feet).

Pitch 3: Climb the crack- and jug-laced slab up and left to a hanging corner that leads to the top. (5.8; 70 feet).

20. King Pump   5.11d
This one demands every trick in your bag.

First ascent: Kris Kline, Thomas Kelley (1988).

Start: 40 feet down the descent gully from *Land of the Little People*. Locate the bolt left of a crack and about 10 feet up.

Pitch 1: Climb the face past the bolt to join the crack about 20 feet up. Follow the crack to nearly the top and then move out onto the face and then up to a natural belay. (5.11d; 110 feet).

Pitch 2: Finish on *Trinidad*, *Cryptic Trip*, or *This One Goes To Eleven*.

21. Rock Like an Egyptian   5.11d
The first-ascent party gives this route high praise but cautions about strenuous gear placements.

First ascent: Kris Kline, Thomas Kelley (1987).

Start: Same as *King Pump*.

Pitch 1: Climb up the *King Pump* corner for 15 feet and then traverse right (strenuous pro) to a shallow corner. Climb this shallow corner to its top and head across easier terrain to a shared belay with *King Pump*. (5.11d; 110 feet).

Pitch 2: Finish on *Trinidad*, *Cryptic Trip*, or *This One Goes to Eleven*.

22. Jewel of the Nile   5.11a
An overlooked classic with a great mix of face and crack climbing.

First ascent: Kris Kline, Thomas Kelley (1988).

Start: 40 feet right of *King Pump* at jumbled boulders below an overhang.

Pitch 1: Step up over the roof at the low point on the right side and head up and left to a series of vertical cracks and seams. Climb straight up thin face moves to easier terrain and a big ledge just below *Cryptic Trip*. (5.11a; 110 feet).

Pitch 2: Finish on *Cryptic Trip* or *This One Goes to Eleven*.

23. Trinidad   5.10a
Linked with *Jewel of the Nile* and *Land of the Little People*, *Trinidad* makes for one of the best routes on the Mummy Buttress.

First ascent: Thomas Kelley, Ralph Fickel (1985).

Pitch 1: Climb *King Pump, Rock Like an Egyptian,* or *Jewel of the Nile.*

Pitch 2: From the belay, climb to the base of a shallow corner/crack left of the arête. Climb straight up this crack/corner to the large horizontal and traverse 20 feet left and pull the roof to a shared belay with *Land of the Little People.* (5.10; 100 feet).

Pitch 3: Finish on *Land of the Little People* or *Simple Minds.*

24. Cryptic Trip   5.11c

Nothing Cryptic here . . . steep pulls on beautiful stone!

First ascent: Brady Robinson (1996).

Start: Directly above *Jewel of the Nile,* on the far-left side of the ledge at the top of the second pitch of *The Mummy.*

Pitch 1: Climb the corner right of the arête to the large horizontal. Power up and right past amazingly incut finger jugs and great horizontals to a pod. Climb straight up to a 5.8 left facing corner and ramp to the top. (90 feet).

25. This One Goes to Eleven   5.12a

Can you hear the sustain? A wild and pumpy ride through an improbable wave of overhanging rock.

First ascent: Harrison Shull, Dudley Hammon (2001).

Start: At a pine tree on the large ledge 30 feet left of the second-pitch belay of *The Mummy.*

Pitch 1: Climb the seams behind the small pine to a short left-facing corner below a huge roof. Power up and right past a rail and up to a bolt. Move up past good horizontals to a small roof (death flake on your right) and then traverse left 8 feet to another huge rail. Climb straight up through the center of the overhanging headwall to the top. (90 feet).

26. Brothers Start   5.7+

A good a variation to *The Mummy* on busy days.

First ascent: John and Terry Ferguson (1974).

Start: At the vegetated crack 30 feet left of *The Mummy.*

Pitch 1: Head up the face to the base of the crack and follow this to a belay stance where it ends. (5.7; 80 feet).

Pitch 2: Move up past moss clumps and rhododendrons (better than it sounds!) to the large ledge shared by *Cryptic Trip, This One Goes to Eleven,* and *The Mummy.* (5.4; 70 feet).

Pitch 3: Finish on any of the routes that leave from the ledge.

27. The Mummy   5.5

One of the most popular routes in Linville Gorge, if not in the entire state—and deservedly so! This route offers moderate terrain, great pro, and dizzying exposure in a wilderness setting.

First ascent: Bob Gillespie, Bob Mitchell, Steve Longenecker (1971).

Start: At the base of the Mummy Buttress descent gully, head down and around

left to a gravel-covered cleared area below a slabby face that leads up to a nice crack.

Pitch 1: Climb the slab to the crack, which leads to a gear belay at a nice stance. (5.5; 150 feet).

Pitch 2: Move up and left to the base of the clean cracks. Follow these up to the large ledge. (5.3; 70 feet).

Pitch 3: Climb right of the arête for easier moves or for more challenge, head straight up off the ledge, heading for the left side of a large block. Above the large block, climb the face up to a large ledge with a pine for a belay. (5.3 to 5.5; 110 feet).

Pitch 4: Third-class past vegetated rock to the top. (50 feet).

28. The Daddy   5.6

Only a touch harder than *The Mummy*, but every bit as classic.

First ascent: Art Williams, Mike Holloway (1972).

Start: 200 feet down and around to the right of *The Mummy* at a large left-facing corner with an obvious trampled spot at its base.

Pitch 1: Climb the blocky corner or the face right of the corner (easier) and continue up the upper crack to a large ledge. (5.4; 140 feet).

Pitch 2: Head up the wall on flakes and good horizontals, then angle right toward a pine tree on a ledge. (5.5; 80 feet).

Pitch 3: Traverse blocky ledges up and right and then back left to a belay stance at a pile of blocks on the left end of a ledge. (5.3; 90 feet).

Pitch 4: Move up through the bulge and then angle up and right following blocky, cracklike features onto a featured face leading to a belay in a pod. (5.5; 80 feet).

Pitch 5: Climb the face to either side of this large broken crack and head up to a clean corner. Follow the crack above the corner up through a series of bulges to the top. (5.6; 80 feet).

29. Good Heavens   5.5 (no topo)

An excellent alternative to *The Mummy* and *The Daddy* on crowded weekends.

First ascent: Bob Mitchell, Bob Gillespie (1970).

Start: Hike about 5 minutes down and past *The Daddy* and look for the most obvious large, right-facing corner past a big overhang.

Pitch 1: Climb the dihedral to a small tree with a natural gear belay. (5.4; 100 feet).

Pitch 2: Head up and right, passing below a roof. Exit out right and head up to a belay stance just over the roof. (5.5; 100 feet).

Pitch 3: Climb a short bit of face to a large tree-covered ledge. (5.4; 50 feet).

Pitch 4: Follow the dihedral and blocky face to broken terrain to another large ledge. (5.4; 90 feet).

Pitch 5: Climb path of least resistance to the top. (5.3; 150 feet).

Variation: At the top of pitch 3, make a weird traverse hard left to a tree-filled ledge/corner. Climb up past the trees into a hidden 5.8 chimney and into a huge

Opposite: *Biff Farrell wishes this route went to ten*—This One Goes to Eleven *(route 25)*.

Linville Gorge
The Amphitheater:
Mummy Buttress Area (right)

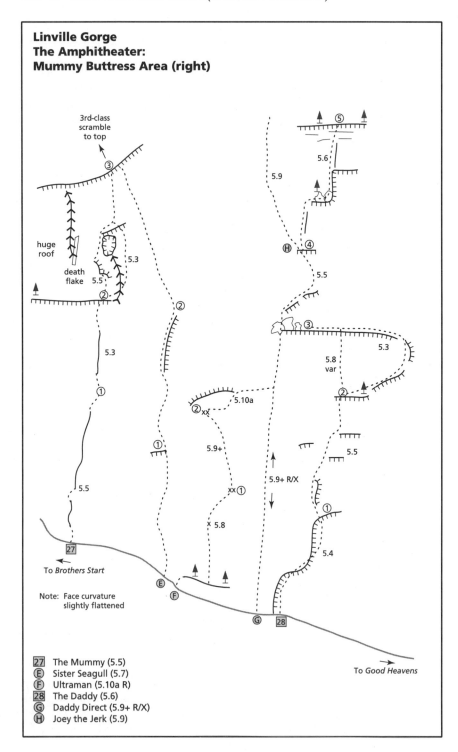

27 The Mummy (5.5)
Ⓔ Sister Seagull (5.7)
Ⓕ Ultraman (5.10a R)
28 The Daddy (5.6)
Ⓖ Daddy Direct (5.9+ R/X)
Ⓗ Joey the Jerk (5.9)

cavelike room. You can't believe you are in North Carolina! Climb out the top where you can either traverse left to the ledge on pitch 3 of *The Daddy* or climb straight up to a ledge and then up and left following a ramp approximately 200 feet to the summit.

Shortoff Mountain

Climbing type: Multipitch traditional
Rock type: Chilhowie quartzite
Height: 450–500 feet
Number of routes: Approximately 70 (28 this guide)
Climbing season: Year-round (best in fall and spring)
Camping: See Linville Gorge introduction. Camping is allowed anywhere from the parking lot up to the top of the cliff as long as you are on Forest Service property. Most of the land along Wolf Pit Road is private property and not open to camping.

Shortoff Mountain, sitting atop the far downstream end of Linville Gorge and overlooking beautiful Lake James, holds some of the tallest rock faces and has some of the cleanest sections of unbroken rock in the gorge. Many locals will describe it as an amazing place to go to avoid crowds and sample some fine adventure climbing and world-class bushwhacking. Despite the long uphill approach, Shortoff features long traditional routes of all grades. Plus, the steep and wild Tilted World offers high-end climbing in a fantastic position.

History

Despite its striking presence as seen from the more popular Linville Gorge crags like Table Rock and The Amphitheater, Shortoff Mountain saw spotty development in the early years. The more obvious lines like *Little Corner*, *Maginot Line*, and *Big*

The cliffs of Shortoff Mountain as seen from the Gold Coast

Corner were undoubtedly the first to fall—probably in the early 1970s. Unfortunately, Shortoff lies off the beaten path and was visited independently by tiny and often fragmented groups of climbers, so most of the details on the earliest exploration in the area have been lost to posterity. However, most climbers from that era reminisce about the aura of impregnability that surrounded the cliffs at Shortoff back then. They were big, steep, and committing—even more so than the walls of The Amphitheater that had so intimidated climbers earlier.

As climbers pushed the limits at crags like Moore's Wall, the North Carolina Wall, and Looking Glass Rock, their skills and confidence grew. Soon they started to make forays in to Shortoff to tap the potential of the steep quartzite walls. No climber in this group had as great an impact on the development of routes on Shortoff as Tom Howard—his name appears on nearly half the first-ascent credits and on nearly every classic line. Howard teamed up with a variety of partners but really found his groove with Jim Okel and Bruce Meneghin. Starting in 1976, Howard led a seemingly one-man crusade to pick off all the classic natural lines on the wall, which lasted well into the mid-1980s. Routes like *Straight and Narrow, Paradise Alley,* and *Dopey Duck* fell with remarkable ease. Howard's confidence grew and his vision and tenacity on steep terrain knocked down barriers that led to some of the really steep test pieces such as *Built to Tilt* and *Scream Dream* (aka *Supercrack*).

Word soon spread, though, and climbers began to flock to Shortoff in greater numbers, seeking the opportunity to push their own limits. Doc Bayne, Bruce Burgess, Thomas Kelley, and others from the western part of state came to fill in many of the blanks. Epitomizing the ethical ideal of limiting the placement of bolts, they established lines that are often as audacious as they are difficult. They regularly balanced on the thin line between bold and dangerous, leaving a legacy of routes that demand your full attention in the middle of arm-blowing terrain hundreds of feet in the air. Such a frenetic pace soon spent itself; activity died down in the late 1980s, and Shortoff experienced a lull in traffic.

The early '90s were quiet with a handful of parties coming in and generally climbing the established classics each year. Sporadic route development rekindled in the mid- to late '90s at the hands of a few hard-driven climbers. Of special note are the few routes that Kris Kline established while climbing rope solo. Most notable of these would be *Espresso Grinder,* which checks in at a stout 5.12 and has seen few repeats. Imagine being in there all alone pushing this hard line from the ground up. As usual, Kline's daring combination of difficulty and commitment set a bold precedent for future climbers to emulate.

Not all the development at the high end of the grades came at the hands of these dedicated locals. In a brief but dazzling weekend in April of 1997, two visiting Californians, Scott Lazar and Jose Pereya, knocked off the last "Great Problem" at Shortoff— the stunningly overhanging orange shield of quartzite left of *Cascading Colluvial Kaleidoscope.* Over two days, they established two hard 5.11s through this improbable wave of steep rock, *Raven 13* and *Ginger Rush.* The two routes have a total of two bolts, showing that the visitors were quite adept at the ground-up trad game!

Today Shortoff gets a tiny fraction of the traffic seen at Moore's Wall, Table Rock, or Looking Glass Rock. This is less an indication of the quality of the climbing than it is a statement on the popularity of an area that requires a longish approach and an inclination for adventure trad climbing. Yet with its abundance of classic routes and a dearth of crowds, Shortoff awaits a renaissance in the early twenty-first century.

Weather and Climbing Season

The Shortoff Mountain access road is never blocked, so you can chase sun or shade depending on the season. Even so, high summer is hot no matter what you do.

Getting There

From Asheville, take Interstate 40 east to exit 90 for Nebo/Lake James. From here, travel north on Harmony Grove Road for about 0.5 mile to a right turn (still signed as Harmony Grove Road). Continue approximately 3 miles until you can cross over US 70 at a traffic light and then continue another 0.4 mile to a stop sign. Turn right onto NC 126. Follow NC 126 east past Lake James State Park at about 2.5 miles and eventually cross the Linville River on a narrow bridge at about 10 miles.

Continue another mile and turn left onto Wolf Pit Road (a dirt/gravel road on your left). If you come to the Linville Access Boat Ramp on the right, you have gone too far.

Follow Wolf Pit Road all the way to a dead end at a cul-de-sac. The very last bit of this gravel/dirt road can be impassible for low-clearance vehicles and be even more difficult after wet weather.

Approach

Hike north out of the parking area up an old logging grade. At your first fork, take the right-hand choice, which curls back uphill to the right. About 0.5 mile of hiking on this switchback-laden, eroded logging grade leads you to a four-way intersection. Hike straight across onto a white-blazed, single-track trail—this is the Mountains-to-Sea Trail. Another 0.25 mile will bring you across the top of the cliff to the approach gully, which is marked by a seasonal spring set up with a pipe. Third-class your way down this steep gully to the base of the wall.

Routes are numbered continuously from south to north along the full length of the cliff. The approach gully comes down between routes 13 and 14.

South of the Approach Gully

Routes 1 through 13 are south of the gully (climber's right as you face the wall). Routes 10 through 12 are in the Tilted World, which is essentially the final 80–100 feet of a 400-foot wall. Some experienced parties hike down along the cliff top to the top of these Tilted Wall routes and then rap in to climb only the last pitch.

Descent: Rack up and stash your gear at the top before descending gully to routes.

1. Bonsai   5.10a (no topo)

This nice route is often overlooked due to its remote location. This is the farthest downstream route listed in this guide—a dozen more lie farther downstream awaiting exploration.

First ascent: Thomas Kelley, Rodney Lanier (1993).

Start: Hike about 0.2 mile to the right of *Construction Job*, past a large, dirty,

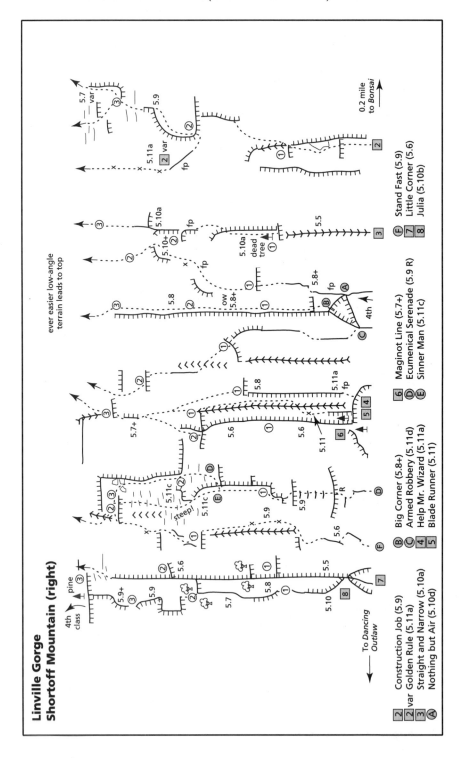

Linville Gorge
Shortoff Mountain (right)

0.2 mile
to Bonsai

ever easier low-angle
terrain leads to top

To Dancing
Outlaw

2 Construction Job (5.9)
2 var Golden Rule (5.11a)
3 Straight and Narrow (5.10a)
Ⓐ Nothing but Air (5.10d)

Ⓑ Big Corner (5.8+)
Ⓒ Armed Robbery (5.11d)
4 Help Mr. Wizard (5.11a)
5 Blade Runner (5.11)

6 Maginot Line (5.7+)
Ⓓ Ecumenical Serenade (5.9 R)
Ⓔ Sinner Man (5.11c)

Ⓕ Stand Fast (5.9)
7 Little Corner (5.6)
8 Julia (5.10b)

left-facing corner, and downhill until you can scramble 15 feet up onto a ledge. Locate a bolt below a large flake.

Pitch 1: Climb up to the bolt and then across the loose flake. At the top of the flake climb straight up past three bolts and gear to a belay in a left-facing corner. (5.10a; 120 feet).

Pitch 2: Step out right, climbing past two bolts (second has no hanger). Once on the easier face above, traverse up and left to hit *Escape Corner* (not in this guide). (5.9+; 150 feet).

Pitch 3: Scramble off to the top.

2. Construction Job   5.9

Three pitches of stellar climbing that offer a bit of everything: slab, roofs, corners, and a lot of exposure.

First ascent: Rich Gottlieb, Tom McMillan (1977).

Start: 50 feet right of *Straight and Narrow* below two inside corners that face each other.

Pitch 1: Climb up the right-hand dihedral to a nice ledge at the base of a grassy corner. (5.5; 100 feet).

Pitch 2: Head up the right arête and then up the face aiming for a crack with some vegetation in it that leads to the base of an arching corner. (5.7; 90 feet).

Pitch 3: Move up this arching dihedral through golden brown rock and then fire straight up jugs through the gray roofs above. Move up and slightly right to below a blocky corner. (5.9; 180 feet).

Pitch 4: Easier, but loose, terrain leads to the top. (5.6; 100 feet).

Variation: Joe Lackey and Glenn Ritter did the first ascent of the third-pitch *Golden Rule* variation in 1998. From the second belay, traverse left to a steep, diagonal crack with a fixed pin. Then head straight up the face passing three bolts and then easier terrain to the top. (5.11a; 130 feet).

3. Straight and Narrow   5.10a

One of the best 5.10s in Linville Gorge if not in the state! Sweet finger and hand cracks spiced up with a few roofs.

First ascent: Tom Howard, Bruce Meneghin (1977).

Start: 100 feet right of *Big Corner* (topo only). Locate the crack system that leads "straight as an arrow" to the top of the wall.

Pitch 1: Follow the obvious wide, vegetated crack to an alcove with a small dead tree. (5.5; 100 feet).

Pitch 2: Move up the crack to a roof and then out right onto the face. Head up and left passing a fixed peg to a small belay stance. (5.10a; 100 feet).

Pitch 3: Continue up the crack and corner to the roof. Pull through the roof on wildly exposed jugs and then on up easier terrain. (5.10a; 140 feet).

4. Help Mr. Wizard   5.11a

Burly moves on a steep wall eventually link up with *Maginot Line*.

First ascent: Lyle Dean, Kitty Calhoun (1982). Jim Okel, Tom Howard, and Thomas Kelley made the first free ascent later that same year.

Mark Owen pulls through the final roof on pitch 3 of Construction Job *(route 2).*

Start: On the steep face 20 feet right of *Maginot Line.*

Pitch 1: Boulder up the steep wall and then climb up the corner past a fixed pin to more moderate ground. (5.11a; 100 feet).

Pitch 2: Continue up to join *Maginot Line.* (5.7; 80 feet).

Pitches 3 and 4: Finish on *Maginot Line.*

5. Blade Runner   5.11

Deceptively steep and sustained moves with a lot of exposure.

First ascent: Bruce Burgess, Thomas Kelley, Victor Moore (1990).

Start: 15 feet right of *Maginot Line*, up on a small tree ledge.

Pitch 1: Boulder up into a dihedral, follow it past a bolt, and then move out right onto the arête. Ride the striking arête for 40 feet then move right onto the face and continue up to belay just below a bulge. (5.11; 140 feet).

Pitch 2: Power up titanic buckets and then up easier ground to merge with *Maginot Line*. (5.10; 40 feet).

6. Maginot Line   5.7+

Excellent rock, great protection throughout, and dizzying exposure might qualify this as the best route of the grade in Linville Gorge.

First ascent: Brad Shaver, Tony Pidgeon (1970).

Start: 100 feet to the right of *Little Corner* beneath a huge left-facing corner with a large pine at the base.

Pitch 1: Climb up past a small pine 20 feet up and continue up the dihedral to a belay stance near the chockstone. (5.6; 90 feet).

Pitch 2: Follow the dihedral to a belay in an alcove. (5.6; 50 feet).

Pitch 3: Angle out right and up the face to a finger-sized crack that leads through the overhang and up to mossy ledges. (5.7; 75 feet).

Pitch 4: Scramble to the top. (5.5; 75 feet).

7. Little Corner   5.6

This large blocky corner is the easiest full-length route at Shortoff. It offers good climbing with fantastic exposure despite its vegetated appearance. Bring extra hand-sized pieces.

First ascent: Unknown.

Start: In the first full-cliff-length, left-facing corner system south of the descent gully.

Pitch 1: Follow the nice hand crack on the slabby right face of the corner to a belay ledge. (5.5; 120 feet).

Pitch 2: Continue up blocky corner past two bulges to an alcove. (5.6; 100 feet).

Pitch 3: Climb corner on blocky jugs following easiest terrain to a ledge with a huge pine. (5.6; 100 feet).

Pitch 4: Climb corner to top. (5.4; 100 feet).

8. Julia   5.10b

Nice liebacks and corners that parallel *Little Corner* to the left.

First ascent: Bruce Meneghin, Tom Howard (1977).

Start: Same as *Little Corner*.

Pitch 1: Climb *Little Corner* until you can move left to an overhanging lieback crack. Follow this crack to a stance below a right-facing corner. (5.10; 110 feet).

Pitch 2: Climb the corner/crack up to a belay stance. (5.8; 90 feet).

Pitch 3: Continue up the blocky and roofy flakes past a bulge and up to belay in a recess. (5.9; 100 feet).

Pitch 4: Follow the flakes to the tree-covered ledge. Easier terrain leads to the top of the cliff. (5.9; 130 feet).

9. The Dancing Outlaw 5.10c

The roof moves on the second pitch alone makes this route very worthwhile.

First ascent: Joe Lackey, Ron Dawson, Zachary Lesch-Huie (1999).

Start: 20 feet left of *Julia* and *Little Corner*.

Pitch 1: Climb up past five bolts and gear to a left-facing crack/corner above a ledge. Continue up and right another 25 feet to a small stance. (5.10c; 120 feet).

Pitch 2: Climb the crack to the roof (fixed pin). Pull the roof and climb up ever-easier terrain to a roomy ledge with a large pine. (5.9+; 180 feet).

Pitch 3: Climb straight up to the top of the cliff. (5.7; 100 feet).

Tilted World

Most parties rap in to Tilted World, *Serentripitous* is the best access from the ground.

10. Built to Tilt 5.10b

This is the original line through the intimidating roofs.

First ascent: Tom Howard, Jim Okel (1981).

Start: At ground level, 300 feet south of the descent gully at a wet corner with an off-width above.

Pitch 1: Head up the slabby face to join the off-width crack 30 feet up. Follow the off-width to its top and then head up face to the vegetated ledge. (5.7; 120 feet).

Pitch 2: Move right to gain a left-facing corner. Follow this for 25 feet and then step out right and head up face holds to a ledge in a corner. (5.7; 100 feet).

Pitch 3: Climb the dihedral and then place pro out in the large roof. Monkey-bar your way through the stupendous overhangs, turn the lip, and head to the top. (5.10b; 90 feet).

11. Full Tilt Boogie 5.11c

A high-octane dash through viciously steep terrain.

First ascent: Doc Bayne, Buddy Price (1994).

Start: On *Built to Tilt*.

Pitches 1 and 2: Climb *Built to Tilt*.

Pitch 3: Climb the face just left of the *Built to Tilt* dihedral. Cross a small ledge and continue straight up into a left-facing corner in the roof and clip a bolt. Power out the roof and on up to the top. (5.11c; 90 feet).

12. Pinball Wizard 5.11

Maybe the best of the three roof routes on this wall.

First ascent: Thomas Kelley, Lee James (1991).

Start: On *Built to Tilt*.

Pitch 1: Climb first pitch of *Built to Tilt*.

Pitch 2: Start up pitch 2 of *Built to Tilt*. At the arch, head up and left along the arch and then up horizontals to a stance. (5.8; 60 feet). *Note:* Can be linked up with pitch 1.

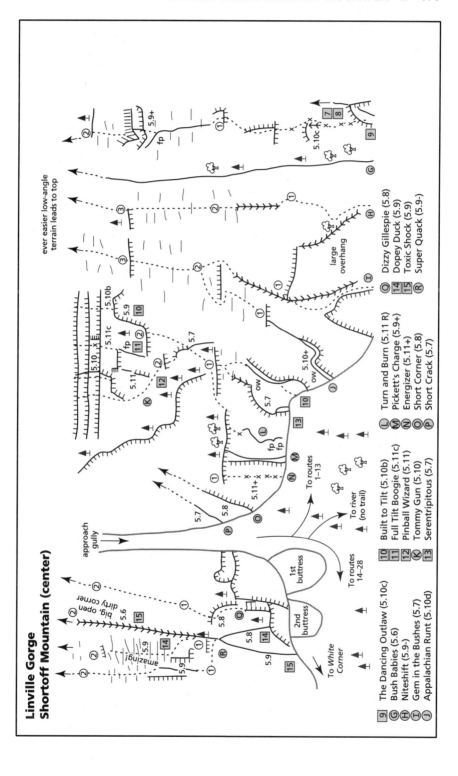

Linville Gorge
Shortoff Mountain (center)

ever easier low-angle terrain leads to top

large overhang

approach gully

big, open dirty corner

amazing!

1st buttress

2nd buttress

To routes 1–13

To river (no trail)

To routes 14–28

To White Corner

⑨ The Dancing Outlaw (5.10c)
Ⓖ Bush Babies (5.6)
Ⓗ Niteshift (5.9-)
Ⓘ Gem in the Bushes (5.7)
Ⓙ Appalachian Runt (5.10d)

⑩ Built to Tilt (5.10b)
⑪ Full Tilt Boogie (5.11c)
⑫ Pinball Wizard (5.11)
Ⓚ Tommy Gun (5.10)
⑬ Serentripitous (5.7)

Ⓛ Turn and Burn (5.11 R)
Ⓜ Pickett's Charge (5.9+)
Ⓝ Energizer (5.11+)
Ⓞ Short Corner (5.8)
Ⓟ Short Crack (5.7)

Ⓠ Dizzy Gillespie (5.8)
⑭ Dopey Duck (5.9)
⑮ Toxic Shock (5.9)
Ⓡ Super Quack (5.9-)

Bruce Burgess pulls into the maze of horizontals on Full Tilt Boogie *(route 11).*

Pitch 3: Climb out left to a left-facing corner that turns into a right-facing corner. Take this to a ledge and then continue up and left to another small ledge. Power through the roof above. (5.11; 90 feet).

13. Serentripitous   5.7
A more aesthetic, ground-up alternative to *Built to Tilt*'s first pitch.
First ascent: Tom Howard, Trip Collins (1981).
Start: 30 feet left of the off-width start to *Built to Tilt*.
Pitch 1: Climb up to the right-arching crack and follow this until it ends. Then follow moderate face climbing to a brush-covered ledge. (5.7; 120 feet)
Pitches 2 and 3: Finish on *Built to Tilt*.

North of the Approach Gully
Routes 14 through 28 are to the north of the approach gully (climber's left when facing the wall).
Descent: Rack up and stash gear at the top before descending to routes.

14. Dopey Duck   5.9
If you only have time to do one 5.9 at Shortoff, this should be the one. The second pitch is like *High Exposure* at the Gunks—only harder and longer! Bring extra small cams.
First ascent: Tom Howard, Jim Okel (1981).
Start: Hike past the second buttress north of the descent gully, and cut uphill at your first opportunity. Scramble up and right onto a large block and locate a blocky hand crack.
Pitch 1: Follow the crack up to a stance above a small birch tree. (5.8; 100 feet).
Pitch 2: Climb up the blocky crack 20 feet until you can traverse left to a small right-facing corner. Then swing up through imposing overhangs and very steep face to a belay stance just above a small roof. (5.9; 100 feet).
Pitch 3: Move up on even bigger holds, passing through some moss hummocks on your way to the top of the cliff. (5.6; 150 feet).

15. Toxic Shock   5.9
A nice journey up a bucket-laced crack. The first pitch serves as a more aesthetic approach for *Dopey Duck*.
First ascent: Unknown.
Start: At a right diagonalling finger crack immediately left of the block where *Dopey Duck* starts.
Pitch 1: Climb the finger crack to join the crack on *Dopey Duck*. Continue to the shared belay stance at the tree. (5.9; 110 feet).
Pitch 2: Continue up the large, blocky crack to a stance. (5.6; 150 feet).
Pitch 3: Climb to the top of cliff. (5.5; 130 feet).

16. White Corner   5.10a
A stellar second pitch with very dirty and loose pitches both before and after. Start on *White Russians Gone Bananas* for the best variation and finish on *Sword of the Lord*.

Doc Bayne checks into jugville on the steep pitch-2 headwall of Dopey Duck *(route 14).*

First ascent: Ralph Fickel, Jeep Barrett (1982).

Start: On *Early Times* (topo only) or *White Russians*.

Pitch 1: Climb either *Early Times* or *White Russians* to the ledge. (80 feet).

Pitch 2: Stem and jam the obvious "white corner" above and step right to a ledge for a gear belay. (5.10a; 80 feet).

Pitch 3: Climb up and right a bit and then straight up on somewhat dirty and loose rock. (5.9; 180 feet).

Pitch 4: Scramble easy fourth-class terrain to the top.

17. White Russians Gone Bananas   5.11a
An excellent route that avoids the chossy *Early Times* (topo only) start to *White Corner.*

First ascent: Nathan Brown, Steve Beesen, Keith Bestal, John Anderson (1997).

Start: 150 feet left of *Toxic Shock* and next to a twin-trunked pine tree at the right end of a corridor formed by a huge boulder.

Pitch 1: Climb the open corner past the second bolt and then traverse left under the roof and up the corner to a fixed peg. Pull through the bulge via a finger crack and move up past another bolt to a ledge to belay. (5.11a; 80 feet).

Pitches 2 through 4: Climb *White Corner.*

18. Sword of the Lord   5.10+
A great finish to *White Corner* that avoids the rubbly rock on the normal finish.

First ascent: Harrison Shull, Bruce Burgess, Dave Wendelin (2001).

Start: At the belay on top of *White Corner* pitch.

Pitch 1: From the belay, head out left and over a bulge up to a bolt. Then climb up some very steep pulls straight up a clean face to a small roof and shallow left-facing corner. Pull right around the roof and corner and climb the blunt arête to a good ledge. (5.10+; 180 feet).

Pitch 2: Climb to the top. (5.6; 100 feet).

19. Lost and Found   5.9
An unheralded classic! The quality climbing stays consistent all the way to the very last move of this gem.

First ascent: Ken Pitts, Karl Lail (1994).

Start: In the "water streak" 30 feet right of the large *Cascading Colluvial Kaleidoscope* corner (topo only).

Pitch 1: Climb the obvious water streak past three bolts to a belay stance above the roofy section of *CCK*. (5.9; 100 feet).

Pitch 2: Move up and right until you are below a very steep bucket-infested wall. Jungle gym your way up this steep headwall to a belay at a ledge with a pine. (5.9; 140 feet).

Pitch 3: Traverse right a bit and aim for the obvious hand crack through the roof to the top. (5.6; 50 feet).

20. Ginger Rush   5.11+ R
This intimidating route has yet to see a known second ascent. The first-ascent party remarked that it is harder and scarier than *Raven 13.*

First ascent: Scott Lazar, Jose Pereya (1997).

Start: On *Cascading Colluvial Kaleidoscope* (topo only). Scramble up to a small stance about 40 feet up.

Pitch 1: From the small stance on *CCK*, traverse out left to a bolt below a small roof. Climb up and left to another bolt and power up steep ground to a small belay stance. (5.11+; 100 feet).

Pitch 2: Climb up steep face to the roofs above. Pull the roofs via corners right

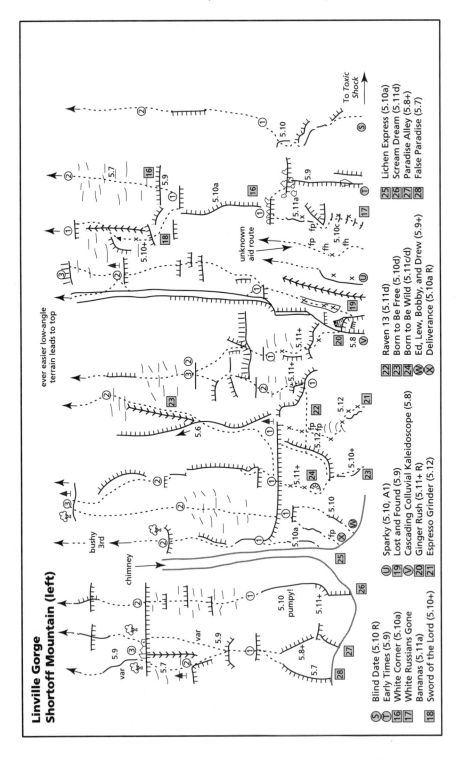

Linville Gorge
Shortoff Mountain (left)

To Toxic Shock

ever easier low-angle terrain leads to top

bushy 3rd

chimney

S Blind Date (5.10 R)
T Early Times (5.9)
16 White Corner (5.10a)
17 White Russians Gone
18 Bananas (5.11a)
   Sword of the Lord (5.10+)

U Sparky (5.10, A1)
19 Lost and Found (5.9)
   Cascading Colluvial Kaleidoscope (5.8)
20 Ginger Rush (5.11+ R)
21 Espresso Grinder (5.12)

22 Raven 13 (5.11d)
23 Born to Be Free (5.10d)
24 Born to Be Wild (5.11c/d)
W Ed, Lew, Bobby, and Drew (5.9+)
X Deliverance (5.10a R)

25 Lichen Express (5.10a)
26 Scream Dream (5.11d)
27 Paradise Alley (5.8+)
28 False Paradise (5.7)

of *Raven 13* and belay at your first chance to reduce drag. (5.10; 90 feet).
Pitch 3: Head up easy ground to join the finish on *Raven 13*.

21. Espresso Grinder 5.12

A standard setting climb. The first ascent was done ground-up on a Rope Soloist™.
It is reportedly quite sustained through the first 50 feet.
First ascent: Kris Kline (1998).
Start: At flakes on the left side of the wall below the huge orange *Raven 13*
overhangs.
Pitch 1: Head up and left past two bolts following sharp flakes. Traverse left
around a rounded arête past two more bolts and fire straight up the thin face, pass-
ing two fixed pins and two more bolts.
Descent: Rap from the pine. (100 feet).

22. Raven 13 5.11d

A jaw-dropping line with dizzying exposure! Bring your big guns for this burly outing. A 4- and a 3-inch cam are needed for the first belay.
First ascent: Jose Pereya, Scott Lazar (1997).
Start: On *Born to Be Free*.
Pitch 1: Climb *Born to Be Free* until you are 20 feet shy of the first belay ledge,
and make an easy traverse 40 feet right to a gear belay below a 5-foot, flat, horizontal
roof above a lichen-covered face. (5.10d; 120 feet).
Pitch 2: Boulder over the roof at a shallow left-facing corner and then move up
the overhanging face on jugs to a good stance at a horizontal crack below an even
bigger roof. (5.11d; 80 feet).
Pitch 3: Ape out awkward and powerful moves through double roofs and pull
up onto a lichen-covered slab to build a belay about 25 feet above the final roof at a
good stance. (5.10d; 60 feet).
Pitch 4: Climb up low-angled jugs to a final steep headwall. Follow the faint,
left-facing corner feature to the top of the buttress. (5.8; 200 feet).

23. Born to Be Free 5.10d

A great route that has some heady opening moves over a nest of brass nuts. The first-
ascent party took the easier, dirty, blocky corner system that trends up to the left.
The first free ascent tackled the steeper corner to the right. This latter, more aesthetic
option, is described below. Bring brass wired nuts.
First ascent: Tom Howard, Bill Newman (1980). Bruce Burgess and Chris
Caldwell made the first free ascent in 1987.
Start: Just around the corner to the left from *Espresso Grinder.*
Pitch 1: Scramble up onto a ledge and build a mini life station with brass in
the old pin scars. Boulder up into the pod and then follow the crack up to a ledge.
Move up and right into a corner that leads to a good belay ledge. (5.10d; 100 feet).
Pitch 2: Climb up easy corners until you can access a steeper corner to the right.
Take this up to its end and then power through handlebar jugs on a steep face to a
stance. (5.10; 150 feet).

Pitch 3: Climb past some left-facing flakes to the top. (5.8; 120 feet).

24. Born to Be Wild   5.11c/d
A stout variation to *Born to Be Free*'s first pitch on bullet-hard golden quartzite.
First ascent: Bruce Burgess, Andy Kluge (1999).
Start: On *Born to Be Free.*
Pitch 1: Boulder the start to *Born to Be Free* and continue 20 feet to the ledge. Move up and left to below a steep golden face. Blast up this steep face on small natural pro and two bolts. Then manage the pump through the final overhangs to the ledge. (5.11c/d; 100 feet).
Pitches 2 and 3: Continue straight up lichen-covered corners (see topo). Or traverse right and rappel from the pine above *Espresso Grinder.*

25. Lichen Express   5.10a
This route's obscurity is a tragic casualty of a lack of information. It is a great route that stays cooler than most due to its location in a shaded gully.
First ascent: Ed Begoon, Jim McArthur (1985).
Start: On the right face of the gully, 100 feet left of *Born to Be Wild.*
Pitch 1: Climb up the face to the finger crack and follow the tenuous, shallow locks without stemming off the opposite wall. Climb up and out of the chimney to a ledge. (5.10a; 120 feet).
Pitch 2: Head up and left to join a water streak with amazing in-cut finger buckets. Follow this up to the vegetation. (5.8; 120 feet).
Pitch 3: Scramble off brushy ground to the very top. (5.4; 100 feet).

26. Scream Dream (aka Supercrack)   5.11d
This stout line really keeps at you. The boulder-problem start may be the technical crux, but the pumpy crack above is the real business!
First ascent: Tom Howard, Jim Okel, Bill Newman (1980).
Start: 30 feet left of the *Lichen Express* chimney.
Pitch 1: Head up a short corner to a bulge, power through the thin holds, and move up and right to the crack. Blast the crack straight up to a stance with slings on a horn. (5.11d; 100 feet).
Pitch 2: Climb the heavily featured face straight up to a pod below a bulge. Pop over the bulge and head straight to the top of the buttress. (5.8; 140 feet).
Pitch 3: Walk back 50 feet, step across a chasm, and climb the short, steep headwall to the very top of the buttress. (5.8; 50 feet).

27. Paradise Alley   5.8+
As good as *Maginot Line,* only slightly harder.
First ascent: Tom Howard, Bill Newman (1979).
Start: 50 feet around the left from *Supercrack* at a left-leaning dihedral.
Pitch 1: Head up and left following the steep corner. Then head straight up good face holds to a ledge with some large blocks. (5.8; 120 feet).
Pitch 2: Climb up and left to a small roof and then follow a corner up and left

to a small ledge a few small pines. (5.7; 100 feet). *Variation:* Head up and left to the roof and then climb straight up and a bit right through steep rock on good holds to the ledge on top of pitch 3. (5.9; 200 feet).

Pitch 3: Climb up steep face holds to a good ledge. (5.7; 70 feet).

Pitch 4: Move around right and finish the same as for *Supercrack.* (5.8; 60 feet). *Variation:* Follow a left-trending crack off the belay ledge. (5.9; 70 feet).

28. False Paradise   5.7

A milder version of *Paradise Alley.*

First ascent: Tom Howard, Bill Newman (1979).

Start: At the corner 40 feet left of *Paradise Alley.*

Pitch 1: Follow the arching corner until it ends. Then cross some heavily featured face to the belay at the top of pitch 1 of *Paradise Alley.* (5.7; 120 feet).

Pitches 2 through 4: Finish on *Paradise Alley.*

SOUTHERN BLUE RIDGE

Opposite: *Alden Pellet jams the super-classic* Out to Lunch *(route 56) on the Sun Wall at Looking Glass Rock.*

6. RUMBLING BALD MOUNTAIN _____

Climbing type: Mostly single-pitch traditional and sport, excellent bouldering
Rock type: Henderson gneiss
Height: 40 to 300 feet
Number of routes: Approximately 150 (65 this guide)
Season: October through April
Camping: Do not camp at Rumbling Bald. There are numerous private campsites nearby (see appendix B).

Although its claim to fame lies partly from being a movie location for *The Last of the Mohicans* and *Dirty Dancing*, Hickory Nut Gorge is also popularly known for Chimney Rock Park and some quaint mountain ambiance. But climbers converge on this area for one reason: Rumbling Bald. A jumble of cliffs and boulders on the gorge rim, Rumbling is widely considered the best winter climbing area in the state and earned its name after some sizeable earthquakes shook the mountain around 1874. The nature of climbing at Rumbling Bald is technical face and splitter cracks. In the late 1990s, bouldering became *the* reason to visit, and crash pads started outnumbering ropes. Whatever reason you come, Rumbling Bald is worth a trip.

History
Listening to locals talk about the early years at Rumbling Bald is like hearing about the '60s: free camping, adventure all around, no crowds, and few rules. Sounds nice, huh? Yes, Rumbling Bald has always been one of the state's coolest climbing areas in part because its central location drew climbers of all backgrounds and the cliff line itself is tailor-made for both sport and traditional climbing. Although the first developers were old school to the bone, the "sweepstakes" years at Rumbling took place just as sport climbing was becoming very popular. That's partially why many a Tarheel climber will tell you Rumbling Bald is their favorite destination in the state. The different personalities and development styles resulted in an excellent assortment of routes. It also doesn't hurt that the rock is some of the best around.

Like most areas in North Carolina, it is hard to determine who actually climbed here first. According to area pioneer Jeep Gaskin, there were a handful of routes in Art Williams's earliest guide, all climbed in 1971 or 1972 and located on the slab left of *Nuclear Arms*. One rainy day in the spring of 1976, Don Hunley, Grover Cable, and Gaskin walked most of the wall from about *Hanging Chain* to the slabs east of the Cereal Buttress. Gaskin recalls being floored by their find and, upon returning to Asheville, telling Asheville Outward Bound instructor Brad Shaver that they had discovered a "surreal" buttress. Shaver, in jest, responded, "What kind of cereal?" Hence the name.

Cable and Hunley brought Shaver to Hickory Nut Gorge in the fall of that year and the trio climbed *Fruit Loops* on their first visit, followed soon after by *Frosted Flake*. Gaskin climbed his first line at Rumbling around Thanksgiving of that year when he did *Captain Crunch*—at 5.10d it was quite a bit harder than the existing lines! But it

nging Chain Wall

Lakeview and Flakeview Areas

Test Pilots Area

Cereal Wall

Comatose Area

Screamweaver Area

Cereal Buttress

Overview of the crags at Rumbling Bald Mountain

was Christmas 1977 when Gaskin climbed perhaps the area's most famous line: the stunning one-pitch finger crack, *Shredded Wheat*. Although the grade of this climb has fluctuated for years in the 10d/11a range it was certainly stout in the days of EBs and passive protection. Gaskin also recalls that at the time of the first ascent, a nearby tree provided some excellent stems! "Without those rests, I would have been completely overmatched," he said recently. Over time, the limbs were removed.

Charlotte climbers Sean and (the late) Shane Cobourn first started climbing here in 1981 and were responsible for popularizing the area with most of the Piedmont crew. Sean remembers climbing the razor-thin flake of *Whiskey for Breakfast* in 1983 on a string of eighteen RPs (the flake was much longer at that point).

By the mid-1980s, word was out about the excellent potential at Rumbling Bald and the cliffs suddenly swarmed with climbers hot for new rock. Despite the potential for friction, there was actually a lot of camaraderie among these groups. Asheville climber Bruce Burgess remembers that it was common for everyone to converge at a cozy pizza joint in Lake Lure (Rusty's) after a day of climbing. Often, the groups would yell stories to each other across the room. Early on, the ethic at Rumbling Bald was mostly ground-up. Some of the most notable routes to go in this style were *Spiders and Snakes, Hanging Chain,* and *Screamweaver*. Kline—responsible for the latter route—remembers belaying Doug Reed on a brilliant all-afternoon ascent of *Leapin' Lizards* in 1986 and deciding shortly thereafter that he would never subject his own belayers to such misery! Kline turned to climbing mostly roped-solo shortly afterward.

Of these ground-up routes, a few stand out. When it was climbed in the mid-1980s, *Lakeview* had more bolts than any single pitch around. In response, the Asheville set dubbed it "Bolt View." After an early repeat, Monty Reagan worked

out a nice variation start and, upon rappelling from the belay station, noticed a striking face climb to the left. Shortly thereafter, he returned with Jeff Lauschey and the
pair knocked off the spectacular *Edgestacy*—at first known only as *Lauschey-Reagan*.
For years, many climbers theorized that this two-bolt climb with ground fall potential went up as a reaction to *Lakeview*. Not true. In fact, this route was just one of
many similar climbs done by Lauschey and Reagan, possibly two of the state's most
overlooked climbers.

Hanging Chain caused a stir of a whole different sort. Climbed in 1987 and initially rated 5.12+, it was—at the time—thought to be the hardest route in North
Carolina. Reed, Byron Bridges, and Tim Fisher did this route "Australian slingshot"
style, in which the rope was left at its high point (even overnight) on four consecu-
tive days until Reed finally unlocked the technical crack climbing and another stout
face section near the top. (This upper face has since sprouted one additional bolt
that did not exist on the first ascent.) Although the lower two-thirds of this 150-foot
route overhang quite continuously, the *Chain* requires expertise in everything from
tips-crack climbing to friction. Important for more than just its sheer difficulty, the
Chain also convinced many climbers that Rumbling offered incredible potential for
extremely difficult sport climbs. In relatively short order, the Hanging Chain Wall
had three additional routes that, by many accounts, rank among the best such climbs
in the state. Reed's frequent partner Porter Jarrard went on to clean and bolt the possibly unrepeated *Love Wig* and *Distemper*.

Anyone with a history in North Carolina might wonder why these routes did not
cause friction, especially since there have been spotty incidents of bolt chopping into
the millennium. In fact, most climbers have been willing to accept Rumbling Bald as a
"transition" cliff—one that allows for high-end sport climbs, but where easier sport
climbs and squeeze jobs are routinely erased. Back in 1987, Burgess remembers discovering (at least for himself) The Kennel. The next weekend he brought a seasoned
Asheville climber up to the cliff who quickly proclaimed it a pile with potential only
for short aid lines. Young and impressionable, Burgess went on to other things. A few
years later, Burgess learned that Jarrard and Chapel Hill climber Harrison Dekker had
climbed all The Kennel classics in a two-week period, including equipping *Mad Dog*
from hooks because it was too steep to rap-drill! One man's trash . . .

The 1990s and more recent years have been times of sporadic development.
Although some classics went up at the beginning of the decade, Rumbling Bald was
closed for several years because of access issues. Upon its gradual reopening in the
late 1990s, Rumbling Bald underwent a transition into a bouldering mecca led by
Asheville climbers Ned Dowling and Lewis Lankford. Nowadays, crash pads commonly outnumber ropes by three to one! Amazing problems such as the *DRTR, The
French Maid*, and *Redneck Riviera* have spearheaded even more development as
climbers continue to explore the hidden coves of this mountain.

Weather and Climbing Season

The main climbing faces on Rumbling Bald Mountain (elevation 3,200 feet) face
southwest. The climbing season here is October through April. Unlike many local
areas, the rock dries very quickly after rains.

Restrictions and Access Issues

Rumbling Bald has been the scene of some challenging access issues over the course of its existence. After going through a period of intense development, the cliff was closed for several years and only reopened in the mid-1990s at the behest of the Access Fund and the goodwill of the landowner. Please remember that Rumbling Bald is privately owned and the right to climb here is not guaranteed.

Please note that a new landowner has recently acquired land at Rumbling Bald, which includes Cereal Buttress and Cereal Wall. It is especially important that climbers follow the rules below to maintain good rapport with the new landowner:

• No camping anywhere on the property. This is extremely important.
• Park at the main pullouts.
• No hunting.
• Please pack out your trash and stay on the main access trails.

Emergency Services

Call 911. Rutherford Hospital is in Rutherfordton. St. Luke's Hospital is in Columbus. (See appendix C).

Gear

Although many Rumbling Bald routes appear to be sport climbs, it is always wise to bring a light rack. Routes that are fully bolted begin with "sport" in the description.

Getting There

Rumbling Bald is in Hickory Nut Gorge near Lake Lure. From Asheville, follow Interstate 240 east to its terminus with US 74-A. Follow this winding mountain road south toward Chimney Rock/Lake Lure. US 74-A, US 64, and NC 9 all converge into the same road outside the tiny town of Bat Cave. From this intersection, follow the combined highway through Chimney Rock, passing the obvious entrance to the park on your right at 2.6 miles. Continue past the park entrance for another 0.7 mile to Boys Camp Road (SR 1305) on the left. Turn onto Boys Camp Road and continue for 1.4 miles to the top of a hill and a red clay access road on the left. Turn onto this dirt road and follow it a short distance to the first (and larger) of two parking areas. These areas are occasionally very crowded.

From Charlotte, follow Interstate 85 south to exit 10 for US 74 (Kings Mountain). Follow US 74 to Forest City, and veer right onto US 74-A. Continue on US 74-A to a junction with US 64. Follow US 64/74-A to Lake Lure where the road becomes US 64/74-A/NC 9. Follow the combined highway through the town of Lake Lure to Boys Camp Road. Turn right and follow the directions above.

Approach

From the parking areas, you can approach the walls on Rumbling Bald from one of two directions. 1) Aim for the Screamweaver Area to reach Hanging Chain Wall, the Flakeview Area, the Lakeview Area, Screamweaver proper, The Kennel, The Cave, and the Test Pilots Area. 2) Aim for the Cereal Wall to reach the Comatose Area, Cereal Buttress, and Cereal Wall proper.

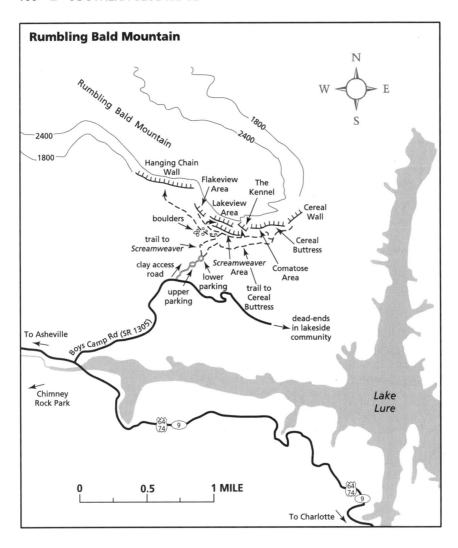

Rumbling Bald Mountain

2400

1800

Hanging Chain Wall

Flakeview Area

The Kennel

Lakeview Area

boulders

Cereal Wall

trail to *Screamweaver*

Cereal Buttress

clay access road

Screamweaver Area

Comatose Area

lower parking

upper parking

trail to Cereal Buttress

To Asheville

Boys Camp Rd (SR 1305)

dead-ends in lakeside community

Chimney Rock Park

Lake Lure

64 74   9

0   0.5   1 MILE

64 74   9

To Charlotte

N
W   E
S

1800

2400

For Screamweaver Area, Hanging Chain Wall, Flakeview Area, Lakeview Area, The Kennel, The Cave, and the Test Pilots Area: From the lower parking area, go left up a steep trail that shortly contours around a shoulder and back to the left (west). Stay on this trail for 0.5 mile until you come to a large boulder on the left called the Trailside Boulder.

For **Hanging Chain Wall,** turn left at the boulder and hike through the entire boulder field. You will eventually pass the huge Washing Machine boulder on your left. Here, continue to contour on the faint trail, following the occasional cairn for about 0.5 mile. It is easy to lose this trail and you should prepare to spend some time bushwhacking on your first visit.

Eventually the trail gains a narrow, steep gully. Climb up this aiming toward the cliff and follow more cairns as they weave through a steep, rocky section. You should emerge at the cliff under the waterfall between *Walk This Way* and *Lavender Dream*. The main Hanging Chain Wall is up and left. *Spiders and Snakes* is to the right. There are no good trails at the base of these cliffs and it is not a good place for dogs or small children.

For the **Flakeview Area,** the **Lakeview Area, Screamweaver** proper, **The Kennel, The Cave,** and the **Test Pilots Area,** continue on the main trail past the Trailside Boulder another 0.2 mile. You'll come to the Screamweaver Area first, near the *Black Planet* and *Boldfingers* routes.

Go left for the Flakeview Area and Screamweaver's left side. Follow the cliff line to the right for Screamweaver's right side, The Kennel, The Cave, and the Test Pilots Area. The Lakeview Area can be approached from either the left or right side of the Screamweaver Area. These trails are all unmarked.

For Cereal Wall, Cereal Buttress, and Comatose Area: From the lower parking area, follow the obvious jeep road that continues to the right. This road contours for approximately 0.75 mile, passing a small drainage, a deep rutted section, and climbing a gradual hill to a flat area.

About 0.1 mile past this flat area, the trail starts up a steep hillside at a boulder field. Follow this well-worn trail to a higher contour line. Go left for the Comatose Area and the left side of Cereal Buttress. Go right for the main Cereal Buttress and Cereal Wall.

Routes are numbered continuously, 1 through 65, starting with Hanging Chain Wall and ending on Cereal Wall.

Hanging Chain Wall

This wall on the far-left side of Rumbling Bald is one of the most impressive at the entire cliff. The routes here are all hard and there is not much in the way of a casual warm-up. This, coupled with a stout approach, usually makes for relatively secluded climbing.

Descent: Rappel the routes. Some routes give additional detail.

1. Spry Look   5.12b
Hold for hold, this route might have the best stretch of face climbing at the Bald. A true endurance fest, with no moves harder than 5.11d but not many that are easier! Bring a few cams 1 to 2.5 inches and a few long draws.

First ascent: Porter Jarrard (1990, rap-bolted).

Start: On the far-left side of the Hanging Chain Wall and just inside a blunt arête.

Pitch 1: Climb the poorly protected slab past several overlaps to gain the slightly overhanging face with a shallow lieback corner. Blitz past the remaining bolts to the double-bolt anchor. (100 feet).

2. Battery Brides   5.12d
Harder moves but with much better rests than its prerequisite to the left. Bring a few 1- and 2-inch cams.

First ascent: Porter Jarrard, Sue Patenaude (1989, rap-bolted).

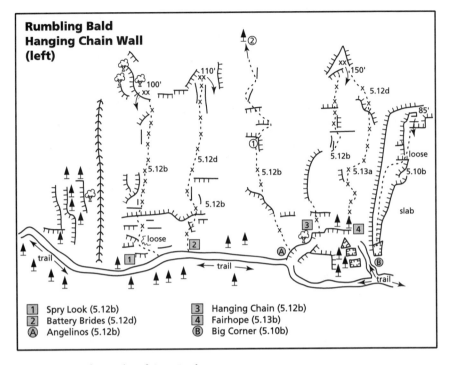

**Rumbling Bald
Hanging Chain Wall
(left)**

1	Spry Look (5.12b)	3	Hanging Chain (5.12b)
2	Battery Brides (5.12d)	4	Fairhope (5.13b)
A	Angelinos (5.12b)	B	Big Corner (5.10b)

Start: 20 feet right of *Spry Look.*

Pitch 1: Saunter up the low face past a bolt and a few pieces of pro to a difficult bulge. Make intricate and bouldery moves the entire way. Nine bolts, double bolt belay. (110 feet). *Note:* To lower, use a 70-meter rope or rappel with two.

3. Hanging Chain   5.12b

A world-class route that stays at you like the first 20 minutes of the movie *Saving Private Ryan.* Wild and intimidating crack climbing leads to a headwall peppered with hard moves. Double ropes recommended.

First ascent: Doug Reed, Byron Bridges, Tim Fisher (1987, ground-up).

Start: 100 feet right of *Battery Brides,* off a high pedestal.

Pitch 1: Work your way up the face past a bolt to a perch beneath the crack. Jam and stem until you can move out right. Blast through the steep section to a good horizontal. Fight the pump past four bolts and finish on a good ledge. Chain anchor. (150 feet).

4. Fairhope   5.13b

Possibly unrepeated, this steep and beautiful route has thwarted some strong attempts.

First ascent: Doug Reed (1989, rap-bolted).

Start: 10 feet right of the Hanging Chain.

Pitch 1: Sport. Work your way up the gorgeous orange wall and past a few heinous sections. Ten bolts; shares anchor with the Chain. (150 feet).

Jack Strifling on the ruthlessly sustained crimps of Spry Look *(route 1)*

5. Walk This Way   5.11b
Long, crimpy, and excellent. It is possible to escape left for a fixed anchor at midheight, but for full credit you have to make the exciting teeter-totter moves near the end. Bring small and midsized cams.

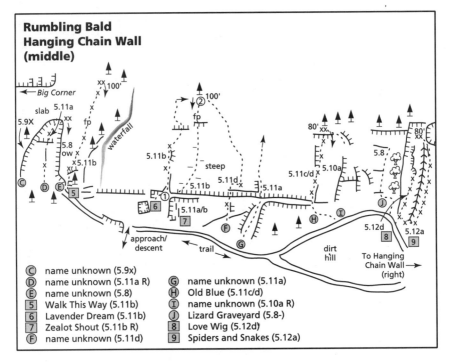

**Rumbling Bald
Hanging Chain Wall
(middle)**

- Ⓒ name unknown (5.9x)
- Ⓓ name unknown (5.11a R)
- Ⓔ name unknown (5.8)
- [5] Walk This Way (5.11b)
- [6] Lavender Dream (5.11b)
- [7] Zealot Shout (5.11b R)
- Ⓕ name unknown (5.11d)
- Ⓖ name unknown (5.11a)
- Ⓗ Old Blue (5.11c/d)
- Ⓘ name unknown (5.10a R)
- Ⓙ Lizard Graveyard (5.8-)
- [8] Love Wig (5.12d)
- [9] Spiders and Snakes (5.12a)

First ascent: Bill Brickey, Tony Ledford (1990).

Start: 100 feet right of previous, on the right side of a gigantic, leaning flake.

Pitch 1: Begin by climbing up a 5.8 corner; step onto a slopey ledge to gain the first bolt. Awkward, steep moves lead to a long stretch of excellent face climbing. (100 feet).

6. Lavender Dream   5.11b

Rarely repeated, but reportedly excellent. Evidently, the corner is not as hard as it looks.

First ascent: Tim Fisher, Doug Reed (1986-87, ground-up).

Start: At the top of the trail, below the clean corner.

Pitch 1: Climb the dirty crack up to the ledge at the base of the corner. Work through a thin section past two bolts and then climb diagonally right to an overlap. Above this, traverse left to reach easier ground. (100 feet).

7. Zealot Shout   5.11b R

If the run-out climbing above doesn't sound appealing, at least sample the excellent, short first pitch. It is not difficult to bail from there.

First ascent: Doug Reed, Tom Howard, Tim Fisher (1986-87, ground-up).

Start: 100 feet right of *Walk This Way*.

Pitch 1: Climb the parallel cracks to the ledge. (5.11a/b; 30 feet).

Pitch 2: Pull the overhang and gain the upper headwall where you can wander right. Keep an eye out for a key stopper placement. A run-out slab will take you up to a ledge with a pin. (5.11b R; 70 feet).

Descent: Rappel from trees.

8. Love Wig   5.12d
The gently overhanging, west-facing wall left of *Spiders and Snakes* with impossibly small holds.

First ascent: Porter Jarrard (1990, rap-bolted).

Start: From where the approach trail meets the base, hike right (east) about 0.2 mile to the unmistakable *Spiders and Snakes* arête. *Love Wig* is on the inside of this arête.

Pitch 1: Sport. Boulder past manky crimpers and imaginary footing. Five bolts to anchor. (80 feet).

9. Spiders and Snakes   5.12a
An obvious and stunning white prow with the best pure arête pinching around. Most stick-clip the first bolt.

First ascent: Bruce Burgess, Chris Caldwell (1988, ground-up).

Start: Right of *Love Wig*, just inside the gully on the face left of the arête.

Pitch 1: Sport. As soon as possible, veer right along small holds, following two bolts to the arête. Roll onto the slabby arête where you can pinch, high-step, and slap your way to the double-bolt anchor. (60 feet). *Note:* An optional medium cam protects a run to the anchor. Also, a certain-to-be very difficult direct start begs to be climbed.

10. Krispy Kreme   5.11d
A good route for the thin-face connoisseur.

First ascent: Bruce Burgess (1988).

Start: The right-most bolted route on the *Spiders and Snakes* buttress.

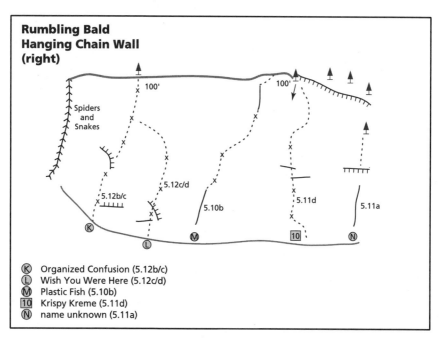

**Rumbling Bald
Hanging Chain Wall
(right)**

Spiders and Snakes

100'   100'

5.12c/d

5.12b/c

5.10b

5.11d

5.11a

(K) Organized Confusion (5.12b/c)
(L) Wish You Were Here (5.12c/d)
(M) Plastic Fish (5.10b)
[10] Krispy Kreme (5.11d)
(N) name unknown (5.11a)

Pitch 1: Fire the bouldery start, then crimp and smear your way up past three bolts and a cam placement.

Descent: Rappel from trees. (100 feet).

Flakeview Area

In recent years, this has become one of Rumbling's most popular areas for its selection of moderate and well-protected routes. Many parties make this their first stop.

Descent: Rappel the routes.

11. Fine Line　　　　　　　　　　　　　　　　　　　　　　　　5.10c

Very popular and a nice entrée to Rumbling's great edge climbing.

First ascent: Steve Orthel, Neil Ofstun, Mike Stewart, Frank Orthel.

Start: On the left side of the Flakeview Buttress, off a flat ledge.

Pitch 1: A slabby start leads over a bulge to cool edging. Five bolts. (100 feet).

12. Drivin' and Cryin'　　　　　　　　　　　　　　　　　　　　5.10a

Surmount a low wave of granite to gain a mellow, lower-angled face.

First ascent: Frank Orthel, Mike Stewart.

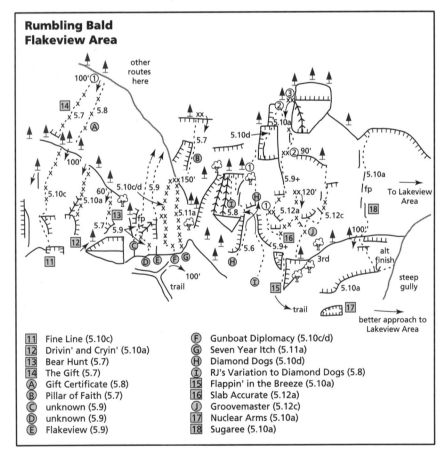

Rumbling Bald Flakeview Area

11 Fine Line (5.10c)	Ⓕ Gunboat Diplomacy (5.10c/d)
12 Drivin' and Cryin' (5.10a)	Ⓖ Seven Year Itch (5.11a)
13 Bear Hunt (5.7)	Ⓗ Diamond Dogs (5.10d)
14 The Gift (5.7)	Ⓘ RJ's Variation to Diamond Dogs (5.8)
Ⓐ Gift Certificate (5.8)	15 Flappin' in the Breeze (5.10a)
Ⓑ Pillar of Faith (5.7)	16 Slab Accurate (5.12a)
Ⓒ unknown (5.9)	Ⓙ Groovemaster (5.12c)
Ⓓ unknown (5.9)	17 Nuclear Arms (5.10a)
Ⓔ Flakeview (5.9)	18 Sugaree (5.10a)

Start: 20 feet right of *Fine Line.*
Pitch 1: Climb the corner beneath a bulge. Balance your way past six bolts. (100 feet).

13. Bear Hunt   5.7

Scamper up the featured face with good pro to another nice section of slab climbing.
First ascent: Martin Penery, Neil Ofstun, Steve Orthel.
Start: 75 feet right of *Drivin' and Cryin'.* Either scramble up a gully or hike around.
Pitch 1: Wander up the low-angled face to a short, difficult section beneath the ledge. (60 feet).

14. The Gift   5.7

This casual jug haul gains excellent position on the upper wall. Bring a light rack.
First ascent: Steve Orthel, Neil Ofstun, Mike Stewart, Frank Orthel.
Start: Off the ledge atop *Fine Line*; it is possible to bushwhack here from the right side of the Flakeview Buttress.
Pitch 1: Climb past four bolts to a tree ledge. (100 feet).

15. Flappin' in the Breeze   5.10a

Three pitches of quality climbing make *Flappin'* a rarity for this section of Rumbling Bald. The second pitch is part of an old route called *Pins R Us.*
First ascent: Bruce Burgess, Andy Kluge (1998).
Start: At the top of a small tree island, about 0.2 mile right (east) of *Bear Hunt.*
Pitch 1: Climb up just right of a large hanging flake, eventually trending left to a bolt. Move up to a small overlap with tricky gear, then continue up and left to a double-bolt belay. (5.9+; 100 feet).
Pitch 2: Move up to a bolt, then traverse right until you can saunter up to a small moss ledge. Move up aiming for a crack, then stem and lieback the beautiful corner system to a nice ledge. (5.9+; 90 feet).
Pitch 3: Climb some short cracks and face past a bolt, then pull straight up to a small left-facing arch aiming for the "golden flake." Jug haul up and right to a double-bolt belay. (5.10a; 50 feet).
Descent: Rap the route.

16. Slab Accurate   5.12a

A variation to the first pitch of *Flappin'* with super high-quality face climbing that demands some precise handiwork.
First ascent: Andy Kluge, Bruce Burgess (1998, ground-up).
Start: Same as *Flappin' in the Breeze.*
Pitch 1: Climb the first pitch of *Flappin'* to the small overlap just above the first bolt. Move right then continue up the super high-quality face following a line of bolts to a double-bolt belay. (120 feet).

17. Nuclear Arms   5.10a

Although often wet, this is a great climb especially when combined with *Sugaree.* Bring double ropes or many long slings.

First ascent: Jeep Gaskin, Jeff Burton (ground-up).

Start: 100 feet right of *Flappin' in the Breeze* and slightly downhill. Begin off a block on the left side of the long, right-arching roof/flake.

Pitch 1: Span past a thin section to gain the excellent, long flake. Continue for about 80 feet, eventually turning the lip at a white streak with good holds. Saunter up the face, aiming slightly left for a ledge and a tree rappel. (100 feet). *Note:* It is possible to follow the flake right and step down to finish.

18. Sugaree   5.10a

From a great position on the upper tier, *Sugaree* follows a series of shallow vertical seams.

First ascent: Jim Proctor, Peter White (1985, ground-up).

Start: Either bushwhack up a third-class gully to the left (not recommended) or climb *Nuclear Arms*.

Pitch 1: Balance your way up the seams to a fixed pin. Load up with several small wires and follow to a ledge. Rappel. (165 feet).

Lakeview Area

Depending on the route you plan to climb, it may be easier to approach either by bush-whacking up and left past *Screamweaver* or up and right past *Finishing School Blues*.

Descent: Rappel the routes unless otherwise noted.

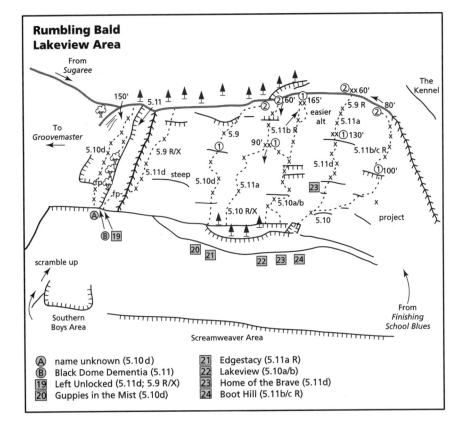

19. Left Unlocked   5.11d (5.9 R/X)

This menacing arête sees relatively little traffic because of its reputation as a death route. But the climbing is reportedly excellent.

First ascent: Doug Reed.

Start: In the corner left of the arête.

Pitch 1: Climb the corner a short way until you can move right past a fixed pin. Labor up the arête past three bolts, then climb carefully to a high bolt. Move left from here, passing a small ledge. (110 feet).

20. Guppies in the Mist   5.10d

This newer route tackles a slate of excellent crimpers just right of the blank bulge.

First ascent: Rodney Lanier, Brad Holroyd (1997).

Start: 50 feet right of the *Left Unlocked* arête.

Pitch 1: Climb the face to a good horizontal. Fight your way past a sustained three-bolt section to another good horizontal. Belay. (5.10d; 75 feet).

Pitch 2: Climb past a bolt to the roofy flakes. Move right for a rappel tree above *Lakeview*. (5.9; 60 feet).

Note: It is possible to combine these into one long pitch.

21. Edgestacy   5.11a R

Bold and brilliant. The holds are all there . . . just don't blow it. Bring a 3.5- or 4-inch piece.

First ascent: Jeff Lauschey, Monty Reagan.

Start: Same as *Guppies in the Mist.*

Pitch 1: Begin as for *Guppies*, but move quickly right trending beneath the bolt. Following the line of least resistance, power up the face past another bolt to the *Lakeview* double-bolt anchor. (90 feet).

22. Lakeview   5.10a/b

A must-do: amazing edging with dramatic position overlooking the Hickory Nut Gorge.

First ascent: Thomas Kelley, Marc Huster, Jonathon Kruegger (1986). Tim Fisher added the direct finish in 1995–96.

Start: 30 feet right of *Edgestacy*. Either chimney behind a tree or climb straight up to the bolt.

Pitch 1: Crimp and pimp your way up the sustained face, wandering slightly. Move left to a double-bolt anchor. (5.10a/b; 90 feet).

Pitch 2: Continue up the face past two bolts to a ledge. (5.10; 60 feet).

Descent: Rappel 165 feet.

Note: The wild and serious direct finish (*Girly Mon Direct*) blasts straight off the sixth bolt into the best position and climbing on this wall. This makes the route nine bolts overall. It is 5.10c R if you go right at the last bolt; 5.11b R if you climb straight to the fixed anchor from the last bolt. (165 feet).

23. Home of the Brave   5.11d

This "land of the free" climb begins with some heady moves but will eventually liberate you.

First ascent: Bruce Burgess, Pascal Robert, Andy Kluge (1998, ground-up).

Start: 20 feet right of *Lakeview.*

Pitch 1: Climb the beautiful and challenging face past natural gear and six bolts to a double-bolt belay. (5.11d; 130 feet).

Pitch 2: Sustained climbing leads past three bolts to a very run-out (5.9) finish. (5.11a; 60 feet).

24. Boot Hill   5.11b/c R

Named for the tombstone-looking rock at the base, this wandering route was never repeated in its terrifying original state—only two bolts on the crux pitch!

First ascent: Tim Fisher, Jim Overby (1986-87, ground-up).

Start: About 20 feet right of *Lakeview* off the tombstone.

Pitch 1: Step off the flake aiming generally right for a shallow horizontal. Climb off the left side of this and make a hairy traverse right to a good pocket. (Note: The bolt was added later for *Home of the Brave.* For full value, don't clip it!) Continue straight and then trend diagonally right a long way to a horizontal at a dish. Natural belay. (5.10 R; 100 feet). *Note:* It is possible to climb a better-protected 5.9 pitch directly up to the ledge atop the first pitch.

Pitch 2: Climb right and up past four bolts to the top. (5.11b/c; 80 feet).

Descent: Rappel *Home of the Brave.*

Screamweaver Area: Left Side

This is a small but action-packed area that you'll see up and left from the approach trail. (There are some new trails here, primarily leading to boulders. Make sure you pick an approach trail that leads left.) Some of the area's most popular routes are here, including *Chickenhead City, Southern Boys Don't Wear Plaid,* and *Black Planet.* There are several routes left of *Southern Boys* that are not in this guide.

Descent: Rappel the routes.

25. Southern Boys Don't Wear Plaid   5.11b

Long considered a testy 5.11+, this prominent, short roof is just not that hard if you use all the available holds.

First ascent: Doug Matthews, Rod Hansen, Jeep Gaskin (1985, ground-up).

Start: On a slab under the roof crack, about 100 feet left from where the approach trail meets the base.

Pitch 1: Fourth-class up the slabs and chimney until you are immediately under the roof. Ape out left to a precarious stance, then blast over the small roof to the upper crack. Wander your way to the top. Rappel from a tree. (80 feet).

26. Pumping in Rhythm   5.11b/c

"Discovered" after rapping down over *Southern Boys,* Eddie Begoon reracked and fired this line in about 10 minutes.

First ascent: Eddie Begoon, Doc Bayne.

Start: In the corner right of *Southern Boys.*

Pitch 1: Chimney up the corner to the first big ledge. Pump your way out left to the rounded arête, and then dash for the top. (85 feet).

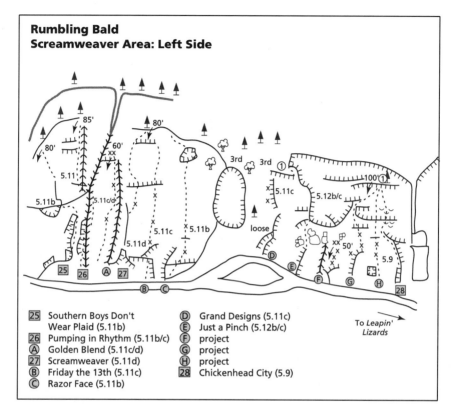

Rumbling Bald
Screamweaver Area: Left Side

25 Southern Boys Don't
    Wear Plaid (5.11b)
26 Pumping in Rhythm (5.11b/c)
Ⓐ Golden Blend (5.11c/d)
27 Screamweaver (5.11d)
Ⓑ Friday the 13th (5.11c)
Ⓒ Razor Face (5.11b)

Ⓓ Grand Designs (5.11c)
Ⓔ Just a Pinch (5.12b/c)
Ⓕ project
Ⓖ project
Ⓗ project
28 Chickenhead City (5.9)

To *Leapin'*
Lizards

27. Screamweaver — 5.11d
If you can get it started, this one is a gem. Fierce finger locks, tenuous face climbing, and an exciting finish.

First ascent: Kris Kline (1986, ground-up). Doug Reed and Clarence Hickman added the direct finish.

Start: Just right of the arête, on top of a block.

Pitch 1: Power up the tips lieback crack to a good pod and eventually a bolt. Load up the pro at the good horizontal under the overlap. Then, either step right for the easier, original finish or crimp your way up the run-out direct finish. (80 feet). *Note:* Another block used to sit at the start, making it somewhat easier.

28. Chickenhead City — 5.9
It's a little broken at first, but this line opens up into an excellent ride. Bring long runners to sling the "chicken heads."

First ascent: Unknown. The name is attributed to Tim Fisher but he believes it may have been climbed earlier.

Start: About 100 feet right of *Screamweaver*, under a left-angling crack.

Pitch 1: Climb the overhanging start to gain a wide hand crack. Move up under a stair-stepped wall until you can trend left and around the roof. Continue to an open ledge with a good crack. Climb steep rock past the "chicken heads" aiming for a tree ledge with a fixed anchor. (100 feet).

Screamweaver Area: *Right Side*

This is the main buttress of this area and home to classics such as *Black Planet* and *Zydygo*. Despite the prominent position, it is usually uncrowded because of the few moderate routes.

Descent: Rappel the routes unless otherwise noted.

29. Leapin' Lizards   5.12b

The first established route on this awesome buttress takes an improbably direct line.

First ascent: Doug Reed.

Start: About 30 feet right of *Chickenhead City*, on the right side of a ledge.

Pitch 1: Climb the devious face up to an overlap with a bolt. Make hard moves past this, continuing straight to a stance at the roof beneath the bulge. Climb past two fixed pins and another bolt to a double-bolt anchor. (80 feet).

30. Boldfingers   5.12a

The opening boulder problem is steep and fun, but a devious seam looms above.

First ascent: Kris Kline, Eddie Begoon (1985).

Start: On the right side of the next wall right of *Leapin' Lizards.*

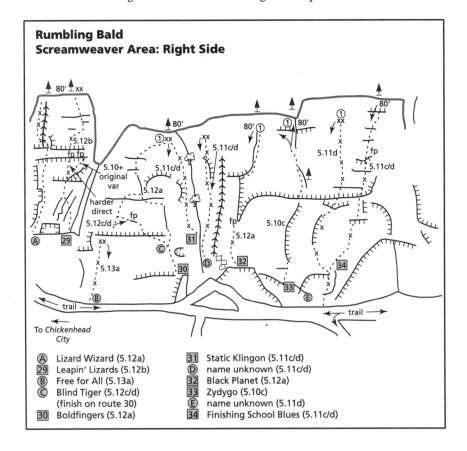

Rumbling Bald
Screamweaver Area: Right Side

Ⓐ	Lizard Wizard (5.12a)	31	Static Klingon (5.11c/d)
29	Leapin' Lizards (5.12b)	Ⓓ	name unknown (5.11c/d)
Ⓑ	Free for All (5.13a)	32	Black Planet (5.12a)
Ⓒ	Blind Tiger (5.12c/d)	33	Zydygo (5.10c)
	(finish on route 30)	Ⓔ	name unknown (5.11d)
30	Boldfingers (5.12a)	34	Finishing School Blues (5.11c/d)

Biff Farrell busts-a-move on the headwall of Leapin' Lizards *(route 29).*

Pitch 1: Either boulder up the overhang to a stance (much harder), or climb an easier crack out right. Move up to a steep hand crack. Exit this and move left to the seam. Devious sequences lead to more hard face climbing and a ledge with a double-bolt belay. (80 feet).

31. Static Klingon   5.11c/d
A great, sporty warm-up for any of the neighboring routes.
    First ascent: Chris Caldwell (1992).
    Start: Just right of *Boldfingers* on the face left of the gully.
    Pitch 1: Easy scrambling over big flakes and briars take you to a good cam placement in the gully. Climb the face to your left past four bolts with a pumpy finish. Double-bolt belay. (80 feet).

32. Black Planet   5.12a
A powerful dyno bars a striking (and all too short) open book.
    First ascent: Doug Reed.
    Start: Off a blocky ledge under the obvious steep corner about 30 feet off the ground and 30 feet left of where the approach trail meets the base.
    Pitch 1: Boulder up to the bolt and throw for an elusive jug and a fixed pin. Stand up, then stem through the awesome corner to a hole. Power out the overhang with jugs, eventually gaining a rappel tree. (80 feet).

33. Zydygo   5.10c
This excellent crescent converts into either a power lieback or jamming test.
    First ascent: Jeep Gaskin, Ralph Fickel, Jeff Burton.
    Start: 10 feet right of *Black Planet.*
    Pitch 1: Climb a short steep section to the crack. Follow until it ends at the roof, then continue via a series of cracks to a cleft.
    Descent: Rappel from an obvious tree. (80 feet).

34. Finishing School Blues   5.11c/d
An overhanging pumpfest with some deceptive moves and pro!
    First ascent: Buddy Brasington.
    Start: *Finishing School* is the right-hand of two bolted lines right of *Zydygo.*
    Pitch 1: Climb up the face past two bolts to a stance below the roof. Hard moves lead past another bolt and a hidden pin to where the angle slackens. Continue to the top and belay from trees. (80 feet).
    Descent: Rappel or walk off.

The Kennel
This area is on a knoll above the main Screamweaver Area cliff line. Hike right and uphill from *Finishing School Blues.* (You can also approach The Kennel by hiking left from the Test Pilots Area.) The concentration of hard routes at The Kennel is quite impressive, but the area will eventually offer an even greater selection when some projects finally fall.
    Descent: Rappel the routes.

35. Mad Dog   5.11d
A steep, mixed line with unbelievable jugs. Save some juice for the end. Bring a handful of small, 0.4- to 1-inch cams.

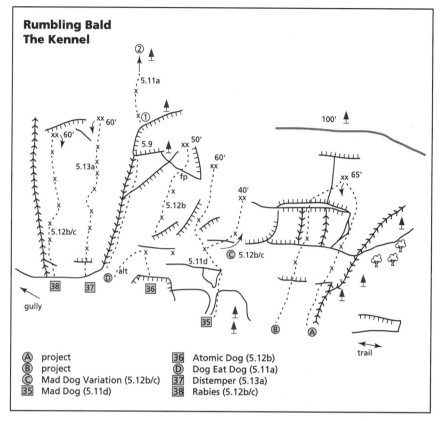

**Rumbling Bald
The Kennel**

Ⓐ project
Ⓑ project
Ⓒ Mad Dog Variation (5.12b/c)
35 Mad Dog (5.11d)

36 Atomic Dog (5.12b)
Ⓓ Dog Eat Dog (5.11a)
37 Distemper (5.13a)
38 Rabies (5.12b/c)

First ascent: Porter Jarrard (1989, ground-up from hooks).

Start: At the top of the gully under an overlap, about 30 feet left of where the approach trail meets the base.

Pitch 1: Wander into position beneath the large roof. Blast over this via big holds, passing two bolts to a flake. Double-bolt anchor. (60 feet).

36. Atomic Dog   5.12b

A crucial hold recently broke on this route leaving it somewhat harder. The jugs are titanic; so is the pump factor leading to the upper crux!

First ascent: Harrison Dekker, Porter Jarrard (1989).

Start: 10 feet left of *Mad Dog*, on the left side of The Kennel.

Pitch 1: Sport. Stick-clip the first bolt, and then crank out the steep wall past two more bolts via the jugs of a lifetime. A bouldery crux protected by a fixed wire leads to a ledge. Double-bolt anchor. (50 feet).

37. Distemper   5.13a

Demands full commitment from the moment you start. With almost nothing easier than 5.12a and still featuring a vicious penultimate crux, this one may put you in a foul mood.

First ascent: Porter Jarrard.

Start: Left of *Atomic Dog*, under a low bulge and 10 feet left of a vegetated off-width.

Pitch 1: Sport. Either stick-clip or use some small cams to surmount the bulge to a stance. Power up the devious face past seven bolts. Double-bolt anchor. (60 feet).

38. Rabies   5.12b/c

A prominent, steep arête that features some incredibly hard moves.

First ascent: Diab Rabie (1998).

Start: 8 feet left of *Distemper.*

Pitch 1: Sport. Stick-clip the first bolt and then fire through steep ground to an angling groove. Five bolts to a double-bolt anchor. (60 feet).

The Cave

The Cave is a small area approximately 200 yards right of *Finishing School Blues.* Instead of bushwhacking up to The Kennel, stay on the same contour lines as the main Screamweaver Area and move right as you're facing the cliff.

Descent: Rappel the routes.

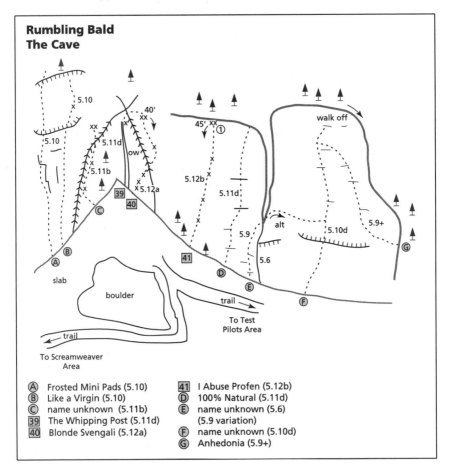

**Rumbling Bald
The Cave**

Ⓐ	Frosted Mini Pads (5.10)	41	I Abuse Profen (5.12b)
Ⓑ	Like a Virgin (5.10)	Ⓓ	100% Natural (5.11d)
Ⓒ	name unknown (5.11b)	Ⓔ	name unknown (5.6)
39	The Whipping Post (5.11d)		(5.9 variation)
40	Blonde Svengali (5.12a)	Ⓕ	name unknown (5.10d)
		Ⓖ	Anhedonia (5.9+)

39. The Whipping Post 5.11d

After placing the lone bolt high in the crack, Eddie Begoon lowered and fired the pitch in one go—despite losing his glasses in the upper roof!

First ascent: Eddie Begoon, Paul Piana (1989, ground-up).

Start: On the obvious off-width left of *I Abuse Profen*.

Pitch 1: Levitate up the burly crack using any means necessary. Clip the bolt and then jam and stem through the upper roof. (40 feet).

40. Blonde Svengali 5.12a

This isn't the most aesthetic route. But the first-ascent team included the well-known Wyoming cowboy, Paul Piana, best known for freeing the *Salathé Wall* on El Capitan.

First ascent: Paul Piana, Eddie Begoon (1989).

Start: Left of *I Abuse Profen*. Start on the *Whipping Post* off-width and then move immediately right.

Pitch 1: Sport. The long moves on the low crux access some fun jug hauling. Four bolts to double-bolt anchor. (40 feet).

41. I Abuse Profen 5.12b

A sustained nightmare of razor edges and thin pockets.

First ascent: Diab Rabie, Scott Greenway.

Start: Where approach trail meets the wall, at the obvious line of bolts on the face.

Pitch 1: Sport. Crimp and stab your way past four bolts to a double-bolt anchor. (45 feet).

Test Pilots Area

For the Test Pilots Area continue past The Cave to a steep shoulder. The route *Test Pilots* is directly above you up the hill. This entire buttress is jam-packed with good lines. Routes 44 through 46 are on the backside of the buttress.

Descent: Rappel the routes.

42. Test Pilots 5.11c

Now that *Test Pilots* has been given a face lift, it is an absolute must-do. The original line went left at the fourth bolt; it is harder if you stay straight.

First ascent: Chris Caldwell, Buddy Price (1987).

Start: In a prominent water groove.

Pitch 1: Sport. Boulder up to an old bolt, then move quickly right for the second. Tenuous face moves lead to a short rest and then to a pumpy face with some tricky sequences. Five bolts to double-bolt anchor. (80 feet).

43. Rocket Science 5.10c

A great mixed line and convenient warm-up for the business on *Test Pilots!* Bring protection up to 0.75 inch.

First ascent: Bruce Burgess (1998).

Start: 10 feet left of *Test Pilots*.

Pitch 1: Climb the short flake past a horizontal to a bolt. Blast up the face past

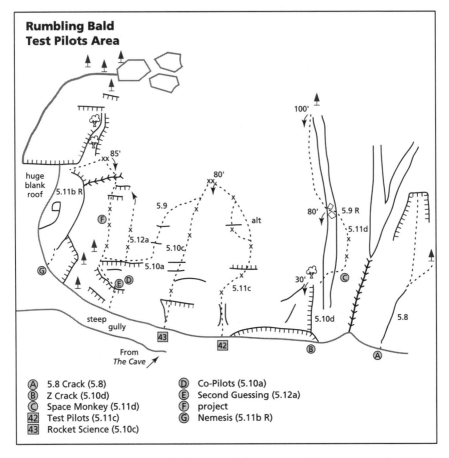

Rumbling Bald
Test Pilots Area

huge blank roof

85'
xx

100'

80'
xx

5.11b R

5.9

alt

80' 5.9 R

5.11d

5.12a

5.10c

5.10a

5.11c

30'

C

steep gully

5.10d

5.8

43

42

B

A

From The Cave

Ⓐ	5.8 Crack (5.8)	Ⓓ	Co-Pilots (5.10a)
Ⓑ	Z Crack (5.10d)	Ⓔ	Second Guessing (5.12a)
Ⓒ	Space Monkey (5.11d)	Ⓕ	project
42	Test Pilots (5.11c)	Ⓖ	Nemesis (5.11b R)
43	Rocket Science (5.10c)		

two more bolts and some textbook TCU placements until you can trend right for the anchor atop *Test Pilots*. (80 feet).

44. Backdoor Man   5.12a

A great choice on warm days, with bold climbing on a steep wall splintered with cracks.

First ascent: Doc Bayne, Nick Williams (1992, ground-up).

Start: Scramble left around the buttress to find the backside routes. This line begins in steep broken rock under some thin cracks.

Pitch 1: Climb past some broken rock to a steep face with excellent long moves and two bolts. Move past a third bolt and into the steep, right-facing corner. Finagle a key small cam and yard for the top.

Descent: Scramble left and rappel from tree. (100 feet).

45. Arch Rival (aka Flakes of Wrath)   5.11b/c

Another good bet on warmer days, this intimidating line tackles a smorgasbord of hard moves.

First ascent: Keith Reynolds, Buddy Brasington (1991).

Start: Under a wide flake, 15 feet left of *Backdoor Man*.

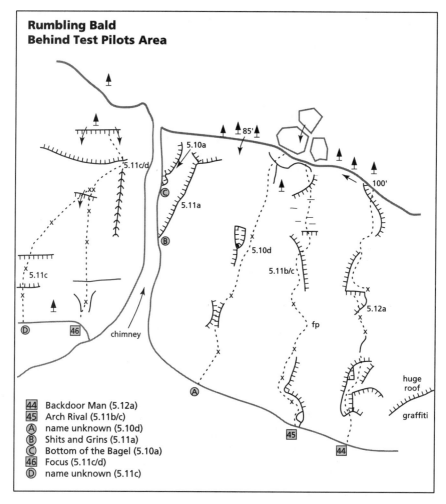

**Rumbling Bald
Behind Test Pilots Area**

5.11c/d

5.10a

85'

100'

5.11a

C

B

5.10d

5.11b/c

5.11c

5.12a

fp

D

46

chimney

huge
roof

graffiti

44 Backdoor Man (5.12a)
45 Arch Rival (5.11b/c)
Ⓐ name unknown (5.10d)
Ⓑ Shits and Grins (5.11a)
Ⓒ Bottom of the Bagel (5.10a)
46 Focus (5.11c/d)
Ⓓ name unknown (5.11c)

45

44

Pitch 1: Climb up to the first, high bolt, then ape past two more to a stance at a fixed pin. Trend left passing the last bolt to gain the left-facing arch. Power your way up this until you can exit onto a pedestal. Continue up the excellent face via horizontals.

Descent: Move left and rappel from the tree. (100 feet).

46. Focus   5.11c/d

Excellent face climbing leads to an impossibly thin crux just feet from the top.

First ascent: Doug Reed.

Start: On the buttress behind *Arch Rival*, off a ledge just right of a tree.

Pitch 1: Climb up the face past three bolts and a double-bolt anchor (use for pro) to a featureless roof. Load up on pro and climb delicate moves to a ledge. (90 feet).

Comatose Area and Cereal Buttress (Left)

This is a broken area of slabby rock split by many gullies and downed trees. It is also popular among the local rednecks as a romantic hideaway. Many additional lines exist

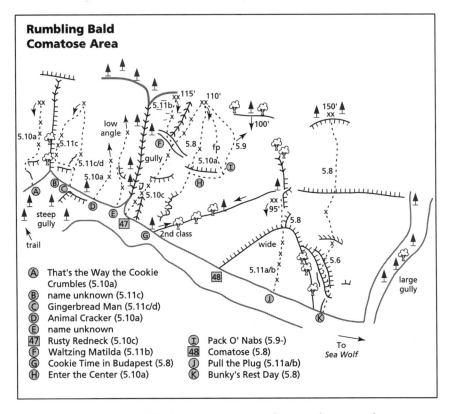

Rumbling Bald
Comatose Area

(A) That's the Way the Cookie
Crumbles (5.10a)
(B) name unknown (5.11c)
(C) Gingerbread Man (5.11c/d)
(D) Animal Cracker (5.10a)
(E) name unknown
[47] Rusty Redneck (5.10c)
(F) Waltzing Matilda (5.11b)
(G) Cookie Time in Budapest (5.8)
(H) Enter the Center (5.10a)

(I) Pack O' Nabs (5.9-)
[48] Comatose (5.8)
(J) Pull the Plug (5.11a/b)
(K) Bunky's Rest Day (5.8)

here in between the established ones—even more than are shown on the accompanying topos. Routes are listed left to right starting at the far-left side of the wall.

Cereal Buttress is part of the area at Rumbling Bald recently acquired by a new landowner, boundaries are marked with blue paint. Please pay special attention to Restrictions and Access Issues at the beginning of this chapter.

Descent: Rappel the routes.

47. Rusty Redneck   5.10c

Thin, aesthetic moves on the arête lead to a long section of fun face climbing.

First ascent: Ian McAlexander, Sean Cobourn, Eric Mullis, Greg Mullis (1993).

Start: Toward far-left side of wall, on a blunt arête immediately right of a gully and uphill from *Comatose*.

Pitch 1: Climb the arête to a stance. Wander up the excellent face. Six bolts to double-bolt anchor. (110 feet).

48. Comatose   5.8

A classic moderate featuring a long, arching corner and a wide crack tussle. Double ropes are helpful; at least one 4-inch piece is mandatory.

First ascent: Jeff Burton, Matt Hodges.

Start: At an obvious right-arching corner, about 0.1 mile from where the approach trail meets the base.

Pitch 1: Lieback, jam, and cruise the corner to where it gets wide. Pull the lip at a notch and then wander up the face to a hole. Double-bolt anchor. (95 feet).

49. Sea Wolf   5.8 R

A blunt prow with great face climbing, widely spaced protection, and exposure. Bring small wires (RPs) and a light rack.

First ascent: Thomas Kelley, Bruce Burgess (1991, ground-up).

Start: 10 feet left of a large gully separating the Comatose Area from Cereal Buttress.

Pitch 1: Wander up the face to a ledge, then aim for a vegetated corner. Climb out and over a flake with a bolt, then continue up the run-out face past two additional bolts.

Descent: Rappel from trees. (150 feet).

50. White Fang   5.12c

The approach is a hassle, but oh-what-a-feature! Super-sized, this would be one of the best arêtes anywhere.

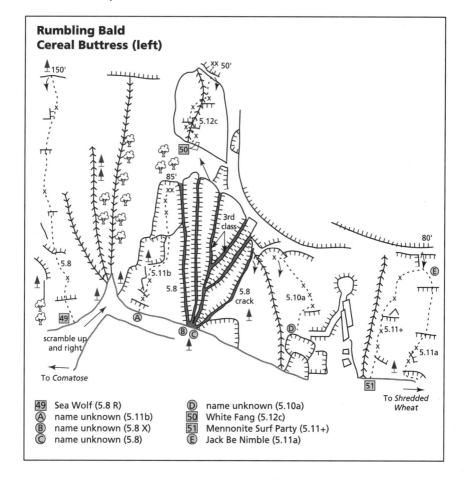

**Rumbling Bald
Cereal Buttress (left)**

49 Sea Wolf (5.8 R)	Ⓓ name unknown (5.10a)
Ⓐ name unknown (5.11b)	50 White Fang (5.12c)
Ⓑ name unknown (5.8 X)	51 Mennonite Surf Party (5.11+)
Ⓒ name unknown (5.8)	Ⓔ Jack Be Nimble (5.11a)

First ascent: Bruce Burgess, Thomas Kelley (1991, ground-up).
Start: Either climb up from the left via the third-class gully, or climb one of several lower routes.
Pitch 1: Sport. Wheedle your way out the arête and past a powerful low crux. Four bolts to double-bolt anchor. (50 feet).

51. Mennonite Surf Party   5.11+
A devilishly thin arête that should be on any slab climber's agenda.
First ascent: Mike Artz, Doug Reed, Eddie Begoon (1987, ground-up).
Start: On the slabby right side of an obvious arête, just above the approach trail.
Pitch 1: Sport. Make delicate moves to gain the first bolt (stick-clip recommended). Slap, lieback, and totter your way past four bolts to slings around a boulder. Bring a 3- or 3.5-inch piece to back up the anchor if you decide to run laps. (80 feet).

Cereal Buttress (Right) and Cereal Wall
Easily the most popular area at Rumbling Bald, the Cereal Buttress and Cereal Wall are actually a collection of walls and buttresses on the far eastern edge (right side) of Rumbling Bald. Visitors will find an excellent assortment of single-pitch crack climbs, including *Fruit Loops* and *Shredded Wheat* on the buttress itself, as well as multipitch classics like *Wild Hickory Nuts* on Cereal Wall.

For the main Cereal Wall, hike right (east) along the buttress and follow a faint climbers' trail about 0.1 mile to the base.

This area of Rumbling Bald has a new landowner; boundaries are marked with blue paint. Please pay attention to Restrictions and Access Issues at the beginning of this chapter.

Descent: Rappel the routes.

52. Shredded Wheat   5.11a
This undisputed classic would be right at home on the Cookie Cliff in Yosemite.
First ascent: Jeep Gaskin, Don Hunley (1977).
Start: Follow the approach trail about 100 feet right after it meets the base and start off a ledge 25 feet above the trail.
Pitch 1: Jam, lieback, and balance your way up the gradually thinning finger crack to a double-bolt anchor. (90 feet).

53. Fruit Loops   5.7
Another three-star crack climb. The rarely-climbed second pitch is funky and excellent.
First ascent: Brad Shaver, Grover Cable (1976).
Start: 50 feet right of *Shredded Wheat* in the low crack.
Pitch 1: Pinch and jam the short steep crack using the occasional thank-god handhold. Continue past a slabby section to a final flaky area and a double-bolt belay in a chimney. (5.7; 80 feet).
Pitch 2: Chimney and stem your way up the slot, eventually emerging onto a lower-angled face. Continue to some pods and a fixed rappel station. (5.7; 70 feet).

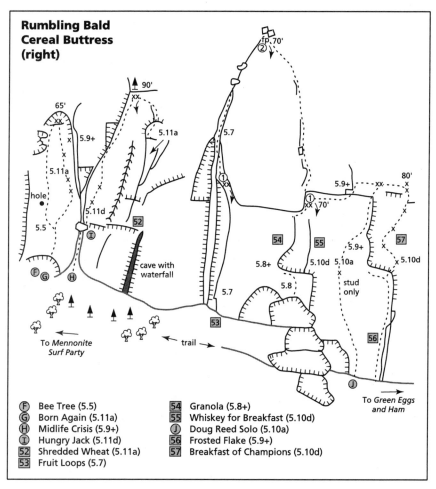

**Rumbling Bald
Cereal Buttress
(right)**

Ⓕ Bee Tree (5.5)
Ⓖ Born Again (5.11a)
Ⓗ Midlife Crisis (5.9+)
Ⓘ Hungry Jack (5.11d)
52 Shredded Wheat (5.11a)
53 Fruit Loops (5.7)

54 Granola (5.8+)
55 Whiskey for Breakfast (5.10d)
Ⓙ Doug Reed Solo (5.10a)
56 Frosted Flake (5.9+)
57 Breakfast of Champions (5.10d)

54. Granola   5.8+

Leaders should be solid at the grade before racking up on this potential bone breaker.

First ascent: Brad Shaver (1976).

Start: 15 feet right of *Fruit Loops*, off a sharp flake.

Pitch 1: Balance your way up to the low roof. Move left along this and pull the left-facing flake onto the face above. Continue up to the inside of the hanging corner with a double-bolt belay. (5.8+; 70 feet).

Pitch 2: Climb broken cracks up the casual face to the same fixed rap station as *Fruit Loops*. (5.7; 70 feet).

55. Whiskey for Breakfast   5.10d

With modern microgear, this highly recommended variation is a reasonable endeavor. Bring small wired nuts or "slider" nuts.

First ascent: Sean Cobourn, Shane Cobourn, Wes Love (1983).

Start: Same as *Granola*.

Frank Carus inserts perfect fingerlocks on Shredded Wheat *(route 52).*

Pitch 1: Climb the slab to the roof and move right until you are underneath the flake. Power lieback your way up the face with the help of some key edges. Double-bolt belay. (5.10d; 70 feet).

Pitch 2: Move out right to the short roof crack. Vault over this and trend right to an old double-bolt anchor. Either rappel here or continue to the anchor over *Breakfast of Champions.* (5.9+; 50 feet).

56. Frosted Flake   5.9+

Bring extra 3- and 3.5-inch pieces for this stunning, pumpy, left-facing corner.

First ascent: Brad Shaver, Grover Cable (1976).

Start: 25 feet right of *Whiskey for Breakfast* in the low crack and corner system.

Pitch 1: Saunter up the easy, low corner to the roof. Move left out this, eventually pulling into a strenuous lieback. Get some pro and book it for better holds. Rappel from old double-bolt anchor or the anchor over *Breakfast of Champions*. (80 feet).

Bryan Haslam on the Daliesque-patterned rock of Granola *(route 54)*

57. Breakfast of Champions   5.10d

Awesome, thin face climbing that is also quite exciting. Probably not a good way
to start your day. Many parties use double ropes to get protection in the *Frosted
Flake* corner.

First ascent: Eddie Begoon, Mike Artz (1987).

Start: On *Frosted Flake*.

Pitch 1: Climb the crack until you can clip the first bolt out right. Trend up
and left to the second bolt (hard, scary clip), then angle back right past two more
bolts to a double-bolt belay. (80 feet).

58. Green Eggs and Ham   5.12a/b

Bail slings that usually adorn the low bolts attest to this route's difficulty and allure.

First ascent: Tripp Halbkat, Mark Owen, Pascal Robert (1990).

Start: Follow a faint trail about 0.1 mile right of *Breakfast of Champions* and
contour around to the buttress's backside to find an arête.

Pitch 1: Sport. Crimpers lead out to the arête, where a few vicious moves gain a
big ledge. Climb past three bolts aiming for the tree ledge. Five bolts total. (80 feet).

59. Captain Crunch   5.10d

No seasoned 5.10 crack climber will be able to walk past this beauty. The steep, locker
jams on the upper section are particularly memorable. Bring extra 3- or 4-inch gear.

First ascent: Jeep Gaskin, Brad Shaver (1976).

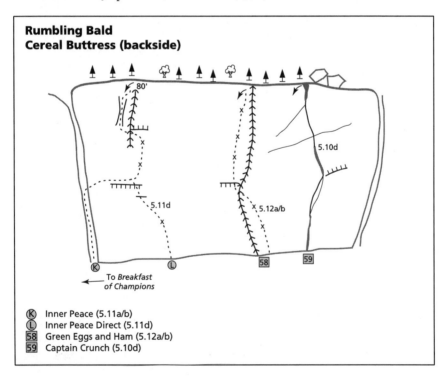

**Rumbling Bald
Cereal Buttress (backside)**

Ⓚ Inner Peace (5.11a/b)
Ⓛ Inner Peace Direct (5.11d)
58 Green Eggs and Ham (5.12a/b)
59 Captain Crunch (5.10d)

Start: 40 feet right of *Green Eggs and Ham.*

Pitch 1: Climb the wide crack with some face holds to a loose block. Step left around this to gain the overhanging crack through the headwall. Jam to the top. (80 feet).

60. Instant Surreal   5.10c/d R

Don't blow it at the first crux of this mini mind bender. An attentive belay is imperative.

First ascent: Thomas Kelley, Ralph Fickel (1991).

Start: Off a grassy ledge opposite *Captain Crunch.*

Rumbling Bald Cereal Wall

Ⓐ Brunch at the Club (5.11d, A0)
Ⓑ name unknown (5.12)
60 Instant Surreal (5.10c/d R)
61 Nut n' Homo (5.10b; 5.8 R)
62 Wild Hickory Nuts (5.11b)
63 Moosehead (5.11b/c)
64 Battle Creek Bulge (5.11d)
65 Snap, Crackle, and Pop (5.11b)
Ⓒ Well Balanced Breakfast (5.11)
Ⓓ Unfinished Breakfast (5.9 R)
Ⓔ Mitey Fine (5.9)

Pitch 1: Thin edges and sloping dishes lead past the lower bolts. Clip the last one and make another long runout to a good crack with a tree. Ignore the bolt studs and set up a natural belay. (100 feet).

61. Nut n' Homo   5.10b (5.8 R)
One of the longest routes at Rumbling Bald and the easiest way to summit this impressive eastern edge of the mountain.

First ascent: Thomas Kelley, John Tainio (1989).

Start: 25 feet right of *Instant Surreal,* on a slab just left of a leaning tree.

Pitch 1: Boulder up easy rock to a narrow ledge at 30 feet, and continue past a short overlap to the first of two bolts. Traverse left to a belay in the good crack (same as *Instant Surreal*). (5.8 R; 100 feet).

Pitch 2: Climb up into the arching roof, traverse left, and roll around onto the face. Bypass a fixed belay (used on the descent) and continue traversing left along good ledges or cracks to the chimney. Follow this to a huge mossy ledge with a tree. (5.7; 120 feet).

Pitch 3: Climb up discontinuous seams and cracks to a ledge. (5.10b; 70 feet).

Pitch 4: Move to the right side of the ledge, then finagle up past a slot to the summit. (5.9; 80 feet). *Note:* It is also possible to wander slightly left to the summit.

Descent: Rappel 150 feet from double bolts above *Moosehead* to the belay station bypassed on pitch 2. Rappel 170 feet from there.

62. Wild Hickory Nuts   5.11b
Sustained climbing and brilliant position make this one of the best routes at Rumbling Bald, especially when combined with *Instant Surreal.*

First ascent: Thomas Kelley, John Tainio (1989, ground-up).

Start: Same as either *Instant Surreal* or *Nut n' Homo.*

Pitches 1 and 2: Climb either route to the mossy tree ledge.

Pitch 3: Step up onto the steep headwall aiming for a bolt. Clip it and move right to a shallow crack system. Continue past two more bolts until the difficulty eases and you gain a belay on the same ledge as *Nut n' Homo.* (5.11b; 75 feet).

Pitch 4: Finish up *Nut n' Homo.* (5.9; 80 feet).

63. Moosehead   5.11b/c
The two final pitches of 5.11 face climbing make this a testy and intimidating affair.

First ascent: Doc Bayne, Jon Miller (1991, ground-up).

Start: On *Instant Surreal* or *Nut n' Homo.*

Pitches 1 and 2: Climb to the fixed belay midway across the second pitch of *Nut n' Homo.*

Pitch 3: Climb straight up on crimpers to a fierce sequence past a bolt. Belay with medium cams on a small shelf. (5.11b/c; 50 feet).

Pitch 4: Step left off the belay and climb past horizontals to a bolt. Trend up and left through a steep section protected by small TCUs. Continue to a bowl with a bolt. Move far to the left to circumvent a blank section, and then trend back right to a double-bolt belay. (5.11b/c; 100 feet).

64. Battle Creek Bulge   5.11d

This menacing face has no outrageous moves, but it's a cumulative pump capped by a balls-to-the-wall finish. Bring triples in 0.5- to 1-inch cams.

First ascent: Bruce Burgess, Thomas Kelley (1992, ground-up).

Start: On *Instant Surreal* or *Nut n' Homo.*

Pitches 1 and 2: Climb to the fixed belay midway across the second pitch of *Nut n' Homo.*

Pitch 3: Climb up and right about 40 feet to a bulge near the base of a faint, left-rising corner. Pull the bulge and continue up the left-rising feature for another 20 feet. Follow the line of bolts through a sustained face to a slab. Continue to fixed belay. (130 feet).

65. Snap, Crackle, and Pop   5.11b

Though it has a reputation for brittle flakes on the crux pitch, this is another stunning multipitch line. Double ropes recommended.

First ascent: Thomas Kelley, Mark Stroud, Sam Stevenson, John Tainio (1990, ground-up).

Start: At a low-angled corner right of *Nut n' Homo.*

Pitch 1: Climb the corner past a small roof to gain a tree ledge with some loose flakes. (5.8; 100 feet).

Pitch 2: Scramble up the flakes to two overlaps separated by a fixed pin. Climb up the exposed face past three bolts, angling slightly left, to a series of horizontals. Double-bolt belay on the right side of a roof. (5.10a; 100 feet).

Pitch 3: Climb past a bolt and through a notch in the roofs to gain the upper headwall. Spectacular face climbing leads to a bolt, where you can step right to lower-angled ground. Continue past one run-out section to a ledge with a bolt and then on to the summit. (5.11b; 120 feet).

7. LOOKING GLASS ROCK _____

Climbing type: Multipitch traditional
Rock type: Granite
Height: Up to 500 feet
Number of routes: Approximately 180 (78 this guide)
Season: Year-round
Camping: Camping is allowed anywhere in Pisgah National Forest so long as you are 1,000 feet (or more) from the road or in designated campsites. The USFS Davidson River Campground (fee) on US 276 across from Pisgah Ranger Station offers full amenities (see appendix B).

The large expanses of exposed granite at Looking Glass Rock offer an incredible amount of variety to the visiting climber. "The Glass" is a nearly 500-foot dome thrust up into densely vegetated Pisgah National Forest near Brevard. It holds Grade V hook and head nightmares on the North Side, mellow cracks on the South Face, and the

Hidden Wall
and North Side

Nose Area

Sun Wall

South Side

FR 475B

Overview of Looking Glass Rock as seen from the Blue Ridge Parkway

infamous perplexing eyebrows at the Nose Area and Sun Wall. But this is only scratching the surface. The countless faces and coves around the base of Looking Glass Rock will provide a lifetime of exploration for even the most dedicated climbers.

History

Looking Glass Rock is certainly the best-known climbing area in North Carolina and in the South in general. It would not be a huge stretch to say that it might offer the most variety of any crag east of the Mississippi. Strong words, you say? Well, consider where else you can climb true multiday, granite, big wall routes that require a full arsenal of aid skills, jam hundreds of feet of splitter cracks, smear and pull up 500-foot walls of eyebrows at every difficulty level, and crimp up desperate face-climbing test pieces. Somehow despite all of this potential, climbing development at Looking Glass was a bit late to arrive even by eastern standards.

When Bob Watts finally stood atop *The Nose* in December of 1966 to belay Steve Longenecker and Bob Gillespie up the last pitch, more well-known eastern venues like the Gunks, Cathedral Ledge, and Seneca Rocks had already pushed into the ethereal realm of 5.10 and were knocking at the door of 5.11. These accomplishments had obvious import, but Looking Glass remained off the map for the rest of the climbing world. The locals could not have been happier. Prolific Looking Glass activist Jeep Gaskin recalls, "we all reveled in our little climbing backwater knowing that what we were doing was good and that the world did not care. We just gave it the finger and kept going."

While most climbing areas can neatly divide their histories into little blocks of time that coincide with spurts of motivated development, the development at Looking Glass might best be subdivided into waves of strong-willed characters. The first wave—the three *Nose* pioneers, along with Brad Shaver, Will Fulton, Bob Mitchell, Jim McEver, and a handful of others—pushed the standards of both aid and free routes at The Glass well into the mid-1970s. To a man, they all credit Bob Mitchell as the dominant climber of the generation. Bob Gillespie remembers that Mitchell never really fell, even on the hardest routes of the day. While he was obviously climbing at a level beyond most of his peers' abilities, he really never was climbing at his own limit. Such drive brought about free routes like *Dum Dee Dum Dum, Sundial Crack,* and fine aid routes like *The Odyssey* and *The Seal.*

Brad Shaver was another very talented climber from the early days who ran the first climbing shop in the South, Mountaineering South in Asheville. By the age of twenty he had climbed extensively across the United States, soloed *Tis-sa-ack* on Half Dome, and made lasting friendships with other great climbers like Henry Barber. While he contributed to fewer first ascents at The Glass than some others, he was certainly a catalyst for climbing more difficult routes as he brought an outside perspective into the area. Shaver, tragically, perished on a Himalayan expedition in 1978 before he could fully reach his potential, but not before he pushed others to do so here in western North Carolina.

Another first waver, Jim McEver, also deserves note because in the early 1970s he almost single-handedly developed the now very popular South Side at Looking Glass with the help of Ron Cousins, Stan Wallace, Art Williams, and a few others. Keeping the area relatively low-key, he managed to head in there over and over again to pluck gems like *Second Coming, Rat's Ass, Gemini Crack, Bloody Crack,* and several more appealing lines. McEver was notably committed to the switch to hammerless free climbing, which was under great debate at the time. "We never carried hammers, pins, or bongs," he said. "Not only did I not carry it with me, I did not even have it in my car. I left all that shit at home."

The frenetic first-ascent activity from 1977 to 1988 signaled the second wave and would yield the bulk of the routes that we see on Looking Glass today. The scene during this time was considerably larger than before, yet was still comfortably intimate. Characters the likes of Jeep Gaskin, Monty Reagan, Whitney Heuermann, Doc Bayne, Chris Caldwell, and Bob Rotert dominated route development in this era. While they took their cues from the drive and ethical legacy of their predecessors, they took their first ascents to levels that few can imagine even today. None led the charge any more than Jeep Gaskin, whose name appears on the first ascent of over a third of the routes on The Glass. He started his assault on the upper levels of free-climbing difficulty with the first free ascent of *The Odyssey* in 1977 with Don Hunley, and *The Womb* with Joe Myers.

Gaskin had been deeply impressed by the 1976 visit of Henry Barber, who shattered all conceptions of what was possible with his back-to-back free ascents of *Out to Lunch* and *Cornflake Crack,* both longstanding aid routes. Gaskin remembers "watching this otherwise ordinary guy launch himself at another chunk of The Glass. On *Out to Lunch,* Barber went up to the roof, hung off that rattly fist jam, and tried throwing a hex into the vertical crack above. I could not believe what I was seeing! The hex finally stuck on the exact throw when Henry came off. So there he was hanging from a hand wrapped in perlon, his feet dangling. He pulled up the rope and made the clip, and finished the route."

After a wild night of partying in Asheville, the group went back out to the North Side, where Barber asked about freeing *Cornflake*. Gaskin continues, "Freeing such a demanding aid route was beyond our comprehension but we had already witnessed things from Barber that we could not have imagined so why the hell not? Henry placed a tiny Crack-n' Up above the flaring jam that opens the route, and as soon as he stepped out onto the smears his feet blew. There was nothing else between him and the ground, so we were sure he was going onto his head in the rhodos, but the Crack-n' Up held. Henry became hysterical, lowered off, and took a solitary walk toward the hidden wall. He came back and blew the route away. After the first pitch it was hard to follow [the team's] progress, but I remember shouts of encouragement and crows of pleasure."

Taking inspiration from Barber's whirlwind visit, Gaskin went on to establish or help establish classic hard test pieces like *Aerospace Cadet, Labia, Legendary Nuclear Bomb, Danger Dog,* and *Glass Menagerie,* among others. Not to be outdone, Rotert, Reagan, and Bayne were also hard at work—often with Gaskin—on establishing routes that, even by modern standards, are as difficult as they were audacious. Couple the fiercely adhered-to ground-up ethic with rock that does not lend itself to 5.13s, and you end up with a climbing era that placed a premium on head space over brawn. Bayne, an active local who was establishing cutting-edge routes until his tragic death in 2001, related that the conditions dictated that the "only logical way to push the limits was to see how far out you were willing to push the boat."

While these difficult and committing free climbs were appearing at The Glass, a tight fraternity of devoted and talented aid climbers were working their way up the imposing sheer walls of the North Side. Aid climbers were few and far between in the South in the 1980s, therefore there are few climbs on this face whose first ascents do not belong to the trio of Whitney Heuermann, Jeff Burton, and Forrest Gardner. Starting in the early 1980s, these three developed their skills and confidence establishing routes like *Secret Alloys, Chieftains of Creep, Creatures of Waste,* and *Brain Wall* that are standard trade routes today. Such experience led to more daring lines and eventually to such standard-setting (or one might argue death-defying!) lines as *Brain Dead, Panic Value, Carolina Hog Farm,* and *Grand Slam of Sheep*—all of which have significant sections of very strenuous aid over terrain that would likely result in serious injury in the event of a fall. Packing a lot of bang-for-the-buck into its 500 feet, the North Side remains the premiere eastern aid-climbing venue offering a bit of everything for both first timers and seasoned wall vets alike.

While the pace of route development at The Glass slowed in the 1990s, Looking Glass was by now firmly established as one of the holy shrines of North Carolina traditional climbing. Climbers were coming from all over the East to sample a stunning array of routes at all grades. Yet, true to the area's exploratory precedents, the late 1990s brought a new wave of climbers with a fresh perspective who were not content to repeat routes time and time again. Armed with triple sets of small TCUs that opened up many new options for protection, they began sniffing around the "blank" faces that earlier climbers had dismissed as unprotectable. Combining the standard ground-up ethic with a willingness to drill bolts where needed on the lead has allowed Bruce Burgess, Andy Kluge, Bryan Haslam, and Harrison Shull to add well over a dozen high-quality routes in the past several years. Some of the gems from this crop that are worth seeking out are *Hidden Agenda, Irish Jig, Mainline Express, Bombelay, Prey,* and *Liquid Anal Crowbar.*

The latest wave's willingness to bolt where needed, however, was taken to its illogical and unfortunate extreme when the well-protected 5.5 first pitch of *Sundial Crack* and the 5.8 *Gemini Crack* sprouted bolts overnight. The added bolts did not last thirty-six hours, but they left the climbing community shaken and concerned about a new generation of climbers weaned from gyms to outdoor sport areas. It is hoped that all climbers will realize that retro-bolting established traditional lines has no place in North Carolina and certainly no place at The Glass. This huge dome of eyebrow-laced granite always has been a place where climbers come to tune into the inner strengths and desires that fuel their climbing ambitions, and it will hopefully remain so for generations to come.

Weather and Climbing Season
The best season for the South Side, Sun Wall, and Nose Area runs September through May. During the heat of the summer, you will find some shady relief at the North Side and Hidden Wall. The South Side can stay wet for days after a rain while other faces dry more quickly.

Restrictions and Access Issues
There are seasonal closures of sections of the North Side for peregrine falcons. Contact the Pisgah Ranger District or check the websites listed in appendix B for the closure dates and affected routes.

Emergency Services
Call 911. The closest phone is at the Pisgah Forest Wildlife Education Center. Climbers should be self-rescue ready and able to get an injured climber to the ground where the waiting rescue squad members will be ready to help. The Transylvania Community Hospital in Brevard is the closest medical facility (see appendix C).

Gear
A standard North Carolina rack will work well at Looking Glass, but the infamous eyebrows can eat up your collection of small to medium cams. Also consider bringing Tri-Cams, as they work very well in flaring eyebrows where cams will not.

Getting There
A few miles east of Brevard, or 25 miles southwest of Asheville, locate the intersection of NC 280 and US 276; take US 276 north. After passing through the large stone "gates" marking the entrance to the Pisgah National Forest, continue about 5 miles to a road on the left (FR 475) that is signed for the Pisgah Forest Wildlife Education Center. Follow FR 475 a few miles past the left turn into the education center—the road turns to gravel here and soon splits. Take the right-hand fork—

FR 475B—and drive a little over 1 mile to the first big parking area signed "Slickrock Falls Trail." Park here for the South Side. For the Nose Area and Sun Wall, continue on FR 475B another 1.8 miles to a parking area on the right. The trailhead is signed "Sunwall Trail." For the North Side and Hidden Wall, continue along FR 475B about 0.18 mile to a small pullout on the right that is bordered by landscape timbers and has a wooden kiosk.

Approach

For the Hidden Wall and the North Side: From the parking area on FR 475B, hike down into the grassy clearing and cut left to follow an old logging grade. Almost immediately, look for a worn footpath that veers right onto a single-track trail through the woods. Follow this trail about 20 minutes to the base of the wall.

For the South Side: From the parking area at Slickrock Falls, hike approximately 0.7 mile to the base of the rock. Please stay on the trail that switchbacks up to the base rather than beelining straight up to the cliff—this will help reduce erosion. This main trail meets the base of the wall near *Left Up* and *Bloody Crack.*

For the Nose Area: From the parking area on FR 475B, take the trail signed for the "Sunwall" from the parking area approximately 0.4 mile to the rock. You will arrive at the base of the wall at *Sundial Crack.*

For Sun Wall: Start as for the Nose Area, but immediately after the trail passes a large downed tree and you scramble over a large granite slab, look for a much smaller trail that heads out right into the woods at the first left-hand switchback immediately above the granite slab. Take this trail, which contours up and then around the hill to your right and deposits you at the base of *Legendary Nuclear Bomb.* Traverse right around the base of the wall to reach the Sun Wall proper. You can also hike all the way to the base of *Sundial Crack* at the Nose Area and traverse the entire wall to the right.

Routes are numbered 1 to 78 and move counterclockwise around Looking Glass Rock, starting from the left end of the Hidden Wall and finishing at the right end of the South Side.

Hidden Wall

To access the Hidden Wall traverse left along the base of the North Side. The first obvious gully you pass after *The Sperm* will be the descent gully off the top of the North Side. Continue on a trail past a small grungy buttress and through a section of forest with no rock over to the Hidden Wall. The trail hits the wall just uphill from *Carboman* and *Pepper Pot Tube* (topo only).

Descent: Rappel routes noted, or descend the gully to the right.

1. Anne Marie   5.8

It's a bit off the beaten path, but excellent nonetheless.

First ascent: Peter Young, Peter Prandoni.

Start: Farthest-left route on Hidden Wall, 300 feet left of *Tarheels* at a rocky meadow. Scramble left up a vegetated ramp to a spacious ledge below a crack/corner system.

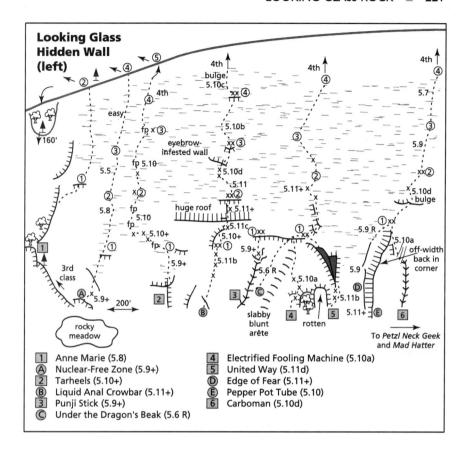

Looking Glass Hidden Wall (left)

1. Anne Marie (5.8)
A. Nuclear-Free Zone (5.9+)
2. Tarheels (5.10+)
B. Liquid Anal Crowbar (5.11+)
3. Punji Stick (5.9+)
C. Under the Dragon's Beak (5.6 R)
4. Electrified Fooling Machine (5.10a)
5. United Way (5.11d)
D. Edge of Fear (5.11+)
E. Pepper Pot Tube (5.10)
6. Carboman (5.10d)

Pitch 1: Head up the initial corner until it gets steep. Then move out right and move up past water-sculpted rock and eyebrows to a ledge. (5.8; 80 feet).

Pitch 2: Stay right of the obvious crack system and follow eyebrows to the top. (5.8; 150 feet).

Descent: Bushwhack down and left to the lowest point possible on a tongue of trees and rappel 160 feet to the ground.

2. Tarheels   5.10+

An excellent but very convoluted route that demands your utmost attention in route finding. Be prepared to spend the better part of a day on this one.

First ascent: Gary Slate, Dave Black, Alan Bartlett (1986, ground-up).

Start: 150 feet left of *United Way* at a left-facing corner.

Pitch 1: Climb the corner and escape right through a crack. Climb the crack for a few moves and then head up left on eyebrows to a gear belay. (5.9+; 100 feet).

Pitch 2: Traverse left past a fixed pin and three bolts before heading up past two more fixed pins to a belay with a single bolt and some gear. (5.10+; 120 feet).

Pitch 3: Leave the belay to the left and clip a bolt. Weave up and a bit left past another bolt and fixed pin before moving right and up to a belay at a bolt and fixed pin. (5.10; 100 feet).

Pitch 4: Head up and left and as the terrain gets easier, head straight up and right past unprotected face to a belay. (5.9; 100 feet).

Pitch 5: Climb off to the top. (5.6; 150 feet).

Descent: Same as for *Anne Marie*.

3. Punji Stick   5.9+

Another good single-pitch route at the Hidden Wall—a little more traffic should clean it up nicely.

First ascent: Bryan Haslam, Harrison Shull (2001, ground-up).

Start: Uphill to the left of *The Slash* in an obvious corner.

Pitch 1: Climb the corner to a bulge, pass a bolt, and head up right to a pod. Continue up through eyebrows to bolted anchors. (70 feet).

4. Electrified Fooling Machine   5.10a

This eyebrowless slab is unique for Looking Glass.

First ascent: Harrison Shull, Bryan Haslam (1999, ground-up).

Start: 25 feet left of *United Way* below obvious bolted slab.

Pitch 1: Climb straight to the second bolt and break left to get out to the third bolt. Then climb much easier terrain to belay at anchors for the first pitch of *United Way* (aka *The Slash*). (100 feet).

5. United Way   5.11d

A long and winding road through steep and technical eyebrows. Bring three to four 0.25-inch cams.

First ascent: Chris Caldwell, Ed Begoon, Kris Kline, Doc Bayne, Bruce Burgess (1986, ground-up). Earlier the same year, Jim MacArthur and Freddie Young made the first ascent of the first pitch, also known as *The Slash*.

Start: 80 feet left of the obvious off-width, *Pepper Pot Tube* (topo only).

Pitch 1: Slab past two bolts to a nice hand crack in a V slot that leads to a bolted anchor. (5.11b; 100 feet).

Pitch 2: Move up and right across two crescent corners to a shallow right-facing corner and a bolt. Climb up and left to another bolt and then follow thin technical brows up and right for about 30 feet to a gear belay in an eyebrow. (5.11d; 80 feet).

Pitch 3: Climb up and left 40 feet to a bolt. Continue up and left through sustained eyebrows and belay when you find a suitable stance with good gear. (5.11a; 100 feet).

Pitch 4: Continue up and right through steep brow climbing. (5.9; 150 feet).

Pitch 5: Climb the final slabs to the top. (5.6; 80 feet).

Descent: Bushwhack right and descend the gully between the Hidden Wall and the North Side.

6. Carboman   5.10d

The first-ascent party reports that the bong and the first belay bolts were already in place. Nothing has been learned of their origins.

First ascent: Jeep Gaskin, Joe Coates (1978).

Start: 15 feet right of the obvious off-width, *Pepper Pot Tube* (topo only).

Pitch 1: Climb the obvious hand crack past a bong to the shared anchors above *Pepper Pot Tube*. (5.10a; 80 feet).

Pitch 2: Traverse right around a bulge and head up to a bolt. Climb up and out right then on incut horizontals to a bolted belay. (5.10d; 90 feet).

Pitch 3: Move up and right to a gear belay. (5.9; 120 feet).

Pitch 4: Same as pitch 3 only a bit easier. (5.7; 150 feet).

Pitch 5: Scramble up easier terrain to the top.

Descent: Bushwhack right and descend the gully between the Hidden Wall and the North Side.

7. Petzl Neck Geek   5.11d, A0

The A0 rating is due to a wild dyno from standing in a sling on a bolt to a jug.

First ascent: Jeep Gaskin, Jon Miller (1989).

Start: First bolted route uphill from *Carboman*.

Pitch 1: Climb to the second bolt; make the A0 move. Then climb up and left past two bolts and pass a slight bulge on the right to another bolt. Climb up and left past three more bolts and head to a belay at a stance. (165 feet).

Descent: Finish on *Carboman* or rappel.

8. The Mad Hatter   5.11a

Unbelievably cool horizontals and crisp edges make this route and its three uphill brethren real treats!

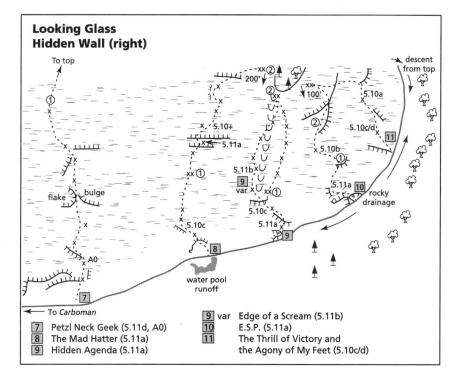

**Looking Glass
Hidden Wall (right)**

7	Petzl Neck Geek (5.11d, A0)
8	The Mad Hatter (5.11a)
9	Hidden Agenda (5.11a)
9 var	Edge of a Scream (5.11b)
10	E.S.P. (5.11a)
11	The Thrill of Victory and the Agony of My Feet (5.10c/d)

First ascent: Thomas Kelley, Bruce Burgess (1990, ground-up).
Start: 150 feet uphill from *Carboman* at a small water runoff pool at the base. The first bolt has a homemade black hanger on it.
Pitch 1: Climb the slab and flakes to the first bolt. Pass two more bolts and then a long stretch of great eyebrows to a belay at a tiny stance. (5.10c; 100 feet).
Pitch 2: Move up to a bolt and into the double-tiered roof. Pull the bulge, clip a bolt, and then move up and right past two horizontals. Continue up past three more bolts and a necky 5.9 section to a bolted belay. (5.11a; 100 feet).

9. Hidden Agenda   5.11a
The first pitch is good, but the two second pitches are even better.
First ascent: Harrison Shull, Bruce Burgess, Pascal Robert (2001, ground-up). In the same year, Burgess, Andy Kluge, and Shull made the first ascent of the second-pitch variation known as *Edge of a Scream*.
Start: 50 feet uphill from *The Mad Hatter* at a flat spot below right-facing flakes.
Pitch 1: Climb over flakes to a bolt. Make some tenuous slab moves to gain a small corner and ramp. Move up the ramp to a bolt and then left to the base of a water groove with a two-bolt anchor. (5.11a; 70 feet).
Pitch 2: Head out right of the dirty groove to good horizontals with surreal Tri-Cam placements. Then climb straight up past five bolts to a two-bolt anchor in the groove. (5.10c; 100 feet). *Variation:* Climb up the left edge of the groove following gear and five bolts. At the fifth bolt, step to the right side of the groove following knobs past one bolt to anchors. (5.11b; 100 feet).

10. E.S.P.   5.11a
Named in honor of Bruce Burgess's unflappable faith that this apparently blank face would yield climbable features. The horizontal edges on this route are nothing short of amazing. Tri-Cams up to no. 2.5 are especially helpful.
First ascent: Bruce Burgess, Kris Kline (1988, ground-up).
Start: 30 feet uphill from *Hidden Agenda* at left-leaning flakes and cracks.
Pitch 1: Move up and left across flakes to a good horizontal above a bulge. Then bust-a-move up and left onto the seemingly blank face. Move up past a short arching flake and then head up and right to a belay ledge. (5.11a; 80 feet).
Pitch 2: Climb the face up and left 50 feet to a bolt. From the bolt climb up and right to a belay ledge. (5.10b; 90 feet).
Pitch 3: Climb the corner up right and then straight up to join the double-bolted belay on *Thrill of Victory*. (5.9+; 45 feet). Pitch 3 can be linked with pitch 2.
Descent: Rappel *Thrill of Victory*. (100 feet).

11. The Thrill of Victory and the Agony of My Feet   5.10c/d
More of the same fantastic edge pulling as *E.S.P.* The fixed gear recently got an up-grade, which should increase this route's appeal.
First ascent: Bruce Burgess, Noel Dent (1988, ground-up).
Start: 30 feet uphill of *E.S.P.* below a bolt and a short left-facing corner.
Pitch 1: Climb up to the bolt and then up into the small left-facing corner. At

LOOKING GLASS ROCK ▲ 225

the top of the corner, head up to a bolt and either move left and up (easier) or climb
directly above the bolt. Then move up and right to a good stance (optional belay).
From the stance, climb up and left across a ramp for another 35 feet to a bolted station. (5.10c/d; 110 feet).

Pitch 2: Moderate yet run-out climbing continues to a tree ledge. (5.8; 120 feet).

Descent: Rappel the route. A 60-meter rope gets you down with stretch.

North Side

The North Side of Looking Glass looks, feels, and climbs as though a little piece of
Yosemite landed in the Southeast. On its left flank, you'll find some of the best pure
crack climbing in the state.

With a few exceptions, the overhanging shield of granite right of *Shrimp Cocktail*
is almost exclusively the domain of the aid climber. The grade IV and V ratings found
here owe more to commitment and difficulty than length. It is also extremely important to note that this guide uses a different and more modern aid ratings system than
previous North Carolina climbing guides (see appendix A for an explanation).

Fixed gear is often left in place at Looking Glass due to the incipient and delicate
nature of many of the rock features. Repeated nailing or heading would quickly yield a
trashed placement that could only be surmounted via the drill. Please take the time to
work through the grades rather than jumping on routes that are too difficult. In the
past, fixed gear has been added to existing aid lines, neutering once-proud aid climbs
such as *Invisible Airways, Remember Appomattox,* and *Glass Menagerie.* If you cannot
repeat a route without adding "chicken bolts," then please do not get on it.

Descent: For all routes, hike left along the faint rhododendron tunnel trail at
the top of the wall until it takes you down the scramble between the Hidden Wall

Overview of the North Side of Looking Glass Rock

and the North Side. Or hike directly up to the tourist trail, turn right, and then over to the *Nose* rappel stations.

12. The Sperm   5.9+

Don't let the chimney on the first pitch deter you from this enjoyable line.

First ascent: Brad Shaver, Bob Mitchell (1971). Shaver and Grover Cable made the first free ascent in 1976.

Start: At the large crack/chimney on far-left side of the North Side, 130 feet left of *Safari Jive.*

Pitch 1: Scamper up to the wide crack and squirm up the chimney to a belay at the base of a right-leaning crack. (5.9; 80 feet).

Pitch 2: Climb the right-leaning crack to its end at bolted anchors. (5.9; 80 feet).

Pitch 3: Climb up the vertical crack and then angle up and left to a bolted belay. (5.9+; 100 feet).

Pitch 4: Climb easier terrain off to the top. (5.7; 100 feet).

13. Pooter the Poacher   5.10c

This is a direct line up to the second-pitch belay anchors of *The Sperm*. Double ropes and extra TCUs recommended.

First ascent: Andy Kluge, Becky Barth (2000, ground-up).

Start: In a short crack at ground level 20 feet right of *The Sperm.*

Pitch 1: Head up the initial crack and then traverse up and left to a short, shallow corner. Pull over this and head back 25 feet right to pull over a bulge with horizontals. Traverse back left and step up onto the face above an overhang. Climb straight up past four bolts to the anchors on top of the second pitch of *The Sperm*. (165 feet).

Pitches 2 through 4: Finish on *The Sperm* or rappel the route.

14. The Womb   5.11b

Good climbing on every pitch, but the third-pitch corner is simply amazing. You'll swear you are in Yosemite!

First ascent: Tony Pidgeon, Steve Longenecker, Bob Gillespie (1970). Jeep Gaskin and Joe Meyers made the first free ascent in 1977.

Start: On face and flakes right of a vegetated crack and 30 feet left of *Safari Jive.*

Pitch 1: Climb to the right of the vegetated crack up to a ledge. (5.8; 65 feet).

Pitch 2: Follow the diagonal crack up and right to a left-facing corner that leads up to an alcove. (5.9; 100 feet).

Pitch 3: Pull out the overhanging off-width into 50 feet of perfect finger locks leading to a belay stance. (5.11b; 80 feet).

Pitch 4: Climb eyebrows to the top. (5.7; 120 feet).

Descent: Instead of descending via the gully, some parties traverse right on the ledge after pitch 3 to a large pine and rappel to the *Safari Jive* ledge.

15. Safari Jive   5.11c

The short finger crack on the second pitch sure packs a pump! If you are top-roping the first pitch, please allow leading parties to climb through.

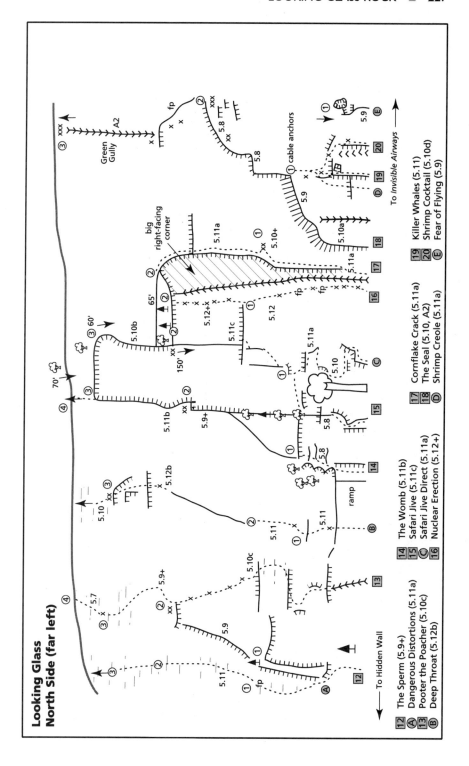

Looking Glass
North Side (far left)

To Hidden Wall

Green Gully A2

fp

To Invisible Airways →

12 The Sperm (5.9+)
Ⓐ Dangerous Distortions (5.11a)
13 Pooter the Poacher (5.10c)
Ⓑ Deep Throat (5.12b)

14 The Womb (5.11b)
15 Safari Jive (5.11c)
Ⓒ Safari Jive Direct (5.11a)
16 Nuclear Erection (5.12+)

17 Cornflake Crack (5.11a)
18 The Seal (5.10, A2)
Ⓓ Shrimp Creole (5.11a)

19 Killer Whales (5.11)
20 Shrimp Cocktail (5.10d)
Ⓔ Fear of Flying (5.9)

Adam Fox, with Carl Bogue belaying, stems the flawless pitch-3 corner of The Womb *(route 14).*

First ascent: Jeep Gaskin, Don Hunley (1979).

Start: In cracks 50 feet left of *Cornflake Crack.*

Pitch 1: Climb the alternating cracks and corners to the tree with slings. Move out right to a short crack and then up to a gear belay at a good stance. (5.8; 110 feet).

Pitch 2: Move up and right to access the finger crack through the bulge. Fire through the overhang and follow the fine crack to the belay ledge. (5.11c; 65 feet).

Descent: Rappel with two ropes from the bolted anchors.

16. Nuclear Erection   5.12+, A2

A stout route that should rank among the hardest free climbs on Looking Glass. Despite our best efforts, we could not confirm that the second pitch of this stunning line has ever received a true redpoint free ascent. Maybe you're the one to do it?!

First ascent: Whitney Heuermann, Lyle Dean, Jeff Burton, Max Bradburn (1991).

Start: At *Cornflake Crack* 20 feet left of *The Seal*.

Pitch 1: Follow the line of bolts, fixed pins, and some gear on the arête just left of *Cornflake Crack*. Belay on natural pro at a large horizontal below the right end of a bulge. (5.12b; 100 feet).

Pitch 2: Exit right around the bulge and head up past five bolts to the huge ledge on top of the Cornflake Buttress. (5.12+?; 65 feet).

17. Cornflake Crack   5.11a

A classic in every sense of the word. Hot Henry Barber snatched this gem out from under the noses of the flabbergasted locals.

First ascent: Art Williams, Mike Holloway (1972). Henry Barber and Ric Hatch did the first free ascent in 1976.

Start: In a huge right-leaning corner 20 feet left of *The Seal*.

Pitch 1: Move up to a tenuous tips undercling that accesses the lieback corner. Follow the corner to a small alcove. Exit the alcove out right to anchors. (5.11a; 80 feet).

Pitch 2: Stem and jam your way up the clean-cut corner to a ledge. (5.11a; 100 feet).

Pitch 3: Climb the dirty corner at the back of the ledge to the top. (5.10b; 60 feet).

Descent: Rappel once on single rope from the pine, and then once on two ropes from bolts above *Safari Jive*.

18. The Seal   5.10, A2

The first pitch is a very popular and classic single-pitch climb in its own right.

First ascent: Bob Mitchell, Will Fulton (1969).

Start: About where the approach trail hits the rock look for a large, right-arching crack under a huge roof.

Pitch 1: Follow the arch up and right to threaded cables for a belay. (5.10a; 90 feet).

Pitch 2: Continue up the corner as it zigzags up and right to a belay at the second set of bolted anchors. (5.8; 95 feet).

Pitch 3: Aid up a crack past old fixed gear to a stance at the base of the Green Gully. Climb the Green Gully to a bolted belay. (A2; 120 feet).

Pitch 4: Scramble past licheny rock to the top. (5.7; 80 feet).

19. Killer Whales   5.11

The best of the three routes below the anchors to *The Seal*.

First ascent: Jim MacArthur, Mike McCormick, Chris Caldwell, Monty Reagan (1986).

Start: In the right-facing corner directly below the anchors to *The Seal*.

Pitch 1: Climb the corner with small wires, TCUs, and few brass nuts to the roof. Exit left over the roof to a stance and climb past two bolts to the cable anchor on *The Seal*. (70 feet).

20. Shrimp Cocktail   5.10d

A bit run-out to the first bolt, but great climbing.

First ascent: Whitney Heuermann, Lyle Dean, Jeff Burton, Max Bradburn.

Start: 10 feet right of *Killer Whales* in a corner.

Pitch 1: Climb the dihedral (harder) or the blunt arête to the left (easier) to the first bolt. Face climb to another bolt before pulling the small roof. Angle up and left to the anchors on *The Seal.* (70 feet).

21. Invisible Airways   5.10c, A2

The arching dihedral on pitch 2 is every bit as sweet as it looks. The first pitch is a popular 5.10c free climb.

First ascent: Whitney Heuermann, Jeff Burton (1984). Eddie Begoon and Mike Artz made the first ascent of the first-pitch variation in 1988; the bolt was added later.

Start: Around the corner to the right from *Killer Whales* is a blank corner with a bolt 20 feet up. Start on the flakes 15 feet left of this corner.

Pitch 1: Climb up past the left-facing flakes to a sling nest. Traverse right along a horizontal to a ledge at the corner. Climb this corner to the ledge and bolted anchor above. (5.10c; 80 feet). *Variation:* A 5.12a direct start climbs the very thin corner past a bolt to join the original line.

Pitch 2: Follow the arching dihedral to a bolted belay. (A2; 80 feet).

Pitch 3: Move up and right over a small bulge. Continue following the rising blocky corner to a bolted belay at its top. (A2; 80 feet).

Descent: Rappel the route. Sixty-meter ropes are nice.

22. Brain Wall   5.10+, A3

A milestone in its day that is now much tamer by modern aid standards. Still, don't take this one for granted.

First ascent: Forrest Gardner, Greg Allen, Bob Ordner (1985).

Start: At the top of pitch 3 of *Invisible Airways.*

Pitch 1: Follow the fixed gear out right and then up through the wildly overhung roof. Climb straight up the headwall to a belay below the corner. (A3; 120 feet).

Pitch 2: Follow the corner as it slowly disappears. Clip a bolt and head up and right to a sloping stance and belay. (A3; 120 feet).

Pitch 3: Scramble off to the top. (5.6, A1; 100+ feet).

23. Waste Not, Want Not   5.12b/c

Just enough gear to keep you off the ground, and spaced out enough to keep your full attention on technical climbing.

First ascent: Kris Kline (1987).

Start: 20 feet right of the *Invisible Airwaves* direct start corner.

Pitch 1: Climb right up a small ramp to a sloping shelf and then up good edges left to a bolt. Move up to a fixed pin at the base of the left-leaning seam. Follow it past two bolts and some brass nuts to the large belay ledge on *Invisible Airwaves.* (80 feet).

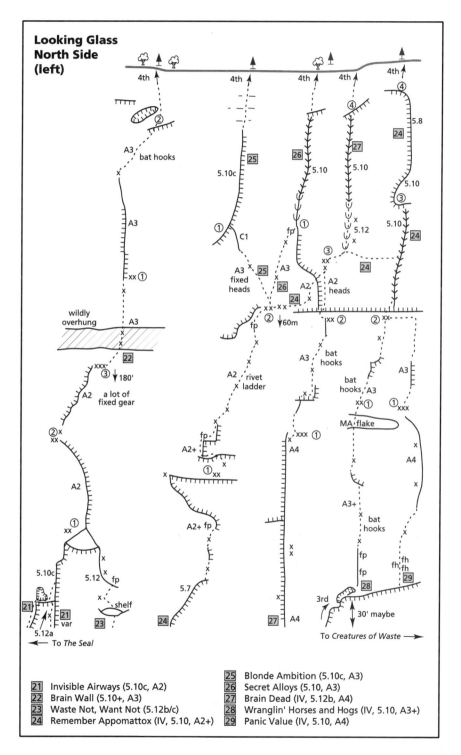

Looking Glass North Side (left)

21 Invisible Airways (5.10c, A2)
22 Brain Wall (5.10+, A3)
23 Waste Not, Want Not (5.12b/c)
24 Remember Appomattox (IV, 5.10, A2+)
25 Blonde Ambition (5.10c, A3)
26 Secret Alloys (5.10, A3)
27 Brain Dead (IV, 5.12b, A4)
28 Wranglin' Horses and Hogs (IV, 5.10, A3+)
29 Panic Value (IV, 5.10, A4)

24. Remember Appomattox (aka Rowins's Route)   IV, 5.10, A2+

If *Glass Menagerie* and *Invisible Airways* are in the bag, then this might be the next candidate on your hit list. The real route name only recently came to light and shows Chris Rowins's sense of humor: He named this route after the Stone Mountain locals renamed his *Bombay Groove* as *Yankee Go Home.*

First ascent: Chris Rowins, Steve Schneider, Bill Fisher (1979).

Start: 30 feet right of *Waste Not, Want Not* at a left-facing ramp/corner.

Pitch 1: Follow the blocky corner up and right until you are below a bolt. Climb up past two bolts to the base of the flexible flake. Ride the flake up and left to a bolt. Traverse the large shelf back to a bolted belay. (A2+; 150 feet).

Pitch 2: Move up and left from the belay following fixed heads and bolts. Move back right and hit the base of a rivet ladder. Follow this rivet ladder to its top and then up a corner and out right to anchors. (A2+; 150 feet).

Pitch 3: Traverse right on fixed gear and bat hooks past the first water groove and up past the pitch-3 anchor on *Brain Dead* onto the second groove. Continue right and climb up this groove to a belay. (A2; 100 feet).

Pitch 4: Continue up the corner/groove to a stance. (5.10; 120 feet).

Pitch 5: Climb to the top. (5.4; 90 feet).

25. Blonde Ambition   5.10c, A3

This fine line went unnoticed for so long due to a dense covering of lichen. It now might be one of the more aesthetic ways to finish *Remember Appomattox.*

First ascent: Toby Grohne, Jeff Weathersbee (1998).

Start: At the top of pitch 2 of *Remember Appomattox.*

Pitch 1: Traverse up and left past a bolt to gain a vertical seam. Continue up a seam on fixed heads to a natural belay at a horizontal crack. (A3; 70 feet).

Pitch 2: Free-climb the shallow corner to the top. (5.10c; 200 feet).

26. Secret Alloys   5.10, A3

Like *Blonde Ambition*, this route is really a direct finish to *Remember Appomattox.* Done the summer after *Remember Appomattox*, Forrest Gardner recalls that they had no circleheads, so he led off the belay on a string of twenty-eight RURPs placed in horizontals. Luckily, today there are fixed heads over this section.

First ascent: Forrest Gardner, Rob Robinson (1980).

Start: Same as *Blonde Ambition.*

Pitch 1: Climb up and right on a field of fixed heads and a bash cam (a Tri-Cam coerced into a small pod!) to a fixed anchor at the base to the groove. (A3; 80 feet).

Pitch 2: Climb the groove to the top. (5.10; 150 feet).

27. Brain Dead   IV, 5.12b, A4

One look at the rusting wires festooning this clean corner should be enough to make you want to puke . . . or maybe it will make you want to grab your aiders and a stiff drink. This route is one of the classic hardman test pieces on Looking Glass.

First ascent: Whitney Heuermann, Jeff Burton, Lyle Dean (1989).

Start: 75 feet right of *Remember Appomattox* in a clean corner above Camp Squalor, the obvious, flat, dirt camping spot.

Pitch 1: Gain the bottom of the shallow corner, and then follow the obvious line of fixed heads passing four bolts to a bolted belay. (A4; 120 feet).

Pitch 2: Continue straight up passing three bolts and fixed heads to a belay in a large horizontal. (A3; 100 feet).

Pitch 3: Pull the roof on some rivets and climb up to a belay. (A2; 50 feet).

Pitch 4: Crank the water runnel to gain a crack in the groove to a natural belay. (5.12b or A1; 120 feet).

Pitch 5: Scramble to the top.

28. Wranglin' Horses and Hogs   IV, 5.10, A3+

This serious endeavor is a two-pitch direct up to the groove at the top of *Remember Appomattox*. It gained some notoriety when it was featured on the cover of *Climbing* magazine in March 1998.

First ascent: Jeff Burton, Whitney Heuermann, Max Bradburn (1989).

Start: At a seam 30 feet up on a ledge and 40 feet right of *Brain Dead*.

Pitch 1: Scramble up and right onto a ledge with large blocks. Follow a seam past fixed RURPs, and then across a blank headwall to a bolted anchor. (A3+; 100 feet).

Pitch 2: Continue following a dark streak past fixed heads to a bolted anchor. (A3; 100 feet).

Pitch 3: Finish straight up to join up with *Remember Appomattox*.

29. Panic Value   IV, 5.10, A4

One experienced local aid aficionado said there are several spots on this route where falling simply is not an option. Another calls it "possibly the most heads-up route on the North Side."

First ascent: Jeff Burton, Whitney Heuermann, Max Bradburn (1990).

Start: 40 feet right of *Wranglin' Horses and Hogs* and 40 feet up on top of flakes. Look for the nest of heads 20 feet up off the flakes.

Pitch 1: Ease past the nest of circleheads and then follow a terrifying string of no. 1 circleheads to a bolt. Continue up another nauseating line of heads in a shallow arching seam past two more bolts to a belay. (A4; 120 feet).

Pitch 2: Climb up past easier aid to a large horizontal that can be traversed left on good gear to the *Horses and Hogs* belay. (A3; 80 feet).

Pitch 3: Finish straight up on *Remember Appomattox*.

30. Creatures of Waste   IV, 5.10, A3

The first pitch is an enjoyable free climb that stays dry in all but the worst rain.

First ascent: Whitney Heuermann, Monty Reagan.

Start: About 40 feet right of *Wranglin' Horses and Hogs* and a bit downhill. Look for easy flakes that traverse up and out right.

Pitch 1: Scramble up and right along the easy flakes to the base of the corner. Pass a bolt and power lieback the corner to a bolted belay. (5.10c; 95 feet).

Pitch 2: Move left a bit and climb up a blank face past two bolts to the base of a seam. Follow the seam to a bolted anchor. (A3; 100 feet).

Pitch 3: Climb up easier aid to the base of a large, dirty water groove. Take this to a bolted anchor. (A2+; 100 feet).

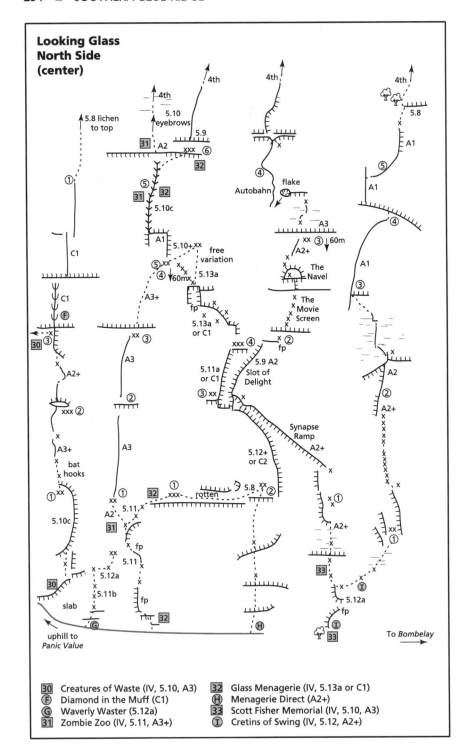

**Looking Glass
North Side
(center)**

30 Creatures of Waste (IV, 5.10, A3)
Ⓕ Diamond in the Muff (C1)
Ⓖ Waverly Waster (5.12a)
31 Zombie Zoo (IV, 5.11, A3+)

32 Glass Menagerie (IV, 5.13a or C1)
Ⓗ Menagerie Direct (A2+)
33 Scott Fisher Memorial (IV, 5.10, A3)
Ⓘ Cretins of Swing (IV, 5.12, A2+)

Pitch 4: Move left to *Horses and Hogs* or climb straight up *Diamond in the Muff* (topo only).

31. Zombie Zoo   IV, 5.11, A3+
A great introduction to harder aid routes at Looking Glass.
>**First ascent:** Whitney Heuermann, Jeff Burton, Max Bradburn, Lyle Dean.
>**Start:** On *Glass Menagerie*.
>**Pitch 1:** Climb *Glass Menagerie* up to the bolt ladder on the first pitch. Move up and left 30 feet to a bolted belay. (5.11, A2; 80 feet).
>**Pitch 2:** Follow a seam past fixed heads to a bolted anchor. (A3; 90 feet).
>**Pitch 3:** Follow the same seam to another bolted belay. (A3; 70 feet).
>**Pitch 4:** Tackle a roof on aid with some trickery heading up and right. Then climb up to a shared belay with *Glass Menagerie*. (A3+; 120 feet).
>**Pitch 5:** Climb up the crack to a horizontal. Traverse left to a large crack. Follow this to the top and make a gear belay. (5.10c; 90 feet).
>**Pitch 6:** Climb straight up over bulge and follow eyebrows to the top. (5.10, A2; 200 feet).

32. Glass Menagerie   IV, 5.13a or C1
The first route to push through to the top of this intimidating wall and the first to be freed as well. This is by far the most traveled aid route in the state and is unfortunately the poster child for how the repeated addition of fixed gear can emasculate a great aid climb.
>**First ascent:** Jeep Gaskin, John Borstelman (1980). First free ascent by Pascal Robert, Arno Ilgner, and Kris Kline in 1995 (team ascent).
>**Start:** Walking right from *Brain Dead* you will start going downhill. Where the ground levels off, go another 20 feet to a few small pines below a shallow right-facing corner with some fixed pins in it.
>**Pitch 1:** Climb the shallow corner to a bolt. Wander generally up left, climbing past two more bolts and a fixed pin. Then a bolt ladder will take you up and right to the belay on a nice ledge. (5.11; 80 feet).
>**Pitch 2:** Traverse a gravelly and somewhat rotten ledge right to a bolted anchor. (5.8; 30 feet).
>**Pitch 3:** Head up the "Open Book" pitch past numerous bolts and fixed gear. At the top of the corner, head left 15 feet and up into a left-facing corner to a belay. (5.12d; 70 feet).
>**Pitch 4:** Head up the crack and corner above to a perch below the roof. (5.11a; 50 feet). *Note:* Pitches 4 and 5 can easily be linked.
>**Pitch 5:** Climb left out the roof past much fixed gear. At the end of the corner, head up to the base of the bolt ladder that leads up and left to a belay. (5.13a or C1; 60–70 feet). *Variation:* At the base of the bolt ladder, the free variation climbs straight up an unprotected face to a bolted belay. (5.13a; 100 feet). Then the next free pitch traverses left along a ledge until you can step down in eyebrows and then over to the anchors on top of the original pitch 5. (5.10+; around 100 feet).
>**Pitch 6:** Climb straight up the cracks 15 feet to a horizontal that leads left 20

feet to a large vertical crack. Follow this crack to its end and traverse right to a bolted belay. (5.10c; 120 feet).

Pitch 7: Pull the bulge above the belay and savor the sweet hand crack above. When the crack peters out, start slabbing to the top (5.9; 165+ feet).

33. Scott Fisher Memorial   IV, 5.10, A3

A relatively new independent line that has received high praise from the early repeats. Todd Wells named the route after his friend, Scott Fisher, who died on Everest the spring before he and Wells had planned to establish this route.

First ascent: Todd Wells (led all pitches), Joe Lackey, Rick Mix, Lee Munson (1997).

Start: 50 feet right of *Glass Menagerie* at a small tree.

Pitch 1: Climb an arching right-facing corner past a fixed pin. Climb the corner to a bolt at the top, where *Cretins of Swing* traverses right. Move out left and up to a short bolt ladder that leads to a corner and a belay above. (A2+; 70 feet).

Pitch 2: Move up the corner to a rivet and then follow the Synapse Ramp up and left for 30 feet to a bolt. Then head up the huge off-width/chimney known as the Slot of Delight to a fixed belay below a bulge. (A2+; 90 feet).

Pitch 3: Cross The Movie Screen on heads, hooks, and rivets to gain The Navel. Climb out the left side of this hole and then up and right to a bolted belay. (A2+; 90 feet).

Pitch 4: Move out left to a rivet then over a bulge to a discontinuous seam. Climb past a pair of rivets and traverse left to access the Autobahn crack that leads 80 feet to a belay. (5.10, A3; 120 feet).

Pitch 5: Follow the crack to its end at a horizontal and step left and up to gain a small right-facing corner. Take this to its end and then weave your way to the top. (5.9, A1; 165 feet).

34. Extracrimpy Chicken   5.11d/12a

A delicacy of southern fried face climbing. If you like sustained, steep, granite face climbing, this one's for you.

First ascent: Bruce Burgess, Andy Kluge (1999).

Start: 45 feet right of *Scott Fisher,* at a large flake shaped somewhat like the state of South Carolina, 8 feet up on a ledge. This is the leftmost of the three bolted routes.

Pitch 1: Scramble up to the flake and traverse left to a shallow right-facing flake with a bolt. Move through high-test pulling straight up past four bolts and a few tiny units to the anchors. (90 feet).

Descent: Lower from anchors.

35. Bombelay   5.11c

An excellent and challenging pitch with great variety.

First ascent: Bruce Burgess, Andy Kluge (1999).

Start: Same as *Extracrimpy Chicken.*

Pitch 1: Climb to the short, right-facing corner directly above the South

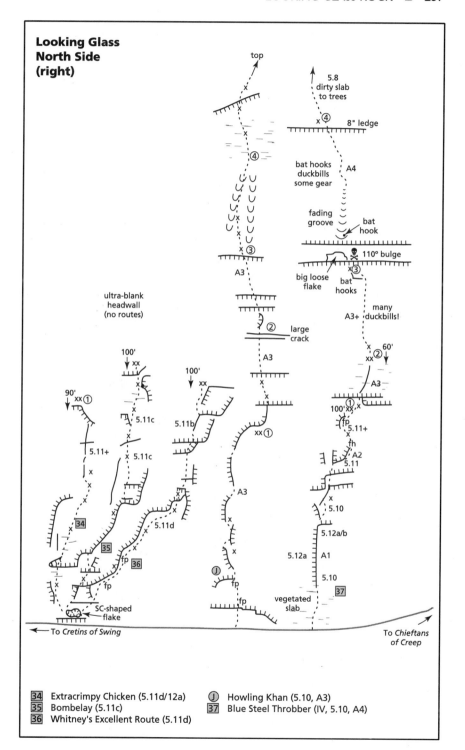

Looking Glass North Side (right)

top

5.8
dirty slab
to trees

8" ledge

bat hooks
duckbills
some gear

A4

fading
groove

bat
hook

110° bulge

big loose
flake

bat
hooks

A3

many
duckbills!

A3+

ultra-blank
headwall
(no routes)

large
crack

A3

60'

A3

100'

100'

5.11c

100'

5.11b

5.11+

A2

5.11+

5.11

90'

5.11c

5.11d

A3

5.10

5.12a/b

5.12a   A1

5.10

34

35

36

37

vegetated
slab

SC-shaped
flake

← To *Cretins of Swing*

To *Chieftans of Creep* →

34	Extracrimpy Chicken (5.11d/12a)	**J**	Howling Khan (5.10, A3)
35	Bombelay (5.11c)	**37**	Blue Steel Throbber (IV, 5.10, A4)
36	Whitney's Excellent Route (5.11d)		

Carolina–shaped flake. Move up past a bolt into a right-facing corner. Lieback the corner up past a bolt, over a roof, and mantel onto the ledge above. Fire past four bolts up the face to the anchors. (100 feet).

Descent: Lower from anchors.

36. Whitney's Excellent Route 5.11d

An overlooked predecessor to the previous two routes that offers stellar climbing reminiscent of Yosemite.

First ascent: Whitney Heuermann (1993).

Start: Same as *Bombelay.*

Pitch 1: Gain the right-arching corner up and right of *Bombelay.* Lieback and undercling out the steep corner past two fixed pins and five bolts. Move up and right where good pump management will bring you over a series of tiered roofs to the anchors. (100 feet).

Descent: Lower from anchors. Due to the lowering angle, this takes every bit of a 60-meter rope. Watch the ends of your rope!

37. Blue Steel Throbber IV, 5.10, A3+

Old circleheads with few, if any, repeats means that you stand a good chance of doing some real aid climbing on this one. Unskilled climbers with a chisel and drill could make this route as tame as *Glass Menagerie* if not careful.

First ascent: Forrest Gardner, David Hoover (1985). Harrison Shull and Bryan Haslam dubbed the first pitch *Straight Up and Stiff* when they did the first free ascent of this pitch in 2001.

Start: At a tall, shallow, right-facing corner 50 feet right of *Whitney's Excellent Route.*

Pitch 1: Follow right-facing corners to a ledge below a roof. Pull the roof and climb up and right across flakes and up to a bolted belay. (A1; 100 feet). *Variation:* Climb it free at 5.12a/b.

Pitch 2: Move out the roof via an arching crack and belay at the end of the crack at a bolt and a fixed hex. (A3; 65 feet).

Pitch 3: Move straight up the face to a large horizontal below an overhang. Belay at old and questionable anchors. (A3+; 120 feet). *Note:* Pitches 2 and 3 are commonly linked into the first pitch.

Pitch 4: Climb out left past a nasty expanding flake and then up the blankness above on heads and hooks to an 8-inch ledge. (A4; 150 feet).

Pitch 5: A dirty scramble gets you off to the top. (5.8; 100+ feet).

38. Chieftains of Creep IV, 5.11a, A3

Forrest Gardner and Rob Robinson showed up on their first trip to the North Side in 1980, and in one week established both *Secret Alloys* and this fine line. Quite the week's work!

First ascent: Forrest Gardner, Rob Robinson (1980).

Start: At the low-angle ramps 50 feet right of *Blue Steel Throbber.*

Opposite: *Bruce Burgess moves through the burly underclings of*
Whitney's Excellent Route *(route 36).*

Looking Glass
North Side (far right)

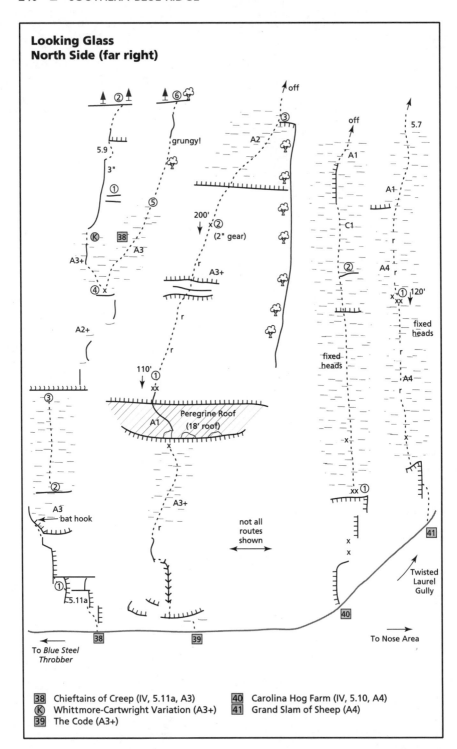

38 Chieftains of Creep (IV, 5.11a, A3)
Ⓚ Whittmore-Cartwright Variation (A3+)
39 The Code (A3+)

40 Carolina Hog Farm (IV, 5.10, A4)
41 Grand Slam of Sheep (A4)

Pitch 1: Climb up the ramps to a ledge and belay at a blocky corner on the far-left side. (5.11a; 120 feet).

Pitch 2: Move up and out left following the weird blocky corner to an overhanging bombay flake. Then pull straight up over this on a bat hook to a belay in a horizontal. (A3; 120 feet).

Pitch 3: Continue straight up the face above to a belay below a bulge. (A2; 100 feet).

Pitch 4: Traverse right to gain a vertical crack above the bulge and follow this feature as it winds up and right to a belay with a bolt. (A2+; 120 feet).

Pitch 5: Climb through horizontals up and right to a belay. (A3; 100 feet).

Pitch 6: Claw up through fields of lichen to the top. (5.9; 80 feet).

39. The Code   A3+

Another standard-setting route by two of the most prolific aid climbers in the East.

First ascent: Todd Wells, Forrest Gardner (1993).

Start: At the plumb line under the largest part of the Peregrine Roof, 100 feet right of *Chieftains of Creep*.

Pitch 1: Gain the left-facing corner and then climb the face above on circleheads to a bolt beneath the intimidating roof. Move out this roof and belay on the face above. (A3+; 140 feet).

Pitch 2: Climb straight up the headwall past a couple of rivets to a belay at a bolt and some gear. (A3+; 100 feet).

Pitch 3: Easier aid leads up and slightly right to a gear belay at a stance. (A2; 120 feet).

Pitch 4: Scramble to the top. (5.8; 80 feet).

40. Carolina Hog Farm   IV, 5.10, A4

A relatively early route that still stands the test of time as one of the more serious aid routes on the North Side.

First ascent: Forrest Gardner, Shannon Stegg (1985).

Start: 50 feet right of *The Code,* in the right-facing corner below the right end of the Peregrine Roof.

Pitch 1: Follow the corner up and right past two bolts to a ledge. (5.10. C1; 80 feet).

Pitch 2: Climb fixed gear for 100 feet and then past some good horizontals to a gear belay. (A4; 150 feet).

Pitch 3: Step right off the belay and climb good horizontals to the top. (A1; 60 feet).

41. Grand Slam of Sheep   A4

Forrest Gardner says, "If you pull out a drill between the belays . . . it ain't A5! There are lots of blind, over-your-head placements on this one. If any one of them fails, you will hit the deck . . . hard."

First ascent: Forrest Gardner, Todd Wells (1997).

Start: The next line of fixed gear up the gully right of *Carolina Hog Farm.*

Bart Bledsoe and Tyler Stracker proudly fly the Jolly Roger on Grand Slam of Sheep *(route 41).*

Pitch 1: Follow the line of fixed gear past one bolt and two rivets to a three-bolt belay. (A4; 120 feet).

Pitch 2: Step left off the belay and up to a rivet and then straight up horizontals and to the top. (A4; 140 feet).

Nose Area

It's a good bet this is the best-known climbing area in the state due to its namesake route. This area sees exceptionally high traffic by both guided groups and regular parties.

42. Dum Dee Dum Dum   5.10c

The first-pitch crack gets most of the praise for this gem, but the whole route is worthy.

First ascent: Brad Shaver, Bob Gillespie (1972). Bob Mitchell and Ron Cousins made the first free ascent the same year.

Start: 300 feet left of *The Nose*, scramble up through the trees to reach a brushy ledge. This route is the obvious crack at the far-left end of the tree ledge.

Pitch 1: Pass a bolt to gain the crack that leads to a ledge with fixed gear. (5.10c; 60 feet). *Variation:* Move out right at the bolt, up, and then back left to the crack. (5.10a).

Pitch 2: Climb the wide crack up and left following an "arch" to a stance with bolted anchors. (5.8; 70 feet).

Pitch 3: Pull a slight bulge and follow eyebrows up to a gear belay. (5.9; 100 feet).

Pitch 4: Scramble up easier terrain to the top of *The Nose*.

Descent: Same as for *The Nose*.

43. The Nose   5.8

The best-known route at Looking Glass and maybe in the entire state—and justifiably so! Take a number on busy weekends for this classic.

First ascent: Steve Longenecker, Bob Watts, Bob Gillespie (1966).

Start: 130 feet left of *Sundial Crack* at a section of lower-angled stone and heavily impacted area below the rock.

Pitch 1: Climb straight up slabs to a big ledge with a bolted belay at the base of the right-angling quartz dike. (5.5; 110 feet).

Pitch 2: Move out right from the belay and then up to the quartz band passing a fixed pin. Follow this quartz band up and right until you can move straight up to a bolted belay. (5.8; 90 feet). *Note*: The first-ascent party climbed left off the belay to reach the dike and then traversed back right above the belay.

Pitch 3: Climb straight up and a bit right to a belay with old eyebolts next to a big flake below the Parking Lot. (5.8; 80 feet).

Pitch 4: Climb straight up the water groove above the Parking Lot. (5.7; 180 feet). *Variation:* Escape left at the Parking Lot and climb fourth-class terrain to the top.

Descent: Please do not rappel the route. To alleviate congestion, a new rap line has been added on the far-right side of the Parking Lot (see topo).

44. Peregrine   5.9

A nice route to hit if *The Nose* did not sate your eyebrow fixation.

First ascent: Steve Longenecker, Brian Lee, Sean Coffey (1989).

Start: 50 feet right of *The Nose,* locate a sharply pointed flake at waist level. Start just right of this.

Pitch 1: Climb eyebrows past two ledges to a belay 75 feet left of the *Sundial Cracks* anchor. (5.7; 80 feet).

Pitch 2: Climb 50 feet up so that the new rap anchors are to your right. Continue up and cross over the dike, and belay on gear at a stance. (5.9; 120 feet).

Pitch 3: Climb directly to the right edge of the Parking Lot to a bolted anchor. (5.7; 120 feet).

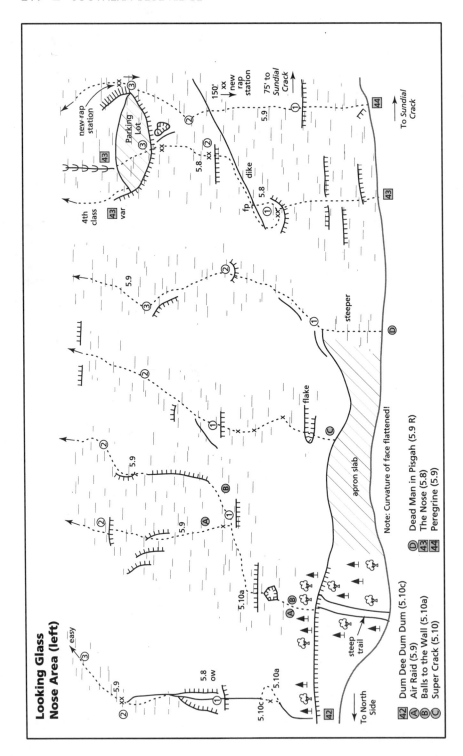

Looking Glass
Nose Area (left)

42 Dum Dee Dum Dum (5.10c)
Ⓐ Air Raid (5.9)
Ⓑ Balls to the Wall (5.10a)
Ⓒ Super Crack (5.10)

Ⓓ Dead Man in Pisgah (5.9 R)
43 The Nose (5.8)
44 Peregrine (5.9)

Note: Curvature of face flattened!

apron slab

steeper

flake

To North Side

steep trail

5.10a
5.10c
5.8 ow
5.9
easy
5.9
5.9
5.10a

To Sundial Crack

75' to Sundial Crack
150'
new rap station
5.9
5.8
5.8
dike
fp
4th class
var
Parking Lot
new rap station

Pitch 4: Step right of the arch and climb homogenous eyebrows trending up and left to end at the top of *The Nose*. (5.7; 150 feet).

Descent: Use the new rappel line that has been installed along Peregrine to alleviate congestion on *The Nose*. It starts on the right side of the Parking Lot (see topo). *Note:* There are good natural pro anchors that keep ascending parties on route and out of the way of descending parties.

David Zamsky on the pitch-2 dike of The Nose *(route 43)*

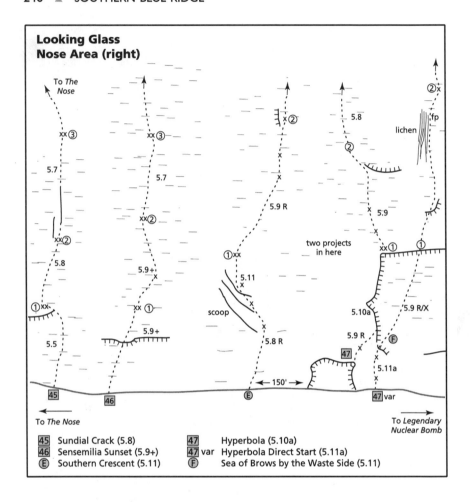

Looking Glass Nose Area (right)

45 Sundial Crack (5.8)
46 Sensemilia Sunset (5.9+)
Ⓔ Southern Crescent (5.11)
47 Hyperbola (5.10a)
47 var Hyperbola Direct Start (5.11a)
Ⓕ Sea of Brows by the Waste Side (5.11)

45. Sundial Crack   5.8

This great line is overshadowed by the popularity of *The Nose,* but it is every bit as classic. Somewhat confusingly named, the "crack" is only about 20 feet long and is on the third pitch.

First ascent: Bob Mitchell, Will Fulton (1972).

Start: Right where the approach trail hits the base of the wall. Locate the chains on top of pitch 1 about 80 feet up.

Pitch 1: Climb up deep eyebrows and horizontals passing the final bulge to the chains on the right. (5.5; 80 feet).

Pitch 2: Diagonal up and right to a bolted station at the base of the "crack." (5.8; 100 feet).

Pitch 3: Move up through some eyebrows, climb the nice crack, and then climb straight up to a natural gear belay in an eyebrow. (5.7; 120 feet).

Pitch 4: Move up and left aiming for the top of *The Nose.* (5.6; 150 feet).

Descent: Same as for *The Nose.*

46. Sensemilia Sunset   5.9+

A carbon copy of the climbing style on *The Nose* and *Sundial Crack* only at a stiffer grade. Rarely crowded on busy weekends.

First ascent: Peter White, Whitney Heuermann.

Start: 50 feet right of *Sundial Crack.*

Pitch 1: Aim for a scoop in the bulge 75 feet up. Once through the scoop, head up and right to the bolted anchor. (5.9+; 150 feet).

Pitch 2: Move up and a bit right passing a bolt. Aim for another bolted anchor. (5.9+; 150 feet).

Pitch 3: Climb straight up ever-easier terrain to another bolted anchor. (5.7; 150 feet).

Pitch 4: Head to the trees. (5.5; 165 feet).

Descent: Same as for *The Nose.*

47. Hyperbola   5.10a

The stellar first pitch dihedral is a "must-do" route. Many parties opt for the harder but better protected direct start.

First ascent: Percy Wimberly, J. Seay (1975). Grover Cable and Dave Black did the first free ascent in 1977. Eddie Begoon and Mike Artz made the first ascent of *Hyberbola Direct Start* in 1988.

Start: 200 feet right of *Sensemilia.* On top of some very large flakes just left of the obvious left-facing corner.

Pitch 1: At the top of the flakes, slab up and right to a bolt and then cast off right to join the dihedral. Climb the incredible locks, jams, and liebacks to the bolted anchor at the top. (5.10a; 100 feet). *Hyperbola Direct Start:* Climb directly up to the corner past two bolts and a funky stance with gear. (5.11a; 100 feet).

Pitch 2: Climb up and left past two bolts and then straight up to the left end of a roof. Break up and left and climb 30 feet to a gear belay. (5.9; 120 feet).

Pitch 3: Climb eyebrows generally straight up. (5.8; 200 feet).

Pitch 4: Scramble off to the top. (5.6; 150 feet).

Descent: Rappel *The Nose* or *Prey.* Anchors for *Prey* are to the right below two short pines that grow side-by-side by themselves on the slab about 150 feet below the tree line.

Sun Wall

Feared and conveniently overlooked by most modern climbers, this stunning section of Looking Glass is one of the cliff's hardman hangouts. Although it boasts everything from splitter cracks to steep jug-hauling to intimidating "jellyrolls," the Sun Wall doesn't offer much in the way of moderate climbing.

48. Psychedelic Delusions of the Digital Man   5.9, A2+

To the best of our knowledge, the first pitch (aka *Electric Kool-Aid Acid Test*) of this stunning line has never truly been sent free on redpoint. It has, however, been lead cleanly on preplaced gear by Jeep Gaskin and Eddie Begoon.

First ascent: Jeff Burton, Lyle Dean, Mark Stroud, Bill Tennent (1985).

Start: 60 feet right of *Hyperbola Direct,* in an obvious right-facing corner.

Pitch 1: Stem, smear, and crimp tiny pin scars past four bolts (only two were placed by the first-ascent party) up this steep corner of white granite. (C2; 100 feet).

Pitch 2: Climb up to a bolt ladder and then up and right to another bolt ladder. Free-climb through eyebrows to a belay. (5.9, A2+; 120 feet).

Pitch 3: Climb eyebrows straight up. (5.8; 200 feet).

Pitch 4: Scamper off to the top.

Descent: Rappel *Prey*. Walk right and look for two short pines growing side-by-side by themselves on the slab about 150 feet below the tree line. Two bolts on top of *Prey*'s pitch 4 are below these trees.

49. Predator   5.12a

Thin face climbing on an intimidating steep wall.

First ascent: Whitney Heuermann, Jeff Burton.

Start: 25 feet right of *Psychedelic Delusions* below an obvious line of bolts.

Pitch 1: Climb through small edges and eyebrows past six bolts and some gear until you can traverse to the anchors for *Psychedelic Delusions*. (100 feet).

50. Prey   5.12d or 5.11c, A0

Stout moves on the first-pitch roof can easily be French-freed. The second pitch offers steep and sustained pure eyebrow climbing.

First ascent: Bryan Haslam, Harrison Shull (1999). Kris Kline did the first free ascent of pitch 1 in 2000.

Start: 150 feet right of *Psychedelic Delusions* on the right side of the roots of a fallen hemlock below the Ravens Roost roof.

Pitch 1: Climb the slab to the base of a short, sharp arête. Pull up into the Ravens Roost and then up past a bolt to a jug at the lip. Mantel onto the jug and then move up and right to a belay. (5.12d or 5.11a, A0; 90 feet).

Pitch 2: Move right up into the dark streak. Follow this stripe up sustained eyebrows past two bolts to a belay. (5.11c; 90 feet).

Pitch 3: Climb the hand crack and move onto an insecure slab that leads to a water groove through a blank bulge. Clip three bolts as you head through the bulge and climb up much easier terrain to a belay. (5.10c; 180 feet).

Pitch 4: Scramble straight to the top. (5.6; 180 feet).

Descent: Rappel the route—three rappels with double 60-meter ropes.

51. Legendary Nuclear Bomb   5.11 R

This laser-straight groove combines hard moves over scant pro and has seen some serious flight time over its few repeats. *The Bomb* is considered by many to be the granddaddy of Looking Glass mind-control routes.

First ascent: Jeep Gaskin, Monty Reagan, Whitney Heuerrman (1986).

Start: 40 feet right of *Prey* at the right end of the brushy ledge.

Pitch 1: Climb up and right past large eyebrows to a bulge. Pull through the bulge and follow the groove past three bolts to a gear belay. (5.10c; 150 feet).

Pitch 2: Stay in the groove past three bolts to a bolted anchor. (5.11a; 100 feet).

Pitch 3: Climb steeper terrain past two bolts and then over a bulge to pass the

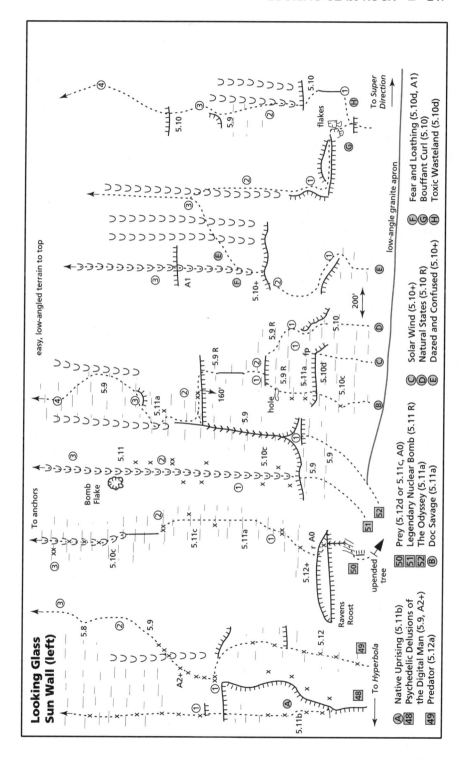

**Looking Glass
Sun Wall (left)**

To anchors

easy, low-angled terrain to top

To *Hyperbola*

To *Super
Direction*

flakes

Bomb
Flake

Ravens
Roost

upended
tree

low-angle granite apron

hole

5.8
5.9
5.9
5.10
5.10
5.10+
5.11
5.11a
5.11c
5.10c
5.12+ r A0
5.12
5.11b
A2+
5.11a
5.9
5.10c
5.9
5.9 R
5.9 R
5.10d
5.10c
5.11a
fp
A1
160'
200'

(A) Native Uprising (5.11b)
(48) Psychedelic Delusions of
the Digital Man (5.9, A2+)
(49) Predator (5.12a)

(50) Prey (5.12d or 5.11c, A0)
(51) Legendary Nuclear Bomb (5.11 R)
(52) The Odyssey (5.11a)
(B) Doc Savage (5.11a)

(C) Solar Wind (5.10+)
(D) Natural States (5.10 R)
(E) Dazed and Confused (5.10+)

(F) Fear and Loathing (5.10d, A1)
(G) Bouffant Curl (5.10)
(H) Toxic Wasteland (5.10d)

Bryan Haslam attempting to free-climb Electric Kool-Aid Acid Test *(5.12+ish; route 48)*

Bomb Flake. Continue up to a good horizontal for a belay. (5.11; 150 feet).

Pitch 4: A long pitch of groove climbing to the top. (5.8; 200 feet).

Descent: Rappel *Prey*. Walk left toward *The Nose* keeping an eye out for two short pines growing side-by-side on the slab about 150 feet below the tree line. Two bolts on top of pitch 4 of *Prey* are located below these trees. Or hike to *The Nose* rappel station.

52. The Odyssey   5.11a

If there were one full-length Sun Wall route that you had to do, then this might be the one. A classic in every sense.

First ascent: Bob Mitchell, Art Williams (1972). Jeep Gaskin and Don Hunley made the first free ascent in 1977.

Start: Just right of *Legendary Nuclear Bomb*, below a crack that starts 50 feet up.

Pitch 1: Climb moderate eyebrows up to the base of the crack. (5.9; 60 feet).

Pitch 2: Climb the crack/corner to its end and traverse right to a fixed belay. (5.9; 120 feet).

Pitch 3: Traverse back left to the corner and head up passing a bolt. Continue up and move left to a bowl and then up and right to a good belay stance. (5.11a; 100 feet).

Pitch 4: Climb up and right to a shallow water groove. Follow this a short way before heading back across the slabby face to a good belay stance at a horizontal in the left-hand water groove. (5.9; 140 feet).

Pitch 5: Easier ground leads to the top of the rock.
Descent: Same as for *Legendary Nuclear Bomb.*

53. Labia   5.11d

A steeper and harder version of *Aerospace Cadet.* A most impressive line.
   First ascent: Bob Rotert, Jeep Gaskin (1983).
   Start: On *Aerospace Cadet.*
   Pitch 1: Same as for *Aerospace Cadet.* (5.9+; 75 feet).
   Pitch 2: Traverse up and left across orange rock to a bolt at the base of the water
groove immediately to the left of *Aerospace Cadet.* (5.10a; 60 feet).
   Pitch 3: Pull very powerful and devious moves through the overhanging water
groove and head up to a belay stance with natural gear. (5.11d; 80 feet).
   Pitch 4: Climb the water groove to the tree island above. (5.6; 130 feet).
   Descent: Same as for *Out to Lunch.*

54. Aerospace Cadet   5.10d

A stunning line through an impressive water groove. The protection is much better
than you might think from below.
   First ascent: Jeep Gaskin, Don Hunley (1978, on-sight).
   Start: 50 feet left of *Out to Lunch,* on the right side of the slabby apron.
   Pitch 1: Climb up the lighter colored streak to a funky mantel up and right
over a bulge. Head up and right to a horizontal crack below a bulge for a gear be-
lay. (5.9+; 75 feet).
   Pitch 2: Climb up and left a move or two and then angle up to the overhanging
groove. Power over the lip and up to a gear belay at a stance. (5.10d; 120 feet).
   Pitch 3: Climb the water groove to the tree island above. (5.8; 130 feet).
   Descent: Same as for *Out to Lunch.*

55. Le Pump   5.11

Appropriately named and much steeper than it looks from below!
   First ascent: Jeff Lauschey, Monty Reagan (1987).
   Start: On the face climb just left of *Out to Lunch.*
   Pitch 1: Climb up deep horizontals to the first bolt then traverse up left to the
second. Pull some stiff moves onto the slab and climb easier ground to the bolted
anchors on *Out to Lunch.* (90 feet).

56. Out to Lunch   5.11a

A great route with tons of variety and great pro. For twenty-four hours in 1975, *Out
to Lunch* was the state's hardest climb . . . until Henry Barber sent *Cornflake Crack*
the very next day.
   First ascent: Brad Shaver (1974, pitch 1). Henry Barber, Ric Hatch (1975, full route).
   Start: 1,000 feet right of *The Odyssey* below a series of left-leaning cracks above
a flat granite apron with a stunted pine tree.
   Pitch 1: Climb the left-leaning cracks to a bolted belay on the large ledge.
(5.10d; 80 feet).

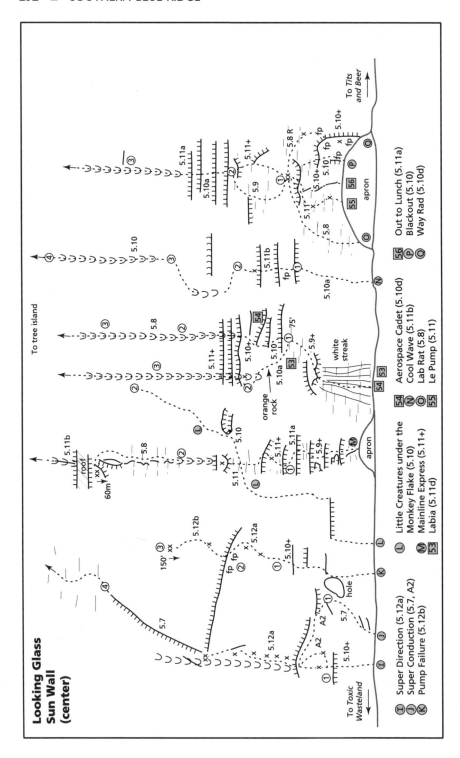

**Looking Glass
Sun Wall
(center)**

Ⓛ Little Creatures under the
   Monkey Flake (5.10)
Ⓜ Mainline Express (5.11+)
53 Labia (5.11d)

54 Aerospace Cadet (5.10d)
Ⓝ Cool Wave (5.11b)
Ⓞ Lab Rat (5.8)
55 Le Pump (5.11)

55 Out to Lunch (5.11a)
Ⓟ Blackout (5.10)
Ⓞ Way Rad (5.10d)

Ⓘ Super Direction (5.12a)
Ⓙ Super Conduction (5.7, A2)
Ⓚ Pump Failure (5.12b)

Pitch 2: Traverse left up the ramp for about 50 feet until you can climb up easier terrain for a few moves. Traverse back right and over some tenuous terrain to a good ledge. (5.9; 100 feet). *Variation:* Fire straight up the steep wall above. (5.11+; 50 feet).

Pitch 3: Climb up to the roof and then out the groove/crack above to a stance and a belay at a horizontal crack. (5.11a; 100 feet).

Pitch 4: Moderate water-groove climbing. (5.8; 200 feet).

Pitch 5: Even easier terrain up and left to a tree island. (5.6; 80 feet).

Descent: On the far-left side of the tree island, locate slings at head height up in a maple tree. Rappel from here to a set of bolted anchors about 190 feet directly below. Rappel 200 feet from here to the ground. This rappel descends *Mainline Express* (see topo).

57. Tits and Beer   5.9

This superb route provides the easiest way to the top of the Sun Wall. Don't take the grade for granted though—it used to be known as the "world's hardest 5.8." The name comes from a Frank Zappa tune.

First ascent: Bob Rotert, Randy Mann (1977).

Start: On the far lower right side of the Sun Wall apron, right of *Out to Lunch*.

Pitch 1: Traverse up and right to a stance below the crack at bolts. (5.4; 60 feet).

Pitch 2: Climb the crack and follow it until its starts to end and you can step out onto the face to the left. Climb up to the horizontal below the bulges and belay. (5.9; 100 feet).

Matt Gentling heads up through the Michelin Man bulges on Tits and Beer *(route 57).*

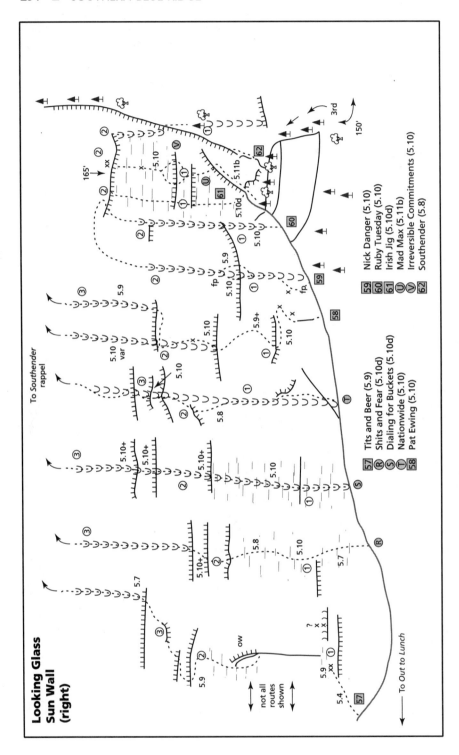

Looking Glass
Sun Wall
(right)

57 Tits and Beer (5.9)
Ⓡ Shits and Fear (5.10d)
Ⓢ Dialing for Buckets (5.10d)
Ⓣ Nationwide (5.10)
58 Pat Ewing (5.10)

59 Nick Danger (5.10)
60 Ruby Tuesday (5.10)
61 Irish Jig (5.10d)
Ⓤ Ⓥ Mad Max (5.11b)
Irreversible Commitments (5.10)
62 Southender (5.8)

Pitch 3: Traverse left 25 feet and pull the "Michelin Man" bulges trending right following the gear and holds. Continue up and right to a stance below a final, smaller bulge. (5.9; 70 feet).

Pitch 4: Move up and right to a groove that you follow for a full rope-length. (5.7; 200 feet).

Pitch 5: Continue up easier ground until you can literally walk around. At this point you should head right (maybe 500 feet) to gain the *Southender* rappel, which is a tree-choked gully in a low-angle corner.

58. Pat Ewing   5.10
Classic water-groove climbing with a few jugs tossed in for good measure.

First ascent: Jeep Gaskin, Julia Gaskin, Whitney Heuermann (1982).

Start: 30 feet left of *Nick Danger.*

Pitch 1: Climb the diagonal crack to its end and then move up and right past two bolts to a small bulge. Traverse left at the bulge 20 feet to a gear belay. (5.10; 80 feet).

Pitch 2: Move up and slightly right over a heady bulge and then back left aiming for a water groove at a bulge. Follow the groove up amazing buckets past a bolt to a belay below another bulge. (5.10; 150 feet).

Pitch 3: Traverse right 25 feet to the rightmost groove and climb it until the terrain eases and you can head up and right to a belay stance. (5.9; 150 feet).

Descent: Traverse right and slightly down to the anchors above *Irish Jig* and rappel.

59. Nick Danger   5.10
The only danger on this gem is having too much fun.

First ascent: Jeep Gaskin, Peter White (1982).

Start: 30 feet right of *Pat Ewing.*

Pitch 1: Climb up and left of the groove passing a fixed pin and a bolt before trending back right into the groove and up to a gear belay below a bulge. (5.10; 100 feet).

Pitch 2: Climb over the bulge straight up (5.10) or a bit right (5.9) and then head up the groove past stacked pins to a gear belay. (5.10 or 5.9; 120 feet).

Pitch 3: Climb up the groove until the terrain eases and you can head up and right to a belay stance on the ledge above *Ruby Tuesday* and *Irish Jig.* (5.8; 100 feet).

Descent: Rappel *Irish Jig.*

60. Ruby Tuesday   5.10
Once given an R rating, modern gear makes this stellar route less sporty. Some locals view this as possibly the best 5.10 water groove on The Glass.

First ascent: Jeff Burton, Peter White (1982).

Start: The first black water groove left of *Southender.*

Pitch 1: Traverse into the water groove from the right or start directly beneath it and then climb the groove up to the obvious horizontal. (5.10; 60 feet).

Pitch 2: Fire up into the steep groove and climb fantastic rock up to the obvious belay ledge. (5.10; 140 feet).

Pitch 3: Traverse up and right to double-bolt rappel anchors. (5.7; 40 feet).

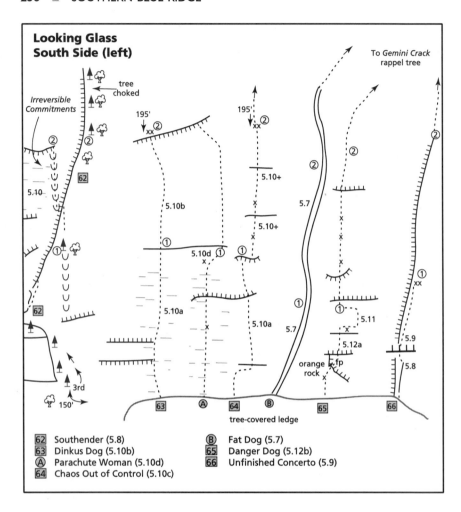

Looking Glass South Side (left)

To *Gemini Crack* rappel tree

Irreversible Commitments

tree choked

195'

195'

5.10+

5.7

5.10

5.10b

5.10+

5.10d

5.11

5.9

5.10a

5.10a

5.7

5.12a

5.8

orange rock

fp

3rd

150'

tree-covered ledge

62	Southender (5.8)	Ⓑ	Fat Dog (5.7)
63	Dinkus Dog (5.10b)	65	Danger Dog (5.12b)
Ⓐ	Parachute Woman (5.10d)	66	Unfinished Concerto (5.9)
64	Chaos Out of Control (5.10c)		

61. Irish Jig   5.10d

Full-bore, in-your-face steep eyebrows!

First ascent: Bruce Burgess, Andy Kluge (Saint Patrick's Day 1998).

Start: On *Southender*.

Pitch 1: Climb up *Southender* for 15 feet and step left into a short crack. Place gear up high and right, step back down, and then power up and left over steep eyebrows to a belay. (5.10d; 80 feet).

Pitch 2: Pull through a bulge to an obvious horizontal. Step left and continue up on amazing jugs that turn to slab before reaching a ledge. (5.10b; 70 feet).

Descent: Rappel once with two ropes from bolts on the right end of ledge.

South Side

This is probably the second most popular and heavily impacted climbing area at The Glass. The South Side of Looking Glass offers a slate of three-star multipitch routes all at rather moderate grades. The area's one drawback is its tendency to run with water after rain.

62. Southender   5.8

A good moderate route that is unfortunately often wet and a bit dirty.

First ascent: Stan Wallace, Ron Cousins (1972).

Start: This is the large, brushy corner that marks the boundary between the South Side and the Sun Wall several hundred yards left of *Bloody Crack*.

Pitch 1: Climb the crack up and right to a belay at some rhododendron bushes. (5.8; 80 feet).

Pitch 2: Climb to more bushes with sling anchors. (5.4; 80 feet).

Pitch 3: Continue up the corner to another growth of rhodos. (5.4; 100 feet).

Descent: Rappel the route.

63. Dinkus Dog   5.10b

One of the finest pure eyebrow routes at Looking Glass.

First ascent: Jeep Gaskin, Jeff Burton (1979, on-sight).

Start: 250 feet left of *Rat's Ass* and about 30 feet up on a tree-covered ledge. Third-class terrain leads up jumbled blocks. *Dinkus Dog* is 40 feet left of the huge *Fat Dog* crack (topo only) below the right side of a small roof.

Pitch 1: Move up to pass the small roof on its right side, and then follow the left side of a dark streak up to a gear belay. (5.10a; 100 feet).

Pitch 2: Climb amazing in-cut eyebrows and trend left to anchors. (5.10b; 100 feet).

Descent: Rap the route with two 60-meter ropes.

64. Chaos Out of Control   5.10c

Stay in control of your mind on this one.

First ascent: Monty Reagan (1987).

Start: Third-class up the tree-covered ledge left of *Rat's Ass* and find the first black water streak left of the *Fat Dog* crack (topo only).

Pitch 1: Climb up eyebrows to a bulge and on up to a gear belay at a small stance. (5.10a; 90 feet).

Pitch 2: Climb steep eyebrows past two bolts and up to bolted anchors. (5.10c; 100 feet).

Descent: Rap the route with two 60-meter ropes.

65. Danger Dog   5.12b

This steep face has sent many a hardman scurrying away with his tail between his legs.

First ascent: Monty Reagan, Jeep Gaskin.

Start: On the tree-covered ledge left of *Rat's Ass,* at the bolt in orange rock between *Fat Dog* and *Unfinished Concerto.*

Pitch 1: Crank past a bolt, a pin, and another bolt where you traverse a bit right. Then head up and back left to a natural pro belay. (5.12a; 80 feet).

Pitch 2: Climb straight off the belay over a bulge into a scoop and then past three bolts and more stout moves. (5.12b; 100 feet).

Pitch 3: Start moving right to get to the *Gemini Crack* rappel tree.

66. Unfinished Concerto   5.9

A really nice first pitch followed by moderate cracks to the top.

First ascent: Peter Farrah, Henry Foreshipps.

Start: On the tree-covered ledge to the left of *Rat's Ass*, at the obvious crack on the right side of the ledge.

Pitch 1: Climb the crack up into the corner. Pass the block and move on up to a bolted belay. (5.9; 70 feet).

Pitch 2: Follow the crack until you run out of rope. (5.5; 200 feet).

Pitch 3: Trend right on moderate terrain to the *Gemini Crack* rappel tree.

67. Windwalker   5.9

A much-overlooked route that is quite good—especially on busy days.

First ascent: John Tainio, Peter White.

Start: Same as *Rat's Ass*.

Pitch 1: Move left out of the *Rat's Ass* corner to a shallow right-facing corner as soon as possible. Move up the corner until you can escape to the face on the left. Follow the white streak to the base of a large corner. (5.9; 110 feet).

Pitch 2: Climb crack to end of rope. (5.5; 200 feet).

Pitch 3: Trend right to the *Gemini Crack* rappel tree.

68. Rat's Ass   5.8

A must-do classic offering thin fingertip locks in a beautiful stemming corner.

First ascent: Stan Wallace, John Ferguson, Jim McEver, Ron Cousins (1973).

Start: 20 feet left of *Second Coming* and about 400 feet left of where the approach trail meets the wall near *Bloody Crack*.

Pitch 1: Climb up the slabs to a tree-covered stance. Climb the thin corner above to a belay on lower-angled terrain. (5.8; 120 feet).

Pitch 2: Climb the crack up and right for a full rope-length. (5.5; 200 feet).

Pitch 3: Trend right to the *Gemini Crack* rappel tree.

69. Second Coming   5.7

With bigger jams, this one's a tad bit easier than *Rat's Ass*, but every bit as classic. The first pitch has probably yielded more broken ankles than the rest of The Glass combined—don't get complacent with your protection!

First ascent: Stan Wallace, Ron Cousins, Art Williams, Jim McEver (1972).

Start: Rightmost of the pair of tall, right-trending crack/corner systems 75 feet left of the Sentry Box Ledge area.

Pitch 1: Climb up the slabby crack to some vegetation and then step left into a right-facing corner that leads up and over a bulge to a belay ledge. (5.7; 100 feet).

Pitch 2: Follow the crack up and right past two precarious flakes. (5.5; 200 feet).

Pitch 3: Trend right to the *Gemini Crack* rappel tree.

70. First Return   5.8

A great route with a lot of variety. Be careful with your pro on the opening moves.

First ascent: Ron Cousins, Art Williams (1972).

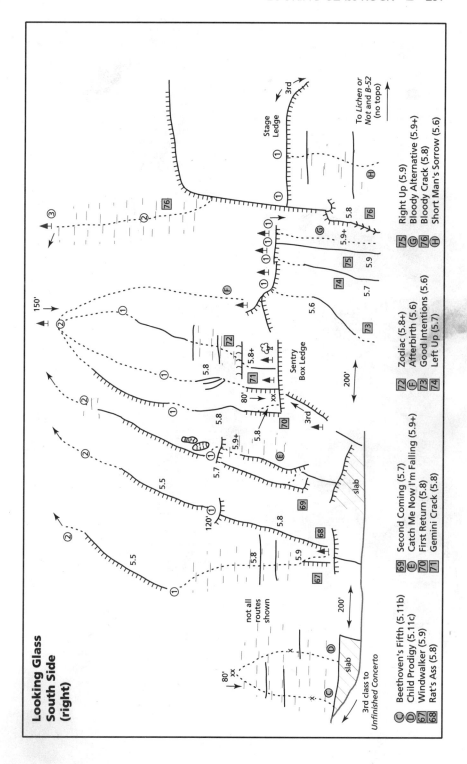

**Looking Glass
South Side
(right)**

Ⓒ Beethoven's Fifth (5.11b)
Ⓓ Child Prodigy (5.11c)
🔲67 Windwalker (5.9)
🔲68 Rat's Ass (5.8)

🔲69 Second Coming (5.7)
Ⓔ Catch Me Now I'm Falling (5.9+)
🔲70 First Return (5.8)
🔲71 Gemini Crack (5.8)

🔲72 Zodiac (5.8+)
Ⓕ Afterbirth (5.6)
🔲73 Good Intentions (5.6)
🔲74 Left Up (5.7)

🔲75 Right Up (5.9)
Ⓖ Bloody Alternative (5.9+)
🔲76 Bloody Crack (5.8)
Ⓗ Short Man's Sorrow (5.6)

Susan Haslam in the pitch-1 corner of Second Coming *(route 69)*

Start: On far-left end of Sentry Box Ledge at a right-facing corner. Sentry Box Ledge is 50 feet up off the ground and 120 feet left of *Bloody Crack*. Be careful scrambling up fourth class onto the ledge.

Pitch 1: Climb the corner on thin tips and face holds up to a steep crack. Exit the crack to the left and aim for the base of large corner system. (5.8; 100 feet).

Pitch 2: Follow the corner up and right to the *Gemini Crack* rappel tree. (5.5; 150 feet).

71. Gemini Crack   5.8
Well protected, never outrageous, and certainly a worthy tick. Often done as one pitch.
First ascent: Jim McEver, David Broemel (1973).
Start: On Sentry Box Ledge right of the rappel bolts in a right-facing corner.
Pitch 1: Climb the corner to a series of discontinuous cracks and then angle to
the left. At the top of the cracks, move up horizontals to a gear belay. (5.8; 100 feet).
Pitch 2: Head for the rappel tree. (5.6; 70 feet).
Descent: A 150-foot rappel puts you on the Sentry Box Ledge.

72. Zodiac   5.8+
The hardest of the trio of routes on Sentry Box Ledge.
First ascent: Buddy Price, Doc Bayne (1977).
Start: At a shallow finger crack in black rock 20 feet right of *Gemini Crack*.
Pitch 1: Climb the finger crack up to a bulge. Top out the bulge and head up
eyebrows to another, steeper crack. At the top of the crack step up to eyebrows for a
gear belay. (5.8+; 110 feet).
Pitch 2: Climb the face up and left to the *Gemini Crack* rappel tree. (5.6; 70 feet).

73. Good Intentions   5.6
A good introduction to slabby eyebrow climbing at The Glass.
First ascent: Buddy Price, Doc Bayne (1977).
Start: Right of and below Sentry Box Ledge, 25 feet left of *Left Up*.
Pitch 1: Move up the diagonal crack to a nice stance and then up the face to
vegetated ledge. (80 feet).
Descent: Rappel from the *Right Up* tree.

74. Left Up   5.7
A nice crack-climbing primer, but it stays wet longer than most Glass routes after
rain. The opening moves are not to be taken lightly—this route has been the scene
of more than one broken ankle.
First ascent: Stan Wallace, Ron Cousins, Jim McEver (1973).
Start: 30 feet left of *Right Up*.
Pitch 1: Climb the obvious finger and hand crack to the ledge. (80 feet).
Descent: Rappel from the *Right Up* tree.

75. Right Up   5.9
A bit harder version of *Left Up*. Be careful with your pro in the first 20 feet.
First ascent: Jim McEver, M. Wousey, Blair Ritter (1974).
Start: 15 feet left of *Bloody Crack*.
Pitch 1: Climb the obvious hand crack to a tree with slings. (80 feet).
Descent: Rappel from the tree.

76. Bloody Crack   5.8
A nice route, but the scene of way too much congestion on busy weekends. The route
is harder than it might appear due to years of polishing by hands and feet.

First ascent: Stan Wallace, Jim McEver, Ron Cousins (1973).

Start: Under the left end of Stage Ledge.

Pitch 1: Climb the prominent hand crack up to the left end of Stage Ledge. (5.8; 50 feet).

Pitch 2: Head up the big corner above Stage Ledge for about 40 feet until you can exit left onto a low-angled face with eyebrows. (5.6; 100 feet).

Pitch 3: Head to the top and bushwhack over left to the *Gemini Crack* rappel tree. (5.5; 150 feet).

77. Lichen or Not   5.5 (no topo)

Another great moderate route when other South Side routes are crowded.

First ascent: Will Leverette.

Start: 100 feet right of the Stage Ledge area, just right of a tree island 20 feet up.

Pitch 1: Climb past a blocky, diagonal crack, and then up low-angled face up to bolted anchors. (5.5; 90 feet).

Pitch 2: Climb up and a bit right to trees at top. (5.5; 100 feet). *Note:* Few do more than pitch 1.

Descent: Rappel the route.

78. B-52   5.10a (no topo)

It is too bad that the beautiful hand crack through a roof on pitch 2 is so short.

First ascent: Ed Begoon, John Gratz (1984).

Start: 500 feet right of the Stage Ledge area, on the front of the next large buttress.

Pitch 1: Climb up the face left of the brushy crack to a ledge with jumbled boulders. (5.8; 80 feet).

Pitch 2: Move up and right to pull the roof via a splitter hand crack. (5.10a; 70 feet).

Descent: Rap from trees.

8. CEDAR ROCK ━━━━━━━━━━━━━━━━━━━━━━━━

Climbing type: Multipitch traditional

Rock type: Granite dome

Height: 50 to 300 feet

Number of routes: Approximately 35 (16 this guide)

Climbing season: Fall through spring

Camping: Wilderness camping is allowed anywhere in Pisgah National Forest so long as you are 1,000 feet or more from the road or in designated campsites. See appendix B for contact information. There is also an A-frame shelter on the Art Loeb Trail located 0.2 mile south of Butter Gap and underneath Cedar Rock.

Tucked away in a deep, lush cove of Pisgah National Forest, this intimidating shield of black and white streaked granite is one of the best face-climbing destinations in the state. In fact, if you're into extremely technical, vertical face climbs, Cedar Rock is *the* place to hone your craft. Unlike nearby Cashiers Valley domes (see chapter 9), where the emphasis is often on padding your way up water grooves, or Looking Glass, where you're constantly high-stepping into eyebrows, Cedar Rock is blessed with laser-cut crimpers and sinker—though widely spaced—horizontals. That's not to say all the routes at Cedar Rock are like this. In fact, you can scare yourself silly on many of the Cedar's slabby "trad moderates" such as *Cedar Pie*. Meanwhile, test pieces such as *Pawing the Void* or *Passion and Warfare* are visionary lines that will demand outrageous crimp strength and a willingness to drop the clutch.

While you're in the Cedar Rock area, check out the nearby Stone Depot and John's Rock areas. Outward Bound often takes students to the Stone Depot, which is a 400-foot, mostly low-angled, north-facing cliff on the flanks of Cedar Rock. In recent years, climbers have also done some new routes at John's Rock, which is visible from FR 475 on the drive from Pisgah National Forest. Explore a little.

History

Considering its proximity to Looking Glass Rock, it is no wonder that climbers began exploring the various faces of Cedar Rock as long as forty years ago. In the early 1960s, Jim McEver, Stan Wallace, and Ron Cousins did an unprotected, one-pitch, 5.8 fist crack on one of the northern tiers of the mountain. Reports of first ascents on other, lower-angled sections of the mountain occasionally pop up, too. But for the most part, climbers missed the hidden southwest face until a serendipitous discovery in 1986.

During a hiking trip, Charlotte climber Charles Ivey discovered the face and a relatively easy access trail. Ivey quickly passed on the discovery to Spartanburg, South Carolina, attorney and climber Sean Cobourn, who has always been hot for new

Overview of the Southwest Face of Cedar Rock

Caught Up in the Air

Cedar Pie

Wild Ginger Root

rock. The duo returned soon afterward and marveled at the untouched wall, which at the time towered over a gorgeous mountain meadow teeming with tall grasses and wildflowers. In walking the base, Cobourn and Ivey pointed out some obvious features and even attempted the imposing slot that would later become *Rawhide Arch*. At the time of their first visits, the climbers were only seeking natural features and their first foray onto the face was tentative. *Oh! Mr. Friction* follows a short arch and then slabs off to gain the summit.

Cobourn recalls that he and his brother Shane were enamored of the cliff and spent every available weekend there for two years. Still, the climbers did not relish the thought of launching up onto Cedar's apparently blank headwall armed with hooks and hand drills. Instead, they decided to experiment by bolting a few lines on rappel to see if they would go in this manner. Unfortunately, their efforts did not really help; the smooth granite and paucity of holds still repelled them and they left the lines as open projects. These lines later became *Glass Dancer* and *Stockings on the Mantle.*

Clarence Hickman and Mark Pell were the other climbers who had the greatest early impact at Cedar Rock. In 1986, the Cobourns had presented Cedar Rock as a birthday present to Hickman (known to friends as "Scrappy Cloggins"). Soon afterward, Hickman and Pell set to work picking the cherries. For their first route, *Cedar Pie,* the duo actually placed the well-spaced bolts on rappel. Yet from that point forward, Hickman did most of his lines ground-up in deference to the ethic at nearby Looking Glass. Hickman said that the climbers would occasionally rappel and clean a potential project, but classics such as *Toads-R-Us, Caught Up in the Air,* and *New Creatures* went in as ground-up lines.

All these efforts opened the floodgates at Cedar Rock, and soon some of the best climbers in the East were visiting. Virginia climber Eddie Begoon arrived one weekend and—in a single trip—completed vicious (and scary) face climbs such as *Surfin' with the Alien* and *I Wanna Be Sedated.* Over a few years in the early 1990s, locals such as Chris Caldwell, Bruce Burgess, and Doc Bayne really pushed the limits and came up with *Cajun Style, Wild Ginger Root,* and the cliff's coup-de-grace, *Passion and Warfare.* Possibly the best line of the wall, this route by Burgess and Caldwell is an ocean of sculpted crimpers. Burgess remembers that this line took almost an entire season just to equip because all the bolts save the third on the second pitch were drilled by hand. Caldwell—who still complains of neck problems from the effort—drilled that lone power-assisted bolt from a stance high on the second pitch with a nasty, sloping eyebrow in one hand and a drill in the other. Burgess managed to redpoint the line first despite a sickening 5.11 runout at the top. He later returned to re-bolt the upper section in order to eliminate both some unintentional rope drag and the runout.

Caldwell also later added the amazing *Pawing the Void* in an inspired effort. Caldwell, who now lives in Durango, Colorado, remembered that he first decided to rappel the route in a rainstorm just to see if a line existed. He then had Greenville, South Carolina, climber Buddy Price hold him against the wall with a stick so Caldwell could drill the first, tenuous bolt. The route (previously known incorrectly as *Fondling the Void*) got its name because Caldwell laid out of work for several days to rope solo *The Void* accompanied only by his dog—the sole witness to Caldwell's repeated 20-footers!

Weather and Climbing Season

Cedar Rock (elevation 4,056 feet) faces southwest. The face gets sun for much of the day, but some of the water-groove routes seep in the mornings. This area receives approximately 80 inches of rainfall every year, mostly in the form of afternoon thundershowers in spring and summer.

Restrictions and Access Issues

Cedar Rock is part of the Pisgah National Forest and there are no current raptor closures or other restrictions. For resource and safety concerns as well as courtesy to other climbers, the forest service encourages climbing in small groups.

Emergency Services

Call 911 to reach the Transylvania County Rescue Squad. Climbers should be self-rescue ready and able to get an injured climber to the ground where the waiting rescue squad members will be ready to help. The closest hospital is Transylvania Community Hospital just off US 64 in Brevard (see appendix C).

Gear

Bring a standard North Carolina free-climbing rack. As at Looking Glass Rock, Tri-Cams are especially helpful.

Getting There

From Brevard at the junction of NC 280, US 64, and US 276 (near the main entrance to Pisgah National Forest), drive west on US 64 through Brevard for approximately 5.5 miles to Cathey's Creek Road (FR 471) on the right. A good landmark is a sign for Kuykendall Group Campground. Drive on Cathey's Creek Road for 5.9 miles (only a short distance is paved) to an obvious pullout for about four cars on the right. Vehicles parked in the roadway or blocking the gate may be subject to citations.

It is also possible to reach Cedar Rock from inside Pisgah National Forest. From the three-way highway intersection noted above, follow US 276 west into Pisgah for 5.5 miles, passing the Pisgah Ranger Station. Turn left at FR 475 signed for the fish hatchery. Continue on FR 475 for 5.6 miles to a large, unmarked intersection. (This is marked as the Gloucester Gap area on USGS maps and is on the Art Loeb Trail; look for the trail signs.) Turn left onto FR 477 and continue for 2.2 miles to the pullout (now on the left) noted above.

Approach

From the parking area, hike around the Forest Service gate and follow the obvious jeep road uphill about one mile and into Low Gap. Here you will see an intersection with the Art Loeb Trail. Continue straight across the clearing on the main road (still an old jeep road) for another 0.25 mile toward Butter Gap. This is a large clearing and the junction for seven different roads and trails.

From Butter Gap, continue straight across the intersection on the unmarked, main jeep road passing several large downed trees. If you are on a marked trail, you're going the wrong direction. The Art Loeb Trail should be below you and to your right.

The road you are on eventually contours right and, at 0.4 mile, ends at a tiny clearing that can serve as a campground. Here, look to your left (east) for a small side trail through the rhododendron. This trail climbs the hillside through a scree field and eventually arrives at the base of Cedar Rock at *Surfin' with the Alien.*

Southwest Face
Routes are listed right to left, with routes 1 through 5 to the right of the approach trail and routes 6 through 16 to the left.

Descent: Rappel the route unless otherwise noted.

1. Cedar Blossom   5.9+
Sustained and continuous, this all-natural line is a recent addition and great stepping stone for the harder grades. Bring extra 0.5-inch to 1-inch cams.

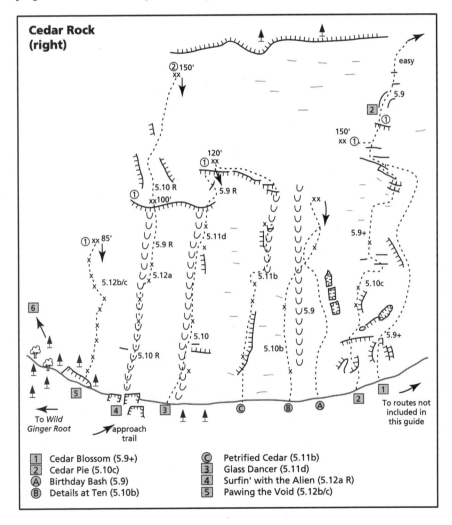

1	Cedar Blossom (5.9+)	Ⓒ	Petrified Cedar (5.11b)
2	Cedar Pie (5.10c)	3	Glass Dancer (5.11d)
Ⓐ	Birthday Bash (5.9)	4	Surfin' with the Alien (5.12a R)
Ⓑ	Details at Ten (5.10b)	5	Pawing the Void (5.12b/c)

First ascent: Bruce Burgess, Bryan Haslam (1999).
Start: Approximately 100 feet uphill from where the approach trail meets the base.
Pitch 1: Delicate slab moves take you up to a small right-facing corner. Continue up right to avoid a large hollow flake. Move up the featured face for another 25 feet to a left-rising ramp. A beautiful face leads to a good horizontal for a directional. (120 feet). Traverse 20 feet up left to the belay anchors of *Cedar Pie*.

2. Cedar Pie   5.10c
A full day's work in one long and intricate pitch! Named for the famous *Skunkpie* at Crowders Mountain, this excellent route has good pro if you're willing to wander. Tri-Cams, long runners, and double ropes are recommended.
First ascent: Clarence Hickman, Mark Pell (1986, bolted on rappel).
Start: 20 feet left of *Cedar Blossom*.
Pitch 1: Saunter up to a short corner crack. Make some hard moves past a large hole (4- to 5-inch cam) to gain a right-facing arch. Climb left around this past two bolts and gun for a small scoop (optional belay if climbing on a single rope). Move up a bit and traverse hard right then up again to better horizontals and natural gear. Excellent moves take you left past a bolt to a bomber cam. Move right again, following the best holds and gear eventually cutting back left to a fixed anchor. (150 feet).
Note: It is possible to climb a second pitch and walk off. See topo. (5.9; 70 feet).

3. Glass Dancer   5.11d
A prominent water groove that's hard to pass by without gawking.
First ascent: Sean and Shane Cobourn (bolted on rappel). Kris Kline got the first free ascent.
Start: At the water groove 20 feet right of *Surfin' with the Alien*.
Pitch 1: Climb past a low bolt to gain a small ledge. Climb past another bolt into the water groove where you can crimp and stretch past two bolts in one steep section to gain a bowl. Follow the weakness past a short runout to the double-bolt anchor. (120 feet).

4. Surfin' with the Alien   5.12a R
There are several ways to make the heady opening moves. Some gear at 20 feet takes the edge off if you're approaching from below. Though unprotected, it is easiest to trend up and right. If you blow it, prepare for a bone-rattling slide into the base . . .
First ascent: Eddie Begoon, Mike Artz, Chris Caldwell (1989).
Start: Where the approach trail meets the base and under a water groove.
Pitch 1: Pad your way up the face to gain a high bolt. Three more bolts up the beautiful water streak lead through the steep crux to a double-bolt belay. (5.12a R; 100 feet).
Pitch 2: Continue directly off the belay through an hourglass feature to gain a crack. Moderate climbing leads to an anchor. (5.10b R; 150 feet).

5. Pawing the Void   5.12b/c
With multiple cruxes and tiny holds, this astoundingly difficult and invigorating line makes you realize what's possible on "blank" rock elsewhere in North Carolina.

First ascent: Chris Caldwell (early 1990s, rope-solo, ground-up).
Start: Look for the obvious line of bolts 20 feet left of *Surfin' with the Alien.*
Pitch 1: Sport. Crimp up the steep face. Nine bolts to a double-bolt anchor. (85 feet).

6. Wild Ginger Root   5.11b

Two pitches of diverse climbing—plus one wild section on the headwall—make this route a real journey into the heart of Cedar. The third bolt on the second pitch of this route was drilled from a stance. . . . Think about that when you're struggling to clip it!

First ascent: Mike McCormick, Doc Bayne.
Start: Off a rhododendron ledge, 30 feet left of *Pawing the Void.*
Pitch 1: Climb delicately to the first bolt and finagle your way past a small, right-facing overlap. Once under position at the roof, move up and right following a tiny corner. Pull the roof past a bolt and romp to a double-bolt belay. (5.11a; 100 feet).
Pitch 2: Climb up and left following the unprotected face beneath the corner. Gain a small pillar to clip the first bolt and follow the line right. Palm and crimp your way up the excellent corner until it is easy to traverse left to an anchor. (5.11b; 90 feet).
Descent: Move left and make a 165-foot rappel from *Frijolitos de Amor* (topo only).

7. Stockings on the Mantle   5.11c

Even as the first route on Cedar's amazing headwall, we could get away with including *Stockings* only because of its second pitch.

First ascent: Shane and Sean Cobourn made the first ascent and established most bolts by rappel. Sam Stevenson and Victor Moore returned and Stevenson onsighted the route on Christmas Eve 1987.
Start: 50 feet left of *Wild Ginger Root.* Follow obvious right-facing flakes and corners through the lower-angled wall.
Pitch 1: Climb a flake up onto a ledge. Clip a bolt and move out right a few feet; then continue straight up to the corner overhead. Stem and jam your way to a bolt. (5.9+; 110 feet).
Pitch 2: Pull onto the headwall and climb past some short vertical cracks. Negotiate the devious face past four bolts to gain a large ledge with loose blocks. Double-bolt belay. (5.11c; 55 feet).
Descent: Same as *Wild Ginger Root.*

8. Passion and Warfare   5.12c

This is the mother's milk of steep face climbing. Many feel this is the best route at Cedar Rock for both its position high on the bulging headwall and the incredible holds.

First ascent: Bruce Burgess, Chris Caldwell (1989, ground-up with some aid).
Start: 15 feet left of *Stockings on the Mantle.*
Pitch 1: Climb the low-angled face past one bolt, gaining a series of shallow vertical cracks. Belay from a small stance with good medium-sized gear. (5.11b; 90 feet).
Pitch 2: Let the games begin. Climb up past a weird corner to gain the world-class face above. Nobody ever said true love came easy! Six bolts total. (5.12c; 80 feet).

Jesse McGahey pulls through the steep headwall on pitch 2 of Wild Ginger Root *(route 6).*

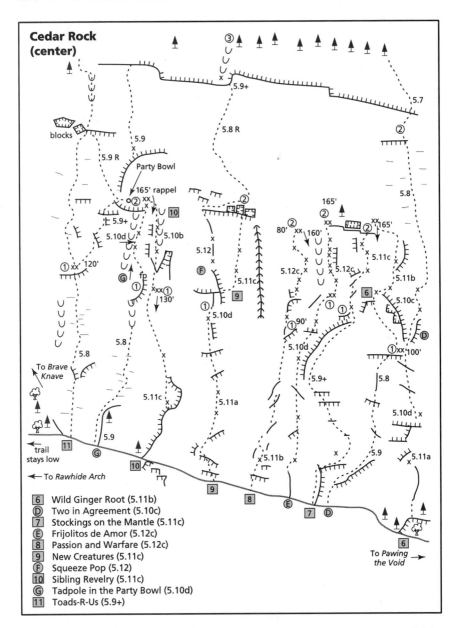

Cedar Rock (center)

blocks
Party Bowl
165' rappel
5.9+
5.7
5.8 R
5.8
5.9
5.9 R
5.10d
5.10b
5.9+
120'
130'
5.8
5.8
To Brave Knave
5.9
trail stays low
To Rawhide Arch
5.11c
5.11c
5.10d
5.11a
5.11b
5.12
5.12c
5.11c
5.11c
5.10d
90'
5.10d
5.9+
5.8
100'
80'
160'
165'
5.11c
5.11b
5.10c
5.10d
5.9
5.11a
To Pawing the Void

6   Wild Ginger Root (5.11b)
D   Two in Agreement (5.10c)
7   Stockings on the Mantle (5.11c)
E   Frijolitos de Amor (5.12c)
8   Passion and Warfare (5.12c)
9   New Creatures (5.11c)
F   Squeeze Pop (5.12)
10 Sibling Revelry (5.11c)
G   Tadpole in the Party Bowl (5.10d)
11 Toads-R-Us (5.9+)

9. New Creatures   5.11c

Despite the old bolts on the second pitch, *New Creatures* gains some excellent position on the left side of Cedar's rounded headwall. This route is perhaps less popular due to the lack of fixed belays, which means a walk off the summit.

First ascent: Clarence Hickman, Mark Pell.

Start: 20 left of *Passion and Warfare* and 20 feet right of the obvious *Sibling Revelry* corner.

Pitch 1: Balance your way up the featured face past several overlaps and one thin section to gain a vertical crack for the belay. (5.11a; 100 feet).

Pitch 2: Step right and continue up a slot for a short distance until you can escape right around the bulge. Climb up past two bolts to a natural belay on a ledge. (5.11c; 70 feet).

Pitch 3: Wander up the face above (5.8 R) to an obvious cleft in the roof. Pull this and continue up the final water groove to the summit. (5.9+; 100 feet).

Descent: Walk off left to gain a short, fourth-class slab that takes you to the base.

10. Sibling Revelry   5.11c
Memorable corner climbing leads up to a spicy face.

First ascent: Shane Cobourn, Mark Pell.

Start: In the obvious (though often wet) corner as you continue left along the base.

Pitch 1: Lieback and undercling the excellent Yosemite-style corner. Just as the going gets thin, move out left onto the face past a pin and bolt. Trend up and left along the weakness past another bolt to a three-bolt belay station. (5.11c; 130 feet).

Pitch 2: Continue straight off the belay past two bolts to an anchor in the Party Bowl. (5.10b; 90 feet).

11. Toads-R-Us   5.9+
Many parties do only the first 5.8 pitch, which is the best moderate at Cedar Rock. Several variations exist from there.

First ascent: Chris Little, Clarence Hickman, Mark Pell.

Dave Wendelin discovers the stellar edging on pitch 1 of Toads-R-Us (route 11).

Andy Kluge launches the sideways dyno on his test piece, Frijolitos de Amor *(topo only).*

Start: Off a slab where the trail detours away from the main wall; 30 feet left of *Sibling Revelry.*

Pitch 1: Climb past a shallow, right-facing corner to gain the appealing face laced with good horizontals (a lot of good gear from 0.45 to 2 inches) to a double-bolt belay. (5.8; 120 feet).

Pitch 2: Climb one of two variations (see topo). The recommended route angles up and right to gain the Party Bowl ledge. (5.9+; 50 feet).

Descent: Rappel 165 feet from the Party Bowl.

12. Rawhide Arch   5.10d

One of the earliest routes attempted at Cedar Rock for its obvious—though aptly named—feature. Ouch!

First ascent: Thomas Kelley, Sam Stevenson. Danny Caldwell is credited with the second pitch.

Start: Follow the main trail as it skirts away from the wall, and then move up to a higher tier. *Rawhide* starts at the right side of this narrow tree ledge.

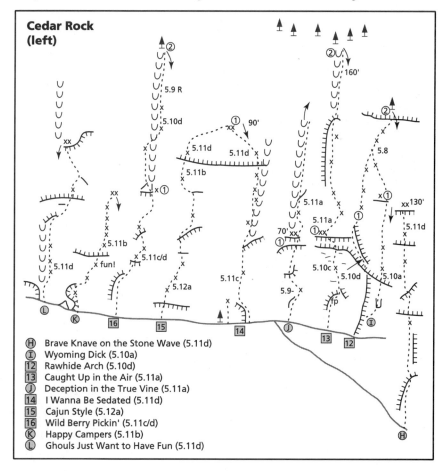

Cedar Rock (left)

Ⓗ Brave Knave on the Stone Wave (5.11d)
Ⓘ Wyoming Dick (5.10a)
12 Rawhide Arch (5.10d)
13 Caught Up in the Air (5.11a)
Ⓙ Deception in the True Vine (5.11a)
14 I Wanna Be Sedated (5.11d)
15 Cajun Style (5.12a)
16 Wild Berry Pickin' (5.11c/d)
Ⓚ Happy Campers (5.11b)
Ⓛ Ghouls Just Want to Have Fun (5.11d)

Pitch 1: Chickenwing and jam your way up the wide slot to a difficult section past the bulge. Single-bolt belay. (5.10d; 60 feet).

Pitch 2: Continue up the face passing five bolts to a tree ledge. (5.8; 100 feet).

13. Caught Up in the Air 5.11a

Although a key flake on the second pitch has finally broken, if you can finagle your way up, this pitch is one of the best around: excellent exposure and magical holds!

First ascent: Clarence Hickman, Mark Pell.

Start: 50 feet left of *Rawhide Arch* under a right-arching flake.

Pitch 1: Climb the flake past a fixed pin, tiptoe out right to gain a stance and protection. Continue up the face past a bolt and some excellent horizontals, passing a small bulge to a double-bolt anchor. (5.10c; 80 feet).

Pitch 2: In the past, standing on a thin flake allowed you to clip the first bolt. This flake is now gone. A difficult reach gains the upper face. (5.11a; 160 feet)

Descent: Rap from trees to gain the first-pitch anchor.

14. I Wanna Be Sedated 5.11d

"Hurry hurry hurry before I go insane / I can't control my fingers / I can't control my brain. . . . " Could the Ramones have described this route any better? Despite the weird start, *Sedated* deserves a go.

First ascent: Eddie Begoon, Tony Barnes (1989, ground-up).

Start: 25 feet left of *Caught Up in the Air.*

Pitch 1: Climb up to a bolt on the left side of a right-facing flake, clip it, and climb back down. This is your pro for the first crux, which is getting to the second bolt! Back on the ground now, this time climb up the right side of the flake using fierce crimpers to gain the second and third bolts. Here, follow a good 1- to 2-inch horizontal right and into a superb water groove. Climb to an ominous bulge, where you can move left and pass a final bolt to gain anchors. (90 feet).

15. Cajun Style 5.12a

Like it spicy? This bayou babe is thin and extremely technical down low and opens up to gain two devious cruxes near the end. Bring single cams 0.45 to 1.5 inches.

First ascent: Chris Caldwell, Thomas Kelley (1990, ground-up with hooks).

Start: 20 feet left of *Sedated.*

Pitch 1: Climb up to the first bolt and make some very difficult friction moves out right past two more bolts. Continue up the face past two more bolts and occasional small horizontals to a bulge. Power through to a bulge where some final hard moves will allow you to move right for a fixed anchor. (90 feet).

16. Wild Berry Pickin' 5.11c/d

The name describes the nature of the first-ascent activity on the one day that this climb and *Sedated* went up simultaneously.

First ascent: Chris Caldwell, Doc Bayne (1989, ground-up from hooks).

Start: 20 feet left of *Cajun Style.*

Pitch 1: Climb past the right-facing corner and then past three bolts to gain good horizontals. Belay at one bolt and a slung horn. (5.11c/d; 70 feet).

Pitch 2: Continue up the water groove past three bolts and one runout (5.9 R) to gain the top. (5.10d; 80 feet).

Descent: Rappel from trees.

9. BIG GREEN MOUNTAIN

Climbing type: Multipitch traditional
Rock type: Granite dome
Height: 70 to 300 feet
Number of routes: Approximately 50 (15 this guide)
Climbing season: October through April
Camping: Free camping is allowed on Forest Service land in the Panthertown Valley (see appendix B). There is an excellent **A**-frame shelter large enough for fifteen people on the trail to Big Green (see Approach below). There are many other flat spots in the area as well. Please use the fire rings and pack out your trash. Do not camp in the parking lot.

Big Green Mountain is the region's flagship cliff for hairball face climbing. Where Whiteside Mountain (chapter 10) at least has some casual routes and Stone Mountain's (chapter 2) moderate routes remain well liked, Big Green is woefully short on both moderates and popularity. In fact, this cliff is probably more obscure now than ever. For some reason, tales of desperate first ascents, long runouts, and

Overview of Big Green Mountain's West Face

padding up polished water grooves have given Big Green something of a reputation. But if slabby-to-vertical face climbing ever comes back into vogue, Big Green is one cliff that deserves a second look.

This granite dome stands over beautiful Panthertown Valley near the town of Cashiers. A west-facing, three-season cliff at 4,200 feet, Big Green has great atmosphere and some of the best face climbing you can shake a stick at, *if* you're up for the excitement. Long runouts are quite common here, especially when the difficulties are less than 5.9.

History

Part of the larger Cashiers Valley, Panthertown Valley is a 6,300-acre backcountry area formerly owned by the electric utility Duke Power and now under management by the U.S. Forest Service. Since its conversion to public land in 1989, the area has become quite popular, although it still maintains an untrammeled flavor. Big Green is just one of several large domes in the area.

According to longtime area climber Jeep Gaskin, the first documented visit into Big Green came in April 1987. At the time, the property was still privately owned and trespassing was rumored to be especially challenging because of two guard dogs. Undeterred, a foursome including Gaskin and Monty Reagan made the three-hour bushwhack into Big Green and—with only three bolts—the Gaskin-Reagan team immediately jumped on one of the wall's most alluring water grooves. At 5.10b, this line became *Bigeminy* (formerly known incorrectly as *By Jimminy*) and set the tone for the type of Big Green route that went up afterward. On the third pitch, Reagan went for it through 50 feet of steep and unprotected climbing until the water groove narrowed. Then he cleverly wedged a figure-eight rappel device into the lips of the groove so he could hang and drill a bolt. Today, Gaskin says the lack of hardware limited bolting at least as much as ethical considerations.

The ensuing development of Big Green occurred at an interesting time in North Carolina climbing history. Fresh off investing a lot of time and energy in areas such as Looking Glass, climbers such as Gaskin, Reagan, Thomas Kelley, and Doc Bayne turned their attention to Big Green and all its virgin rock. Previous experience meant that the climbers' face-climbing chops and ability to bolt on lead from atrocious stances were at all-time highs. So in a very real sense Big Green became *the* proving ground for old-school, ground-up climbing. Routes such as *Green Revolution* (5.11b R), *Gangrene* (5.11c X), and *Black Widow* (5.12a) each raised the bar in terms of commitment, difficulty, and style. Even today, a successful ascent of one of the area test pieces involves a healthy combination of confidence, arrogance, dread, and wisdom.

In 1991, Gaskin managed a free ascent of one of the area's hardest routes, *Live at Leads* (5.13a), which is still likely unrepeated. Not long afterward, most of the main protagonists at Big Green moved on to other areas. It's possible, of course, that they merely lost interest. But it's more likely that they finally reached a point of diminishing returns—it was time to make a choice between difficulty and style and Gaskin, for one, chose the latter. Since he ruled the roost, most climbers acquiesced out of sheer respect and very few new routes have since gone up at Big Green. Today,

Gaskin still refers to the "Green Standard" as a style of climbing in which commitment outweighs everything.

This is not to say the cliff is climbed out; it is not. But if you are thinking about adding your own first ascent here, consider some of these issues (with all due respect to Atlanta climber Jim Corbett, who articulates them better than anybody): (A) Like most of the climbing areas in the Panthertown Valley, Big Green is a granite dome, which means the routes are tenuous and delicate but less than vertical. Bolting on rappel is *verboten* because virtually any line would be climbable here if this style were accepted. (B) As elsewhere in the valley, strength of mind is equally as important as your current redpoint ability. As Corbett has said, "Can you imagine anything more boring and pointless than a water groove with a bolt every 10 feet?"

Weather and Climbing Season

Although the cliff faces west, it is often climbable in warm weather because of its elevation and early-morning shade. In the event of rain, options are limited, but often lines such as *Nature Bats Last, Green Revolution, Between the Ditches,* or *Full Shred* will offer a bit of dry rock. Jackson County sees approximately 47 inches of precipitation annually, most of it in the summer.

Restrictions and Access Issues

There are no current restrictions or access issues. The U.S. Forest Service manages the entire Panthertown Valley as a backcountry area in the Highlands Ranger District of Nantahala National Forest.

Emergency Services

Call 911. Highlands-Cashiers Hospital is on US 64 near Highlands (see appendix C).

Gear

A typical North Carolina free climbing rack will suffice. Although bolts abound, nearly every route at Big Green involves placing some protection.

Getting There

Big Green Mountain is in Jackson County near Cashiers, which is approximately 28 miles west of Brevard on US 64. From the intersection of US 64 and NC 107 in Cashiers, follow US 64 east for 2 miles and turn left onto Cedar Creek Road (SR 1120). Follow Cedar Creek Road for 2.3 miles to an intersection with Breedlove Road (SR 1121) and turn right. Follow Breedlove Road for approximately 3.4 miles until it turns to gravel. Continue another 0.2 mile to its end at a small circular parking lot at a gated access road. The parking is tight and you may have to be creative if there are many other vehicles in the lot. There is a kiosk and map at the gate.

Approach

The approach to Big Green is easy but not well marked, and although the way is primarily downhill, numerous side trails occasionally make for interesting going. If all goes well, the walk should take you approximately 20 minutes.

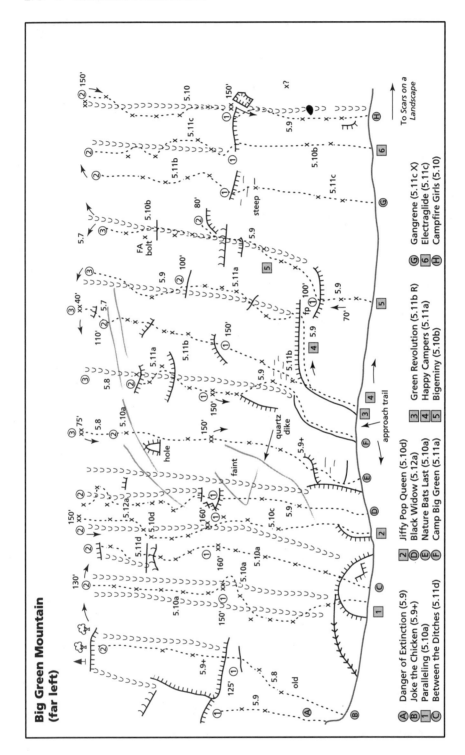

Big Green Mountain
(far left)

Ⓐ Danger of Extinction (5.9)
Ⓑ Joke the Chicken (5.9+)
1 Paralleling (5.10a)
Ⓒ Between the Ditches (5.11d)

2 Jiffy Pop Queen (5.10d)
Ⓓ Black Widow (5.12a)
Ⓔ Nature Bats Last (5.10a)
Ⓕ Camp Big Green (5.11a)

3 Green Revolution (5.11b R)
3 Happy Campers (5.11a)
4 Bigeminy (5.10b)

Ⓖ Gangrene (5.11c X)
6 Electraglide (5.11c)
Ⓗ Campfire Girls (5.10)

Follow the main access road around the gate and down into the valley. (At approximately 0.4 mile, look on the left for a great overlook and view east to Big Green.) At approximately 0.75 mile, turn right (south) at the first obvious fork.

Follow this road (which quickly pinches down) and at 0.2 mile, come to another fork. Turn left (east) onto an unmarked single-track trail. This trail briefly skirts a field and then turns into the woods. Though unmarked, this trail is easy to follow and continues gently downhill, eventually passing through rhododendron tunnels. At approximately 0.4 mile, this trail dead-ends at a larger double-track trail.

Turn left to follow this trail and cross Panthertown Creek in about 50 yards. In just over 0.1 mile, pass an A-frame shelter on the right. Continue on the trail to a sandy spot at 0.3 mile, where you turn left at an unmarked but obvious single-track trail.

From here, you can see the wall through the trees. Continue another 150 yards to a trail that follows the base of the cliff. For routes 1 and 2, turn left. For routes 3 through 15, turn right.

1. Paralleling   5.10a

This excellent line is Big Green's "entrance exam" for 5.10. It climbs between two side-by-side black grooves on the steep, left side of the cliff. Two long, enjoyable pitches with barely adequate protection will keep you guessing. Bring small wires or brass.

First ascent: Joe Lackey, Thomas Kelley.

Start: Beneath mossy flakes in an overlap.

Pitch 1: Climb directly up between the two water runnels past five bolts to a two-bolt belay. (5.10a; 150 feet).

Pitch 2: Continue straight up past five more bolts and a difficult steep section to the belay on a tree ledge. Move right and rappel from *Jiffy Pop Queen* double-bolt anchors. (5.10a; 130 feet).

Descent: Rappel the route.

2. Jiffy Pop Queen   5.10d

One of the area's finest routes with a combination of water-groove friction, steep face, and flake pulling! Bring extra TCUs and medium stoppers.

First ascent: Thomas Kelley, Bruce Burgess, Sam Stevenson (1989).

Start: At an obvious left-facing corner beneath a quartz band; 30 feet right of *Paralleling.*

Pitch 1: Climb a flake through two quartz bands until you can trend left about 30 feet. As the wall steepens, continue past three bolts to a double-bolt anchor. (5.10c; 160 feet).

Pitch 2: Continue up the steep groove past six more bolts to a double-bolt belay. (5.10d; 150 feet).

Descent: Rap the route.

3. Green Revolution   5.11b R

An awesome face climb sandwiched in between two of the area's best water runnels.

First ascent: Doc Bayne, Corinne Webb (1990).

Stephen Scoff finesses his way up the intimidating second pitch of Paralleling *(route 1).*

Start: At a long, low, right-arching corner under a series of water grooves, just right of the approach trail.

Pitch 1: Follow the ramp right of the *Camp Big Green* (topo only) groove to where it turns into a roof. Look for a bolt on the steep face to your left and continue past one more bolt to gain a good overlap. Natural belay. (5.11b; 150 feet).

Pitch 2: Teeter your way up the face via some excellent edges and the occasional sloper. Five bolts lead over a bulge and past two quartz bands where you can get a natural belay. (5.11b; 110 feet).

Pitch 3: Romp up the slab above to gain a double-bolt rappel station. (5.7; 40 feet).

Descent: Rappel down and left over *Camp Big Green* or scramble farther left over to *Nature Bats Last* (topo only).

4. Happy Campers   5.11a

Prepare for steep knobs and wild, off-balance water-groove climbing with some excellent exposure.

First ascent: Thomas Kelley, Bruce Burgess (1989).

Start: Same as *Green Revolution*.

Pitch 1: Follow the *Green Revolution* corner system to where it ends at a bowl and belay. (5.9; 100 feet).

Pitch 2: Move up past a fixed pin and four bolts, eventually gaining a water groove and a large horizontal. Belay with natural gear (medium and large cams). (5.11a; 100 feet).

Pitch 3: Follow the groove until the angle slackens. (5.9; 100 feet).

Descent: Move left to the established rap lane over *Nature Bats Last*.

5. Bigeminy   5.10b

Long erroneously called *By Jimminy*, this route is actually named after a serious cardiac arrhythmia. Have the crash cart ready . . .

First ascent: Jeep Gaskin and Monty Reagan were the first to climb this groove in 1987, although their line avoided some of the difficulties on the lower section because they were conserving bolts. Unaware of that ascent, Thomas Kelley and partners returned not long afterward and straightened out the line . . . until they realized their folly high on the second pitch. The standard climb now follows Kelley's route.

Start: 50 feet right of *Happy Campers*.

Pitch 1: Start beneath two bolts just left of a water groove and climb a short pitch to a sloping ledge beneath a bulge. This is the *Happy Campers* belay. (5.9; 70 feet).

Pitch 2: Climb into the water groove and past three bolts. Natural gear helps negotiate past two more bulges at which point you can step right to a good ledge and belay. (5.9; 80 feet).

Pitch 3: Reenter the water groove and negotiate increasingly steep terrain with the occasional good edge and four bolts. Belay at an obvious horizontal. (5.10b: 90 feet).

Pitch 4: Move left to the rap lane over *Camp Big Green*. (5.7; 50 feet).

Descent: Rappel *Camp Big Green*.

6. Electraglide   5.11c

A knobby (and knee-knocking) first pitch gives way to a faint water streak on the second. Brace for subtle face climbing on laser-cut edges in a shallow, steep groove.

First ascent: Jeep Gaskin, Jon Miller (1990).

Start: 50 feet right of *Happy Campers*.

Pitch 1: Climb past a horizontal and quartz knobs to gain two bolts. Continue to a double-bolt belay on a ledge atop *Campfire Girls*. (5.10b; 150 feet).

Pitch 2: Step left off the belay to gain the shallow water groove. Climb past five bolts and make a run to easier ground. (5.11c; 150 feet).

Descent: Rappel *Campfire Girls*.

7. Scars on a Landscape   5.10b

Two quality pitches of similar difficulty make this an enjoyable outing. However, many parties do only the first pitch, which is an excellent 5.9+.

First ascent: Monty Reagan, Whitney Heuermann (1988).

Start: 200 feet right of *Electraglide*, under a block about 50 feet up the face.

Pitch 1: Climb flat edges past two bolts to gain a hanging block. Follow a right-facing corner past two more bolts and then dash to a double-bolt belay. (5.9+; 100 feet).

Pitch 2: Follow the water groove past two bolts to gain the summit. (5.10b; 150 feet).

Descent: Scramble left to fixed anchors atop *Whip-O-Will* (see topo).

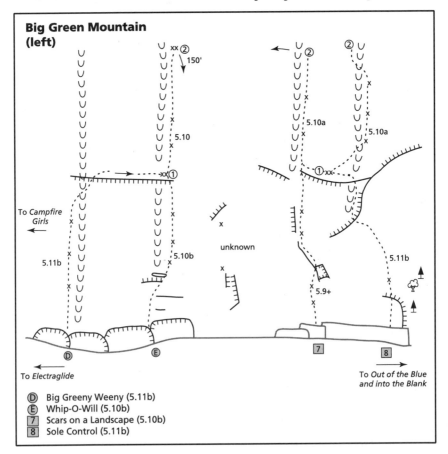

Big Green Mountain (left)

To *Campfire Girls* ←

5.11b

5.10

5.10b

unknown

5.10a

5.10a

5.11b

5.9+

To *Electraglide* ←

To *Out of the Blue and into the Blank* →

Ⓓ   Big Greeny Weeny (5.11b)
Ⓔ   Whip-O-Will (5.10b)
7   Scars on a Landscape (5.10b)
8   Sole Control (5.11b)

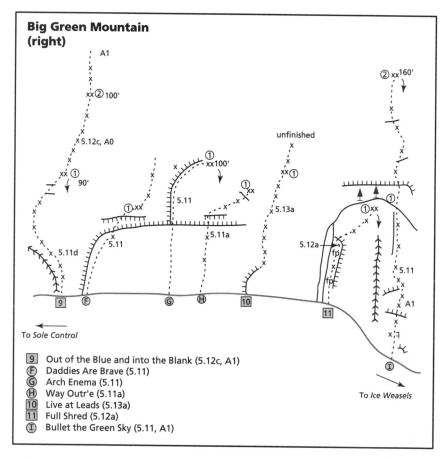

Big Green Mountain (right)

9. Out of the Blue and into the Blank (5.12c, A1)
F. Daddies Are Brave (5.11)
G. Arch Enema (5.11)
H. Way Outr'e (5.11a)
10. Live at Leads (5.13a)
11. Full Shred (5.12a)
I. Bullet the Green Sky (5.11, A1)

8. Sole Control   5.11b

The improbable first pitch features a bare-minimum face followed by a tiger-striped roof.

First ascent: Chris Caldwell, Doc Bayne.

Start: 30 feet right of *Scars in a Landscape*.

Pitch 1: Climb the face inside a left-facing overlap to a horizontal that takes small cams. Crank past the lone bolt and wander up the slab to a corner. Roll around the excellent roof to the belay on *Scars on a Landscape*. (5.11b; 100 feet).

Pitch 2: Climb a water groove past three bolts. (5.10a; 150 feet).

Descent: Rappel the route.

9. Out of the Blue and into the Blank   5.12c, A1

This route starts on a harmless-looking ramp and keeps getting harder. *Blank* claimed some long leader falls and remains an unfinished masterpiece, since it was never free climbed. This route has gone by several names including *The Wheelchair Ramp* and *Jeepers Creepers* for Jeep Gaskin's unyielding determination to complete the project.

First ascent: Jeep Gaskin, Jon Miller, Doc Bayne.

Start: 100 feet right of *Sole Control* at a low, bulging ramp.

Pitch 1: Awkward, steep and demanding climbing along the ramp leads past seven bolts to a double-bolt belay. (5.11d; 90 feet).

Pitch 2: With no move easier than 5.11a and two long sections of sustained 5.12 separated by an A0 bolt, this pitch still awaits a motivated suitor. Twelve bolts to anchor. (5.12c, A0; 100 feet).

Pitch 3: Free-climb past three bolts to a four-hole bat hook ladder. Four more bolts protect the upper part where the difficulty eases. Seven bolts total. (5.12a, A1; 90 feet).

Descent: Rappel the route.

10. Live at Leads   5.13a

Among the hardest slabs in the state . . . or maybe anywhere! Bring a light rack.

First ascent: Jeep Gaskin (1991, ground-up).

Start: 50 feet left of the gully that separates the main wall from *Full Shred.*

Pitch 1: Climb past a right-facing overlap and seven bolts to a double-bolt anchor. (70 feet).

Descent: Rappel the route.

11. Full Shred   5.12a

With intricate stemming, fingertip liebacks, and powerful face climbing, this stunning corner is atypical for the cliff and quite a sandbag to boot. Bring pro to 1 inch.

First ascent: Monty Reagan, Whitney Heuermann (1991).

Start: Follow the trail to the right along the base to the obvious pillar. *Full Shred* is the left-facing crack and corner that starts off a pedestal.

Pitch 1: Move into the corner system past a fixed pin and corner until it ends, then step right and blast across the face past two bolts for a two-bolt anchor. (70 feet).

Descent: Rappel.

12. Ice Weasels   5.11b

A hard section down low gives way to mellow climbing followed by the redpoint crux higher up. Beautiful edges, body tension, and friction all help negotiate this demanding route.

First ascent: Andy Kluge.

Start: Follow the trail to the right along the base and through an obvious cleft between some boulders. *Ice Weasels* starts at the blank face just right of a black streak and climbs to a hidden double-bolt rappel station.

Pitch 1: Sport. Climb past eleven bolts to anchor. (150 feet).

Descent: Rappel.

13. Panthertown Knobs   5.9

Big Green's classic two-pitch moderate. This wall never gives routes away easily, but this one is a gem. Be sure to bring long runners to sling knobs for pro.

Doc Bayne negotiates the deceptively thin dihedral on Full Shred *(route 11).*

First ascent: Thomas Kelley, Sam Stevenson (1989).

Start: 200 feet right of *Ice Weasels* beneath an overlap with a crack.

Pitch 1: Climb past a bolt missing its hanger and negotiate a devious face past horns and a narrow water groove to a double-bolt belay. (5.9; 150 feet).

Pitch 2: Continue past one more bolt and a flake (go right) to where the angle lowers. Move left to reach top. (5.9; 150 feet).

Descent: Rappel from tree.

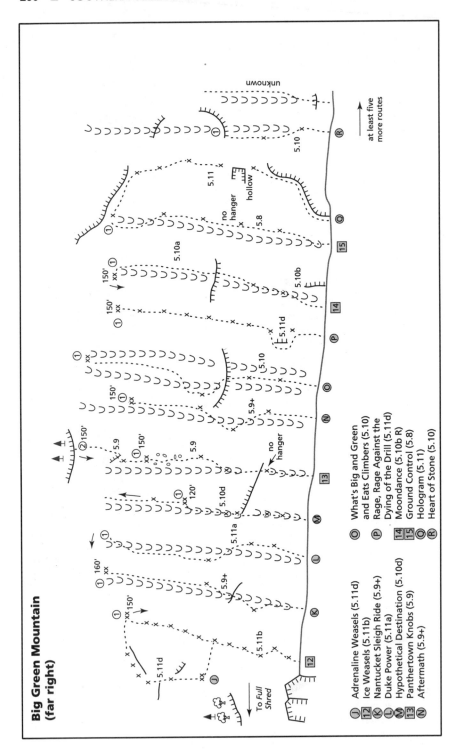

Big Green Mountain (far right)

Ⓙ Adrenaline Weasels (5.11d)
⑫ Ice Weasels (5.11b)
Ⓚ Nantucket Sleigh Ride (5.9+)
Ⓛ Duke Power (5.11a)
Ⓜ Hypothetical Destination (5.10d)
⑬ Panthertown Knobs (5.9)
Ⓝ Aftermath (5.9+)

Ⓞ What's Big and Green and Eats Climbers (5.10)
Ⓟ Rage, Rage Against the Dying of the Drill (5.11d)
⑭ Moondance (5.10b R)
⑮ Ground Control (5.8)
Ⓠ Hologram (5.11)
Ⓡ Heart of Stone (5.10)

at least five more routes

14. Moondance 5.10b R

It is a long 30 feet to the first bolt, and cruxy, too. Falling is not an option.

First ascent: Doc Bayne, Corinne Webb (1990).

Start: 100 feet right of *Panthertown Knobs.*

Pitch 1: Climb left of a left-leaning flake to gain a bolt way off the deck. Continue past another bolt and some good horizontals to reach a double-bolt anchor. (5.10b; 150 feet).

Descent: Rappel the route.

15. Ground Control 5.8

Friction aficionados will enjoy this pitch.

First ascent: Thomas Kelley, Sam Stevenson (1989).

Start: 20 feet right of *Moondance.*

Pitch 1: Pad your way up the water groove past four bolts and make a long run (some gear) to gain a final bolt in a roofy crack system. (150 feet).

Descent: Rappel.

10. WHITESIDE MOUNTAIN ─────────────

Climbing type: Multipitch traditional

Rock type: Whiteside granite (quartz diorite gneiss)

Height: 70 to 700 feet

Number of routes: 50+ (24 this guide)

Climbing season: Year-round

Camping: Do not camp in the parking lot. There is free Forest Service camping nearby. Ammons Branch is a primitive area about 9.5 miles east of Highlands with four sites and no drinking water. (Follow Main Street east out of town for about 8 miles through Horse Cove. When the pavement ends, bear right on Bull Pen Road and go 1.5 miles). Blue Valley is 5.5 miles south of Highlands on NC 28. (See appendix B.)

With a reputation for loose rock, steep routes, skimpy gear, and wild weather Whiteside Mountain remains among the most feared and revered climbing areas in the Southeast. Visible from as far away as Greenville, South Carolina, this mountain in Nantahala National Forest is atypical for the Cashiers Valley area because of its steepness and featured terrain. The mountain's 700-foot Southeast Face sees most of the action, but in recent years climbers have developed routes on its North Face, known as Devil's Courthouse.

All the rock routes here have a serious aura about them due to both the objective dangers and Whiteside's reputation as the local flight school. Whiteside's most popular routes—*The Original Route* and *Traditions*—are easily aided when the going gets tough and are relatively straightforward multipitch ticks for modern rock climbers. If you're willing to up the ante, you will find a host of long and committing routes, perhaps unequaled on the East Coast for sheer ambiance. Ice climbing is also

Boulder Problem Area

Southeast Face

Wildcat Cliffs
private property
no climbing

Wright Wall
private property
no climbing

Overview of the Southeast Face of Whiteside Mountain

popular at Whiteside during the winter, both on the North Face and in some lesser-known corners of the mountain.

History

Whiteside Mountain has a colorful climbing history. Note that we did not say "long." In fact, climbing at Whiteside is only about thirty years old, and most of the action took place in the late 1980s and '90s.

Although Piedmont climber George DeWolfe and two companions made a brief attempt on the wall in 1964, a group of climbers based around the North Carolina Outward Bound School at Table Rock first began climbing Whiteside in earnest in 1968. In that year, English expatriate John Lawrence and John Whisnant began wandering their way up the cliff's obvious—but disconnected—line of weakness. Their chosen line, now known as *The Original Route,* began at the great gray slabs on the wall's far right and climbed through a series of corners and arêtes. Lawrence and Whisnant started the route using polypropylene rope and would hand-over-hand to their high point on each subsequent attempt. The party turned back three times because Lawrence was unwilling to drill high on the face where most parties now pull through the bolt ladder. On one attempt, Lawrence and Whisnant were pinned for several nights by a snowstorm that plastered the wall in ice. Fortunately, the climbers were able to extricate their fixed lines and rap the route. When they returned to their base camp in the woods (which was then below the face), they arrived to find a search and rescue team ready to perform a body recovery. Once the climbers explained how they had made it off alive, they gave the rescuers a lesson in rappelling!

Later, Peter Young and Jim Marshall took over from Lawrence and Whisnant's high point and finally finished the route on a summer night in 1971. Young later recalled that on the advice of a nonclimbing friend, the group had climbed much of the route barefoot because they thought it might help overcome wet rock. "Oh it hurt," Young said. "Especially where we put that shitty bolt ladder in." Once named *Gom Jabber*, the route is now known simply as *The Original Route* (or the *OR*).

Around 1973, Bob Rotert landed on the scene and began cozying up to some of the locals in hopes that their climbing prowess would rub off. It did. Within three years Rotert had completed an early ascent of the *OR* and his own first ascent, *New Perversions* (originally 5.8, A2 and now free at 5.11a/b). This route followed a wandering line right of the *OR* and, in a style that would later come to define Whiteside, took just three protection bolts. *New Perversions* had no protection on five of its eight pitches. In keeping with this difficult and unprotected climbing, the *OR* saw two solo ascents in 1981. The first was by Ted Anderson and Rotert repeated the feat soon after. Anderson aided his way through the bolt ladder and Rotert freed the bolt ladder, although he clipped in with a long sling while he climbed.

The wall was quiet for a few years until Nashville climber Arno Ilgner arrived in 1985. An aspiring caver, Ilgner had first seen Whiteside up close when he was a college student at Tennessee Tech in 1973. Ilgner, like many other cavers before and since, had rappelled down Whiteside via the caver's rappel, a 700-foot, mostly free-hanging rap lane established so cavers could train for the Southeast's many deep pits. Ilgner left the East Coast soon after that first visit, but Whiteside never strayed far from his thoughts. Twelve years later, when he finally felt up to the challenge, Ilgner talked two of his brother's climbing friends and fellow Tennesseans, Mark Cartwright and Eddie Whittemore, into returning to Whiteside.

At the time the wall had several routes, but none through the steep, foreboding headwall. The only attempt had been an 80-foot bolt ladder to nowhere. Ilgner, however, decided on an all-out assault on this impressive swath of stone. He arrived a day early and rappelled the wall again, this time with an eye for connecting features. Armed with that knowledge, the trio started up the wall with three days of supplies and twenty-five ¼-inch bolts, each fitted with homemade hangers. The climbers made quick progress until they reached the headwall, where the hooking became difficult and the exposure intense. After a third day—and one 50-footer by Ilgner on the Jump Pitch—the trio summitted on *The Volunteer Wall* (V, 5.10+, A4).

With Whiteside's aura of impasse broken and climbing standards on the rise, Ilgner began systematically completing successively more difficult Whiteside routes, and the wall underwent a slow but steady development. But let's not forget one notable ascent in 1989: Mark Lassiter's *Traditions*. Loath to battle the horror-show Headwall routes and convinced that Whiteside needed a stronger free climb than the *OR*, Lassiter began working his way up the wall. An Atlanta native who had recently moved to Cashiers, Lassiter was a Rotert disciple with a twist. When the free-climbing difficulty pushed into the 5.11 range, Lassiter was willing to bolt as needed, much to the chagrin of some locals.

When word of *Traditions* leaked out, Lassiter began receiving nasty letters from Tarheel climbers upset about his "over drilling." Lassiter eventually compromised, removing about six bolts from two pitches he had aided, and watched as

Greenville, South Carolina, climber Doc Bayne managed to free the route at 5.11c. Ironically, *Traditions* has since become the wall's second most popular route.

In a way, the incident helped usher in a new era of excitement at Whiteside as Ilgner and crew worked on Headwall routes while others amused themselves with nearby projects. More than other North Carolina cliffs, Whiteside has been a magnet for out-of-state climbers, and several different factions operated here, sometimes completely unaware of the others' actions. Most of the credit goes to the Tennessee crowd led by Ilgner and the Carolina bunch led by Bayne. But a group of Atlanta climbers including Lassiter, Jim Corbett, and Shannon Stegg also made significant additions at Whiteside.

In particular, Stegg's contribution to Whiteside is impossible to ignore: Nearly fifty pitches overall including (with Jerry Roberts) *Arm and Hammer* (5.12a) on the Southeast Face, *Crown of Thorns*, which is the only line on the Southeast Face with no bolts, and numerous ice routes. Stegg continues to find shorter lines such as *One Pitch Wonder* (5.10c) and *Red Dog* (5.9+) in less-explored corners of Whiteside. He and Corbett were also the prime movers on Whiteside's North Face, which was the site of renewed interest in the 1990s when climbers realized that the face offered good face climbing in addition to the well-established ice routes. Painfully obvious from an overlook on US 64, the North Face is one of the most visible—and inaccessible—formations in the area. Save the ice climbs *Starshine* and *Mother Russia* (ice climbers being a particularly motivated breed), little climbing activity occurred before 1990.

The complex North Face is divided by a narrow tree ledge called the Catwalk, which separates the upper Devil's Courthouse section of the face from the lower main North Face. Devil's Courthouse is an outlying cap of Whiteside gneiss, and the lower part of the face was formed by the same intrusive granite pluton that is part of the first couple pitches of the Southeast Face routes. Below and left of Devil's Courthouse, this granite forms a steep, immaculate, 300-foot-high face characterized by a prominent roof/corner system that stair steps right up the face as a nearly impenetrable 10-foot roof just 50 feet above the ground. This intimidating area was home to the first route on the North Face, *Courthouse Arch*, climbed by Mark Lassiter, Jim Corbett, and Bob Ordner in 1990. Their effort required humping in camping and aid gear on old logging roads and a punishing bushwhack retreat to the US 64 overlook when an early spring thunderstorm dumped several inches of hail on the wall.

During this climb, Corbett scoped the wall right of *Courthouse Arch* and recognized that it could provide one of the premier face climbs at Whiteside. Deciding that he lacked the daring and skill to approach ground-up, he returned in 1991 with Shannon Stegg, but the attempt was aborted because of rain. Shortly thereafter, Stegg returned and—in a highly controversial move—rappel bolted this face and a line to the left, creating the *North Face Direct* and *Crystal Crème* and eviscerating the original *Courthouse Arch*. The uproar continues to this day, but the quality of the routes that Stegg put up cannot be denied; and although rap bolted, the routes retain the sportiness of local ethics and are by no means sport climbs. Stegg returned in 1997 to climb *Conquistador*, the only route from the bottom of the main North Face to the top of the Devil's Courthouse, and punched through the main roof to create *Dirty Love*—both from the ground up.

Meanwhile, on the Southeast Face, Ilgner had long been intrigued with the prospect of free climbing *The Volunteer Wall.* He finally completed that project in 1990 at 5.12a, after some serious falls and numerous attempts, including one top-rope rehearsal on the Jump Pitch—the only such pitch on the entire wall where Ilgner employed this tactic. Ilgner also caused quite a ruckus in 1994 when he established the impressive and very controversial *The Warrior's Way.* Many mistakenly believed this route had been rappel bolted, but it was not. Instead, Ilgner and his partners climbed the route ground-up in "aid-point" style, wherein the leader climbs pitches on aid and places protection in places that would lend themselves to a later free attempt.

The diverse first-ascent styles employed at Whiteside have always been a flash point issue in this area. While unquestionably bold, Ilgner was willing to bend many of the area's strict, traditional rules in pursuit of harder and more impressive lines. During his four-year quest to free climb *Little Miss Dangerous* (which is still 5.12a, A0), Ilgner took 55-foot falls even after first ascending the routes on aid. On newer routes such as *The Great Ah Ha,* Ilgner and his partners occasionally employed a hybrid aid-point style in which they would aid the line with an emphasis on speed—sometimes even placing removable bolts on lead—until a second or third climber followed to place protection bolts. Ilgner's new lines were that steep, featureless, and physically demanding.

For many years, Bayne climbed his routes in bottom-up, traditional, free-climbing style, wherein the leader never previewed and only resorted to aid when placing a bolt. This method did not produce routes as difficult as *The Warrior's Way,* but Bayne felt that a traditional approach would keep things equal for subsequent free climbers while allowing them a chance at matching his adventurous spirit. And sure enough, way up on the Southeast Face's High Anxiety Headwall you'll lean back out over space and search for distant bolts in much the same way Bayne must have as he searched for protection or even just a wobbly hook placement from which he could drill.

This guidebook is no place to choose sides over which first-ascent style is more valid, but it does offer a good opportunity to discuss the future. The first ascentionists at Whiteside invested an extraordinary amount of time and energy, and their efforts have resulted in one of the most challenging climbing areas anywhere. Before discounting their routes as passé, see how climbers pushed themselves at Whiteside. There is plenty of reason to believe that twenty-first century climbers will one-up their predecessors in difficulty, mental commitment, and style. And maybe more than anywhere else in North Carolina, Whiteside is the place to do it.

(Special thanks goes to Jim Corbett for his history of the North Face.)

Weather and Climbing Season

The trailhead at Whiteside Mountain is open year-round but the best time for climbing the Southeast Face is September through April, and prime climbing season on the North Face is May through October.

Even cold winter days are often pleasant on the Southeast Face (which will get afternoon shade). A general rule for climbing at Whiteside is this: The parking lot and first 0.25 mile of the approach trail are always cooler than it is on the wall.

Climbers should be especially vigilant for fast-moving thunderstorms that often approach from the north.

Restrictions and Access Issues

Beginning in late January every year, the National Forest Service closes a portion of Whiteside for peregrine falcon nesting. The closure often lasts until late summer. In 2000, after years of hard work by local climbers, the Forest Service agreed to close just a portion of the Southeast Face instead of the entire face. *Traditions* and routes to the right (east) of it remain open year-round. Please heed these closures. There is a new kiosk in the parking area with climbing routes and closures posted.

Additionally, the Forest Service has identified federally endangered lichen on some parts of Whiteside. *Gymnoderma lineare* (rock gnome lichen) is typically found on vertical rock that is occasionally exposed to seepage and is associated with a very distinct red-colored moss. Please keep an eye out for this important and rare species.

Gear

All routes at Whiteside require a slimmed-down version of the typical North Carolina free-climbing rack. Emphasize small to medium cams. Long runouts are quite common regardless of the climbing difficulty. It is customary to eschew R or X ratings at Whiteside since every pitch would likely qualify.

For Southeast Face routes, rack up in the parking lot and wear a small pack. Retreat from this face is not easy; double ropes or a trail line are highly recommended.

Emergency Services

Call 911. Highland-Cashiers Hospital is on US 64 near Highlands (see appendix C).

Getting There

From Cashiers, travel west on US 64 for 4.7 miles to the Jackson and Macon County line. Turn left (south) onto Whiteside Mountain Road (SR 1600) at a large sign for Wildcat Cliffs Country Club. Drive approximately 1 mile and look for the Forest Service gravel parking lot on the left. Locate pit toilets in the parking lot. The Forest Service charges a small fee for day-use parking ($2 per car in 2001).

Approach

For Boulder Problem in the Sky Area: Follow the summit trail (the main Whiteside loop trail) out of the parking lot, and at 0.1 mile veer right up steep steps. (Do not take the main road.) Continue up switchbacks until the trail reaches the ridgeline. Here, where the trail makes a hard left, the climbers' trail disappears behind two hemlocks. Continue up the main trail about 50 feet to a trail on the right (often obscured by brush) at some large, hidden boulders. Follow a trail between the boulders for 0.1 mile to the wall and then scramble down through rhododendron.

For the Southeast Face: Follow the summit trail out of the parking lot, veer right up steep steps at 0.1 mile, and continue up switchbacks until the trail reaches the ridgeline. Here, where the trail makes a hard left, continue straight through two hemlocks that obscure a wooden post.

Follow this obvious trail down the ridge to reach the base. Hike along the base to reach all routes on the Southeast Face, which are listed left to right. If you are making your first trip to Whiteside and all goes well, it will take approximately 45 minutes to reach the base of *The Original Route.*

For the North Face (aka Devil's Courthouse): There are several approaches to this complex part of Whiteside. If all goes well—and it probably won't—you should arrive at the North Face after about one hour.

Follow the gray-blazed summit trail out of the parking lot. Stay on the road for 0.9 mile until you reach the shoulder on the eastern flank of Whiteside Mountain. To your left, locate a narrow trail leading down into rhododendron.

Descend briefly to an obvious fork where the main trail goes left. (Go right for a short diversion and a stunning view of the Southeast Face.) The trail will contour left (stay high as you scramble over some exposed rock) for 0.4 mile to a gap and the junction of several trails near a fire ring.

For the northeast face ice routes, Courthouse South Face, the east end of The Catwalk, and the Main North Face, descend the trail to your right. Within 100 yards, a faint trail contours right to the ice climbs. Continue on the main trail, walking along the base of the Courthouse South Face on your left. Soon, the trail climbs up to the flat ridge top above the North Face. To reach the east end of The Catwalk, descend left.

For the Main North Face, continue along the ridge top. In 100 yards, you'll encounter a cluster of ten trees on the left, which is often marked by either a sling or tape. Cut sharply left and bushwhack down to a rappel tree above *Crystal Crème.* Two double-rope rappels reach the base. Alternatively, continue straight on the trail to a rock overlook. Descend the right edge of this, wind back left at the base, and drop down a short step. Follow a faint trail straight down (steep) until it curves left to the base of the North Face.

Routes are listed continuously 1 through 24 starting with the Boulder in the Sky Area, through the Southeast Face, and ending on the North Face.

Boulder Problem in the Sky Area

This area is popular as a fallback when weather prevents climbing on the main Southeast or North Faces. A gigantic arête and roof system keeps the wall dry in all but the most terrific rain showers.

1. Boulder Problem in the Sky   5.11a/b (no topo)

A short approach, well-protected climbing and a generally laid-back atmosphere could almost convince you that this isn't Whiteside . . . *almost.*

First ascent: Diff Ritchie, Bob Rotert. Rotert returned for the free ascent in 1976.

Start: Under the obvious corner, scramble up onto a ledge.

Pitch 1: Climb the left-facing corner to a belay at a bolt. (5.8; 90 feet).

Pitch 2: Traverse left past a fixed pin to a small overlap festooned with old fixed gear. Pull it and traverse 20 feet left to a three-bolt belay. (5.11a; 60 feet).

Pitch 3: Face-climb straight off the ledge to gain a crack that leads under the roof. Move left under the roof to a fixed anchor at a huge horn. (5.8; 60 feet).

Descent: Most parties make a double-rope rappel to the ground from the top of the third pitch. It is possible to climb to the summit where you can join the main Whiteside loop.

Southeast Face

This is it: the biggest, baddest wall in the East. Some loose rock, long runouts, and the intimidation factor might make you want to go sport climbing instead . . .

Descent: Walk off from top of face.

2. Ship of Fools Direct   IV, 5.12a/b

When you add up all the business on the direct version of this route (which also includes parts of *Room to Breathe* and *KKK Variation*—routes not included in this book), this route becomes one of the most sustained, long free climbs around.

First ascent: Mark Cartwright, Eddie Whittemore, Arno Ilgner, and Mark Ilgner all assisted in the first ascent in 1987–88. Kris Kline free-climbed the first pitch of the *KKK Variation*. Arno Ilgner made the first full free ascent in November 1991.

Start: On the left end of the main wall, 50 feet right of a right-facing corner.

Pitch 1: Friction up slabby face, eventually pulling past flakes and a weakness in the roof at a left-facing flake to a bolted belay. (5.10c; 80 feet).

Pitch 2: Move up and right off the belay past obvious horizontals and into steeper ground. Climb past four bolts to a bolted anchor. (5.11c; 80 feet).

Pitch 3: Step up and right off the belay into crimpers. Power past two bolts and continue through spectacular black rock above. Eight bolts total. (5.12a/b; 160 feet).

Pitch 4: Climb a left-angling corner and crack system until it ends at a tree. (5.10c/d; 90 feet).

Pitch 5: Walk around a tree ledge and up onto the Port O' Call Ledge. (5.0; 60 feet).

Pitch 6: Step right around a corner and onto a face with two bolts. A small flake leads into knobby terrain with some run-out 5.10 climbing (long fall potential) to a small ledge. Four bolts total. (5.11d; 90 feet).

Pitch 7: Move directly right off the belay, pass some horns (slings for pro), and move to a bolted belay. (5.11a; 80 feet).

Pitch 8: Move left off the belay past three bolts and a bulge to a crack system. (5.11c; 80 feet).

Pitch 9: Move directly right past moss clods and then up to a horizontal for belay. (5.4; 70 feet).

Pitch 10: Climb the lower-angled face above to the summit. (5.5; 40 feet).

3. The Promised Land   IV, 5.12c

Graced with exciting face climbing down low, wildly exposed moderate ground in the middle, and two intense pitches on the headwall, this route is harder than *Ship of Fools Direct* but goes somewhat faster. The headwall pitches are tremendous: overhanging, solid rock that follows beautiful features. Portions of this route follow *Room to Breathe*, a wandering line that climbs only half of the face.

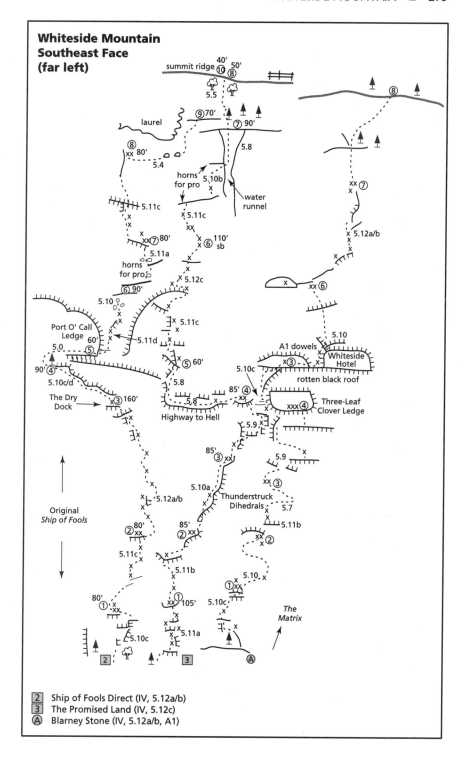

**Whiteside Mountain
Southeast Face
(far left)**

summit ridge

40' 50'
⑩ ⑧
5.5

9 70'
laurel
⑦ 90'
5.8
⑧
xx 80'
5.4
horns
for pro
5.10b
x
water
runnel
x 5.11c
5.11c
xx
x
xx⑦ 80'
x 110'
x ⑥ sb
5.11a
horns
for pro
⑥ 90'
x 5.12c
x
5.10
Port O' Call
Ledge 60'
5.0
⑤
90' ④
5.10c/d
The Dry
Dock
x③ 160'
x 5.11c
x
5.11d
x ⑤ 60'
5.8
5.8
Highway to Hell
85' ④
xx
5.10c
③ xx
5.10a
5.12a/b
Original
Ship of Fools
80'
②
xx
5.11c
85'
②
5.11b
80'
①
xx
105'
①
5.10c
xx
5.10c
5.11a

⑧
xx ⑦
x 5.12a/b
x
xx ⑥
5.10
A1 dowels
x③
Whiteside
Hotel
rotten black roof
Three-Leaf
xxx④ Clover Ledge
5.9 x
5.9
xx ③
Thunderstruck
Dihedrals x 5.7
x
x 5.11b
xx
x ②
5.10
①xx
The
Matrix

2 Ship of Fools Direct (IV, 5.12a/b)
3 The Promised Land (IV, 5.12c)
Ⓐ Blarney Stone (IV, 5.12a/b, A1)

First ascent: Arno Ilgner, Glenn Ritter (1991, mixed aid and free, established over three days).

Start: 20 feet right of *Ship of Fools Direct*, just before the trail drops past a cleft near the base.

Pitch 1: Begin by moving right across a slabby face and past some good, though small, horizontals. Climb a shallow corner system past five bolts to an anchor. (5.11a; 105 feet).

Pitch 2: Blast off the belay via wild, off-balance face climbing. Make a run to the third bolt on this pitch, where you can gain a ledge, and move up and right for a bolted belay. Bring just quickdraws and small cams. (5.11b; 85 feet).

Pitch 3: Move up into the Thunderstruck Dihedrals. Some midsized cams and two bolts protect a weird move in the corner. Bolted belay. (5.10a; 85 feet).

Pitch 4: Climb up past a bolt where the exposure increases dramatically. Do not move too far right or you'll end up in the Three-Leaf Clover Ledge on *Blarney Stone*. Move past another bolt and gun for the bolted belay (5.9; 85 feet).

Pitch 5: Move directly left past one bolt on a narrow ledge system. Continue up disconnected corners to a belay marked by a single bolt. (5.8; 60 feet).

Pitch 6: Climb straight up the increasingly steep face through four bolts. At the fourth, move right and pull the corner and roof system at a weakness with a bolt. Move back left and past four more bolts (sustained face climbing) to a bolted belay. (5.12c; 110 feet).

Pitch 7: Move left off the belay past three bolts to a sloping dike system. Follow this back right slinging horns for pro. Another bolt and a 5.10b move gains a water runnel and a bushy ledge. (5.11c; 90 feet).

Pitch 8: Climb easier terrain to the summit. (5.5; 50 feet).

4. Little Miss Dangerous   IV, 5.12a, A0

A beautiful line with a little of everything, *Little Miss* follows the wall's most natural features. Unfairly saddled with a terrifying reputation, instead prepare for pumpy pitches, adequate protection, and only one short (albeit steep) section of rotten rock. Double ropes are highly recommended.

First ascent: After beginning in 1986, Arno Ilgner, Mark Ilgner, and Doyle Parsons completed the first ascent in 1990. Most of the difficult free pitches were aided. In 1991, the Ilgners returned and eliminated all the aid except two moves on the second pitch.

Start: 250 feet right of *The Promised Land*, look for a huge, right-leaning corner.

Pitch 1: Climb the slab to a thin flake that leads to the dihedral and follow it right to a belay. (5.8; 90 feet).

Pitch 2: The Great Barrier Pitch. Climb up and left past two bolts (A0) to gain a flake. Exit left onto the steep face and continue left another 10 feet where a line of bolts leads through scads of 5.10 and one thin sequence. (5.12a; 80 feet).

Pitch 3: Continue up vertical ground for 20 feet and then begin meandering through some thin face moves and intricate small pro to a good ledge. (5.10d; 165 feet).

Pitch 4: Climb up a vertical wall past two bolts to gain a ledge under a rotten black roof with a fixed piece. Move right and climb gigantic rotten jugs (good cams or slings for pro) to the wall above with a bolt. Pump left for 8 feet to the belay. (5.11c; 70 feet).

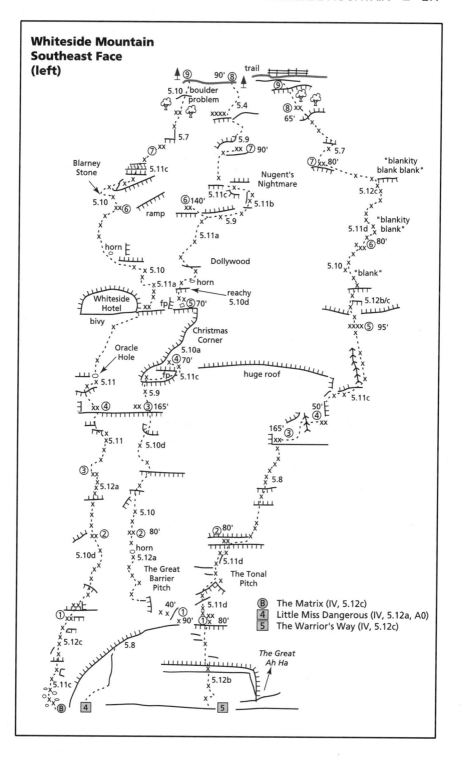

**Whiteside Mountain
Southeast Face
(left)**

9 90' 8 trail

5.10 boulder problem
5.4
9
8 xx 65'

5.7
5.9
7 xx
90' 7
5.7

Blarney Stone
7 xx
5.11c
Nugent's Nightmare
"blankity blank blank"

5.10
6 140'
5.11c
5.11b
5.12cx

xx 6
ramp
5.9
"blankity blank"
5.11d
6 80'

horn
5.11a
5.10 x "blank"

5.10
Dollywood
5.12b/c

5.11a horn
reachy 5.10d
xxxx 5 95'

Whiteside Hotel
bivy
fp 5 70'

Oracle Hole
Christmas Corner
5.10a
4 70'
huge roof

5.11
fp 5.11c
50'
4 xx

5.9
xx 4 xx 3 165'
165'
3

5.11
5.10d
5.8

3
5.12a

5.10
xx 2 80'

2
horn
5.12a
2 80'

5.10d
The Great Barrier Pitch
5.11d
The Tonal Pitch

40' 1
1
5.11d
B The Matrix (IV, 5.12c)

1 xx
x 90'
1 80'
4 Little Miss Dangerous (IV, 5.12a, A0)
5 The Warrior's Way (IV, 5.12c)

5.12c
5.8
The Great Ah Ha

5.11c
5.12b

B **4**
5

Pitch 5: The Christmas Corner. Follow the dihedral up to a large ledge with a single bolt. Back up the anchor by slinging a block. (5.10a; 70 feet).

Pitch 6: Dollywood (As in "big jugs, wild rides . . . "). Make some long moves to a good depression and then take the S path following the best holds. (5.11a; 140 feet).

Pitch 7: Nugent's Nightmare. Climb down off the belay ledge and traverse right for 40 feet underneath a small roof and passing three bolts. A shallow horizontal and two bolts lead up a seam, where you can move left to a bowl with another bolt. Continue 10 feet left to a dirty drainage with one more bolt. Follow this up to a bolt and move right for a double-bolt belay. (5.11c; 90 feet).

Pitch 8: Climb back left to the bolt on the previous pitch and then up to a large flake. Follow it right until the angle slackens. Continue about 75 feet on easy ground, passing a caver's rappel anchor, to the summit. (5.9; 90 feet).

5. The Warrior's Way   IV, 5.12c

An excellent plumb line straight up the steepest portion of Whiteside's Southeast Face. Its reputation as a sport route belies some bold climbing, occasionally weird rock, and intense exposure. Bring some brass or steel wired nuts.

First ascent: Arno Ilgner, Walt Wilkinson (summer 1994, ground-up, mixed aid and free). Ilgner returned for the free ascent in October of that year.

Start: 100 feet right of *Little Miss Dangerous*, beneath a 6-foot roof just 50 feet off the ground.

Pitch 1: Climb the slab past two bolts to a bolt in the roof. Swing over and continue up the face to anchor. (5.12b; 80 feet).

Pitch 2: The Tonal Pitch. This is a nonstop pump with multiple cruxes. Blast up the face past nine bolts to belay. Bring some medium and large cams. (5.11d; 80 feet)

Pitch 3: Move directly right and step off the ledge past two bolts. Flakes, horns, excellent horizontals, and long reaches make this a memorable pitch. Ten bolts. (5.8; 165 feet).

Pitch 4: Climb up and right through lichen-covered, broken rock to the belay. (5.4; 50 feet).

Pitch 5: Move into the corner, then step right past three bolts in increasingly steep rock to a bowl and eventually gain the outside of an arête. Follow to the belay. (5.11c; 95 feet).

Pitch 6: Fire through the overhang and climb past eight bolts to the belay. (5.12b/c; 80 feet).

Pitch 7: Sloping holds, poor edges, and barely featured white rock give this pitch some bite. Eleven bolts. (5.12c; 80 feet).

Pitch 8: Climb out right and past two roofs. Three bolts. (5.7; 65 feet).

Pitch 9: Climb the lower-angled face above to the summit. (5.5; 40 feet).

6. The Great Ah Ha   IV, 5.12b

With protection a little more spread out than on *Warrior's Way* and near that route's difficulty, you may have some "Ah ha" moments on this route! Some say it is harder than *Warrior* overall. Bring 3- and 4-inch cams and long slings on all pitches (some horns for pro).

**Whiteside Mountain
Southeast Face
(center left)**

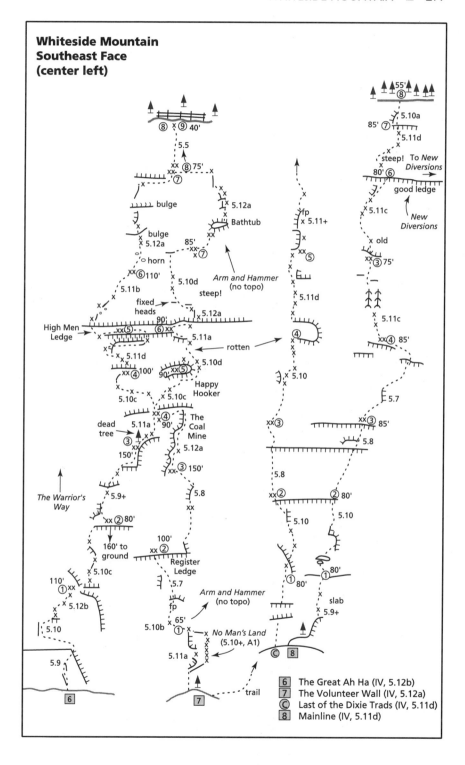

6 The Great Ah Ha (IV, 5.12b)
7 The Volunteer Wall (IV, 5.12a)
C Last of the Dixie Trads (IV, 5.11d)
8 Mainline (IV, 5.11d)

First ascent: Arno Ilgner, Steve Jones (1997). They returned in August 1999 to lead all the pitches free.

Start: 50 feet right of *Warrior*. Begin *Ah Ha* on the face inside the left-facing corner.

Pitch 1: Climb the dihedral to a roof. Pull through where it meets the face and then move up and left toward a flake. Follow this until you can traverse delicately right for the first bolt. Climb up and right through four bolts to the belay. (5.12b; 110 feet).

Pitch 2: Go right 5 feet and then up past four bolts of sustained climbing to a large ledge and the belay. (5.10c; 80 feet).

Pitch 3: Climb a short right-facing corner and continue up past two bolts heading toward a large left-facing corner. Follow to the belay near a dead tree. (5.9+; 150 feet).

Pitch 4: Climb up a ramp and out onto the face where you will continue to the *Volunteer Wall* fourth-pitch belay bolts for pro. Trend left up the steep face with pumpy climbing. Six bolts to double-bolt anchor. (5.11a; 100 feet).

Pitch 5: Fire straight through the strenuous overhang. Trend left to a small right-facing corner and a bolt. Traverse right along a slot that is under a roof. At the far right side, climb out through the roof to gain High Men Ledge. (5.11d; 50 feet).

Pitch 6: Traverse left 15 feet and move off the ledge past a bolt. Continue up the overhanging wall and one bolt to easier ground. Climb up and right to some huge horns and more bolts. A dicey blank section leads right to the belay. (5.11b; 110 feet).

Pitch 7: Climb up and right past two large horns for pro to gain the first of three bolts protecting a steep face. After pulling a bulge, continue up less-than-vertical rock to another bulge. Pull it and continue to a directional bolt. Traverse right along a small roof and gain the caver's rappel bolt belay. (5.12a; 100 feet).

Pitch 8: Climb the easy slab to the summit. (5.5; 40 feet).

7. The Volunteer Wall   IV, 5.12a

This flagship route on Whiteside's Southeast Face was the first to broach the intimidating headwall. Although it is one of the best long free routes in the East, it does have more than its share of run-out 5.10 climbing plus some atrocious bolts and rotten rock. Some bolts on this route have been replaced, but others are in horrible shape, including the belays at the top of pitches 4 and 5.

First ascent: Arno Ilgner, Mark Cartwright, Eddie Whittemore (1985, ground-up in a three-day effort). Arno and Mark Ilgner got the free ascent in 1991 after many tries.

Start: 150 feet right of *The Great Ah Ha*. Scramble up to a tree ledge to start.

Pitch 1: Climb onto a slabby perch and make tenuous moves past a bolt into the left-facing corner. Small wires help back up the single-bolt belay. (5.11a; 65 feet). *Note:* Just right of the first pitch there is a route called *No Man's Land*. This was originally an aid line climbed by Brad Shaver and Dave Buck. Bob Rotert and Ted Anderson freed this pitch at 5.10+ in 1978 by climbing left of the bolts.

Pitch 2: Cruise out left past a bolt and an old fixed angle to gain a short, right-facing corner higher up. Belay at two bolts on Register Ledge. (5.10b; 100 feet).

Pitch 3: Move directly right on the ledge to find a weakness and gain the face above. Climb past an old optional belay, then into some broken rock near a crack.

Move hard to the left aiming for the bolted belay at the base of the Coal Mine corner. (5.8; 150 feet).

Pitch 4: Stem up the corner to a bolt at the crux, then make dicey moves higher to gain stems and much-needed protection. Follow the corner system right and into the rotten black diorite of the Coal Mine. Watch rope drag at the notch. Belay at three poor bolts caked in peregrine feces. (5.12a; 90 feet).

Pitch 5: Climb out left and gain the excellent Happy Hooker face. Climb past two bolts (the second hidden) and find your belay underneath a small roof. (5.10c; 90 feet).

Pitch 6: The infamous Rotten Pitch. You'll soon see why . . . climb right off belay to a bolt. Fire up and left, past another bolt, and into scary, brittle rock. Pull lightly here. Clip a final bolt and move left aiming for a bolted belay at High Men Ledge. (5.11a; 90 feet).

Pitch 7: The (also infamous) Jump Pitch. Swing out over the roof, past three bolts and onto the fantastic face above. Old bashies and heads plus some opportune gear help offset the pump and wild exposure. Gun past two more bolts for the bolted belay. (5.12a; 85 feet).

Pitch 8: Move hard right then up past a bolt and into the Bathtub. Step right and climb slopers through a series of bulges and four bolts to gain a good crack. At another old bolt, move left and belay at the huge caver's bolts. (5.12a; 75 feet).

Pitch 9: Climb the lower-angled face above to the summit. (5.5; 40 feet).

8. Mainline   IV, 5.11d

A sustained, strong line through classic Whiteside terrain: bold face climbing, awkward cracks, and juggy roofs. After doing this 700-foot journey, you may want to mainline! Bring no. 0.5 and no. 1 Tri-Cams.

First ascent: Doc Bayne, Scott Brunet, Nick Williams, Chad Garner (1997, sieged, ground-up with some aid).

Start: 150 feet right of *The Volunteer Wall* and just left of a slab that drops away beneath you.

Pitch 1: Make heady moves to the first of two bolts and find a natural belay in horizontals before the wall steepens. (5.9+; 80 feet).

Pitch 2: Fire up through "holes" and then angle right into a left-facing corner with a ledge. Save some medium and bigger pieces for the belay. (5.10; 80 feet).

Pitch 3: Trend up through easy ground and tackle a crescent-shaped crack through the right-most part of an overhang. Belay at double bolts. (5.8; 85 feet).

Pitch 4: No pro at the start past weird moves. Belay at double bolts. (5.7; 85 feet).

Pitch 5: Move left off belay and power through two bolts. Keep your head on unprotected, bulgy ground above water runnels (5.10) and aim for another double-bolt belay. (5.11c; 75 feet).

Pitch 6: Make a hard, weird move past an old bolt. Trend left and up to the first of three bolts and the base of a right-facing corner. Belay at a luxurious ledge. (5.11c; 80 feet).

Pitch 7: The real steepness! Resist the urge to escape right onto *New Diversions* (topo only). Instead, power up to a bolt, ape through wild, exposed overhangs, and crank to another ledge and natural belay. You're almost home. (5.11d; 85 feet).

Pitch 8: Make a few final delicate and heady moves up a slab and burrow into rhododendrons and the top. (5.10a; 55 feet).

9. Traditions   III/IV, 5.11c

Although also controversial for its time, *Traditions* now sees almost as much traffic as *The Original Route*. Direct and relatively well protected, the route features one steep, exciting pitch down low and a dash of technical face climbing near the summit.

First ascent: Mark and Debbie Lassiter, Bob Ordner (October 1989, sieged, ground-up). Doc Bayne made the first free ascent in July 1990.

Start: Just beneath *Mainline*, the trail drops steeply past some slabs and then continues. The next route is *New Diversions* (topo only), which starts at a slab. For *Traditions*, go 50 feet farther right and look for one bolt in a white slab.

Pitch 1: Climb the slab past one bolt, continue past a bowl, and follow two more bolts to a fixed belay where the wall steepens. (5.9; 165 feet).

Pitch 2: Move out right and up the overhanging wall past four bolts to a single-bolt belay at a tiny stance. (5.11a; 85 feet).

Pitch 3: Traverse right 30 feet and climb up to a big ledge with a bolt. Climb up to a second ledge with a bolt and then make another 50-foot traverse right. Climb up past a fixed pin to a bolted belay. (5.8; 150 feet).

Pitch 4: Move a little right again and then move up the face to a bivy ledge. A pin belay is on the left side of this ledge. (5.8; 150 feet).

Pitch 5: Climb past two bolts to gain a position on the steep, crimpy face above. There's a bolt at your nose for every hard move through the technical crux, then dash for the fixed belay on a ledge. (5.11c; 150 feet).

Pitch 6: Move right about 60 feet along the ledge. Then climb up and belay in a "hole," which is also a belay on *The Original Route*. (5.5; 60 feet). *Note:* From the top of pitch 5, it is possible to take a direct variation straight up to the top of pitch 7. (5.9; 75 feet).

Pitch 7: Climb up and left from the belay to a bolt. Traverse left toward the white ramp, passing two more bolts. Follow the ramp to a long ledge and move left to a belay. (5.9+; 100 feet).

Pitch 8: Continue to the far-left side of the ledge and ape through a flaky corner capped by some steep rock (two bolts). Aim for the tree ledge. (5.10a; 90 feet).

Pitch 9: Follow lower-angled terrain to the summit. (5.8; 100 feet).

10. The Original Route (aka Gom Jabber)   III/IV, 5.11a or 5.9, A1

The *OR* is the closest thing on the Southeast Face to a freeway. Although it is host to both epic and speed ascents, capable climbers will find memorable pitches and wild exposure. More than one party has been rescued off this route, often after unfortunate incidents on pitch 4. It might be a good idea to bring aiders for this section. There is a good bit of traversing on this route, which is something to consider if you plan to take a less-experienced second. There are many sections of poorly protected 5.5 to 5.7.

First ascent: Peter Young, Jim Marshall, John Lawrence, John Whisnant (1968–71, sieged). Although others free climbed certain sections, Bob Rotert free climbed the 5.11a crux in 1977 for the first all-free ascent.

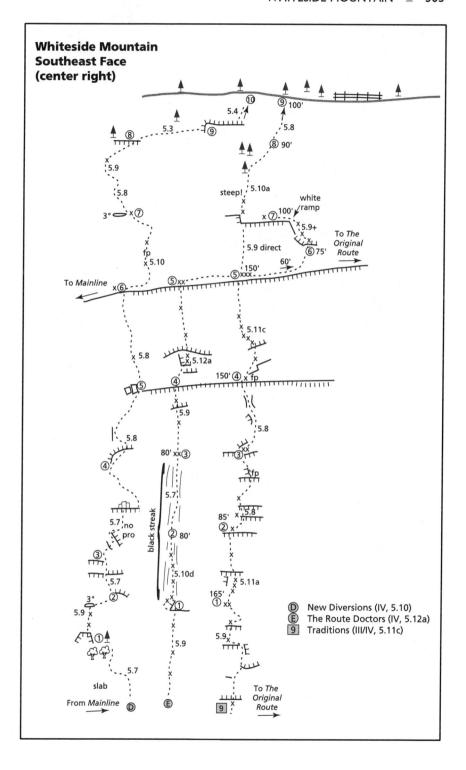

**Whiteside Mountain
Southeast Face
(center right)**

Jimi Combs, with Burton Moomaw belaying, highsteps his way through pitch 5 of Traditions *(route 9).*

Start: On the far-right side of an apron (the Great Gray Slab) and left of a large bushy corner at an open area.

Pitch 1: Pad your way up the slab to the tree ledge. Depending on where you choose to begin, you may be able to find gear on this pitch, which has long been regarded as unprotectable. (5.7; 140 feet).

Pitch 2: Move your belay to the left end of the tree ledge. Climb a short, hollow flake immediately off the belay and then span through the bulge (crux) to better holds. Continue to another good tree ledge. (5.8; 90 feet).

Whiteside Mountain
Southeast Face (right)

summit loop trail

⑥

5.8
off

⑦

steep

5.10a

⑩ 150'

⑦

5.6

5.10 R

⑥ x

white
ramp

5.9+

Traditions

⑦ 75' 10 165'

5.4

xx ⑧

fp ⑨ 150' 5.9

100' x ⑥

5.7

x 5.12a

⑤ 100'

5.9
bulges

x 5.11a

The Bolt
Ladder x xx
xx ⑥ 80'

finish
on *OR*

90'

The Black
Hole

5.10c

⑤ 35' 5.7

90'
④

5.8 R

5.8+ The
Crescent
Pitch

90'

⑤ xx

5.11

5.11c

High
Anxiety
Headwall

5.11d

key #0.5
Tri-Cam

75' ⑤ x

5.7

Ephiphany
Pitch

x 5.8

A0 x blank
band

xx ④ 100'

x A0

White
Dome

xx ③ 90'

5.11

xx ③

prominent
corner

5.7

G

④ 100'

xx ④ 60'

5.6

5.10c

off
route

5.10b

5.9 R
alt

195' ②

x 5.10d

80' ③
xx

③ 150'

②

170'

alternate
belay

5.7

5.8 R

5.11c

5.6 R

original
line

10 90'
②

11

5.8

5.8

①

fp 12

75'

F

To *Catholic
Girls Direct*

①

140'

Great
Gray
Slab

5.7
no
pro

To *Traditions*

10

10 The Original Route
(III/IV, 5.11a or 5.9, A1)
11 Connections (III/IV, 5.11c, A0)
12 Whippin' Boy (III/IV, 5.11d)
Ⓕ New Perversions (5.11a/b)
Ⓖ Dirty Dikes Done Dirt
Cheap (alt finish; 5.12a)

Pitch 3: Scramble about to the left end of the ledge. Then climb short cracks until you can traverse right under an overhang to find a right-facing flake. Follow this to a corner where you can step left and continue up into a bowl with double bolts. (5.7; 80 feet).

Pitch 4: Long rated 5.9+, this pitch has ledge-out potential right off the belay if you're not careful. It is possible to aid the crux corner with some 3-inch gear. Once you pull the corner, continue up the face to a ledge where you can clip a directional bolt and move left to fixed belay. (5.10c; 60 feet).

Pitch 5: Traverse left about 10 feet and then romp up the exposed face above to a double-bolt anchor. (5.7; 75 feet).

Pitch 6: The Crescent Pitch. Move right over the void and then work your way up the amazingly exposed, right-facing corner. Exit left onto the face via a short traverse and face climb straight up to a semihanging belay with several bolts. (5.8+; 80 feet).

Pitch 7: The Bolt Ladder. More high exposure! Face climb (or A0) past three bolts, then diagonal right to a great ledge. If you are concerned about your second, you can belay directly above the bolt ladder. Some parties trend left about 35 feet where you can finagle a natural belay at a "hole." (5.11a or A0; 75 feet). *Note:* From here, many parties opt to finish on *Traditions*, which is better and more direct.

Pitch 8: Traverse right on the airy ledge for approximately 165 feet. Remember your second and find the occasional piece of protection. Belay at triple bolts. (5.4; 150 feet).

Pitch 9: Aim diagonally right up the unprotected face, eventually gaining a grassy crack with a fixed pin where you can belay. (5.6; 150 feet).

Pitch 10: Climb the flake above the belay, then romp up lichen-covered slabs. Bear right of the bushes on the summit. (5.6; 150 feet).

11. Connections   III/IV, 5.11c, A0

Sometimes described as a "super-direct" version of the *OR*, the meat of this route is a 435-foot midsection sandwiched by easier pitches.

First ascent: Doc Bayne, Nick Williams, Jeep Gaskin (1993). In 2001, Bayne and Scott Brunet added the Epiphany Pitch (previewed on top-rope, climbed ground-up).

Start: Same as *The Original Route.*

Pitches 1 and 2: Climb the *OR* to the tree ledge at the top of the second pitch.

Pitch 3: From the tree ledge, climb directly up into a roof and move left into a precarious, overhanging shallow corner (the first-ascent line actually climbed out right and circled around this bulge). Push up to a bolt and then make long moves out left (crux) to gain another bolt. Climb directly up the run-out face above to another good ledge and natural belay. (5.11c; 150 feet).

Pitch 4: Climb up and slightly right to gain a bolt. Move right past another bolt into a corner. Continue up the sparsely protected face above, aiming for the double-bolt belay. (5.10d; 100 feet). *Epiphany variation:* It is best to do this as one long pitch. Climb into the previously mentioned corner, and then aim slightly left for two bolts in a blank band. Aid past these and continue up the steep face past a seam out right. Blast over a juggy bulge and past a bolt to the belay. (5.11c, A0; 180 feet).

Opposite: *David Stewart, with Jake Dumler belaying, free-climbing the bolt ladder on* The Original Route *(route 10)*

**Whiteside Mountain
Southeast Face
(far right)**

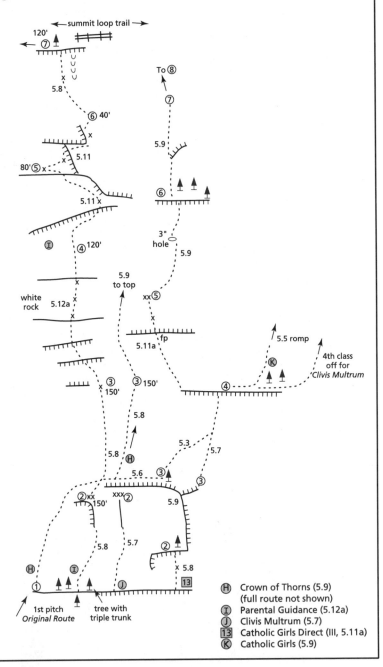

H Crown of Thorns (5.9)
(full route not shown)
I Parental Guidance (5.12a)
J Clivis Multrum (5.7)
13 Catholic Girls Direct (III, 5.11a)
K Catholic Girls (5.9)

Pitch 5: Aid your way past a bolt in the blank band of white quartzite to gain a spectacular face above. Hurry past four well-spaced bolts to gain a ledge. Traverse left here (protect your second) and belay at double bolts just left of The Black Hole. (5.11c, A0; 90 feet).

Pitch 6: Step out right beneath The Black Hole onto a pedestal where you can clip a bolt. Fight the pump and climb past two small overlaps (bring 0.4-inch cams) with a bolt in between to gain the triple-bolt belay at the end of the traverse pitch on the *OR.* (5.10c; 90 feet).

Pitches 7 and 8: Finish on *The Original Route.*

12. Whippin' Boy   III/IV, 5.11d

With only one truly hard pitch, this is a great line to do quickly. But the crux pitch here is a memorable one. The White Dome leads to the High Anxiety Headwall, where you'll better understand the name as soon as you're perched underneath it!

First ascent: Doc Bayne, Mark Lassiter, Nick Williams (1993, ground-up with bolts drilled from hooks).

Start: Same as *The Original Route.*

Pitch 1: Climb first pitch of *The Original Route.*

Pitch 2: Move about 20 feet left on the tree ledge and below a short, left-facing corner with a fixed pin. Climb past this pin to a larger, left-facing corner. Step right around the corner and climb past two bolts to a large ledge. (5.8; 170 feet).

Pitch 3: From the ledge, angle slightly right as the wall steepens. Climb to a right-facing "point" just under a bolt. Gain a double-bolt belay. (5.10b; 90 feet).

Pitch 4: Step left off the belay to gain the steep and exciting White Dome. Continue left to a good ledge under the roof. Here, begin moving right along a ramp past two bolts. Grab the "potato chip" to reach a third bolt. Now you're off to the races: Gun through the High Anxiety Headwall past another bolt until the angle lessens. Move left to set a good natural belay with 2- to 3-inch cams. (5.11d; 90 feet).

Pitch 5: Step right and climb a short pitch to another ledge. (5.7; 35 feet).

Pitch 6: Continue up the face above, passing one bolt and eventually gaining a single bolt just under an overlap that marks the belay. Back up the belay with natural gear. (5.7; 100 feet).

Pitch 7: Make a few bouldery moves off the belay to gain the casual face above. Wander to the summit. (5.9; 150 feet).

13. Catholic Girls Direct   III, 5.11a

If the crux mantel is more than you care to bite off, this route easily converts into a 5.5 romp that allows you to gain altitude the easy way. Bring one or two 3.5- or 4-inch cams.

First ascent: Ted Anderson, Jeep Gaskin, and Bob Rotert climbed the original *Catholic Girls* at 5.8. The trio third-classed off the wall from a belay after the second pitch. In 1990, Mark Lassiter and Shannon Stegg added the more aesthetic direct variation.

Start: Same as the *Original Route.*

Pitch 1: The first pitch of *The Original Route.* Once on the ledge, walk right until you gain an open area under a corner system.

Whiteside Mountain
Main North Face

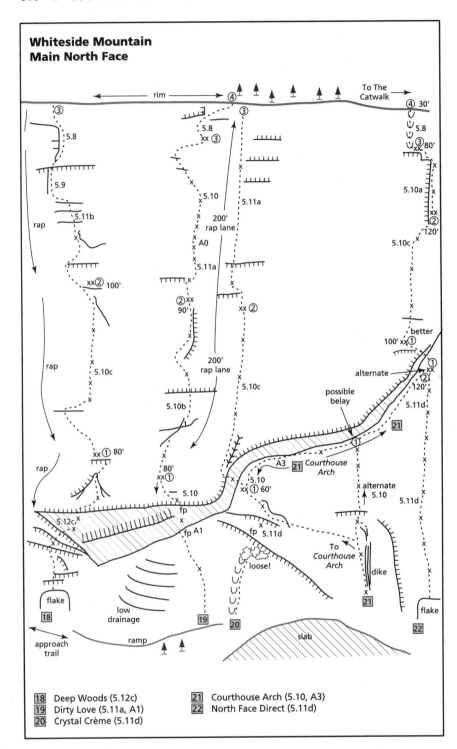

rim

To The Catwalk

5.8
5.9
5.11b
rap
5.10c
rap
rap

③
5.8
xx ③

④

③

5.8
xx ③

5.11a

5.10
200'
rap lane

A0

5.11a

②xx
90'

xx ②

200'
rap lane

5.10c

5.10b

xx① 80'

④ 30'
5.8
③ 80'
xx

5.10a

②
120'

5.10c

better
100' xx①

alternate

①
xx
②
120'
5.11d

possible belay

21

①

A3 21 Courthouse Arch

5.10
xx① 60'

5.12c
fp
fp A1

flake
18

low drainage

80'
xx①
5.10

fp 5.11d

loose!

approach trail

ramp

19

20

alternate
5.10

To Courthouse Arch

dike

21

slab

21

5.11d

flake
22

18 Deep Woods (5.12c)
19 Dirty Love (5.11a, A1)
20 Crystal Crème (5.11d)

21 Courthouse Arch (5.10, A3)
22 North Face Direct (5.11d)

Pitch 2: Climb past a bolt to gain a ledge with a pine tree. (5.9+; 60 feet).

Pitch 3: Continue up the corner until it turns into a roof. Here, make Houdini moves out and right to a horizontal and set up a natural belay. (5.9; 100 feet).

Pitch 4: Climb directly up the unprotected face above to a ledge. (5.7; 150 feet).

Pitch 5: Angle up and left to a stance below a 3-foot roof. Step right to clip a fixed pin and roll onto the upper face with a hard mantel move. Climb past another bolt to a double-bolt belay. (5.11a; 120 feet). *Note:* To take the 5.5 variation to the summit, climb directly up off the fourth pitch belay.

Pitch 6: Trend right up the face above (passing a good hole that offers large cam protection) to a good tree ledge. (5.9; 130 feet).

Pitch 7: Continue up the fluted face via a water runnel and a short right-facing corner. Move left around this and continue up the easier face above. (5.9; 130 feet).

Pitch 8: Wander up the low-angled rock to the summit.

North Face (aka Devil's Courthouse)

This complex area of Whiteside Mountain is visible from an overlook on US 64. It includes several separate areas: a south-facing backside (Courthouse South Face, which is not visible from the overlook), an upper tier to the Main North Face (The Catwalk), and the Main North Face proper. Routes are presented left to right, beginning on the Courthouse South Face.

Courthouse South Face

This face rises above the main (right-hand) trail that descends from the gap described in the approach. Steep and easily accessible, this face has apparently seen a fair amount of activity, with stoppers and other fixed gear mysteriously appearing and disappearing. The rock tends to be more weathered and friable than on the rest of the mountain, making for serious and adventurous outings.

Descent: Walk off from top of wall.

14. Judgment Day   5.11b (no topo)

First ascent: Shannon Stegg, Jim Corbett (1993, ground-up).

Start: At the left-hand edge of the face, below a left-facing dihedral.

Pitch 1: Climb up to the dihedral and follow it to a ledge. Belay on gear. (5.9; 90 feet).

Pitch 2: Step right and climb leftmost of two cracks up the steep headwall. The friable edges of this crack make the going strenuous and it is difficult to place gear. Follow to the top of the Courthouse and belay from bushes. (5.11b; 90 feet).

15. The Gavel   5.11c (no topo)

First ascent: Shannon Stegg, Jim Corbett (1992, ground-up).

Start: At the right-hand edge of the face, below a right-facing corner. Look for a series of flakes below a high, blunt arête with a bolt.

Pitch 1: Climb the corner and flakes to a large ledge. (5.10a; 90 feet).

Pitch 2: Climb overhanging blunt arête past a bolt and up left on desperate moves past a fixed pin. Follow to the top of the Courthouse and belay from bushes. (5.11c; 90 feet).

The Catwalk

This narrow tree ledge traverses the north face below the Courthouse and above the Main North Face. A short, vertical 80- to 100-foot rock band above the ledge has been the scene of much new route activity, most of it anonymous.

Above a grassy area on the west (right) side of The Catwalk is a steep face, below a prominent roof and bounded on the right by a dihedral. The dihedral is *Nirvana Blues* (5.10c), climbed rope-solo by Jim Corbett in 1989 to the roof and avoiding the wide crack at the top, which is usually soaking wet. A later party has climbed into the wide crack and placed permanent anchors. Just to the left of *Nirvana Blues*, unknown parties have installed a few sport routes up the face below the roof. These are all hard, in the 11c to 12b range.

Descent: Walk off from top of wall.

16. Statutory Rape   5.11a (no topo)
First ascent: David Young, Jim Corbett (1996, ground-up).
Start: On the left side of The Catwalk, look for a high, right-facing corner with bolts.
Pitch 1: Begin by bouldering past a bolt into the right-facing corner with another bolt. Move out left and up past a third bolt to a horizontal weakness. Step right to a finger crack and climb up to a ledge with a double-bolt anchor. (80 feet).

17. Fight the Power   5.10d (no topo)
First ascent: Chris Wilson, Jim Corbett (1997).
Start: About 300 feet farther down The Catwalk, the trail passes below an expanse of rock that extends to the top of the Courthouse. Find a right-facing dihedral at a roof just above the trail.
Pitch 1: Climb up and trend up and right to a prominent ledge. The face is steeper and longer than it looks. Belay in trees to right. (5.9; 150 feet).
Pitch 2: Continue to an obvious right-facing corner with an intricate crux and difficult pro. Move left from the top of the corner and belay from an amazing chaise-lounge ledge with awesome views and exposure. (5.10d; 70 feet).
Pitch 3: Follow the face to the top of the Courthouse. (5.7; 80 feet).

Main North Face

With a northern exposure at 4,800 feet, the North Face of Whiteside might be the prime summer crag in the Southeast. The routes are long and serious, and evacuation of an injured climber would be epic. Climb within your limits and don't expect a rescue.

Descent: The descent on these routes depends on your approach: If you hiked the trail in, rappel all routes back to the base. If you rappelled in, climb all routes to regain the rim.

18. Deep Woods (aka Squatter's Flight)   5.12c
A difficult, strong line up the steepest part of the cliff that offers a mix of roofs, thin faces, and crack climbing. Does it get any better? Double ropes, double cams up to 3.5 inches, and one 4-inch cam are recommended.
First ascent: Shannon Stegg, Tony Sykes, Jim Corbett (1992, aid, some top-rope rehearsal).

Start: If you follow the trail in, *Deep Woods* begins just left of the largest roof area. Locate the line of bolts through tiered roofs and starting atop flakes.

Pitch 1: Climb off the flake past several small overlaps to get established under the roof. Make powerful moves and then a hard traverse to escape as the angle lessens. Four bolts to a double-bolt belay. (5.12c; 80 feet).

Pitch 2: Move left off the belay and then back right to gain the first of four bolts. The upper corner and knobby face are excellent. Double-bolt belay. (5.10c; 100 feet).

Pitch 3: Climb around an overlap to gain a left-facing corner and steep face, past wild horizontals. A rack of medium and large cams is the key on this section. Eventually, gain a good but dirty vertical crack and climb to the summit. (5.11b; 170 feet).

19. Dirty Love 5.11a, A1

Two short aid sections are all that prevent this from being one of the best routes around. Double ropes recommended.

First ascent: Shannon Stegg, et al.

Start: From the low drainage, hike ramp up and 75 feet right of *Deep Woods* to below a line of bolts in the roof.

Pitch 1: Climb the face past a bolt to a series of roofs and hanging flakes. Aid past fixed pins and two bolts, turn the lip, and move up to a double-bolt belay. (5.10, A1; 80 feet).

Pitch 2: Climb the face to a wild X-crack feature. Power through this past some long reaches and a small roof to two bolts in a left-facing corner. Double-bolt belay. (5.10b; 90 feet).

Pitch 3: Follow the corner up and right to a hidden bolt. Move right onto the face and yard on bolts to pass a short blank section. Continue past four more bolts and horizontals until you can move right to a double-bolt belay. (5.11a, A0; 80 feet).

Pitch 4: Ape through a fun, steep section with good cracks to the summit rim. (5.8; 40 feet).

20. Crystal Crème 5.11d

An interesting and unique route. If the first pitch crux were on an easily accessible boulder, climbers would come from miles around just to do it. Double ropes recommended.

First ascent: Shannon Stegg, Jim Corbett (1992, bolted on rappel).

Start: From the low drainage, hike the ramp up and right 100 feet, below a flake and high corner to where the main roof turns into a vertical, right-facing corner.

Pitch 1: Climb the obvious water groove into an area of loose blocks. Move right past a fixed pin to a stance below a bulge with a bolt. Boulder an intricate sequence through the bulge to a bolt, then climb past another bolt and left to double-bolt belay. (5.11d; 60 feet).

Pitch 2: Climb out left past a bolt through the huge arch, and then around an arête to a crystal dike. Climb this up and slightly right to a double-bolt anchor. (5.10c; 120 feet). *Note:* Beware many sharp corners on this pitch.

Pitch 3: Climb straight up the face past two bolts to the summit ridge. (5.11a; 180 feet).

21. Courthouse Arch   5.10a, A3

This route follows the wall's natural weakness and was the first line on the face. Many fixed pins and heads, bring knifeblades. Combining pitch 1 of *Courthouse Arch* with pitches 2 and 3 of *Crystal Crème* creates an excellent 5.10+/5.11- route up the face.

First ascent: Jim Corbett, Mark Lassiter, Bob Ordner (1990, ground-up on aid).

Start: 40 feet right of *Crystal Crème* at the quartz dike.

Pitch 1: Climb a quartz dike past two bolts and flake to a stance at a grass pad. Move left 50 feet on a delicate traverse to a bolt, then up the flake to a double-bolt belay. (5.10a; 120 feet).

Pitch 2: Step left into the dihedral, aid up, and then traverse right under a roof to a double-bolt belay. (A3; 120 feet).

Pitch 3: Boulder up and left over a roof to a belay on the *North Face Direct,* then trend up and right past three bolts to a double-bolt belay in a scoop. (5.10; 120 feet).

Pitch 4: Climb a shallow right-facing corner, then move up and left to a double-bolt belay. This is pitch 3 of *North Face Direct.* (5.10a; 80 feet).

Descent: Rappel the route or climb pitch 4 *North Face Direct* to the summit.

22. North Face Direct   5.11d

Perhaps the best route on the North Face, this line offers a long pitch of five-star face climbing. Success is all in your timing, as cool conditions help with the friction.

First ascent: Shannon Stegg.

Start: 40 feet right of *Courthouse Arch.* Look for a line of bolts starting off a large flake.

Pitch 1: Pump your way up the amazingly sustained face past eight bolts to the second of two bolted anchor stations (atop pitch 2 of *Courthouse Arch*). (5.11d; 120 feet).

Pitch 2: Face-climb past three bolts to a bolted belay. (5.10c; 120 feet).

Pitch 3: Follow a right-facing corner past two bolts. (5.10a; 80 feet).

Pitch 4: Climb out via a steep water runnel. (5.8; 30 feet).

23. Subtle Rush   5.10d (no topo)

The little brother of *North Face Direct,* this tackles a long pitch of immaculate white granite. Brace for the same sporty, sustained, and high-quality face climbing.

First ascent: David Young, Chris Wilson, Jim Corbett (1997, ground-up).

Start: Follow a faint trail right of *North Face Direct* for 300 feet, around a brushy buttress to a sweeping granite slab. Start at the left edge.

Pitch 1: Crimp and teeter up a sustained face past seven bolts to tree ledge. 5.10d (150 feet).

Descent: Rappel.

24. Conquistador   5.11b (no topo)

The only route that goes the full distance from the bottom of the Main North Face to the top of the Courthouse. Although two tree-ledge traverses may mar the aesthetics, the interesting and varied climbing and spectacular arête finish at an ancient Spanish inscription produce a memorable route.

First ascent: Shannon Stegg, Stuart Coffield (1997). Stegg, Coffield, and Tom Woodruff made the first free ascent in 1997.

Start: Follow the faint trail past a small cave to a huge hanging block.

Pitch 1: Climb up and left of the block via a roof crack to another crack system up high. Continue to a double-bolt belay just under the tree ledge. (5.11b).

Pitch 2: Traverse to the right side of the tree ledge. Follow a long, right-arching corner system to its end and then climb back left around a roof. Continue past small roofs and a horn to a double-bolt belay. (5.10a).

Pitch 3: Move up past a small roof with a bolt to a larger roof. Traverse left under this and follow the sustained face to the arête. Don't forget to look for a carving on the point. (5.11b).

Descent: Hike down the main trail atop the Courthouse to the main trail junction at the gap.

APPENDIX A: RATINGS

Free Climbs

The Yosemite Decimal System (5.0 to 5.14) gives no information on the protection possibilities for a climb. It is up to each individual leader to ascertain these factors while on lead. It most instances, this guide tries to use the supplemental R or X system to denote the seriousness of a climb. An R rating generally signifies a long section of unprotected climbing with the possibility for a potentially injurious fall. An X rating generally signifies a long section of unprotected climbing (especially a section that might involve a crux) where a fall will almost certainly result in injury or even death.

It is customary to eschew R or X ratings on many pitches in North Carolina. At some cliffs (notably Stone Mountain, Big Green Mountain, and Whiteside Mountain), it is customary to omit "R" ratings since almost every pitch is run-out to some degree. Climb within your ability.

Aid Ratings

In an attempt to modernize the aid ratings, this guide has adopted an updated ratings scheme initially proposed by John Middendorf and now becoming more universal among aid climbers. Please note that these ratings reflect a shift away from the grades found in previous North Carolina climbing guides for the North Side of Looking Glass Rock. Familiarize yourself with the upgraded ratings scale below before venturing onto any of the regraded routes.

The scale is from A0 to A5 or from C0 to C5. The A refers to aid climbs in general, which may use pitons, bolts, or chocks. The C refers to clean aid climbing, using only hammerless protection that does not mar the rock. It is sometimes possible to clean-climb a route that is rated with the A system.

A0: Also known as "French-free," using gear to make progress, but generally no aiders required.

A1: Easy aid. Placements straightforward and solid. No risk of any piece pulling out. Aiders generally required. Fast and simple for C1, the hammerless corresponding grade, but not necessarily fast and simple for nailing pitches.

A2: Moderate aid. Placements generally solid but possibly awkward and strenuous to place. Maybe a tenuous placement or two above good pro with no fall danger.

A2+: Like A2, but possibly several tenuous placements above good pro. Twenty-to 30-foot fall potential, but with little danger of hitting anything. Routefinding abilities may be required.

A3: Hard aid. Testing methods required. Involves many tenuous placements in a row. Generally solid placements (which could hold a fall) found within a pitch. Long fall potential up to 50 feet (six to eight placements ripping), but generally safe from serious danger. Usually several hours required to complete a pitch, due to complexity of placements.

A3+: Like A3, but with dangerous fall potential. Tenuous placements after long stretches of body-weight pieces. Potential to get hurt if good judgment is not exercised. Time required generally exceeds three hours for experienced aid climbers.

A4: Serious aid. A lot of danger with 60- to 100-foot fall potential common and uncertain landings far below.

A4+: More serious than A4. These leads generally take many hours to complete and require the climber to endure long periods of uncertainty and fear, often requiring a balletlike efficiency of movement in order not to upset the tenuous integrity of marginal placements.

A5: Extreme aid. Nothing really trustworthy of catching a fall for the entire pitch. Rating should be reserved only for pitches with no bolts or rivets (holes) for the entire pitch.

A6: Theoretical grade. A5 climbing with marginal belays that will not hold a fall.

APPENDIX B: CONTACT INFORMATION AND RESOURCES

Contact Information
This is the primary contact information for the land management agencies of each climbing area. Where there is no management agency, the agency that has camping information is listed. Please call the agencies or visit their websites for updated information about camping.

Moore's Wall
Hanging Rock State Park
PO Box 278
Danbury, NC 27016
(336) 593-8480
hangingrock@mindspring.com
www.ils.unc.edu/parkproject/haro.html

Stone Mountain
Stone Mountain State Park
3042 Frank Parkway
Roaring Gap, NC 28668
(336) 957-8185
stonemtn@infoave.net
www.ils.unc.edu/parkproject/visit/stmo/home.html
Private campsites: (336) 957-4351 or (336) 957-2536

Crowders Mountain
Crowders Mountain State Park
522 Park Office Lane
Kings Mountain, NC 28086
(704) 853-5375
crowders@vnet.net
www.ils.unc.edu/parkproject/visit/crmo/home.html

Ship Rock
National Park Service
Blue Ridge Parkway
199 Hemphill Knob Road
Asheville, NC 28801-3417
(828) 271-4779
www.nps.gov/blri/

Linville Gorge
Pisgah National Forest
Grandfather Ranger District
109 East Lawing Drive
Nebo, NC 29761
(828) 652-2144
www.cs.unca.edu/nfsnc/

Rumbling Bald Mountain
This climbing area is on private land.
Hickory Nut Gorge Chamber of
  Commerce
2948 Memorial Highway
PO Box 32
Chimney Rock, NC 28720
(828) 625-2725
www.thehickorynutgorge.com/

Looking Glass Rock and Cedar Rock
Pisgah National Forest
Pisgah Ranger District
1001 Pisgah Highway
Pisgah Forest, NC 28768
(828) 877-3265
www.cs.unca.edu/nfsnc/

Big Green Mountain and Whiteside Mountain
Nantahala National Forest
Highlands Ranger District
2010 Flat Mountain Road
Highlands, NC 28741
(828) 526-3765
www.cs.unca.edu/nfsnc/

Resources
In recent years, the climbing community has benefited greatly from the proliferation of climbing-related websites. These sites allow for the rapid exchange of information that previously took weeks or months to circulate, and certain sites can help climbers determine the weather forecast before making a long trip into the mountains. Keep in mind that these sites may change often or even disappear over time.

Carolina Climbers Coalition: *www.carolinaclimbers.org*
Southeastern Climbers Coalition: *www.seclimbers.org*
Boone weather: *www.booneweather.com*

The Access Fund
The Access Fund is a national nonprofit climbers' organization that works to keep climbing areas open and to conserve the climbing environment. For help with land closures, land acquisition, legal or land management issues, funding for trails and other projects, or if you are interested in starting a local climbers' group, call (303) 546-6772 or visit their website at *www.accessfund.org*.

APPENDIX C: EMERGENCY SERVICES

Moore's Wall
Stokes County Emergency Medical
   Services Dispatch
(336) 593-2852

Stokes-Reynolds County Memorial
   Hospital
Highways 8 and 89, Danbury
(336) 593-2831

Stone Mountain
Hugh Chatham Memorial Hospital
180 Parkwood Drive, Elkin
(336) 527-7000

Crowders Mountain
Gaston Memorial Hospital
2525 Court Avenue, Gastonia
(704) 834-2944

Ship Rock
Blue Ridge Parkway's "Parkwatch"
   emergency number
(800) 727-5928

Watauga Medical Center
336 Deerfield Road, Boone
(828) 262-4100

Linville Gorge Climbing Areas
Grace Hospital
2201 S Sterling Street, Morgantown
(828) 580-5000

Rumbling Bald Mountain
Rutherford Hospital
288 S Ridgecrest Avenue,
   Rutherfordton
(704) 286-5000

St. Luke's Hospital
220 Hospital Drive, Columbus
(828) 894-3311

Looking Glass Rock and Cedar Rock
Transylvania Community Hospital
Hospital Drive, Brevard (off US 64)
(828) 884-9111

Big Green Mountain and Whiteside Mountain
Highlands-Cashiers Hospital
Between Highlands and Cashiers on
   US 64
(828) 526-1200

ROUTE INDEX

Page numbers in italics indicate topo and page numbers in bold indicate photo.

Adrenaline Weasels (5.11d), *286*
Adrift (5.9), *64–65*
Adventures with Jake (5.10), *118*
A Friend in Need (5.11d), *135*
Aerial Act (5.10d), 85, *85*
Aerospace Cadet (5.10d), 251, *252*
Afterbirth (5.6), *259*
Aftermath (5.9+), *286*
Aid Raid (5.11c), *41*, 43
Airlie Gardens (5.9), 99, *99*
Air Raid (5.9), *244*
Air Show (5.8+), *35*, 36, 37
Almost Seven (5.7), *41*, 42
Aloof Roof (5.8), *41*
Alternative Man (5.12b/c), *95*, 96
America Under Attack (5.12d/13a), 117, *118*
Anchor Rode (5.6), *65*
Angelinos (5.12b), *188*
Anguish of Captain Bligh, The (5.11b/c), 102
Anhedonia (5.9+), *202*
Animal Cracker (5.10a), *206*
Anne Marie (5.8), 220, *221*
Another Brick in the Wall (5.10d), *76*
Anthrax (5.11d), 73, *74*
Aphid in My Pants (5.10d), *127*, 129
Appalachian Runt (5.10d), *171*
Appalachian Spring (5.12c), 116, *116*
Apricot Jam (5.9+), 145, *145*
Arch Enema (5.11), *283*
Arch Rival (5.11b/c), 204, *205*
Armed Robbery (5.11d), *166*
Artistic Arête (5.13a), 95, *95*
A Tall Climb to Be Good On (5.9), *127*, 128
Atomic Dog (5.12b), 201, *201*
Autumn Speaks (5.9), *65*
A Walk in the Light (5.9+), *41*
Axis (Bold as Love) (5.11c), *82*, 84

Backdoor Man (5.12a), 204, *205*
Balls to the Wall (5.10a), *244*
Balti Porter (5.10), *95*
Banana Breath (5.10a), 61, *64–65*
Bat Attack (5.12a), 45, *45*
Battery Brides (5.12d), 187, *188*
Battle Creek Bulge (5.11d), *213*, 215
Bear, The (5.7), 87, *87*
Bear Hunt (5.7), *192*, 193
Beer Wolf (5.9+), *83*
Bee Tree (5.5), *209*
Beethoven's Fifth (5.11b), *259*
Between the Betwix (5.10), *80*
Between the Ditches (5.11d), *278*
Between the Ways (5.10c), 59, *64*
B-52 (5.10a), 262
Big Corner (Rumbling Bald) (5.10b), *188*
Big Corner (Shortoff) (5.8+), *166*
Big Crack (5.5), *85*
Bigeminy (5.10b), *278*, 281
Big Greeny Weeny (5.11b), *282*
Bimbo's Bulge (5.10c), *18*, *33*, 34
Birthday Bash (5.9), *266*
Black Dome Dementia (5.11), *194*
Black Flag (5.10d), *76*, 78
Black Flag Direct (5.13b), *76*
Blackout (5.10), *252*
Black Planet (5.12a), *198*, 200
Black Sand Beaches (5.11d), *74*
Black Widow (5.12a), *278*
Blade Runner (5.11), *166*, 169
Blarney Stone (IV, 5.12a/b, A1), *295*
Blind Date (5.10 R), *176*
Blind Tiger (5.12c/d), *198*
Block Route (5.8), 57, *64*
Blonde Ambition (5.10c A3), *231*, 232
Blonde Svengali (5.12a), *202*, 203

Blood on the Tracks (5.9), *67*
Blood, Sweat, and Tears (5.7), *127*, 128
Bloody Alternative (5.9+), *259*
Bloody Crack (5.8), *259*, 261
Bloody Hog (5.10 R), *125*
Blue Chock (5.10a), 38, *39*
Blue Steel Throbber (IV, 5.10, A3+), *237*, 238
Boardwalk (5.8), **88**, *95*, 98
B.O.G. Man (5.10d), *99*, 101
Boldfingers (5.12a), 198, *198*
Bolter Problem, The (5.10c), *74*
Bombay Groove (5.10a), **52**, 60, *64*
Bombelay (5.11c), 236, *237*
Bonsai (5.10a), 165
Boogie 'Til Ya Puke (5.12b), 47, *47*
Boot Hill (5.11b/c R), *194*, 196
Born Again (5.11a), *209*
Born Free (5.8, A2), *131*
Born to Be Free (5.10d), *176*, 177
Born to Be Wild (5.11c/d), *176*, 178
Borrowed Time (5.9), *93*, 94
Bottom of the Bagel (5.10a), *205*
Bouffant Curl (5.10), *249*
Boulder Problem in the Sky (5.11a/b), *293*
Brain Dead (IV, 5.12b, A4), *231*, 232
Brain Wall (5.10+, A3), 230, *231*
Brave Knave on the Stone Wave (5.11b), *273*
Breakfast of Champions (5.10d), *209*, 212
Breaking Rocks is Hard to Do (5.9), *41*
Break on Through (5.10a), *35*, 36
Brick in the Wall (5.10d), *76*, 78
Broach, The (5.11d), 98, *99*
Brothers Start (5.7+), *157*, 159
Brown Route, The (5.10), *148*
Brown Sugar (5.10), *67*

Brunch at the Club (5.11d, A0), *213*
Buffalo Nickel (5.7), *95*
Buffalo Time (5.9+), *95*
Built to Tilt (5.10b), 170, *171*
Bullet the Green Sky (5.11, A1), *283*
Bumblebee Buttress (5.8), 148, **150**, *151*
Bumbledink (5.9), 147, *149*
Bumble Fingers (5.10d), *151*
Bunky's Rest Day (5.8), *206*
Burn Crack (5.10c), *76*, 77, 78
Burning Man, The (5.10d), *131*
Bush Babies (5.6), *171*

Cajun Style (5.12a), *273*, 274
Campbell Crack (5.10d), *111*, 115
Camp Big Green (5.11a), *278*
Campfire Girls (5.10), *278*
Captain Crunch (Rumbling Bald) (5.10d), 212, *212*
Captain Crunch (Stone) (5.11a R), *64*
Captain Hook's Nameless Nightmare (5.11d), *145*, 146
Carboman (5.10d), *221*, 222
Carnivore, The (5.12c), *74*, 76
Carolina Hog Farm (IV, 5.10, A4), *240*, 241
Carolina Jam (5.9, A2), *152*
Carpe Freeum (5.11c), 116
Cascading Colluvial Kaleidoscope (5.8), *176*
Castaway, The (5.12a), *102*, 103
Catch Me Now I'm Falling (5.9+), *259*
Caterpillar (5.7), *80*, 81
Catholic Girls (5.9), *308*
Catholic Girls Direct (III, 5.11a), *308*, 309
Catnip (5.11b), *27*
Caught Up in the Air (5.11a), *273*, 274
Cave Route, The (5.5), *131*, 132
Cedar Blossom (5.9+), 266, *266*
Cedar Pie (5.10c), *266*, 267
Champ's Route (5.7), *131*
Changing Corners (5.10b/c), 144, *144*
Chaos Out of Control (5.10c), *256*, 257
Chickenhead City (5.9), 197, *197*
Chieftains of Creep (IV, 5.11a,

A3), 238, *240*
Child Prodigy (5.11c), *257*
Christine's Funky Monkey (5.10), *152*
Chromium Chain (5.11c), 92, *93*
Clivis Multrum (5.7), *308*
Closer to the Heart (5.9), *64–65*
Code, The (A3+), *240*, 241
Cold Turkey (5.8), *125*
Comatose (5.8), 206, *206*
Command Performance (5.11d), *41*
Commitment (5.10b), *152*
Connections (III/IV, 5.11c, A0), *305*, 306
Conquistador (5.11b), 314
Construction Job (5.9), *166*, 167, **168**
Conventional Warfare (5.12d), *118*, 122
Cookie Time in Budapest (5.8), *206*
Cool Wave (5.11b), *252*
Co-Pilots (5.10a), *204*
Corner, The (5.7), *151*
Cornflake Crack (5.11a), *227*, 229
Courthouse Arch (5.10, A3), *310*, 314
Cracker Jack (5.8), 125, *125*
Creatures of Waste (IV, 5.10, A3), *233*, 234
Cretins of Swing (IV, 5.12, A2+), *234*
Crown of Thorns (5.9), *308*
Cryptic Trip (5.11c), *157*, 159
Crystal Crème (5.11d), *310*, 313
Crystal Lizard (5.8), 58, *64*
Cunning Mr. Lingus (5.11a), *118*

Daddies Are Brave (5.11), *283*
Daddy, The (5.6), 161, *162*
Daddy Direct (5.9+ R/X), *162*
Dancing Outlaw (5.10c), 170, *171*
Danger Dog (5.12b), *256*, 257
Danger of Extinction (5.9), *278*
Dangerous Distortions (5.11a), *227*
Dazed and Confused (5.10+), *249*
Dead Man in Pisgah (5.9 R), *244*
Death Wish (5.10c), *45*, 46
Deception in the True Vine (5.11a), *273*

Deep Throat (5.12b), *227*
Deep Woods (5.12c), *310*, 312
Deliverance (5.10a R), *176*
Desperately Seeking Juggage (5.11b), 82, *83*
Details at Ten (5.10b), *266*
Dialing for Buckets (5.10d), *254*
Diamond Dogs (5.10d), *192*
Diamond in the Muff (C1), *234*
Dinkus Dog (5.10b), *256*, 257
Dirty Crack (5.8), 59, *64–65*
Dirty Dikes Done Dirt Cheap (5.12a), *305*
Dirty Love (5.11a, A1), *310*, 313
Discipline, The (5.12a), 54, *55*
Dish, The (5.9 R), *79*
Distemper (5.13a), 201, *201*
Diving Board, The (5.11d), 117, *118*
Dixie Crystals (5.9), 57, *64*
Dixie Fury (5.12a), *74*, 75
Dizzy Gillespie (5.8), *171*
Doan's Pills (5.8), *41*
Doc Savage (5.11a), *249*
Dog Eat Dog (5.11a), *201*
Do or Dive (5.10a), *41*, 42, **43**
Dopey Duck (5.9), *171*, 173, **174**
Doug Reed Solo (5.10a), *209*
Doug's Dihedral (5.11c R), *74*
Dream On (5.9), *55*
Dream Waves (5.9), *55*
Drivin' and Cryin' (5.10a), 192, *192*
Dromedary (5.8), *41*
Duke Power (5.11a), *286*
Dum Dee Dum Dum (5.10c), 243, *244*

Early Times (5.9), *176*
Easy Hard (5.5), *38*, 39
Ecumenical Serenade (5.9 R), *166*
Edge of a Dream (5.7), 102, *102*
Edge of a Scream (5.11b), 223, *223*
Edge of Fear (5.11+), *221*
Edge of Fire (5.11b), *30*, 33
Edgestacy (5.11a R), *194*, 195
Ed, Lew, Bobby and Drew (5.9+), *176*
Egg Wall (5.4), *38*
Elastic Rebound Theory (5.11c), 73, *74*
Electra (5.10c), *80*, 81
Electraglide (5.11c), *278*, 281

Electric Boobs (5.9+), *65, 66*
Electric Kool-Aid Acid Test (5.12+?), 244, *245,* **250**
Electrified Fooling Machine (5.10a), *221, 222*
Ellie Raynolds Memorial Buttress (5.10b/c), *131,* 132
Encore (5.11b), *118,* 119
Enduro Man (Rides Again) (5.11d), *48,* 49
Energizer (5.11+), *171*
Energy Czar (5.10c), *80,* 81
Enter the Center (5.10a), *206*
Entrance Crack (5.4 R), 59, *64*
Eros (5.10d), *111,* 112
Eros Direct (5.12a), *111*
E.S.P. (5.11a), *223,* 224
Espresso Grinder (5.12), *176,* 177
Eureka (5.10c), *152*
Excess Reality (5.10a/b), *135*
Extracrimpy Chicken (5.11d/12a), 236, *237*
Eye Sockets (5.10), 85, *85,* **86**

Face Value (5.11+), *55*
Fairhope (5.13b), 188, *188*
False Impressions (5.8), *125*
False Paradise (5.7), *176,* 179
Fantastic (5.9+), 54, *55*
Fashion (5.12b), *82,* 84
Fat Dog (5.7), *256*
Fat Lady, The (5.11a), 117, *118,* **119**
Father Knows Best (5.8), *64*
Fear and Loathing (5.10d, A1), *249*
Fear of Flying (5.9), *227*
Feature Presentation (5.8+), *144*
Field's Direct (5.7), *131*
Fight the Power (5.10d), 312
Filet-O-Fish (5.12a), *48,* 49
Fine Line (5.10c), 192, *192*
Finger Crack (5.8), *85*
Finger Love (5.10a), *41*
Finishing School Blues (5.11c/d), *198,* 200
Fire Point (5.9+ R), *95,* 96
First Flight (5.11b), 98, *99*
First in Flight (5.12a), 25, **26,** *27*
First Return (5.8), 258, *259*
Fish for Breakfast (5.12a/b), *48,* 49
Five Easy Pieces (5.10d), *41*
5.8 Crack (5.8), *204*
5.11 Roof (5.11), *99*
Flakeview (5.9), *192*
Flappin' in the Breeze (5.10a), *192,* 193

Fleet Feet (5.10), *55,* 56
Focus (5.11c/d), 205, *205*
Fortress Fingers (5.10b), 84, *85*
Freebird (5.11b/c), 151, *152*
Free for All (5.13a), *198*
Fresh Garbage (5.10a), *125*
Freuhlein (5.11a), *74*
Friday the 13th (5.11c), *197*
Frijolitos de Amor (5.12c), *270,* **272**
Frosted Flake (5.9+), *209,* 211
Frosted Mini Pads (5.10), *202*
Fruit Loops (5.7), 208, *209*
Fuddy Mucker (5.9+), *64*
Full Shred (5.12a), *283,* 284, **285**
Full Tilt Boogie (5.11c), 170, *171,* **172**
Future Primitive (5.9), *131*

Gangrene (5.11c X), *278*
Garbage Disposal (5.10 R), *125*
Gastonia Crack (5.4), *76*
Gavel, The (5.11c), 311
Gemini Crack (5.8), *259,* 261
Gem in the Bushes (5.7), *171*
Ghouls Just Want to Have Fun (5.11d), *273*
Gift, The (5.7), *192,* 193
Gift Certificate (5.8), *192*
Gimp, The (5.10d), *82,* 84
Gingerbread Man (5.11c/d), *206*
Ginger Rush (5.11+ R), 175, *176*
Girls in Cakes (5.8, A2), *152*
Glass Dancer (5.11d), *266,* 267
Glass Menagerie (IV, 5.13a or C1), *234,* 235
Go Dog Go (5.12a), *30,* 32
Golden Blend (5.11c/d), *197*
Golden Earring (5.7), *41,* 42
Golden Rule (5.11a), *166,* 167
Golden Shower (5.9), *80*
Good Heavens (5.5), 161
Good Intentions (5.6), *259,* 261
Gorpin Engulfin (5.11d R), *93*
Grand Designs (5.11c), *197*
Grand Funk Railroad (5.9-), *65,* 66
Grand Slam of Sheep (A4), *240,* 241, **242**
Granola (5.8+), 209, *209,* **211**
Great Ah Ha, The (IV, 5.12b), 298, *299*
Great Arch, The (5.5), 61, *64*
Great Brown Way (5.10c), 59, *64*

Great Escape (5.9), *33*
Great White Way (5.9), **58,** 59, *64*
Green Eggs and Ham (5.12a/b), 212, *212*
Green Revolution (5.11b R), 278, 279
Groovemaster (5.12c), *192*
Ground Control (5.8), *286,* 287
Ground Zero (5.11b), 154, *154*
Gumbies Go Home (5.10d), *85*
Gumfighter, The (5.11+), 93, *93,* **94**
Gunboat Diplomacy (5.10c/d), *192*
Gunshy (5.9), *145*
Guppies in the Mist (5.10d), *194,* 195
Guy's Smile (5.4), *127*

Haiku (5.11c), *118*
Hairy Canary (5.11a), 117, *118*
Hanging Chain (5.12b), 188, *188*
Hanging High (5.9), *125,* 126
Hanging Hog (5.10), *125*
Happy Campers (Big Green) (5.11a), *278,* 281
Happy Campers (Cedar Rock) (5.11b), *273*
Hard Rock Cafe (5.12c), 116, *116*
Harpoon (5.10a), 101
Hawksbill Traverse (5.9), *111,* 114
Head and Shoulders (5.9+), *152*
Head Jam (5.5), *38,* 39
Heart of Stone (5.10), *286*
Heckfire (5.7), *157*
Helios (5.12a), *125,* 126
Helmet Buttress (5.6), *131*
Helmet Variation (5.8), *131*
Help Mr. Wizard (5.11a), *166,* 167
Hercules (5.14a), *27,* 28
Hidden Agenda (5.11a), *223,* 224
Hidden Crack (5.7), *127,* 128
Hindu Kush (5.8), *95,* 96
Hindu Kush Direct (5.10d), *95,* 96
Hologram (5.11), *286*
Home of the Brave (5.11d), *194,* 195
Honeymoon, The (5.8+), *127,* 128

Hook and Bladder (5.9), *65*
Hopscotch (5.3), 36, *38*
Howling Khan (IV, 5.10, A3), *237*
Hungry Jack (5.11d), *209*
Hyperbola (5.10a), *246*, 247
Hyperbola Direct Start (5.11a), *246, 247*
Hypothetical Destination (5.10d), *286*

I Abuse Profen (5.12b), *202*, 203
Ice Cream Direct (5.12c), *118*, 120, **121**
Ice Weasels (5.11b), 284, *286*
Impossible Dream (5.9), *55*
Indian Head Direct (5.10+), 44
Inner Peace (5.11a/b), *212*
Inner Peace Direct (5.11d), *212*
Instant Karma Direct (5.10d), *80*, 81
Instant Surreal (5.10c/d R), 213, *213*
Intensive Care Unit (5.10d), *131*, 132
Invisible Airwaves (5.10c, A2), 230, *232*
Irish Jig (5.10d), *254*, 256
Irreversible Commitments (5.10), *254*
I Scream Therefore I Am (5.12a), *118*, 120
I Wanna Be Sedated (5.11d), *273*, 274

Jack Be Nimble (5.11a), *207*
Jeep's Chimney (5.10a), *118*, 120
Jewel of the Nile (5.11a), *157*, 158
Jiffy Pop Queen (5.10d), 279, *278*
Jig Zag (5.11a), *118*
Jim Dandy (5.4), *127*, 130
Jingoist, The (5.11), *93*
Joey the Jerk (5.9), *162*
Joke the Chicken (5.9+), *278*
Judgment Day (5.11b), 311
Julia (5.10b), *166*, 169
Just a Pinch (5.12b/c), *197*
Just Say Moo (5.10a/b), *131*, 132

Karma (5.10b), *80*
KB Capers (5.10a), *95*, 97, **97**
Keep and Arm Bears (5.10), *135*
Killer Whales (5.11), *227*, 229
King Contrary Man (5.11c), *118*

King of Kings (5.11d), **109,** *118*
King Pump (5.11d), *157*, 158
Klingon Traverse (5.12), *76*
Krispy Kreme (5.11d), 191, *191*

Lab Rat (5.8), *252*
Labia (5.11d), 251, *252*
Lakeview (5.10a/b), *194*, 195
Land of the Little People (5.11a), *157*, 158
Last Dance (5.11c X), 55, *55*
Last of the Dixie Trads (IV, 5.11d), *299*
Lavender Dream (5.11b), 190, *190*
Le Pump (5.11), 251, *252*
Leapin' Lizards (5.12b), 198, *198*, **199**
Left of Buffalo Nickel (5.5), *99*
Leftovers (5.10b), *144*
Left Unlocked (5.11d; 5.9 R/X), *194*, 195
Left Up (5.7), *259*, 261
Legendary Nuclear Bomb (5.11 R), 248, *249*
Lichen Express (5.10a), *176*, 178
Lichen or Not (5.5), 262
Life Is Like a Rubber Rope (5.10+), *145*
Like a Virgin (5.10), *202*
Line of Fire (5.12c), 115, *116*
Link, The (5.12), *99*, 101
Liquid Anal Crowbar (5.11+), *221*
Linn Cove Lullaby (5.10a), 99, *99*, **100**
Little Corner (5.6), *166*, 169
Little Creatures under the Monkey Flake (5.10), *252*
Little Miss Dangerous (IV, 5.12a, A0), 296, *297*
Little Titties (5.8 R), *131*
Live at Leads (5.13a), *283*, 284
Lizard Graveyard (5.8-), *190*
Lizard Wizard (5.12a), *198*
Lock or Drop (5.11a), *135*, 137
Look Ma No Bolts (5.10), *135*
Lost and Found (5.9), 175, *176*
Lost at Sea (5.8), 102, *102*
Lost in Space (5.10b), *111*, 112, **113**
Love Wig (5.12d), *190*, 191
Lovers in a Dangerous Time (5.7 R), *127*
Low Brothers (left) (Class 5), *118*

Low Brothers (right) (5.8), *118*

Macho Dorito (5.6), *127*
Mad Dog (5.11d), 200, *201*
Mad Hatter, The (5.11a), 223, *223*
Mad Max (5.11b), *254*
Maginot Line (5.7+), *166*, 169
Maiden Voyage (5.9), *102*, 103
Mainline (IV, 5.11d), *299*, 301
Mainline Express (5.11+), *252*
Mama's Goin' Crazy (5.10), *67*
Man Overboard (5.11), *102*
Master Beta (5.10c), *82*, 83
Master of Puppets (5.10), *144*
Matrix, The (IV, 5.12c), *297*
McGrady's Route (5.11a), *55*
Menagerie Direct (A2+), *234*
Mennonite Surf Party (5.11+), *207*, 208
Mercury's Lead (5.9-), 60, *64*
Middle Road, The (5.12+), 46, *47*
Midlife Crisis (5.9+), *209*
Mighty Mouse (5.11c), *47*, 49
Mike's Crack (5.5), *76*
Mitey Fine (5.9), *213*
Mitzeitzusparen (5.9+), 149, *151*
Moondance (5.10b R), *286*, 287
Moosehead (5.11b/c), *213*, 214
Mourning Maiden (5.10a), *125*, 126
Mu (5.10a R), *151*
Mudbone (5.12b), *74*
Mummy, The (5.5), **140,** 161, *162*
My Route (5.6), *131*, 133

Nantucket Sleigh Ride (5.9+), *286*
Nationwide (5.10), *254*
Native Uprising (5.11b), *249*
Natural States (5.10 R), *249*
Nature Bats Last (5.10a), *278*
Nemesis (5.11b R), *204*
Nevermore (5.11b), *47*
Never Never Land (5.12a R), 147, *149*
New Creatures (5.11c), 270, *270*
New Diversions (IV, 5.10), *303*
New Perversions (5.11a/b), *305*
New World Man (5.12c), 45, *45*
Nick Danger (5.10), *254*, 255
Nicotine (5.13a), *47*, 48
911 (5.8), *82*

Niteshift (5.9-), *171*
No Alternative (5.5), 62, **63,**
65
North Face Direct (5.11d),
310, 314
North Ridge (5.5), *135,* 137
Northeast Passage (5.12), *131*
Nose, The (Crowders) (5.5), *79*
Nose, The (Looking Glass)
(5.8), 243, *244,* **245**
Nothing but Air (5.10d), *166*
Not See (5.11b), *74*
No Workman's Comp (5.6),
131
Nuclear Arms (5.10a), *192,*
193
Nuclear Cottage Cheese (5.9+),
79, *79*
Nuclear Crayon (5.10b), *41*
Nuclear Erection (5.12+, A2),
227, 229
Nuclear-Free Zone (5.9+), *221*
Nut n' Homo (5.10b; 5.8 R),
213, 214
Nutrageous (5.8+), *148*
Nutrasweet (5.10), *99*
Nutsweat (5.9+), *45,* 46

Odyssey, The (5.11a), *249,* 250
Old Blue (5.11c/d), *190*
100% Natural (5.11d), *202*
On Misty Edge (5.11c), 135,
135
Ooga Chocka (5.8), *79,* 80
Opa (5.9+ R), *131*
Open Book, The (5.11b), 153,
154
Opinionated (5.9), *82*
Orange Blossom Special (5.11a
X), *65,* 66
Organized Confusion (5.12b/c),
191
Original Route, The (III/IV,
5.11a or 5.9, A1), 302, *305,*
307
Out of the Blue and Into the
Blank (5.12c, A1), 283, *283*
Out to Lunch (5.11a), **180,**
251, *252*
Overhang Direct (5.8), 79, *79*

Pack O'Nabs (5.9-), *206*
Pandora's Way (5.9), *65*
Panic Value (IV, 5.10, A4),
231, 233
Panthertown Knobs (5.9), 284,
286
Parachute Woman (5.10d),
256
Paradise Alley (5.8+), *176,* 178

Paralleling (5.10a), 279, *278,*
280
Parental Guidance (5.12a), *308*
Pascal's Route (5.12c/d), 115,
116
Passion and Warfare (5.12c),
268, *270*
Pat Ewing (5.10), *254,* 255
Patience (5.12 R), *145*
Patio Roof (5.12b), 92, *93*
Pawing the Void (5.12b/c),
266, 267
Peek-A-Boo (5.5), *127,* 129
Peek-A-Boo Direct (5.10a),
127
Peer Pressure (5.9+ R/X), *55*
Pepper Pot Tube (5.10), *221*
Peregrine (5.9), 243, *244*
Permission Granite (5.10a), *55*
Perplexus (5.11c), *74*
Persistence of Vision (5.9), *127*
Peterbuilt (5.12a), *131,* 133
Petrified Cedar (5.11b), *266*
Petzl Neck Geek (5.11d, A0),
223, *223*
PF Flyers (5.10a), *67*
Phantom of the Opera (5.11c),
118, 120
Phaser (5.9+), *93*
Phasers on Stun (5.11a), *111,*
114
Pick-A-Dilly Prow (5.11b), 87,
87
Pickett's Charge (5.9+), *171*
Pillar of Faith (5.7), *192*
Pinball Wizard (5.11), 170, *171*
Pink Flamingo (5.11a), *80*
Pixie Wall (5.11c/d), 146. *149*
Plastic Cat (5.12b R/X), *38,* 39
Plastic Fish (5.10b), *191*
Playground (5.9+), *76*
Pleasant Dreams (5.8+), 87, *87*
Pooh Corner (5.11a), 25, *27,*
28
Pooter the Poacher (5.10c),
226, *227*
Porter's Pooh (5.11c), 26, *27*
P.O.V. (5.12c), *30,* 31
Predator (5.12a), 248, *249*
Prey (5.12d or 5.11c, A0), 248,
249
Promised Land, The (IV,
5.12c), 294, *295*
Protectorate (5.9), *93*
Prow, The (5.4), 153, *154*
Psychedelic Delusions of the
Digital Man (5.9, A2+),
247, *249,* **250**
Psychotic Reaction (5.10b/c),
80, *80*

Pteranodon (5.11a), *74*
Pull the Plug (5.11a/b), *204*
Pulpit, The (5.8), 62, *65*
Pump Failure (5.12b), *252*
Pumping in Rhythm (5.11b/c),
196, *197*
Punji Stick (5.9+), *221,* 222
Purple Daze (5.11a), 62, *65*
Purring, The (5.10c), *65,* 66
Pygmalion (5.12d), 27, *27*
Pyromania (5.10a), *67*

Quaker State (5.11a), *41,* 42

Rabies (5.12b/c), *201,* 202
Rage, Rage Against the Dying
of the Drill (5.11d), *286*
Rainy Day Women (5.10a),
61, *64–65*
Raise Hell (5.8), *41,* 42
Rapid Transit (5.12a), *135*
Rat's Ass (5.8), 258, *259*
Rattlesnake Crack (5.9), 156,
156
Raven 13 (5.11d), *176,* 177
Rawhide Arch (5.10d), 273,
273
Razor Boy (5.12), *93*
Razor Face (5.11b), *197*
Reckless Abandon (5.11a), 44,
45
Recommendation, The
(5.12b), *48,* 49
Red Red Wine (5.11b), *82*
Red Wall Chimney (5.3), *82*
Remember Appomattox (IV,
5.10, A2+), *231,* 232
Revival (5.11 R/X), 93, *93*
Rice Krispies (5.10c R), *64*
Riders on the Storm (5.11a),
29, *30*
Right Up (5.9), *259,* 261
Rinky Dink Direct (5.11b),
147, *149*
Rinky Dink Original (5.10),
149
Rinky Direct (5.12, A0), *149*
Rip Van Winkle (5.7), *127,*
128
RJ's Variation to Diamond
Dogs (5.8), *192*
Rocket Science (5.10c), 203,
204
Rock Like an Egyptian
(5.11d), *157,* 158
Rocky's Roof (5.10), *80*
Roof Awakening (5.11b), *48*
Route Doctors, The (IV,
5.12a), *303*
Ruby Tuesday (5.10), *254,* 255

Rusty Redneck (5.10c), 206, 206

Sadistic Rhythm (5.9), *80*, 81
Safari Jive (5.11c), 226, *227*
Safari Jive Direct (5.11a), *227*
Saturday Night Live (5.10a), *67*
Scars on a Landscape (5.10b), 282, *282*
Scimitar (5.12a), *55*, **56**, 57
Scott Fisher Memorial (IV, 5.10, A3), *234*, 236
Scramble My Feedback (5.10a), *82*, 83
Scream Dream (5.11d), *176*, 178
Screamin' Meemies (5.11 R), *157*
Screamweaver (5.11d), 197, *197*
SD Modiano (5.9), 156, *156*
Seal, The (5.10, A2), *227*, 229
Sea of Brows by the Waste Side (5.11), *246*
Sea Wolf (5.8), 207, *207*
Second Coming (5.7), 258, *259*, **260**
Second Guessing (5.12a), *204*
Second Stanza (5.8+), 133, **134**, *135*
Secret Alloys (5.10, A3), *231*, 232
Sensemilia Sunset (5.9+), *246*, 247
Sentinel Buttress (5.5), *33*, 34
Sentinel Chimney (5.4), *38*
Serentripitous (5.7), *171*, 173
Sermon, The (5.9), *65*
Seven Year Itch (5.11a), *192*
Shadowdance (5.10c or 5.11c/d R), *45*, 46
Shake and Bake (5.11b/c), 152, *152*
Ship of Fools Direct (IV, 5.12a/b), 294, *295*
Shit Hook (5.8+), 40, *41*
Shits and Fear (5.10d), *254*
Shits and Grins (5.11a), *205*
Short Corner (5.8), *171*
Short Crack (5.7), *171*
Short Man's Sorrow (5.6), *259*
Shredded Wheat (5.11a), 208, *209*, **210**
Shrimp Cocktail (5.10d), *227*, 230
Shrimp Creole (5.11a), *227*
Sibling Revelry (5.11c), *270*, 271
Silence the Critics (5.12b), 82, *83*

Simple Minds (5.7), *157*
Sinner Man (5.11c), *166*
Sister Seagull (5.7), *162*
Skip to My Lou (5.6), 130, *131*
Skunk Crack (5.8), *157*
Slab Accurate (5.12a), *192*, 193
Slabster's Lament (5.12b), *74*, 75
Slabster's Lament Direct (5.12c), *74*, 75
Slimebelly Snakeass Sodhole Skunkpie (5.12a), *76*, 78
Slimey, The (5.9), *152*
Slippin' into Darkness (5.9), 131, *131*
Snag, The (5.12b), *74*, 75
Snap, Crackle, and Pop (5.11b), *213*, 215
So It Goes (5.8+), *76*
Solar Wind (5.10+), *249*
Sole Control (5.11b), *282*, 283
Southender (5.8), *256*, 257
Southern Boys Don't Wear Plaid (5.11b), 196, *197*
Southern Crescent (5.11), *246*
Space Monkey (5.11d), *204*
Space Race (5.10d), *111*
Space Wrangler (5.12a), *145*
Sparky (5.10, A1), *176*
Special Forces (5.11a R), 95, *95*
Special Operations (5.11+), *95*
Spectre Man (5.10), *145*
Sperm, The (5.9+), 226, *227*
Spice (5.11b R), *45*, 46
Spiderman Swings South (5.10d), 68
Spiders and Snakes (5.12a), *190*, 191
Spitter (5.12b), *74*
Spring Break (5.8), *82*
Spring Fever (5.7), *82*
Spring Fling (5.8), *82*
Spring Swing (5.8), *82*
Spry Look (5.12b), 187, *188*, **189**
Squeeze Pop (5.12), *266*
Stab in the Dark (5.10d; 5.8 R), 40, *41*
Standard Deviation (5.8), *152*
Standard Deviation Variation (5.9), *152*
Stand Fast (5.9), *166*
Stars and Bars (5.12b), *27*
Star Trekin' (5.10b), *111*, 112
Static Klingon (5.11c/d), *196*, 198
Statutory Rape (5.11a), 312

Stockings on the Mantle (5.11c), 268, *270*
Storm in a Teacup (5.10a), 60, *64*
Straight and Narrow (5.10a), *166*, 167
Straight Up and Stiff (5.12a/b), *237*, 238
Strawberry Preserves (5.10c), 63, *65*
Stukas over Disneyland (5.10b), *127*, 130
Stun Your Partner (5.10c), *111*
Stupid Roof (5.10b), *79*
Subtle Rush (5.10d), 314
Sufficiently Breathless (5.9+ R/X), *67*, 68
Sugaree (5.10a), *192*, 194
Sundial Crack (5.8), 246, *246*
Super Conduction (5.7, A2), *252*
Super Crack (Looking Glass) (5.10), *244*
Supercrack (Shortoff) (5.11d), *176*, 178
Supercrimp (5.13c/d), 25, *27*
Super Direct (5.8), *33*, 34
Super Direction (5.12a), *252*
Superman is Dead (5.12b), *47*
Super Quack (5.9-), *171*
Surfin' with the Alien (5.12a R), *266*, 267
Swing Your Partner (5.11a), *111*, 114
Swing Your Phaser (5.9+), *111*
Sword of the Lord (5.10+), 175, *176*

Tadpole in a Party Bowl (5.10d), *270*
Taken for Granite (5.9), *67*
Talking about Mudflaps (5.11), 127
Tankslapper (5.11+), *135*
Tarantula (5.10a), *152*, 153
Target Practice (5.8), *82*
Tarheels (5.10+), 221, *221*
Teflon Trip (5.10c), *67*, 68
Temporary Tradition (5.11a), *80*
Terrorist, The (5.13a), *74*, 75
Test Pilots (5.11c), 203, *204*
That's the Way the Cookie Crumbles (5.10a), *206*
This One Goes to Eleven (5.12a), *157*, 159, **160**
Thratcher (5.13a), *74*
Thrill of Victory and the Agony of My Feet, The (5.10c/d), *223*, 224

Time Passage (5.9 R/X), *111*
Tips Ahoy (5.12c/d), 115, *116*
Tits and Beer (5.9), 253, **253,**
254
T.K.O. (5.12a), 82, *83*
Toads-R-Us (5.9+), *270,* 271,
271
Toilet Bowel (5.10), *55*
Tommy Gun (5.10), *171*
Tom Tom Club (5.9 R), *82, 84*
Too Much Fun (5.9), 38, *38*
Top That (5.8), *74*
Top That Direct (5.10b), *74*
Tower Traverse, The (5.8), *135*
Toxic Shock (Crowders),
(5.11d), *74,* 76
Toxic Shock (Shortoff), (5.9),
171, 173
Toxic Wasteland (5.10d), *249*
Traditions (III/IV, 5.11c), 302,
303, **304**
Trinidad (5.10a), *157,* 158
True Grit (5.10), *135*
Turkey Beard (5.12a), 154,
154, **155**
Turn and Burn (5.11 R), *171*
Twist and Shout (5.10a X),
151
Two in Agreement (5.10c), *270*
Two Pitch (5.4), *125*
Two Step (5.10), 80, *80*
Ultraman (5.10a R), *162*
Underdog (5.12b R), *30,* 32
Under the Dragon's Beak (5.6
R), *221*
Unfinished Breakfast (5.9 R),
213
Unfinished Concerto (5.9),
256, 258
United Way (5.11d), *221,* 222
Unorthodox Behavior (5.10),
111
U Slot (5.7), 57, *64*

Vascular Disaster (5.11b/c), 47,
47
Volunteer Wall, The (IV,
5.12a), *299,* 300

Wahoo Start (5.9), *55*
Wailing Wall (5.6), *41, 43*
Walk This Way (5.11b), 189,
190
Wall, The (5.10a), *76,* 78
Waltzing Matilda (5.11b), *206*
Warrior's Way, The (IV, 5.12c),
297, 298
Washboard (5.6), 37, *38*
Wasp, The (5.5), *127*
Waspafarian (5.10b), *74*

Waste Not, Want Not (5.12/c),
230, *231*
Waste-a-Bit (5.10d), *135,* 137
Waverly Waster (5.12a), *234*
Way Outr'e (5.11a), *283*
Way Rad (5.10d), *252*
Wedding Present (5.10), *127*
Welcome to Crowders (5.12a),
82, *83*
Welcome to Moore's (5.10d),
39
Welcome to Watauga (5.11a),
99, 101
Well Balanced Breakfast (5.11),
213
Wet Dreams (5.9+ R/X), *55*
What Else Is There to Do?
(5.7), *80*
What's Big and Green and Eats
Climbers (5.10), *286*
What's Up Doc (5.10d), *131,*
132
Whining, The (5.11d), *74,* 75
Whip-O-Will (5.10b), *282*
Whippin' Boy (III/IV, 5.11d),
305, 309
Whipping Post, The (5.11d),
202, 203
Whiskey for Breakfast (5.10d),
209, *209*
White Corner (5.10a), 173, *176*
White Fang (5.12c), 207, *207*
White Light (5.8), *135*
White Lightning (5.8), *135,*
136, 137
White Russians Gone Bananas
(5.11a), 173, *176*
White Way Direct (5.9), 57,
64
Whitney's Excellent Route
(5.11d), *237,* 238, **239**
Whittemore-Cartwright Varia-
tion (A3+), *240*
Wild Berry Pickin' (5.11c/d),
273, 274
Wild Eyed Southern Boys
(5.12a), *27*
Wild Ginger Root (5.11b),
268, **269,** *270*
Wild Hickory Nuts (5.11b),
213, 214
Wild Kingdom (5.11d), 29,
30, **31**
Wildlife (5.12b R/X), *30*
Windwalker (5.9), 258, *259*
Windy City (5.8), *111*
Winged Mongrel (5.10a), 111,
111
Wish You Were Here (5.12c/d),
191

Womb, The (5.11b), 226, *227,*
228
Wooly Aphid (5.10a), *127,* 129
WOSL (5.8 R), *64*
Wounded Hindu (5.10 R), *95*
Wounded Knee (5.9+), *95*
Wounded Warrior (5.10+), *148*
Wranglin' Horses and Hogs
(IV, 5.10, A3+), *231,* 233
Wyoming Dick (5.10a), *273*

Yardarm (5.8-), 61, **62,** *64–65*

Zagger (5.7), *152*
Z Crack (5.10d), *204*
Zealot Shout (5.11b R), 190,
190
Zeus (5.13b), *27,* 29
Zodiac (5.8+), *259,* 261
Zombie Woof (5.10b), 41, *41*
Zombie Zoo (IV, 5.11, A3+),
234, 235
Zoo Love (5.9- X), *55*
Zoo View (5.7+), **22,** 35, *35*
Zydygo (5.10c), *198,* 200

ABOUT THE AUTHORS

Yon Lambert is a former full-time journalist who has been hiking and climbing in the Appalachians for well over a decade. Cross-country travels and climbing trips have only deepened his appreciation for Carolina rock. Yon currently lives in Spartanburg, South Carolina, where he is the assistant director of a statewide non-profit, the Palmetto Conservation Foundation *(www.palmettoconservation.org)*. He and his wife, Diane, are expecting their first child in the fall of 2002.

From his first experiences climbing at Looking Glass as a thirteen-year-old, **Harrison Shull** has been in love with North Carolina climbing. Whether it is run-out slab at Stone Mountain, overhanging jugs on the headwall at Whiteside, or bulging eyebrows at Looking Glass, Harrison ranks North Carolina climbing as some of the nation's best—best-kept secret that is! He has climbed extensively in the United States and spent six years living and working at Seneca Rocks, West Virginia, as a climbing guide. He moved to Asheville in 1998, where his work as a freelance photographer *(www.shullphoto.com)* specializing in outdoor adventure sports allows him plenty of time to be out in the North Carolina woods.

Yon Lambert   *Harrison Shull* (Photo: Eric Jackson)

THE MOUNTAINEERS, founded in 1906, is a nonprofit outdoor activity and conservation club, whose mission is "to explore, study, preserve, and enjoy the natural beauty of the outdoors. . . . " Based in Seattle, Washington, the club is now the third-largest such organization in the United States, with 15,000 members and five branches throughout Washington State.

The Mountaineers sponsors both classes and year-round outdoor activities in the Pacific Northwest, which include hiking, mountain climbing, ski-touring, snowshoeing, bicycling, camping, kayaking and canoeing, nature study, sailing, and adventure travel. The club's conservation division supports environmental causes through educational activities, sponsoring legislation, and presenting informational programs. All club activities are led by skilled, experienced volunteers, who are dedicated to promoting safe and responsible enjoyment and preservation of the outdoors.

If you would like to participate in these organized outdoor activities or the club's programs, consider a membership in The Mountaineers. For information and an application, write or call The Mountaineers, Club Headquarters, 300 Third Avenue West, Seattle, WA 98119; 206-284-6310.

The Mountaineers Books, an active, nonprofit publishing program of the club, produces guidebooks, instructional texts, historical works, natural history guides, and works on environmental conservation. All books produced by The Mountaineers Books fulfill the club's mission.

Send or call for our catalog of more than 500 outdoor titles:

The Mountaineers Books
1001 SW Klickitat Way, Suite 201
Seattle, WA 98134
800-553-4453
mbooks@mountaineersbooks.org
www.mountaineersbooks.org

The Mountaineers Books is proud to be a corporate sponsor of Leave No Trace, whose mission is to promote and inspire responsible outdoor recreation through education, research, and partnerships. The Leave No Trace program is focused specifically on human-powered (nonmotorized) recreation.

Leave No Trace strives to educate visitors about the nature of their recreational impacts, as well as offer techniques to prevent and minimize such impacts. Leave No Trace is best understood as an educational and ethical program, not as a set of rules and regulations.

For more information, visit *www.LNT.org,* or call 800-332-4100.